Blogging in the Global Society:

Cultural, Political and Geographical Aspects

Tatyana Dumova
Point Park University, USA

Richard Fiordo
University of North Dakota, USA

Senior Editorial Director:	Kristin Klinger
Director of Book Publications:	Julia Mosemann
Editorial Director:	Lindsay Johnston
Acquisitions Editor:	Erika Carter
Development Editor:	Hannah Abelbeck
Production Editor:	Sean Woznicki
Typesetters:	Milan Vracarich, Jr.
Print Coordinator:	Jamie Snavely
Cover Design:	Nick Newcomer

Published in the United States of America by
Information Science Reference (an imprint of IGI Global)
701 E. Chocolate Avenue
Hershey PA 17033
Tel: 717-533-8845
Fax: 717-533-8661
E-mail: cust@igi-global.com
Web site: http://www.igi-global.com

Library of Congress Cataloging-in-Publication Data

Blogging in the global society: cultural, political and geographical aspects / Tatyana Dumova and Richard Fiordo, editors.
   p. cm.
  Includes bibliographical references and index.
  Summary: "This book provides a comprehensive view of blogging as a global practice, looking at the new virtual world--a blogosphere--populated with opinion leaders and information purveyors, political pundits and activists, human and animal rights defenders and abusers, corruption fighters and truth seekers"--Provided by publisher.
  ISBN 978-1-60960-744-9 (hbk.) -- ISBN 978-1-60960-745-6 (ebook) -- ISBN 978-1-60960-746-3 (print & perpetual accesbs) 1. Blogs--Social aspects. 2. Blogs--Political aspects. 3. Internet--Social aspects. 4. Internet--Political aspects. I. Dumova, Tatyana, 1962- II. Fiordo, Richard, 1945-
  HM851.B593 2012
  303.48'33--dc23
                    2011031144

British Cataloguing in Publication Data
A Cataloguing in Publication record for this book is available from the British Library.

All work contributed to this book is new, previously-unpublished material. The views expressed in this book are those of the authors, but not necessarily of the publisher.

Table of Contents

Section 1
The Global Blogosphere: Political, Cultural, Legal, and Ethical Issues

Section 2
Blogs and Blogging: Case Studies

Section 3
Analyzing Blogs: Approaches and Perspectives

Preface

BLOGGING IN THE GLOBAL SOCIETY: CONTEMPORARY ISSUES, INTERPRETATIONS, AND VIEWPOINTS

Blogging in the Global Society

During the last decade, the Internet and the Web have undergone a remarkable expansion, permeating all aspects of people's lives and resulting in an unprecedented growth of social interaction technologies. Social interaction technologies (SIT) are Internet-based tools and techniques that help initiate, share, and maintain interactive and collaborative activities online (Dumova & Fiordo, 2010). New SIT-based social media have notably changed people's information gathering and communication habits by adding a strong interactive and collaborative aspect to the milieu. As perhaps the best-known example of social media globally, blogging has experienced outstanding growth, evolving from an online version of old-fashioned personal journaling into a global mass medium. According to a comprehensive social media survey, the global blogosphere "rivals any mass media in terms of reach, time spent, and wider cultural, social, and political impact" (Wave 3 Social Media Tracker, 2008). The current number of blogs in the world amounts to 168 million (BlogPulse, 2011) with some popular blogs having hundreds of thousands of subscribers.

Merging the storytelling and editorial powers of the newsroom, blogging puts publishing and broadcasting into the hands of any individual who is determined to let the world hear his or her voice. It is not accidental that many ready-to-use templates offered by blog hosting services use the phrase "Hello World" as a header. All one needs to succeed as a blog writer is an Internet connection and the persistence to keep a blog updated several times a week. As bloggers themselves note, there are many types and varieties of blogs aside from a private diary:

While personal blogs are still far and wide across the blogosphere, you will find a lot of non-personal blogs as well. Today, a blog is a platform for news, tutorials, travel tales, articles, video, photos and more. Blogs have several categories similar to what websites had several years ago. You have technology blogs, travelogues, personal blogs, news blogs, videologs, photoblogs etc. (Scocco, 2008)

Blogs create a personalized, two-way multimedia rich online communication channel. People blog for a myriad of reasons, from complex to simple, which is in part documented in this edited volume. As one blogger explains:

I started blogging because I wanted to explore my own point of view on topics around communication, branding, and eventually the emergence of social media. More than anything, writing helps me work through ideas, find clarity, and find connections between threads. It has helped me establish an area of expertise, a personality and point of view, and work through ideas that interest me. Also? I love to write. Words are my chosen medium, so blogging is a natural fit for me. (Naslund, 2011)

Another blog writer mentions that blogging provides her with the opportunity "to share photos and information with anyone, anywhere, at anytime" (Knittingsings.com, 2008). In the words of a scholar explaining the popularity of social media through collaborative Internet technologies, "consumers are producers; audiences are authors; users are developers" (Sunstein, 2006, p. xii). A blog's ability to effortlessly create mosaics with words, images, video, audio, and animation releases the creative energy of the individual, increases human agency, ignites a personal quest for change, and creates social, political, and economical momentum for societal transformation.

For many, blogging has turned into an ample outlet for self-expression and originality in the age of intruding big governments, brazen transnational corporations, ever-growing plutocracies, and diminishing civil and human rights—sometimes to the point of obsession. Blogging has evolved into a platform for social contact, sharing information and opinions, learning from others, and ultimately for creating new knowledge. A blogger reflects:

Now that I have been writing for about 2 weeks I have come to find that blogging is a self-contained community that stretches around the world. Your blog is your window out to the world, so that everyone can see in to your hobbies, interests, and passions. Each blog has its own persona and mine is the nonsensical ramblings of the mind. This is one thing that interests me and now I get to share it with the world, and not only that but the world gets to comment and interact with me. (Scocco, 2008)

Although blogging has been a subject of many scholarly investigations, there is still a noticeable lack of publications that can provide a multidisciplinary and cross-cultural analysis of the phenomenon on a global scale. Aimed to explore the phenomenon of blogging in the contexts and settings of today's society, this book delves into the social, cultural, economic, political, and critical dimensions of blogging around the world. Furthermore, this text examines the similarities, distinctions, implications, and specific characteristics of blogs, bloggers, and blogging from various perspectives and viewpoints.

At the time when blogging as a medium is going through a transition (Technorati, 2010), *Blogging in the Global Society* provides a much-needed forum for sharing ideas and exchanging views among scholars and professionals. The chapters featured in this collection address a subject of keen interest to academics, practitioners, and citizens alike. The authors address a pressing demand for knowledge by offering their international expertise and specialization in areas ranging from communication and computer science to law and religion while applying a cornucopia of research methods. By bringing together contributors from academic and professional fields, this volume advances the fast-growing area of knowledge dealing with the theory and practice of blogging across continents.

Diverse Perspectives and Topics

The editors elicited diverse perspectives from experts on the subject of the global blogosphere with special attention being addressed to political, cultural, legal, and ethical issues. The result is a compilation of state-of-the-art research findings on global blogging. Conceptually, the editors maintain consistency with Tim Berners-Lee's perspective on Web science as being inherently interdisciplinary and aiming to "create approaches that allow new powerful and more beneficial patterns to occur" (Berners-Lee et al., 2006, p. 769). From varied perspectives on the global blogosphere, the elite scholars contributing to this book made a dedicated effort to advance knowledge.

The depth and breadth of the chapter topics in *Blogging in the Global Society* relate the blogosphere to the following significant issues: blogs as a source of democratic deliberation, citizen media and political conflict in Thailand, blogmongering in China, a reflection of women's sports, a code of conduct for bloggers, a case study of the basketball blog KnickerBlogger.Net, a medium of expression among estranged American Hasidim, a case study of blogging in Ireland, a means of communication and influence toward Palestinian sovereignty, a means of grieving, a popular communication medium for political blogging in the USA, a uses and gratification study of Latin American bloggers, a First Amendment perspective on blogging in the U.S., a hermeneutic analysis of the meanings of blogs, and the future of blogging through the lens of social interaction technologies.

Scope

Blogging in the Global Society assumes a worldwide approach to its subject matter. Scholars from divergent geographical regions (such as Europe, North America, Asia, and the Middle East) have contributed to the volume. The overall scope of the geographical areas embraced by the authors in this book includes the United States, Ireland, Latin American countries, China, Thailand, Israel, and the Arab world. The text unites experts ranging from communication and computer science to law and religion; simultaneously, it embodies international perspectives on the timely and crucial subject of blogging around the world. The researchers employ qualitative and quantitative research methods encompassing empirical, interpretative, historical, critical, and philosophical approaches to answering research questions and testing hypotheses.

Chapter Organization

The chapters unfold in a unified format similar to the following: abstract, introduction, background, literature review, main body, conclusion, future research directions, references, and key terms and definitions. The abstract summarizes the content of the chapter and highlights the major findings. The introduction explains the direction of the research reported in the chapter. While the background section contextualizes the challenges behind the research, the literature review covers completed studies relevant to the research topic. The main body of the chapter articulates the position of the author and develops the content. The conclusion entails deductions from the study and its results, and the future research directions outline the implications of the findings for further investigations. Under references, the authors cite their research sources. Finally, the key terms and definitions detail important concepts selected by the chapter authors.

OVERVIEW

The book has three sections. All three sections enhance the reader's comprehension of the global blogosphere and shed light on its political, cultural, legal, and ethical issues. The wisdom and talent of the authors are shared with the readers in the following:

Section 1: The Global Blogosphere: Political, Cultural, Legal, and Ethical Issues

Section 1 highlights blogging worldwide and includes Chapters 1-5, which circumnavigate the world via blogging. Chapter 1 by Barbara K. Kaye, Thomas J. Johnson, and Peter Muhlberger investigates how blog reliance among users influences political participation. The authors maintain that social, cultural, and political contexts in different countries may impact deliberative communication in the blogosphere. For deliberation to be open and fruitful, bloggers must be informed yet willing to listen to opposing points of view, thereby synthesizing all the distinct voices they hear. Unfortunately, much evidence suggests the public stays appreciably apathetic and ignorant, and both apathy and ignorance weaken deliberation—the heart of any democracy. In the final analysis, the learned authors demonstrate a positive correlation between blog reliance and democratic deliberation, which may depend on the motives behind blog use.

In Chapter 2, Melissa Wall and Treepon Kirdnark try to determine how the political crisis that occurred in Thailand during the spring of 2010 might yield information and elicit understanding towards the role and function of current-events blogging in a non-Western country. The themes that emerge from the analysis suggest intriguing explanations and new understanding. Technology alone does not yield enlightenment; rather, illumination follows from a communicator's personal reflections. With respect to the Thai crisis, while blogging may enhance the public sphere by amplifying alternative points of view and voices, the authors find evidence that blogging might merely serve to reinforce existing political opinions and the intensity of the political struggle.

Zixue Tai in Chapter 3 details how the Chinese blogosphere, which developed later than in Western countries, became the largest in the world. Blogs have redefined Chinese cyberculture and revolutionized online user participation. The Chinese blogosphere has afforded netizens with the opportunity for collaborative and collective action in defense of the public interest. Chinese netizens collaborate online to demand public accountability from officials, stop corruption, and encourage positive societal change. Yet, state censorship creates barriers for self-expression that cause many Chinese bloggers to refrain from political topics. For their own safety, most bloggers employ self-censorship and focus on entertainment and amusement – even to the point of "feeding public curiosity for the sexy, the weird, and the bizarre." In all likelihood, this direction taken by the Chinese blogosphere will continue to delineate blogging in China.

Women's sports advocates have envisioned the blogosphere as a place free of the gatekeeping constraints and gender stereotypes of traditional media editors. In Chapter 4, the research of Marie Hardin, Bu Zhong, and Thomas F. Corrigan explores independent sports blogs and contrasts their portrayals of gender with those of mainstream sports media. Findings confirm that the American blogosphere exhibits tendencies inherited from mainstream media including the marginalization of women's sports, and the subsequent objectification of female athletes. The authors reveal that rationalizations, not reasons, have been used to explain why sports writers have not become more progressive on gender issues with the advent of blogging. The researchers conclude that the sports blogosphere is failing to attract bloggers with progressive views on sports; instead, the blogosphere is attracting writers who for one reason or another prefer to maintain the status quo of old-media values.

Gwen L. Shaffer, in Chapter 5, argues that the idea of a universal code of conduct for bloggers can fail to acknowledge the unique freedoms of speech and expression personified by the global and national blogospheres. Even the best-intended rules of conduct can nullify the benefits of having no gatekeepers on the Internet. The lack of central editorial control in blogging permits communities of bloggers to freely connect and decide what boundaries for self-expression they deem necessary. In spite of noble intentions, a blogging code of conduct could diminish free speech in the blogosphere. The author reaches a valuable conclusion: namely, that bloggers should fully understand and accept the expressive boundaries of a given blog before stepping into the fray. Finally, owners of single-authored blogs and moderators of collective blogs must clearly stipulate their rules so that bloggers will understand the consequences of crossing the line.

Section 2: Blogs and Blogging: Case Studies

Section 2 examines specific case studies and encompasses Chapters 6-10. Anastacia Kurylo and Michael Kurylo, in Chapter 6, inquire into whether or not blogs have evolved beyond the personal and idiosyncratic limitations of online journals. The authors decide that in the case of KnickerBlogger.Net, a name derived from a professional basketball team, the New York Knickerbockers, a blog can become a virtual sports fan "classroom" that permits diverse points of view. This case study documents the capacity for sports blogs to educate fan communities and to allow fans to express their personal opinions. The metaphor of a classroom provides a useful viewpoint for understanding how at least one sports blog has joined the mainstream and suggests a measure for interpreting how blogs may become accepted at large.

Naomi Gold probes the depths of blogging as an emotional, expressive release for disgruntled American Hasidim in Chapter 7. Gold maintains that blogging entails "reflection and conversation taken to electronic lengths." With respect to reflection, blogging has opened new communication channels for formerly isolated individuals allowing them to connect and share ideas, perspectives, and life experiences. The researcher reveals these newly found powers of blogging in the context of American Orthodox Jewish communities. Currently, blogging in these communities is availing a platform for weighing in on Hasidic customs, practices, and lifestyles; it is affording members who are "off the path" with a means to reinforce or diversify their beliefs and ways of life. Overall, blogging has provided an equally valuable communication outlet for Hasidic members who choose to stay in their communities or leave them. The author argues that blogging has globalized the former hermitical Hasidic world. Indeed, instead of weakening Hasidic communities, blogging might be bringing the potential to rejuvenate them through dialogue and open discussion.

In Chapter 8, Lori F. Brost and Carol McGinnis report a case study of blogging in Ireland. Some pundits suggest that blogging in Ireland is on the decline, while Twitter and Facebook are on the rise. The authors, however, indicate that blogging is merely changing. Although some bloggers quit, many continue to blog while others adopt new forms, such as live blogging. Along with technologically sophisticated Irish males who were early adopters of blogging, men and woman from all walks of life are now blogging in Ireland. The lively and varied topics in the Irish blogosphere encompass "social, political, and cultural interests, concerns, and activities." It appears that competing traditional media outlets have sensationalized the overly self-critical and reflective commentary on the coming demise of Irish blogging featured in some blogs. In short, blogging is "alive and well in Ireland."

Justin D. Martin and Sherine El-Toukhy, the authors of Chapter 9, inquire into the Palestinian political blogosphere. Although the authors found that most Palestinian bloggers were critical of the State of Israel and its policies, research unveiled that the bloggers' tone on the State of Israel was not as derisive and belligerent as they anticipated. Some Palestinian bloggers seem to be demonstrating empathy, and kindness; in fact, many of these bloggers embrace a restrained style over a vituperative one. The authors infer that at least a fraction of Palestinian bloggers believes that the Israeli-Palestinian conflict in the Middle East is curable and that the Palestinian blogosphere should not be exploited to advance extremist views.

Chapter 10, written by Jocelyn M. DeGroot and Heather J. Carmack, elaborates on blogging as a means of grieving. Individuals experiencing the loss of someone special may be grief-stricken. Since their mourning may require substantial "grief work" to reorient their lives, blogging can become an effective communication channel to help them recover from a loss. The authors indicate that grief blogging functions as a public arena for individuals to help them cope with and recover from grief while keeping the lines of communication with the outside world open. Grief blogs embody the inherent paradox of the Internet—that is, users publicly communicate private information for the sake of personal recovery, despite the number of ethical dilemmas along the way.

Section 3: Analyzing Blogs: Approaches and Perspectives

The chapters in Section 3 utilize various research perspectives and approaches for analyzing, interpreting, and assessing blogs and blogging. The section starts in Chapter 11 with the study of Lynne M. Webb, Tiffany E. Fields, Sitthivorada Boupha, and Matthew N. Stell on the contributions of blog design, rather than content, to the popularity of U.S. political blogs. Aiming to assess channel characteristics associated with popular political blogs, the study finds a positive correlation between internal accessibility, comment opportunities, and blog popularity (gauged by "hits" or page views), as well as between length of a blog's homepage and opportunities for user interaction. Ultimately, this study of channel characteristics indicates that the most popular blog styles for users are those "with more tabs, more links, and greater internal accessibility."

In chapter 12, Jenny Bronstein applies a uses and gratification approach to determine the motivations of Latin American bloggers. The study reveals that Latin Americans blog to satisfy emotional and social needs and that blogging incorporates releasing emotions, building interpersonal relations, and mere information gathering. The motivation that Latin American bloggers rate highest is the need to express what is felt and thought. Other motivations that are equally important include the following: to fulfill a need for self-expression, to open an outlet for communicating frustration, to develop a deeper understanding of oneself through public self-disclosure, to improve writing skills, to document personal life experiences, ideas, and thoughts, and to share information. Interestingly, the majority of Latin American bloggers do not consider "just passing the time" as a motivation for blogging.

Chapter 13, by Joshua Azriel, is written from the U.S. Constitution's First Amendment legal perspective and yields acute information. The author holds that as bloggers enter the publishing field, they should fully realize the legal risks of retribution for distributing hurtful blog content. Since libel, privacy, obscenity, and other speech laws can be applied to blogging, future court cases will adjudicate whether new common law principles will influence the content and boundaries of blogs. Although the 1996 Communications Decency Act exempts Internet service providers from legal responsibility for offensive Internet posts, the U.S. Congress can retune the law by redefining Internet users' liability. In conclusion, Azriel notes that with the First Amendment as a protection of free speech and freedom of the press, the U.S. legal system still contains an abundance of punishing powers for bloggers who decide to venture outside the First Amendment into areas of libel, invasion of privacy, threats, and obscenity.

Richard Fiordo sets forth, in Chapter 14, a hermeneutic perspective in the analysis of a blogging episode. This study demonstrates that blog content can trigger extremely complex discursive interactions. When readers fail to recognize the layered convolutions of blogs in their unique contexts and with their hidden stories, misinterpretations will follow. Since multiple hazards may accompany the extraction of meaning in blogs, blogs might best be critiqued through integrated methods. To determine a blog's overall message and identify the stories behind the stories, a blog should be approached from multiple perspectives. The research into this particular blogging incident shows: (1) that the expressed intention of the blog investigated seems to have boomeranged and resulted in the opposite of its expressed ideal of helping someone in need, and (2) that inquiry into other blogs should carefully seek to discover suppressed flaws like those masquerading as humane efforts in the analyzed blog.

Tatyana Dumova, author of Chapter 15, examines the status quo of the global blogosphere through the lens of the emerging social interaction technologies to ascertain what the future holds for blogging. Surveying global blogging for recent trends, the author concludes that underlying social interaction technologies make blogging especially suitable for grassroots initiatives and innovation. Recent technological developments, such as the convergence of blogging and social networking platforms, network-based peer production, microblogging, and hyperlocal and live blogging, have wide-ranging implications for audiences around the world. For over a decade, Internet users have employed blogs as a ubiquitous social media tool to communicate and interact with others, and there is evidence to expect that they will continue to rely on this medium in the future.

Designed to explore the global potential of blogs for bridging people and cultures in today's world, *Blogging in the Global Society* traces blogging practices across national borders, cultural confines, and geographical constraints. An array of perspectives, research methods, and findings articulate the unique contribution of this book to the understanding of the roles and functions of blogging. On behalf of the authors, the editors express hopes that this volume will attract further scholarly attention to the diverse issues of blogging in a global context. The editors are aware of the limitations of any attempt to cover a global medium in a single book and see its publication as a small step forward into this frontier of knowledge and practice.

Tatyana Dumova
Point Park University, USA

Richard Fiordo
University of North Dakota, USA

REFERENCES

Berners-Lee, T., Hall, W., Hendler, J., Shadbolt, N., & Weitzner, D. J. (2006). Creating a science of the Web. *Science, 313*, 769–770. doi:10.1126/science.1126902

BlogPulse. (2011). *BlogPulse stats*. Retrieved August 18, 2011, from http://www.blogpulse.com

Dumova, T., & Fiordo, R. (2010). Preface. In Dumova, T., & Fiordo, R. (Eds.), *Handbook of research on social interaction technologies and collaboration software: Concepts and trends*. Hershey, PA: Information Science Reference.

Knittsings.com. (2008, August 14). *How to thread a pink passup duomatic 4 color changer*. Retrieved July 10, 2011, from http://knittsings.com/how-thread-pink-passap-duomatic-4-color-changer/

Naslund, A. (2011). *8 lessons learned from the long blogging road*. Retrieved August 10, 2011, from http://www.brasstackthinking.com/2011/08/8-lessons-learned-from-the-long-blogging-road/

Scocco, D. (2008, August 18). *27 definitions for blog*. Retrieved July 10, 2011, http://www.dailyblogtips.com/27-definitions-for-blog/

Sunstein, C. R. (2006). *Infotopia: How many minds produce knowledge*. New York, NY: Oxford University Press.

Technorati. (2010). *State of the blogosphere 2010*. Retrieved July 24, 2011, from http://technorati.com/blogging/article/state-of-the-blogosphere-2010-introduction/

Wave 3 Social Media Tracker. (2008). *Power to the people* (Universal McCann survey report). Retrieved April 10, 2011, from http://www.universalmccann.com/Assets/wave_3_20080403093750.pdf

Acknowledgment

This book would not have been possible without the dedication and assistance of many individuals. First and foremost, the editors would like to express their profound gratitude to the authors who have contributed their knowledge, expertise, and research insights to develop this timely, and in many aspects, remarkable publication. The editors would also like to acknowledge the help of the reviewers involved in the peer evaluation process and thank them for providing constructive critiques and valuable suggestions. Finally, our deep gratitude goes to the IGI Global publishing team representatives for their professional commitment, patience, and support.

We sincerely thank all those who have helped this book come to fruition.

Tatyana Dumova
Point Park University, USA

Richard Fiordo
University of North Dakota, USA

Section 1
The Global Blogosphere:
Political, Cultural, Legal, and Ethical Issues

Chapter 1
Blogs as a Source of Democratic Deliberation

Barbara K. Kaye
University of Tennessee Knoxville, USA

Thomas J. Johnson
University of Texas Austin, USA

Peter Muhlberger
Texas Tech University, USA

ABSTRACT

This chapter examines the deliberative potential of blogs and blog users. It investigates whether heavy reliance on blogs promotes positive characteristics—political efficacy, political interest, and political involvement—needed to foster democratic deliberation, or whether it leads to negative attributes—low trust, selective exposure, and political partisanship—that hinder democratic deliberation. Results show that unlike those who rarely rely on blogs, heavily dependent individuals are more involved in current events and are more trusting of the government, but they are also more likely to practice selective exposure by reading ideologically consistent blogs. Further, heavy reliance predicts involvement and selective exposure. The deliberative potential of blogs is boosted by users' involvement in political issues but impeded by their propensity to seek out blogs that contain agreeable information. Instead of evolving into a public sphere, blogs may be becoming issue-oriented zones in which deliberation is limited to an ideological perspective.

INTRODUCTION

The emergence of the World Wide Web in the mid-1990s resurrected hopes of reinvigorating democracy by creating a space where democratic deliberation—a process in which citizens vol-untarily participate in discussions about public issues—could take place and the voice of the people could be elevated above the din of special interests and have a greater influence on pubic opinion (e.g., Jones, 1995; Rheingold, 1993).

Some envisioned the Internet as a delibera-tive democratic forum where citizens engage in rational debate over common problems leading to

DOI: 10.4018/978-1-60960-744-9.ch001

more informed public opinion that can help guide decision-making by public officials (Dahlberg, 2007; Habermas, 1989). However, more recent research has raised doubt about the Internet's ability to stimulate democratic deliberation. Rather than bringing people together to engage in rational debate, the Internet may be creating communication outposts where likeminded people gather to reinforce their preexisting opinions and attack those who hold opposing ones, leading to increased polarization of political views (Galston, 2003; Sunstein, 2001). Blogs that typically post highly partisan content abet polarization by attracting users who seek out opinions that support their point of view and avoid those that challenge them (Johnson, Bichard, & Zhang, 2009). Thus, political discussion on blogs may represent the antithesis of democratic deliberation ideals.

While several studies have examined whether the nature of blog discussion constitutes democratic deliberation (Koop & Jansen, 2009; Xenos, 2008), what has not been as extensively researched is whether reliance on blogs leads to positive political attributes (such as increased self-efficacy, political interest, and involvement) as well as negative effects (such as low trust, selective exposure, and political partisanship). This study then examines whether reliance on blogs influences political attributes that foster or hinder democratic deliberation.

LITERATURE REVIEW

Democratic Deliberation

Interest in democratic deliberation first began to flourish during the 1970s in response to people becoming less trustful, less interested and less engaged in the political process (Delli Carpini & Keeter, 1996; Putnam, 2000). Democratic theorists argue that political conversation really is the soul of democracy and that for democracy to thrive it must have an engaged and informed citizenry (Fishkin, 1991; Gastil & Dillard, 1999; Kim, Wyatt, & Katz, 1999). Also, decisions derived from democratic deliberation are believed to benefit democratic governance more than simple majority rule or decisions made only by elites (Kim, 2006; Strandberg, 2008).

While theorists have devoted considerable attention to discussing the importance of "democratic deliberation" to the political process, it is not always clear what is meant by the term (Bohman, 1996; Hardy, Scheufele & Wang, 2005). Several studies have used the terms "democratic deliberation" and "public sphere" interchangeably (e.g., Dahlberg, 2007; Vergeer & Hermans, 2008), though the *public sphere* as envisioned by Habermas (1989) is technically the space in which the activity of democratic deliberation occurs.

Democratic deliberation has been defined as "discussion that involves judicious argument, critical listening and earnest decision making. Full deliberation includes a careful examination of a problem or an issue, the identification of possible solutions, and the use of these criteria in identifying an optimal solution" (Gastil, 2000, p. 22). Therefore, deliberative democracy is a process where citizens voluntarily participate in discussions about public issues (Kim, et al., 1999). During deliberative discussion, participants carefully examine a problem or issue, identify possible solutions, establish or reaffirm evaluation criteria, and use these criteria to identify the optimum solution to the problem (Dahlberg, 2001, 2007; Gastil, 2000; Sunstein, 2001). The quality of public deliberation depends on informed participants offering diverse opinions.

Democratic deliberation is typified by several important characteristics including: (1) a diversity of points of view in which people are given equal opportunity to express themselves; (2) a rational and critical debate focusing on an issue or a set of issues; (3) a discussion of issues of social importance; and (4) an arena to develop solutions to problems:

- Participants must represent a wide range of views so that different perspectives are debated and discussed. Deliberation only occurs when participants engage in a constructive manner with differing points of view rather than simply agreeing with and reinforcing views that are similar to their own (Koop & Jansen, 2009; Stromer-Galley & Muhlberger, 2009). Similarly, people must be given both adequate and equal time to voice their point of view rather than having the forum dominated by one or two voices (Dahlgren, 2001; Gastil, 2000; Koop & Jansen, 2009). While public deliberation scholars are concerned with getting a wide variety of viewpoints, public sphere researchers stress the importance of universal access to the deliberation site (Habermas, 1989).
- Democratic deliberation is not an intellectual "free for all," but a forum for rational and critical debate normally focused on a particular issue or set of related issues. Ideally, participants will enter a debate armed with critical, well-reasoned arguments, will express them even in the face of potentially hostile reaction from others, will listen to conflicting viewpoints before reacting, and will be open to revising their preferences in light of new information or perspectives offered by other participants (Chambers, 2003; Hardy et al., 2005; Wright & Street, 2007).
- Democratic deliberation should revolve around areas of social interest that are not normally questioned in the political arena (Habermas, 1974, 1989).
- A deliberation forum is not simply a place to engage in rational debate, but a venue to develop solutions to problems. Democratic deliberation is how the public should "identify, draw attention to and interpret social problems and propose solutions" (Curran, 2000, p. 136).

Blogs and Democratic Deliberation

The potential for the Internet and its components, such as blogs, to serve as a forum for democratic debate has been the subject of recent research. Blogs are considered advantageous for democratic deliberations for the following reasons:

- Blogs eliminate geographic constraints to deliberation, thereby lowering the cost of travel for both organizers and participants (Delli Carpini, Cook, & Jacobs, 2004; Kim, 2006).
- Gatherings can be assembled quickly to discuss pressing issues (Delli Carpini, et al., 2004).
- Blogs are not as subject to commercial pressures or government control as traditional media, which allows people to express their views more freely (Dimaggio, Hargittai, Neuman, & Robinson, 2001; Wojcieszak & Mutz, 2009).
- Personal anonymity and the absence of verbal cues prevent judgments based on race, gender, and attractiveness (Papacharissi, 2004).
- Blogs might increase the participants' abilities to engage in democratic debate (Price & Capella, 2002; Price, Nir, & Capella, 2002).

Therefore, online deliberative discussions are at least equal, if not generally superior, to face-to-face ones.

As blogs have emerged as a legitimate alternative to the mainstream press, so has interest in whether blogs do serve as a site for deliberation. Proponents argue that blogs embody the spirit of the public sphere by providing a "virtually local" forum for public debate missing since the days of coffee houses and salons (Keren, 2004; Thompson, 2003). Blogs foster a sense of community among users who gravitate toward the ones that share their viewpoints (Johnson & Kaye, 2004, 2007;

Johnson, Kaye, Bichard, & Wong, 2007; Kaye & Johnson, 2006; Papacharissi, 2004; Trammell, Tarkowski, & Sapp, 2006). Blogging, then, allows anyone with Internet access to erect a platform online to voice his or her views and provides an easy way for people to comment on posts made by others (Baoill, 2004).

Critics argue, however, that most blogs fall short of serving as forums for democratic deliberation for three major reasons: Blogs are not structured to promote democratic debate; they tend to attract those who share points of view rather than hold a diversity of opinions; and the nature of blog discussions normally fall far short of the deliberation ideal:

- Few blogs serve as forums of discussion and many do not allow comments but simply serve as a soapbox for the blogger. Other blogs allow reader comments to be posted on the blog, but they must first go through a gatekeeping process in which the blogger decides whether the comment is appropriate to post (Baoill, 2000). Even when blog users are allowed to comment on blog entries, their comments are not nearly as prominent as the original post (Barton, 2005). Because bloggers may post comments about a dozen or more topics, blog structure does not foster a sustained, robust discussion. While certain comments may generate a long thread of follow-up remarks most blog users state their views and then move on to another topic (Baoill, 2000).

- Blogs do not typically attract a mixture of individuals who bring a variety of points of view required of a deliberative forum. Most blogs focus on specific interests such as gun control or gay rights that limit the topic of conversation, and like-minded blog users tend to congregate on blogs that represent their points of view, rather than alternative perspectives. Such homogene-

ity within online groups reduces the quality of debate because diverging opinions, which are necessary for a fruitful debate on issues of public concern, are missing (Albrecht, 2006). More importantly, partisan sources such as blogs may create a vicious circle by encouraging likeminded people to gather in "cyber ghettos" and engage in "enclave extremism" where they may have little contact with, or understanding of, outside groups and thus followers may become progressively more extreme in their political positions (Dahlgren, 2005; Sunstein, 2007; Xenos, 2008).

- Critics also claim that blogs fail to achieve perhaps the main deliberative goal: promoting a rational and critical debate that leads to consensus. Blogs, like many other online forums, tend to be dominated by a few individuals who espouse their views without offering supporting evidence. Also, partisan blog users are not often willing to listen to conflicting opinions or revise their views as a result new information. Rather, blog participants attack the positions of those who oppose them (Dahlberg, 2001; Poster, 1997; Strandberg, 2008). Even among those who argue that most online discussion is largely civil (Papacharissi, 2004), blogs at best may offer only a public space for discussion rather than a true site for deliberation.

Characteristics of Blog Users

While Habermas (1989) argued that in the public sphere everyone must have the ability to participate in democratic deliberation, he was aware that elite citizens would be more likely to do so. He argued that those who are more politically interested, who believe they have the ability to influence the political system and who engage in politics are more likely to participate in democratic discussions.

Indeed, blog users appear to be models for democratic discussion. For example, blog users are distinguished from non-blog users by their strong interest in and extensive knowledge about politics, their regular participation in online and offline political activities, especially their work on behalf of candidates or issues (Delli Carpini et al., 2004; Gastil, 2000; Graf, 2006), and their high level of political efficacy (Johnson & Kaye, 2004, 2007). Blog reliance, then, could create a virtuous circle by attracting the political active and interested who read the blogs and become even more interested and active in politics. However, users tend to be more likely than non-users to be distrustful of the media and government institutions (Graf, 2006; Johnson & Kaye, 2004, 2007). Additionally, political blog users tend to be highly partisan and seek out information that supports their already-held political attitudes and avoid information that challenges those views (Iyengar & Hahn, 2009; Stroud, 2006, 2008; Sunstein, 2001, 2007). Indeed reliance on blogs has proven to be a stronger predictor of seeking out supportive information than any other online source (Johnson & Kaye, 2009). Therefore, blog use reinforces users' existing partisan positions rather than leading them to seek both sides of an issue and weighing the merits before reaching a decision (Zhang, Johnson, Bichard, & Gangadharbatla, 2009).

Thus, partisanship and selective exposure may be the antitheses of public deliberation. Additionally, blog users do not demographically resemble the U.S. population as a whole or even the average Internet users. Blog users are young, well-educated males with high incomes (Eveland & Dylko, 2007; Johnson & Kaye, 2004, 2007; Technorati, 2008), whereas Internet users more closely resemble the American mainstream. That is, women and men are equally likely to be online and gaps based on race, age, education and income have narrowed (Pew Research Center, 2008).

Research Questions

Whether blogs are or can become spheres of democratic deliberation largely depends on the users. The blogs themselves are merely a place of convergence. It is the users and the way they participate that distinguish rational deliberation from mere expression of opinion.

This study examines whether those who heavily rely on blogs tend to be more likely to possess positive political attributes that lead to deliberation, such as increased political efficacy, political interest, and involvement, as well as negative attributes such as low trust, selective exposure and political partisanship, which inhibit discussion than those who are less reliant on blogs for political information. Therefore, this study will address the following questions:

RQ1: Do levels of political attributes associated with fostering democratic deliberations (political efficacy, political interest, political involvement) differ between those who rely heavily on blogs and those who rely rarely on blogs?

RQ2: Do levels of political attributes associated with impeding democratic deliberations (political distrust, selective exposure, political partisanship) differ between those who rely heavily on blogs and those who rely rarely on blogs?

H1: Reliance on blogs predicts political attributes associated with democratic deliberation (political efficacy, political interest, and political involvement) after controlling for political ideology, the ideology of the blogs individuals rely on, and demographic variables.

H2: Reliance on political blogs predicts political attributes that may impede demographic deliberation (political distrust, selective exposure, and political partisanship) after controlling for political ideology, the ideology of the blogs individuals rely on, and demographics.

METHOD

An online survey that specifically targeted blog users was posted from April 23 to May 22, 2007. To specifically reach blog users, the authors contacted 109 blog users to request a survey announcement and a link to the survey URL. The survey was linked from 70 blogs of diverse ideologies, such as the conservative *Boortz News* (now called *Nealz Nuze*), the middle-of-the-road *Moderate Voice*, and the progressive *Daily Kos*.[1] Additionally, a "snowball" technique was used, which allowed respondents to automatically forward the survey to fellow blog readers (Babbie, 2002).[2] The survey was completed by 1,989 respondents.[3]

Blog Reliance

The degree to which users rely on blogs for news and information was assessed by a question that asked respondents to mark their level of reliance on a 1-5 scale that ranged from "never rely on" to "very heavily rely on."

Political Attributes

Survey respondents were asked about several political characteristics that have been identified as those that are catalysts of democratic deliberation:

- Political efficacy was measured as a summed index made up of two items from the National Election Studies conducted by the University of Michigan: "People like me don't have any say about what the government does" and "Every vote counts in an election, including yours and mine." The response options ranged from "strongly disagree" to "strongly agree." The polarity was reversed on the first efficacy item. Reliability for the efficacy index is .54.[4]
- Interest in news and current events was measured on a 0-10 scale with 0 as "not interested at all" and 10 as "very interested."

- Involvement in contemporary issues and events was assessed by the following question: As a result of blogging my involvement in general news and current events has "greatly decreased," "decreased," "stayed the same," "increased," "greatly increased."

Respondents were also asked about characteristics that are impediments of democratic deliberation:

- Trust in the government was also assessed as an index comprised of items taken from the National Election Studies: "Most of our leaders are devoted to service," "Politicians never tell us what they really think," and "I don't think public officials care much about what people like me think." The response options also ranged from "strongly disagree" to "strongly agree." The polarity was reversed on the second and third statements. The reliability for the trust index is .74.
- Selective exposure was measured by the question, "How likely are you to purposely connect with blogs that share your point of view on issues?" Respondents selected from a 0-10 scale with 0 as "not likely at all" and 10 as "very highly likely."
- Political partisanship was assessed by asking respondents to mark on a 0-10 scale how strongly tied they are to their political party of choice.

Ideology

Two questions asked about respondents' political ideology and their perceptions of the ideology of the blogs they visit most often. The options for both questions were: "very liberal," "liberal," "moderate," "conservative," "very conservative."

Demographics

Respondents were asked their gender, their age as of their last birthday and estimated their 2007 income. They also selected their highest level of education from among seven options that ranged from "less than high school" to "Ph.D. degree" and "other."

Data Analysis

First, reliance on blogs was recoded as a separate variable that grouped respondents as either very heavily/heavily relying on blogs (those who marked 4 or 5) sometimes/rarely relying on blogs (those who marked 1 or 2). Moderate users (those who marked 3) were excluded from the two group comparisons. Independent samples *t*-tests were then run to ascertain differences between heavy and light blog users on the variables that foster democratic deliberation and on those that inhibit it.

Next, regressions were run to examine the influence of blog reliance on the political attributes that may either impede or lead to deliberation. The regression controlled for demographics and ideology of the respondents and of the blogs they visit most often by entering the independent variables in blocks. For each regression, one of the political attributes (political efficacy, political interest, political involvement, selective exposure, political distrust and political partisanship was entered as the dependent variable. Next, demographics (gender, age, education, income) were entered into the first independent variable block, the second block consisted of blog and personal ideology, and reliance on blogs was entered into the third block for each regression.

RESULTS

The profile of this survey's respondents shows that just over three-quarters (77.3%) are male and almost nine out of ten are white (89.5%).

The respondents are highly educated with 89.7% reporting some college or higher, and they report an annual income of $90,500 on average. Additionally, they average 47.7 years of age and have been accessing blogs for an average of 5.2 years. The demographic characteristics of this survey's respondents are similar to the profiles of blog readers reported by others (Blogads, 2006, Graf, 2006).

Looking at the political attributes that foster democratic deliberation shows that the overwhelming majority of blog users (82.7%) expressed a strong interest in current events and news. Additionally, almost three-quarters (74.8%) credit blogs as a catalyst to greater involvement in general news issues. Respondent also tend to believe they have the power to bring about political change. Just over one-half (51.0%) claim high levels of political efficacy (those who marked 8, 9 or 10 [range 2-10]) and 37.1% report moderate levels (marked 5, 6 or 7).

Although the respondents are highly self-efficacious they do not seem to trust the government. Only 13.2% of the respondents report high to very high levels of trust, 47.0% say they are moderately trustful and four out of ten (39.8%) claim low to very low feelings of trust. Respondents are also moderately likely to connect to blogs that share their worldview ($M = 8.35$, range 1-10). The respondents, however, are not strongly tied to a political party ($M = 5.62$, range 1-10). Further, about one-third (32.1%) expressed weak party ties, 36.0% moderate ties, and 31.9% strong ties.

When asked their political ideology, almost six of ten (57.7%) responded that they are conservative, 24.4% moderate, and 18.0% consider themselves liberals. Their ideology closely matches the ideology of the blogs they read; 63.6% visit blogs that are conservative in nature, while only 18.5% access liberal-leaning blogs, and 17.8% favor ideologically moderate blogs.

Heavy Blog Users vs. Light Blog Users

The first research question investigates differences between respondents who very heavily/heavily rely on blogs and those who sometimes/rarely rely on blogs on their levels of political efficacy, interest and involvement in current events – attributes that are associated with democratic deliberation. Heavy blog users are significantly more involved in issues of the day than light blog users ($t = 8.75$, $df = 1520$, $p < .000$). Heavy and light blog users do not differ on either levels of political efficacy or interest in news and current issues (Table 1).

When looking at the characteristics that impede deliberation heavy blog users are more trusting of the government than light blog users ($t = 2.59$, $df = 1337$, $p < .01$). Neither group, however, is very trusting. On a scale of 3-15, trust levels of heavy blog users average 7.47, and light blog users 6.91. Heavy blog users are also significantly more likely to seek information from blogs

that concur with their own opinions ($t = 11.20$, $df = 1520$ $p < .001$). The combination of low trust in the government and selective exposure to a narrow range of agreeable perspectives may inhibit democratic deliberation. There is no difference between heavy and light blog users on strength of ties to a political party, but there is a significant difference between the two groups on political ideology. Heavy blog users (Table 1) are significantly more conservative ($M = 3.52$) than light blog users ($M = 3.15$).

How much respondents rely on blogs may influence their outlook about world events, and thus their willingness to engage in rational discourse and problem solving. Regression analysis was used in this study to ascertain whether reliance on blogs predicts political efficacy, and interest in - and involvement with news and political events. The first hypothesis is partially supported because blog reliance is a strong and significant predictor of only involvement ($b = .21$, $p < .001$). Individuals who rely heavily on blogs and are heavily

Table 1. Comparisons between heavy blog users and light blog users

	Heavy Blog Reliant (n = 1345) (Means)	Light Blog Reliant (n = 177) (Means)
Variables that Foster Democratic Deliberation		
Political efficacy (mean range 2-10) ($t = -.116$, $df = 1516$, $p = .907$)	7.13	7.15
Interest in news (mean range 1-10) ($t = .763$, $df = 1517$, $p = .446$)	8.73	8.64
Involvement in news (mean range 1-5) ($t = 8.75$, $df = 1520$, $p = .000$)	4.04A	3.46B
Variables that Impede Democratic Deliberation		
Trust in government (range 3-15) ($t = 2.59$, $df = 1337$, $p = .009$)	7.47A	6.91B
Selective Exposure (mean range 1-10) ($t = 11.192$, $df = 1520$, $p = .000$)	7.64A	6.00B
Political Partisanship (range 1-10) ($t = 1.26$, $df = 1446$, $p = .208$)	5.72	5.42
Ideology		
Political Ideology (conservative = 5) ($t = 4.33$, $df – 1458$, $p = .000$)	3.52A	3.15B

* Means scores with capital letters = horizontal comparisons - differ by $p < .05$ independent samples t-test.

involved in world affairs tend to be females (b = .06, p < .05). Reliance on blogs does not predict whether individuals believe they have power to bring about political change, neither does it influence their interest in world events. However, younger respondents who visit conservative blogs are more likely to be highly self efficacious, while males who visit liberal blogs are more interested in news and politics (Table 2).

The study next turns its attention to the variables that tend to inhibit democratic deliberation (low trust in the government, selective exposure and political partisanship) Regression analysis investigated whether reliance on blogs predicts these characteristics. The second hypothesis is partially supported because selective exposure is predicted by reliance (b = .23, p < .001). Those who rely heavily on blogs and who practice selective exposure by visiting blogs that promote like-minded perspectives and opinions (Table 3) tend

to be conservative (b = .11, p < .05) females (b = .07, p < .05) who do not visit liberal blogs (b = -.09, p < .05).

On the other hand, blog reliance does not predict whether blog users are trusting of the government or political partisanship. Although the *t*-tests indicate that heavy blog users are significantly more trusting of the government than light blog users, the regression analysis does not indicate a predictive strength. Controlling for the respondents' ideology and the ideology of the blogs they visit most often weakens the regression. The regression analysis does, however, suggest that highly educated liberals who do not connect to conservative blogs are trusting of the government. Further, older, male conservatives are the most strongly connected to their political party of choice (Table 3).

Table 2. Hierarchical regression analysis of blog reliance as a predictor of variables that boost democratic deliberation

	Political Efficacy	Interest in News and Politics	Involvement in News & Politics
Gender (female = positive)	.01	.06*	.06*
Age	-.08**	.04	.04
Education	.04	.02	.05
Income	.01	.03	.00
R2	.007	.009	.010
Significance	.021	.008	.002
Blog Ideology (conservative = 5)	.20***	-.10*	.00
Political Ideology (conservative = 5)	.03	.03	.03
R2	.054	.014	.010
R2 Change	.047	.005	.000
Significance	.000	.001	.011
Blog Reliance	.00	.05	.21***
R2	.054	.016	.055
R2 Change	.000	.002	.045
Adjusted R	.050	.012	.050
Sig. of Change	.000	.001	.000

*p < .05, **p < .01, ***p < .001

Table 3. Hierarchical regression analysis of blog reliance as a predictor of variables that impede democratic deliberation

	Trust in Gov't	Selective Exposure	Political Partisanship
Gender (female = positive)	.04	.07*	.13***
Age	-.04	.04	.09**
Education	.14***	.00	.04
Income	-.01	-.00	.02
R2	**.024**	**.007**	**.025**
Significance	**.000**	**.032**	**.000**
Blog Ideology (conservative = 5)	.13**	-.09*	-.06
Political Ideology (conservative = 5)	-.10*	.11*	.12**
R2	**.030**	**.014**	**.030**
R2 Change	**.006**	**.007**	**.005**
Significance	**.000**	**.002**	**.000**
Blog Reliance	.04	.23***	.03
R2	**.031**	**.065**	**.03**
R2 Change	**.001**	**.051**	**.001**
Adjusted R	**.027**	**.061**	**.027**
Sig. of Change	**.000**	**.000**	**.000**

*p < .05, **p < .01, ***p < .001

CONCLUSION

Whether blogs have the potential to heighten democratic deliberation is a matter of debate. Blog enthusiasts envision a blogosphere as a focal point of rational persuasion and conversation where social and political issues are discussed among diverse users and consensus is reached (Delli Carpini, et al.; Dimaggio, et al., 2001; Wojcieszak, & Mutz, 2009). Others, however, take a more skeptical look and believe that blogs hinder democratic debate largely because they attract a homogenous audience whose purpose is to push their point of view while discounting other perspectives (Dahlgren, 2005; Sunstein, 2007; Xenos, 2008). This study of 1,989 blog users compares those who heavily rely on blogs to those who rarely rely on blogs. The question is whether reliance on blogs leads to positive political attitudes, such as political efficacy, political interest and political involvement, which have been linked to democratic deliberation or to negative attributes such as low trust, selective exposure and political partisanship.

This chapter reveals three main findings that bear on the deliberative potential of blogs:

- Whether comparing means with a *t*-test or controlling for other variables via regression, users who rely heavily on blogs are significantly more likely than light blog users to report greater involvement in news and politics as a consequence of their use of blogs.
- Heavy blog users are significantly more likely than light blog users to report exposing themselves selectively to like-minded blogs. Overall, while effects found here are significant they are not very strong. Blog reliance explains 4.5% of the vari-

ance of involvement in news and politics and 5.1% of the variance of selective exposure. While these are respectable levels of explanatory power for a single variable, the relationships are weakly determinative. Heavy blog users are only somewhat more politically involved and somewhat more selective in information exposure on average than light blog users.

- Regression results find no significant relationship between blog reliance and four other indicators of positive or negative deliberative potential—political efficacy, interest in news and politics, trust in government, and political partisanship.

These results oppose a vicious circle interpretation of blog use—namely, that the more people read blogs, the more they become politically disaffected and selective in what they read, and these negative attributes lead them to read blogs more often, which further reinforces the negative attributes. As discussed in the literature review, some observers believe the objective and structure of blogs lead to growing polarization, partisanship, and 'enclave extremism' (Dahlgren, 2005; Sunstein, 2007; Xenos, 2008). If such views are correct, it should be the case that those who use blogs more heavily would show dramatically higher levels of information selectivity than lighter users, but findings here indicate only a moderate impact, at best. Also, partisanship and low trust in government, particularly among conservative bloggers, should be appreciably greater among heavy users. No such effects were found here. The findings, then, do not suggest that greater reliance on blogs leads to a vicious circle of extremism, partisanship, and distrust.

While perhaps blog users differ from the general public in these negative attributes, increasing reliance on blogs does not seem to lead reliably to the negative attributes among blog users. If blog users are different from the general public, the findings are most consistent with the view

that blog users differ largely due to self-selection and not as a consequence of the causal impact of blog reliance. If blog reliance causes escalating negative attributes among blog users, then those who rely more heavily on blogs should have markedly more negative attributes, but instead the differences between heavy and light blog users are moderate and mixed.

Neither, however, do the findings support a virtuous circle interpretation of blog use. Again, the literature review indicates that some observers believe that the structure of blogs lends itself to encouraging deliberative engagement (Johnson & Kaye, 2004, 2007; Kaye & Johnson, 2006; Papacharissi, 2004). Some researchers (Muhlberger, 2005; Neuman, 1986) suggest that political engagement follows a virtuous circle—one in which more engagement yields more positive attributes such as political knowledge and political efficacy, which in turn encourage yet greater engagement. The interactive nature of blogs creates the expectation that heavy blog users would be sharply more involved in news and politics than light blog users, while the data here indicate only a moderate impact. Likewise, the virtuous circle interpretation anticipates that heavy blog users would be appreciably more politically efficacious and interested in news and politics, on average. The findings here indicate no significant relationship. Again, the findings are most consistent with the view that certain types of people are drawn to blogs, not that blogs greatly reshape people into virtuous citizens.

To the extent that blogs have a causal impact on the deliberative fitness of participants, blog reliance pulls in two opposing directions with respect to such fitness—it moderately increases engagement, a positive outcome, but it also moderately increases selectivity, a negative outcome. These findings are not consistent with a view of blog participants as motivated to engage a diversity of others in public problem solving—a key part of the definition of deliberation. If blog users were seeking out deliberations with the aim of solving public problems by critical and rational discussion with opponents, heavier blog users would not show higher levels of ideological selectivity and there should perhaps be more evidence of a virtuous circle from blogging. Additionally, the finding of high homogeneity among blog users, who are predominantly male, white, educated, and conservative, reinforces the conclusion that diversity, and thus deliberation, does not draw blog users. On the other hand, if blog users were primarily focused on confirming their own presuppositions, the findings should perhaps show stronger evidence of heightened selectivity among heavy blog users, which they do not.

A final issue is whether this chapter correctly stipulates, in its regression analyses, that blog reliance affects engagement and selectivity rather than the reverse. Certainly, it is imaginable that the direction of causality may be reversed or bidirectional, as suggested by other research (Zhang, et al., 2009). This chapter, however, starts with literature that suggests that structural features of blogs may enhance such factors as engagement and selectivity. Granting these authors' supposition that blog use drives such factors related to deliberative potential, the analyses here find moderate and conflicting effects of blog use on deliberative potential—even granting that all the effect is in this direction.

Solutions and Recommendations

This chapter begins with a puzzle: the view, from one quarter, that blog users might be supercharged deliberators and the view, from another quarter, that bloggers are deliberatively unfit—that they are polarized, focused on confirming their presuppositions, and unwilling to interact with a diversity of others. It appears that both views cannot be simultaneously accurate. The findings in this chapter leave yet another puzzle: bloggers do not appear to be strongly deliberative or anti-deliberative, and the activity in which they are engaged does not appear to be meant as either

a deliberation or purely for the confirmation of presuppositions. As a potential solution to these puzzles, a third interpretation of the motives behind blog use is proposed.

Rather than motivation to deliberate, a motive to become more informed might explain both moderately higher engagement and selectivity. Engagement follows directly from a desire to be informed. Also, as people become more knowledgeable about an issue, they begin to rule out certain positions based on consistency with their other beliefs and values. Thus, as people become more informed, they become more selective (Johnson, et al., 2009). For example, those who have studied biological evolution may find creationist websites of little interest. To the extent that information on political issues in the United States is largely organized into two ideological camps with deeply different readings of available data, it is not surprising that selectivity tends to follow these ideological lines. Selectivity, then, is not necessarily a feature imposed by blogs on users, but a feature of the organization of political disagreement by interest groups, politicians, and various quarters of the public sphere.

The implications of a possible information motive for the deliberative potential of the Internet is mixed, given that the motive in this case appears to direct people along ideological cleavages. For successful deliberation, people must be informed but also willing to listen to opposing points of view, synthesizing a more defensible view from all they hear. Apathy and ignorance are not conducive to deliberation, yet, regrettably, much evidence suggests the public is appreciably apathetic and ignorant. Thus, if a desire to be informed drives intensity of blog reliance or is enhanced by greater blog reliance, it does contribute toward knowledge and points of view that could be leveraged for deliberation. The selectivity of the information motive is not conducive to deliberative potential, but blogs are not, it appears, deliberative forums. An important question is whether the selectivity of bloggers would adversely affect their engagement in more deliberative forums. To the extent that such selectivity is not intense and is driven by a desire for more information rather than the reverse, it might not adversely affect such deliberative potential—an issue that may deserve further research. For recommendations, then, this chapter moves to a discussion of future research possibilities.

FUTURE RESEARCH DIRECTIONS

This chapter examined the impact of blog reliance among blog users on characteristics that can boost or hinder democratic deliberation. The respondents to this study were those who were eligible to vote in the United States. This study should be replicated in countries with differing political structures and elite organizations.

The social, cultural, and political environments within various countries may influence the deliberative potential for blog users. The two-party political structure that exists in the U. S. is sharply divided ideologically, which may very well influence democratic deliberation among U. S. citizens. To fully understand the role blogs play in deliberation, comparisons should be made among users in different countries. Tracked over time and across multiple countries, such research could clarify democratic trends in the global blogosphere and the root causes of these trends.

Additionally, the relationship between the political structural features organizing a given issue and the polarization of blog discussion should be studied. Such research can compare blog user reactions and blog treatment of issues in a given country that involve differing degrees of elite polarization. Such research could provide valuable insights on the dynamics of how blogs affect their users within a given culture, could more firmly establish the causal direction of blog effects and ascertain whether users are drawn into virtuous or vicious circles of blog reliance.

Another potentially fruitful area for further research, suggested in the conclusion, would involve a more detailed experimental examination of the selectivity and deliberative potential of blog users. The conclusion sketches an alternative explanation to both the view that blog users are more deliberatively fit and the view that blog users are more highly selective and polarized. That alternative is that blog users are simply people who seek out information on an issue in which they are interested, which typically involves some selectivity. Blog users of differing persuasions could be experimentally given information of varying quality both consistent and contrary to their views. Heavy blog users could be compared with light blog users to determine whether they show more resistance to attitudinal shifts and less sensitivity to the quality of information.

Lastly, blog reliance and the potential for democratic deliberation may depend on the motives behind blog use. An examination of self-reported motives and how they track with deliberative fitness or lack thereof could provide insights on the deliberative potential of blog users and provide additional evidence regarding the "information seeking" interpretation of blog users' motives advanced. The current dataset contains information on blog users' motives in the United States, and preliminary analysis suggests that information seeking is an important motive.

REFERENCES

Albrecht, S. (2006). Whose voice is heard in online deliberation? A study of participation and representation in political debates on the Internet. *Information Communication and Society*, *9*, 62–82. doi:10.1080/13691180500519548

Babbie, E. (1990). *Survey research methods*. Belmont, CA: Wadsworth.

Babbie, E. (2002). *The basics of social research*. Belmont, CA: Wadsworth.

Baoill, A. O. (2000). Slashdot and the public sphere. *First Monday, 5.* Retrieved April 1, 2004, from http://www.firstmonday.org/ issues/ issue5_9/baoill /index.html

Baoill, A. O. (2004). *Into the blogosphere: Rhetoric, community, and culture of weblogs.* Retrieved March 6, 2004, from http://blog.lob.umn.edu/ blogosphere/ weblogs_and_public_sphere.html

Barton, M. D. (2005). The future of rational-critical debate in online public spheres. *Computers and Composition, 22,* 177–190. doi:10.1016/j.compcom.2005.02.002

Blogads. (2006). *Political blogs reader survey 2006.* Retrieved January 18, 2008, from http://blogads.com/survey/2006/2006_political_blogs_ reader_survey.html

Bohman, J. (1996). *Public deliberation: Pluralism, complexity, and democracy.* Cambridge, MA: MIT Press.

Chambers, S. (2003). Deliberative democratic theory. *Annual Review of Political Science, 6,* 307–326. doi:10.1146/annurev.polisci.6.121901.085538

Curran, J. (2000). Rethinking media and democracy . In Curran, J., & Gurevitch, M. (Eds.), *Mass media and society* (pp. 120–154). London, UK: Arnold.

Dahlberg, L. (2001). The Internet and democratic discourse: Exploring the prospects of online deliberative forums extending the public sphere. *Information Communication and Society, 4,* 615–655. doi:10.1080/13691180110097030

Dahlberg, L. (2007). Rethinking the fragmentation of the cyberpublic: From consensus to contestation. *New Media & Society, 9,* 827–847. doi:10.1177/1461444807081228

Dahlgren, P. (2001). Media and the transformation of democracy . In Axford, B., & Huggins, R. (Eds.), *New media and politics* (pp. 64–88). London, UK: Sage.

Dahlgren, P. (2005). The Internet, public spheres, and political communication: Dispersion and deliberation. *Political Communication, 22,* 147–162. doi:10.1080/10584600590933160

Delli Carpini, M. X., Cook, F. L., & Jacobs, L. R. (2004). Public deliberation, discursive participation, and civic engagement: A review of the empirical literature. *Annual Review of Political Science, 7,* 315–344. doi:10.1146/annurev. polisci.7.121003.091630

Delli Carpini, M. X., & Keeter, S. (1996). *What Americans know about politics and why it matters.* New Haven, CT: Yale University Press.

DiMaggio, P., Hargittai, E., Neuman, W. R., & Robinson, J. P. (2001). Social implications of the Internet. *Annual Review of Sociology, 27,* 307–336. doi:10.1146/annurev.soc.27.1.307

Eveland, W. P., & Dylko, I. (2007). Reading political blogs during the 2004 election campaign: Correlates and political consequences . In Tremayne, M. (Ed.), *Blogging, citizenship, and the future of media* (pp. 105–126). New York, NY: Routledge.

Fishkin, J. S. (1991). *Democracy and deliberation: New directions for democratic reform.* New Haven, CT: Yale University Press.

Galston, W. A. (2003). If political fragmentation is the problem, is the Internet the solution? In Anderson, D. M., & Cornfield, M. (Eds.), *The civic web: Online politics and democratic values* (pp. 35–44). Oxford, UK: Rowman & Littlefield.

Gastil, J. (2000). Is face-to-face deliberation a luxury or a necessity? *Political Communication, 17,* 357–361. doi:10.1080/10584600050178960

Gastil, J., & Dillard, J. P. (1999). Increasing political sophistication through public deliberation. *Political Communication, 16*(1), 3–23. doi:10.1080/105846099198749

Graf, J. (2006). *The audience for political blogs: New research on blog readership.* Washington, DC: Institute for Politics Democracy & the Internet.

Habermas, J. (1974). The public sphere: An encyclopedia article. *New German Critique, NGC, 3,* 49–55. doi:10.2307/487737

Habermas, J. (1989). *The structural transformation of the public sphere: An inquiry into a category of bourgeois society. (Trans. Thomas Burger).* Cambridge, MA: MIT Press.

Hardy, B. W., Scheufele, D. A., & Wang, Z. (2005, May). *Defining deliberation: Key determinants and distinct dimensions.* Paper presented to the annual convention of the International Communication Association, New York, NY.

Iyengar, S., & Hahn, K. S. (2009). Red media, blue media: Evidence of ideological selectivity in media use. *The Journal of Communication, 49,* 19–39. doi:10.1111/j.1460-2466.2008.01402.x

Johnson, T. J., Bichard, S. L., & Zhang, W. (2009). Communication communities or cyberghettos? A path analysis model examining factors that explain selective exposure to blogs. *Journal of Computer-Mediated Communication, 15,* 60–82. doi:10.1111/j.1083-6101.2009.01492.x

Johnson, T. J., & Kaye, B. K. (2004). Wag the blog: How reliance on traditional media and the Internet influence perceptions of credibility of weblogs among blog users. *Journalism & Mass Communication Quarterly, 81*(3), 622–642.

Johnson, T. J., & Kaye, B. K. (2007). Blogs of war: Reliance on weblogs for information about the Iraqi War . In Tremayne, M. (Ed.), *Blogging, citizenship, and the future of media* (pp. 165–184). New York, NY: Routledge.

Johnson, T. J., & Kaye, B. K. (2009, November). *The dark side of the boon? Credibility, selective exposure and the proliferation of online sources of political information.* Paper presented at the Midwest Association for Public Opinion Research, Chicago, IL.

Johnson, T. J., Kaye, B. K., Bichard, S. L., & Wong, W. J. (2007). Every blog has its day: Politically interested Internet users' perceptions of blog credibility. *Journal of Computer-Mediated Communication, 13*(1), 6. Retrieved December 15, 2007, from http://jcmc.indiana.edu/ vol13/ issue1/ johnson.html

Jones, S. G. (Ed.). (1995). *CyberSociety: Computer-mediated communication and community.* Thousand Oaks, CA: Sage Publications.

Kaye, B. K., & Johnson, T. J. (2006). The age of reasons: Motives for using different components of the Internet for political information . In Williams, A. P., & Tedesco, J. C. (Eds.), *The Internet election: Perspectives on the Web in campaign 2006* (pp. 147–167). Lanham, MD: Rowman & Littlefield.

Keren, M. (2004). Blogging and the politics of melancholy. *Canadian Journal of Communication, 29,* 1–15.

Kim, J., Wyatt, R. O., & Katz, E. (1999). News, talk, opinion, participation: The part played by conversation in deliberative democracy. *Political Communication, 16,* 361–385. doi:10.1080/105846099198541

Kim, J. K. (2006). The impact of Internet use patterns on political engagement: A focus on online deliberation and virtual social capital. *Information Polity, 11,* 35–49. doi:10.1108/09593840610700800

Koop, R., & Jansen, H. J. (2009). Political blogs and blogrolls in Canada: Forums for deliberation? *Social Science Computer Review, 27,* 155–173. doi:10.1177/0894439308326297

Muhlberger, P. (2005). Human agency and the revitalization of the public sphere. *Political Communication, 22*(2), 163–178. doi:10.1080/10584600590933179

Neuman, W. R. (1986). *The paradox of mass politics: Knowledge and opinion in the American electorate.* Cambridge, MA: Harvard University Press.

Papacharissi, Z. (2004). Democracy online: Civility, politeness, and the democratic potential of online political discussion groups. *New Media & Society, 6*(2), 259–283. doi:10.1177/1461444804041444

Pew Research Center. (2008). *Trend data: Demographics of Internet users.* Retrieved April 28, 2010, from http://www.pewinternet.org/ StaticPages/Trend-Data/ Whos-Online.aspx

Poster, M. (1997). Cyberdemocracy: Internet and the public sphere . In Porter, D. (Ed.), *Internet culture* (pp. 201–218). New York, NY: Routledge.

Price, V., & Capella, J. (2002). Online deliberation and its influence: The electronic dialogue project in campaign 2000. *IT & Society, 1,* 303–328.

Price, V., Nir, L., & Capella, J. (2002). Does disagreement contribute to more deliberative opinion? *Political Communication, 19,* 95–112. doi:10.1080/105846002317246506

Putnam, R. D. (2000). *Bowling alone: The collapse and revival of American community.* New York, NY: Simon & Schuster.

Rheingold, H. (1993). *The virtual community: Homesteading on the electronic frontier.* Reading, MA: Addison-Wesley.

Strandberg, K. (2008). Public deliberation goes online? An analysis of citizens' political discussions on the Internet prior to the Finnish parliamentary elections in 2007. *Javnost/The Public, 15,* 71-90.

Stromer-Galley, J., & Muhlberger, P. (2009). Agreement and disagreement in group deliberation and its consequences: Satisfaction, engagement, and opinion reevaluation. *Political Communication, 26,* 173–192. doi:10.1080/10584600902850775

Stroud, N. J. (2006). *Selective exposure to partisan information.* Unpublished doctoral dissertation, University of Pennsylvania.

Stroud, N. J. (2008). Media use and political predispositions: Revisiting the concept of selective exposure. *Political Behavior, 30,* 341–366. doi:10.1007/s11109-007-9050-9

Sunstein, C. (2001). *Republic.com.* Princeton, NJ: Princeton University Press.

Sunstein, C. (2007). *Republic.com 2.0.* Princeton, NJ: Princeton University Press.

Technorati (2008). *State of the blogosphere.* Retrieved April 10, 2008, from http://technorati.com/blogging/ state-of-the-blogosphere

Trammell, K. D., Tarkowski, A., & Sapp, A. M. (2006). Rzeczpospolita Blogow [Republic of Blog]: Examining Polish bloggers through content analysis. *Journal of Computer-Mediated Communication, 11*(3), article 2. Retrieved April 13, 2007, from http://jcmc.indiana.edu/vol11/ issue3. trammell.html

Vergeer, M., & Hermans, L. (2008). Analyzing online political discussions: Methodological considerations. *Javnost/The Public, 15,* 37-56.

Wojcieszak, M., & Mutz, D. (2009). Online groups and political discourse: Do online discussion spaces facilitate exposure to political disagreement? *The Journal of Communication, 59*(1), 40–56. doi:10.1111/j.1460-2466.2008.01403.x

Wright, S., & Street, J. (2007). Democracy, deliberation and design: The case of online discussion forums. *New Media & Society, 9*, 849–869. doi:10.1177/1461444807081230

Xenos, M. (2008). New mediated deliberation: Blog and press coverage of the Alito nomination. *Journal of Computer-Mediated Communication, 13*, 485–503. doi:10.1111/j.1083-6101.2008.00406.x

Zhang, W., Johnson, T. J., Bichard, S. L., & Gangadharbatla, H. (2009). *The seclusion illusion: The influence of selective exposure to political web sites and blogs on political attitudes and behavior.* Paper presented at the 18th Asian Media Information & Communication Center Annual Conference New Delhi, India.

KEY TERMS AND DEFINITIONS

Democratic Deliberation: A process in which citizens voluntarily participate in discussions about public issues. During deliberative discussion, citizens examine a problem or issue, identify possible solutions, establish evaluation criteria and use these criteria to identify the best solution to the problem.

Online Deliberation: An online forum that focuses on a particular issue or related set of issues and brings informed people with a variety of political points of view together to debate the issue and develop solutions to the problem.

Political Blogs: Blogs typically created by individuals that discuss politics and that normally have political preferences.

Political Debate: Ideally, political debates that engage participants in a critical and well-reasoned discussion. The participants are willing to express themselves in spite of potential hostile reactions, listen to conflicting viewpoints before reacting, and be open to revise their views in light of compelling perspectives offered by other participants.

Public Discourse: The activity of sharing ideas of community interest with a community of people in a public setting.

Public Sphere: An area in social life where people can get together to identify social problems, engage in reasoned and critical debate, and reach consensus on issues of public concern that can help guide decision-making by public officials.

ENDNOTES

1. Links to the survey were posted on the following blogs: A Family in Baghdad, A Family in Iraq, Ace of Spades HQ, Ann Althouse, AOL, Appalachian Scribe, Betsey's Page, Blogometer, Boortz News, Brian's Blog, Center for Citizen Media, Citizen Journalism, CNN, Crooks & Liars, Daily Kos, Dan Gillmor, DC Metblogs, Democratic Underground, Fark, Firedoglake, Hassenpfeffer, Highclearing, Hotline Blogometer, brianhornback.blogspot, edwardwillett.blogspot, journalism.nyu.edu/pubzone/weblogs/pressthink, Nofishnonuts, Secrets In Baghdad, Joanne Jacobs, Newshounds, www.wakeupamericans-spree.blogspot, Huffington Post, Hullabaloo, Infomaniac, Instapolit, Instapundit, Jay Rosen's Press Think, Jesus General, Journalism.co.uk, Khalid Jarrar, Knox News No Silence Here, KnoxViews, Mike the Mad Biologist, Mindy McAdams, Moderate Voice, MoveOn.org, NewsHounds, NewsBusters, NewsDissector, Obsidian Wings, Oraculations, Outside the Beltway, Poliblogger, Political Mavens-Steven Taylor, Politics in the Zeros, PowerLine, Power of Narrative, Poynter.org/Romenesko, Pressthink.org, Raw Story,

Skippy the Bush Kangaroo, Slate, Teaching Online Journalism (UNC), Tell Me a Secret, tojou.blogspot, Unqualified Offerings, Wake Up America.

2.   The survey's first question asked respondents to enter their e-mail addresses; all but 17 (99.1%) complied. The respondents' e-mail addresses together with a computer generated ID (programmed to appear on every completed survey) were used to delete duplicated surveys. Additionally, after sending the completed survey a Web page would immediately appear thanking the respondents for their participation and verifying that the survey had been sent so respondents would not retransmit the survey.

3.   This method of convenience sampling was appropriate for specifically reaching a narrow group of blog users (Babbie, 1990). Any attempt at random sampling of this small group of Internet users would result in a large non-qualification rate (At the time of data collection only about one-third of Internet users were connected to blogs). Therefore, posting announcements of the survey on various types of blogs was an appropriate method.

4.   The efficacy index is below the normal .70 standard for internal reliability. However, low reliability scores are not unusual for an index of only two items. One of the main ways to ensure reliability is to use measures that have proven reliable in previous research (Babbie, 1990). Therefore, the authors combined the two items into an index because these two items from the National Election Studies have proven reliable in past studies.

Chapter 2
The Blogosphere in the "Land of Smiles":
Citizen Media and Political Conflict in Thailand

Melissa Wall
California State University – Northridge, USA

Treepon Kirdnark
Bangkok University, Thailand

ABSTRACT

Since the turn of the century, Thailand, dubbed as the "Land of Smiles," has been racked by internal political instability, turmoil, and violence. This study assesses how an ongoing political crisis in Thailand is deconstructed via blogs. A qualitative content analysis of 45 blogs (838 posts) about Thailand indicates that during a peak period of massive anti-government protests in the spring of 2010, blog posts about the crisis tended to fall under three categories: (a) creating a partisan view of the political conflict, which largely mirrored the dominant discourses already present in mainstream media; (b) presenting a dispassionate account that often provided a synthesis of different viewpoints; or (c) offering improvised accounts of what expatriate-tourist bloggers perceived to be important yet having little context to explain. It is argued that although blogging potentially offers new spaces for representing political perspectives in and about Thailand, these perspectives do not always enhance the public's understanding of the political processes and in some cases fan the flames of inflammatory rhetoric.

DOI: 10.4018/978-1-60960-744-9.ch002

INTRODUCTION AND BACKGROUND

Since the turn of the century, the Kingdom of Thailand, known to the outside world by its optimistic tourism moniker, the "Land of Smiles," has been racked by internal political turmoil and violence. Among the most dramatic moments were: a 2006 military coup that overthrew a democratically elected prime minister and imposed martial law; an occupation of the Bangkok's Suvarnabhumi international airport in 2008 by anti-government protesters, which paralyzed the tourism and export industries; massive political demonstrations in March-May 2010 in Bangkok organized by the opposition movement with the demands of immediate elections. The crackdown by the government led to 88 protesters being killed and more than 200 injured during the street clashes between demonstrators and security forces (Amnesty International, 2010a; Ministry of Public Health, 2010). As Allan (2006) argues, sudden spikes in citizen journalism, such as blogging, are frequently triggered by violent political crises.

While Thailand's mainstream print and broadcast media have long operated within zones of official control and self-restriction, the government has purposely used the public protests to curtail the freedom of the press and the Internet. Indeed, attempts to contain oppositional political groups have resulted in what was a relatively free media state becoming increasingly less so (Klangnarong, 2009). At the same time, online media (such as independent websites, blogs and bulletin boards) have taken on a larger role, serving as alternatives that foster open discussions and provide criticism of the government, but also, in some cases, fan the flames of inflammatory rhetoric. The issues underlying the political conflicts in Thailand as well as the growth of social media such as blogs can be linked to the changes wrought by Thailand's embrace of the global economy, which has been followed by mounting income inequalities (Nostitz, 2009). The rise of a new urban middle class has brought demands for a greater say in their country's political decision making and started political clashes with the old political class rallying around Thailand's monarchy.

Political disputes in Thailand reflect a long-standing power struggle among the country's elites representing different social and ethnic groups that crystallized during Thailand's 19th century colonial period (Connors, 2008). The most recent disturbance is traced to the 2001 election of a billionaire businessman and communications tycoon, Thaksin Shinawatra, to become the country's prime minister. As an outsider representing a rising new business class, Thaksin threatened the existing power structure, particularly the network surrounding the royal family. Portraying Thaksin as an authoritarian populist, a coalition of opponents, known as the "Yellow Shirts" (yellow represents the monarchy) rallied against him. Thaksin's political foes organized mass protests against him, eventually leading to Thaksin's removal from the office after a military coup in 2006. This gave rise to the anti-coup "Red Shirt" movement seeking immediate elections. The "Red Shirts" staged popular demonstrations culminating in a massive march on Bangkok in the spring of 2010, when an encampment was formed in the city center. After weeks of intense confrontation and clashes with the police, the demonstrators were forcibly removed from the streets by the army.

While it has been argued that citizen media such as blogs potentially offer a means of expanding the range of voices and points of view available, we should also keep in mind researchers' warnings that communication technology does not automatically empower or provide democratic alternatives (Nakamura, 2002; Slack & Wise, 2002). The aim of this chapter is: a) to critically explore how blogs focused on Thailand's internal political affairs depicted a peak period of a decade-long political conflict; b) to consider the ways in which blogs commenting on or documenting such political conflicts can potentially challenge or reinforce patterns of information flow maintained by the mainstream media.

MEDIA, THE MONARCHY AND POWER IN THAILAND

Thailand's news media and especially its privately owned print component have been considered to be among the freest in Southeast Asia (McCargo, 2001; Servaes, Malikhao, & Pinprayong, 2008). However, traditional reporting routines frequently focus on elite sources and oftentimes merely string together quotes with little analysis or context (McCargo, 2001). For example, the monarchy is heavily covered by the Thai media, furthering the King's role in maintaining unity (Jory, 2001). Important, too, in the current political context, there has been little reporting on the provinces, a gap some sought to fill in recent years with community radio (Brooten & Klangnarong, 2009). Broadcast journalism has historically been tightly controlled by the state with newer satellite channels maintained by communications tycoons, some with the close ties to the government or opposition groups (Klangnarong, 2009). The deficiencies in mainstream news coverage of political life have laid the groundwork for the arrival of Internet news sites and the proliferation of social media such as blogs (Thammo, 2009). However, these have been hampered by a lack of countrywide Internet access. Around a quarter of the population or 16 million are Internet users and many of them access the Internet at work or school (other popular spots are Internet cafés, as well as hotels and coffee shops with Wi-Fi services). Internet users in Thailand tend to be more educated, young, and live in Bangkok (International Telecommunications Union, 2010; National Electronics and Computer Technology Centre, 2008), which suggests that blogging and other social media are primarily used by elites and media professionals.

Over the last few years, what media scholars identify as a "media crisis" has occurred in Thailand. The crisis has affected both traditional and new media. At its core was the fact that mainstream news media have become increasingly politicized,

first under Thaksin Shinawatra who used his communications empire to rise to power during the 2001 elections and then to maintain it. The partisan and politically polarized media practices continued under the leaders who replaced Thaksin after the 2006 military coup. Indeed, some Thai media observers believe that the partisan media increasingly engage in the practice of hate speech and incite followers toward violence (Klangnarong, 2009). Because newspapers, cable and broadcast TV in Thailand failed to expose the underlying roots of the decade-long political crisis, online news sites, particularly social media, have been used to fill this gap (Journalists under attack, 2010). Neither the Thaksin administration nor the one that replaced it welcomed the turn to the Internet as a means of collecting and disseminating information. Thousands of websites have been blocked under a 2007 Computer-Related Crimes Act (Amnesty International, 2010b), which holds website owners liable even for posted comments. The government has also used periodic declarations of a state of emergency to filter blogs and independent news sites, prosecute individuals running the sites and shut down other, traditional media.

The key to the government crackdown on the freedoms of the press and expression has been the invocation of Thailand's *lèse majesté* law, which forbids defamation of the Thai King and his family. In other words, "nothing connected to the monarchy can be criticized or held up to public scrutiny" (Preechasuksakul & Streckfuss, 2008, p. 12). Not a historical Thai tradition, *lèse majesté* was introduced in the 1950s and has been part of a systematic effort to present the monarchy as being above politics and unquestioningly beloved by the Thai people (Preechasuksakul & Streckfuss, 2008; Rojanaphruk, 2008). Yet behind the scenes, the King has been heavily involved in Thai politics, which allowed him to survive through military coups and multiple revisions of Thailand's constitution. With *lèse majesté*, a curtain has been drawn over the political activities of the monarchy. In essence, the *lèse majesté* concept forbids any discussion of movements toward democracy because such discussions would lessen the monarchy's political influence (Winichakul, 2008). This law has become increasingly important as the King of Thailand, Bhumibol Adulyadej, nears his ninth decade, and the future of the constitutional monarchy is unclear since it has relied so heavily on the King's charisma and political prowess (Winichakul, 2008). Many political commentators say that Thailand urgently needs an open public discussion of the future of the monarchy, but the law forbids it (Klangnarong, 2009).

Online communications in Thailand have been particularly targeted by the introduction of the 2007 Computer-Related Crimes Act, which combined the *lèse majesté* law with the "national security" rhetoric in an effort to control online political discussions (Impact of defamation law on freedom of expression, 2009). In the following years, hundreds of cases were brought against Thais netizens and some digital activists were taken to court and sentenced to 10 or more years in prison (Thailand: Reverse backward slide, 2010). Many Internet users have been placed under surveillance, taken into police custody for questioning or simply had their website taken down (Montesano, 2009). Even global social media sites, such as YouTube, have found themselves blocked for months because they were accused of containing content that insults the Thai King.

BLOGGING BEYOND THE WEST

While a growing body of research has focused on political or current events blogs, such studies have mainly examined them as new iterations of online journalism (Carlson, 2007; Eveland & Dylko, 2007; Lowrey & Latta, 2008). In that context, research often focuses on blogging's relationship with mainstream journalists and news (Davis, 2008; Robinson, 2006; Singer, 2005; Wall, 2006). Nearly all of this research has focused on blogging within the Western blogosphere. Some

initial probes of political blogging in non-Western contexts parallels these findings (Gurleyen & Emre, 2010). However, researchers should exercise caution about the blanket application of blog patterns in the West to rest of world, in part, because other places often have less freedom of expression, less well developed media systems, less access to technologies, etc. (Russell, 2009). Besides, Internet access does not necessarily guarantee accompanying democratic political practices (Kluver & Banerjee, 2005). That said, researchers tend to agree that a key impetus in the rise of blogging outside the West is the demand for broader political participation and media representation that old, centralized state-controlled media systems failed to provide (Nguyen, 2009).

Citizen media, such as blogs, have gained large audiences in some countries as they provide a space to articulate grievances and perspectives on economic, political and social changes, as part of what Sonwalker (2009, p. 77) calls the "politics of recognition." Because of their perceived ability to provide grassroots voices a potentially global audience, blogs and other citizen media have become more prominent as a growing range of political actors expect their voices to be heard. While cautioning against an overly optimistic view, media researchers have recently begun to make preliminary assessments of the increase in citizen media in non-Western parts of the world (Douai, 2009; Ibrahim, 2009).

In Southeast Asia, for example, Nguyen (2009) argued that bloggers in Vietnam opened new communication spaces. While they did not generate news per se, they did create a space for debate that previously didn't exist in that country's government-controlled news media system. Nevertheless, Nguyen found that mainstream media were still necessary to amplify those voices in order for them to truly be heard. Sonwalker (2009) also found that blogs in India needed amplification beyond the domestic blogosphere in order to be heard, particularly by members of the Indian diaspora. Douai (2009) argues that the dissent expressed in the Arab blogosphere is misleading and has yet to materialize in equivalent actions in the real world, although the overthrow of dictators in Tunisia and Egypt suggest he was overly pessimistic. Zayyan and Carter (2009) found that one of the most important roles Palestinian blogs serve is as a "window for outsiders to look in" (p. 89), rather than as a tool for internal democracy building.

METHOD

Our consideration of Thai blogging during a political crisis was informed by a cultural studies approach to communication, reflecting the belief that communication is the symbolic process whereby society is maintained (Carey, 1992). The assumption that technology is equivalent to progress tends to color much of the available research about technology and communication so that new media forms, such as blogs, are frequently treated as if they are without precedent. Further, their dissemination and application are assumed to flow evenly across borders despite the inequalities existent in economic and cultural structures of non-Western societies. Thus, the sorts of questions and approaches taken to study of new media lean toward the celebratory, ignoring controversial consequences and critical points of view (Mosco, 2005). Because of that widespread perspective, less optimistic views derived from other approaches, including cultural, are often ignored or de-emphasized in new media research. The cultural model of communication is appropriate for attempting to assess the intersection of new media forms with a specific social context of a non-Western society such as Thailand.

Research Questions, Design, and Procedures

Our goal in this chapter was to explore the following questions: In what ways did bloggers characterize the Thai political conflict in the spring of 2010? More broadly, what can we learn about political blogging in a non-Western context from Thailand's experience? To assess the discourses on these blogs, the authors employed qualitative content analysis of the collected blog posts. We drew on the recommendations of Altheide (1996) in terms of a close careful reading and re-readings of the texts being studied. The authors scrutinized each blog post for patterns concerning the ways blogs characterized the anti-government protests and protesters as well as the actions of the government, security forces, and political leaders. As we did this, we took notes to highlight particular portions that appeared to reflect ongoing patterns in terms of discourses being employed. From these readings, we collaboratively developed initial analytical categories, which were redefined in an ongoing process of constant comparison, until arriving at our conclusions presented below (Corbin & Strauss, 2007).

Sampling

To be included in the analysis, the blog had to have posted written content (not just photographs) focusing on the crisis at its height between March and May 2010. This time period encompasses the mid-March massing of the Red Shirt protesters in Bangkok; the protesters' occupation of areas of central Bangkok; the state of emergency that was declared in early April, followed by shootings of protesters later that month; grenade and other retaliatory attacks by some Red Shirt protesters in early May, followed by a government crackdown and more deaths; and the final dispersal of the demonstrations by the end of May.

Two different blog aggregators were used to locate blogs. The first was *Thai Blog Search*, a blog directory run by an expatriate resident in Thailand. It is part of Paknam Web Network, a gathering of English-language blogs, forums, chat rooms, and photo albums devoted to all aspects of Thailand's culture and life. *Thai Blog Search* identified 100 different blogs about Thailand; 48 of them had content about the political crisis in March-May 2010. We also examined Thailand blogs that were linked to by *Global Voices*, an international network of bloggers and a blog directory based at Harvard University's Berkman Center for Internet and Society. *Global Voices* asks activists from around the world to curate blog content focused on politics and current events in their specific countries. The search of the *Global Voices* directory generated 36 blogs. Because we wanted to integrate as many Thai voices as possible, we also included all blogs we could identify as written by Thais. This produced six blogs (four from *Thai Blog Search* and two from *Global Voices*) with a total of 199 relevant posts. Next, we randomly sampled the remaining blogs on both lists and included half of the blogs from each list. Combined with the Thai-authored blogs, the total number of blogs in the final sample was 45 and produced 838 posts.

FINDINGS

The following themes were identified through the analysis to describe the blog posts about the Thailand crisis in the spring of 2010: (a) a partisan lens; (b) reflective analysis; and (c) improvised accounts.

A Partisan Lens

One of the ways blogs depicted the crisis was through a partisan lens. This is not surprising since blogs have been viewed as a means of expressing a personal opinion and, even when used by mainstream news outlets, tend to employ editorializing voices (Davis, 2008). What is of note here is because the mainstream media in Thailand heavily favored the government throughout the crisis of March-May 2010, bloggers invoking a partisan point of view either were reinforcing that perspective or were offering an oppositional view.

The latter case also meant that blogging potentially could open a new window onto Thai politics.

The partisan lens serves as a means for mainstream news outlets and professional journalists using blogging to give a sharper edge to their one-sided coverage. The *Nation* newspaper in particular, which is known for its use of multimedia and online reporting, deployed blogs that consistently favored the government's position. While it is not surprising to see blogs as a form of editorializing, what is notable is that their use by a mainstream news outlet did not include blogs articulating the other side as well. For example, the paper's managing editor, Khanthong (2010a) described the Red Shirts as "barbarians at the gate, ready to storm into the City of Angels and destroy everything within sight" (2010b, para. 1). Consistently in his blog posts, the Red Shirts were outsiders and not really a part of Thailand, depicted as seeking to enter and sully, as he wrote in one overblown post "the inner corridors of Heaven that is Old Bangkok. Many Bangkokians are about to come out to defend the capital" (Khangthong, 2010b, para. 1). Such biased writing by a senior editor is notable because *The Nation* is considered to be a traditional mainstream news outlet aiming for balance and objectivity. Granted these are writings from a blog, which may contain a more personal opinion, but there is no other blog on the site providing a different point of view of this very contentious, serious political conflict in the country.

The Nation executive editor Suthichai Yoon blogged in a similar vein as well for the newspaper but then he also employed a personal blog, *Musings from Thailand*, to redistribute an even harsher condemnation of the Red Shirt opposition. On his personal blog, Yoon reported the claims made in a meeting of a political faction that the oppositional Red Shirts were aiming to overthrow the current government (Yoon, 2010a). He also ran side-by-side photographs of a Bangkok shopping center that the protesters set on fire next to a photograph of the smoldering Twin Towers in the U.S. just after the 9/11 terrorist attacks. Even though he titled his post "Two pictures, two different stories," running them next to each other implies that they were equivalent to the author. Yoon (2010b) writes, "The WTC's fiery destruction was brought about by foreign terrorists. Bangkok Central World was torched by Thais against Thais" (Yoon, 2010b, para. 2). The construction of that sentence implies that the Thais who committed property damage in Bangkok are somehow equivalent to the hijackers who murdered thousands in New York. (A frequent charge in the immediate aftermath of the Thai crisis was that the Red Shirts were terrorists.) Yoon's own blog reinforces the government-created frame that called the Red Shirts terrorists, rather than legitimate political actors with real grievances. While some radical elements within the Red Shirts became violent, the intra-elite conflict was never discussed, the discourse of the mainstream media focused only on the street violence. This is important because not only are these partisan posts reflecting a skewed media point of view, the personal blog shows how an elite actor is able to rebroadcast his opinion across multiple blogs, each supporting the current power structure. That is, elite cultural actors appear able to draw on their social capital to further distribute a particular point of view.

Of course, employing a partisan lens was not limited to those supporting the current regime. Those favoring the opposition, however, faced a trickier situation; if they were in Thailand they could potentially be censored or even jailed for their blogging. Even if blogging from outside the country, they could put at risk others inside of Thailand who were communicating with them. The group blog, *Political Prisoners in Thailand* (2010), just like the *Nation* bloggers, employs inflated language such as with a post about the country's current leader titled, "Abhisit's dictatorial face." *Political Prisoners* posted anonymous and bylined content. An example of the latter came from a well-known Thai academic and activist Giles Ungpakorn, who is half Thai, with a British

mother, and a father who was once rector at one of Thailand's leading universities. Ungpakorn fled Thailand when brought up on *lèse majesté* charges and currently resides in England. His opinion on the conflict was further disseminated when it was reposted or cited on other oppositional blogs and amplified by the Western news media. In a post on the blog, *Political Prisoners in Thailand*, Ungpakorn used a hyperbolic style of writing: "The bloodthirsty royalist tyrants who are ruling Thailand can only cling to power by the use of force and blanket censorship" (Ungpakorn, 2010a, para.7).

Interestingly, such critical blog posts shatter the image of a placid Thailand that the country's elites have traditionally sought to offer to the public and especially the outside world (Jackson, 2004). Statements such as the one above that are a direct condemnation of the country's leaders would be unlikely to be made—unless anonymous—in Thailand, and, in the past, even those outside the country would hesitate to do so because it violates not only the legal boundaries but Thai norms of public communication. This suggests that Thai blogging potentially may be reflecting a more openly confrontational form of political communication, which, obviously, is part of the dramatic, confrontational real world political actions.

Reflective Analysis

Another way that blogs constructed content was by offering a synthesis of viewpoints on events, generally taking a step back from one-sided partisan rhetoric. In this way, this new cultural form —the blog—seems to take on some of the functions of the older, legacy media. Blogs of this sort tended to be run by elites such as journalists, academics and students, some by Thai authors and others by foreigners or a mix of both. This suggests that some bloggers are attempting to position themselves as outside the conflict, or above the fray, so to speak. For example, *Tumblerblog, a Thai Political and*

Current Events Blog written by Panuwat, offers criticism of both sides in the conflict. His stated goal is to "add my voice to the ongoing public debate regarding where our country is headed... it is highly important for people to be allowed and even encouraged to engage freely in debates on the topics of their choice" (Panuwat, n.d., para.1). With that aim, it is not surprising that his blog supports a more open media system, as seen in this post about the harassment of Thailand's journalists:

Channel 3 reporter Thapanee Eiadseechaialso got into hot water over her reporting of the grenade attacks at Silom on 22 April. As far as I know, what got her into trouble was a series of tweets (which have since been removed) on her twitter account documenting the confrontation between police forces and army forces. (Panuwat, 2010, para. 3)

By adopting a measured tone, *Tumblerblog* seems to offer an ideal Thai for locals and foreigners to read. Thoughtful and reasoned, *Tumblerblog* appears not be involved in the messy confrontation. Panuwat is not advocating a dramatic change in Thailand's governance so much as a more moderate acceptance of basic freedoms. The blog can be seen as an intermediary between Thailand and the outside world as it interprets events. *Saiyasombut*, a blog by a Thai university student studying in Germany who had previously worked as a journalist, also took a similar approach, writing on his blog about speeches supporting the Red Shirts given to the Thai community in that country, "Due to legal reasons I cannot translate and post many parts of the speeches (instead read it yourself), but I found this part noteworthy" (2010, para. 2). Thus, simply being outside the country does not necessarily mean the blogger will reflect a dissident point of view. Of course, with the resources to pursue an advanced degree in another country, such bloggers, even if wishing for mild reforms, would likely become part of the ruling elite and would see no reason to dramatically change or challenge the existing order.

Some of the foreign authored or foreign-Thai collaborative blogs also offered the same concil-

iatory sort of tone. *New Mandala* was created by two Australian National University professors and included a large number of posts written by academics and graduate students from the Western countries and from Thailand about the conflict. Some of the most highly regarded professors of Thai Studies such as Thongchai Winichakul who teaches at the University of Wisconsin – Madison and Charles Keyes of the University of Washington participated in the online discussions, providing an especially sophisticated level of commentary. For example, when the Red Shirts collected their own blood and then splattered the Prime Minister's residence and Parliament with it, participants on the site's comments debated the nature of a ritual previously unknown to Thailand and sought to interpret its possible significance through a historically informed cultural analysis (mainstream media coverage tended to merely document the action with no mention that this was not a traditional Thai action). The blog also employs some journalism techniques such as first-hand reporting, providing an independent, informed and on-going account of what was happening. Such content might previously have been a one-time op-ed appearing in the mainstream news media. This is particularly interesting if compared with the blog of a Western journalist, Newley Purnell, who blogged at *Topic: Thailand*. Purnell's posts focused on immediate happenings ("Red Shirt update: Clashes with police"), offering info graphics such as a map of where bombs were said to have gone off and linking to various other mainstream news media. While he clearly aims for an objective voice, in comparison with *New Mandala*, his readers would receive little information to help them truly understand the complicated politics underlying the violence.

Improvised Accounts

The final theme that emerged from the analysis was a type of blog post that offered less of an attempt at understanding and more of an impromptu focus on the turbulence. Such accounts seem to be written because the expatriate author lives in Thailand or was visiting when the conflict erupted. In fact, such ordinary citizen accounts of dramatic events have become a well-known type of blogging in which a person happens to be in a place suddenly undergoing a dramatic disaster or political conflagration. We have seen this kind of blogging with the South Asia Tsunami in December 2004, London bombings on July 7, 2005, etc.

In particular, we found pre-existing expatriate blogs diverting from their usual content—mostly promoting tourism or living in Thailand—to comment on the protests and violence. For example, the anonymously written *Absolutely Bangkok*, which describes its usual mission as featuring "some girlie talk" in reference to Thailand's prostitution industry, turns its attention to the anti-government demonstrations. Typical of an outsider perspective, the blogger's posts on the crisis generally consisted of shallow observations, such as comparing the protests to the current political schisms in the United States. The blogger followed the dominant frame in Thailand's mainstream media when he ran a photo of the central business district billowing smoke and titled the post "Bangkok's 911." These posts with low fidelity to Thailand are not surprising since much of Thailand's expatriate population is ensconced in foreigner enclaves, never fully learning Thai and relying on their experiences with the tourist-nightlife culture to be their gauge of what they see as the "real" Thailand.

Other foreign residents sought out the action such as 23-year-old German journalism student Florian Witulski, who posted photos and text on his blog, *Vaitor*. While his images were raw and current, they often provided no background or nuance, such as when he wrote, "The military was mostly hidden on the Skywalk and investigating about the explosions + observing the violence between anti-red shirts and police. Some of them were patrolling at the road" (Witulski, 2010, para. 8). There is immediacy in such reports, but it's unclear what readers would gain in understanding what was happening. They would see a police-military crackdown documented through on-the-spot photographs. Granted these are images that the Thai government would likely discourage from appearing in the mainstream media, yet *Vaitor*'s posts contain too little background to help audiences make sense of what the photos mean. In fact, it could be argued that he replicates the problems long identified with mainstream news coverage of conflict: an approach focusing on the most dramatic visual aspects without much background or explanation of the underlying issues.

Other impromptu blogs were temporary visitors, passing through. Annalisa Bluhm (2010) happened to be in Bangkok for her job with General Motors' consumer media division in March 2010 and wrote,

Fortunately, my hotel has a really nice mall, pool and wireless access:) I have moved hotels for the weekend so i'm no longer in the heart of the protest and registered with the US Embassy and have taken necessary precautions in unlikely case of government overthrow or violence. (para. 6)

Jotman, an anonymous blogger who travels the world, paused from writing about rabies in Bali and malaria in Cambodia to post about the impact of the Thai protests on tourists. He asks if Khao San Road (a well known backpacker area in Bangkok) is safe, and writes, "Here is a video taken by a foreigner in the Khao San area as he was shot; this post gives you some idea of the extent to which foreign tourists were terrorized by the crackdown" (2010, para. 4). *Riding out the Economy*, a joint blog coauthored by two recent college graduates from the United States, saw the conflict as another adventure, hitching rides with the protesters, chatting with police and juxtaposing their experiences with the travel advisories from the U.S. State Department. Thus, the improvised accounts provided little understanding of the complexities of the conflict or its players, and served instead to give a limited view of the conflict.

DISCUSSION AND RECOMMENDATIONS

As Thailand continues its long journey toward democracy, the role of the media, particularly news forms such as blogging, will play an important role in the transition. The following actions could help nurture more open and constructive online political communication in Thailand's public sphere: (a) protecting freedom of expression; (b) supporting and amplifying diverse voices; and (c) identifying trustworthy online sources. In these ways, social media such as blogs might contribute to the development of democracy in the kingdom.

Protect Freedom of Expression

While blogging has been said to offer an alternative space for political communication, the government's use of website blocking, censorship and intimidation means that it is likely those who support the regime in power may have a greater ability to have their voices heard. In sum, critical Thai voices may be muted, while pro-government ones are allowed to shout. In this way, the non-anonymous domestic Thai blogging examined here mirrors mainstream news in Thailand. Obviously, the revising of the 2007 Computer Crime Act would be a major step in allowing more voices to be heard. Perhaps a broader coalition with outside groups might bring more pressure on the Thai government to do so.

Support and Amplify Diverse Voices

Simply enabling blogging or using any other social media alone isn't enough. A foundation of fostering citizen voices needs to be laid and those voices need the chance to be heard. This has partly begun under the early 21st century moves

to establish citizen radio broadcasts in regions beyond Bangkok and Central Thailand (Brooten & Klangnarong, 2009; Siriyuvasak, 2007). Those sorts of grassroots projects would benefit from linkages with other entities – be they media or other sorts of organizations – in other parts of Thailand as well as outside the country. Already, some community radio stations have started to become connected to some Thai political websites so that their broadcast is over the air and online. In this way, they can leverage the resources found elsewhere to amplify their voices. For example, a regionally based organization could partner with the radio stations to have someone translate and repurpose locally created radio content onto their blog. Still, many of these radio stations, which are meant to represent the rural, and other disenfranchised communities do not actually serve those communities; others that are trying to are actually shut down by elites within the regional areas.

Identify Trustworthy Online Sources

The democratic possibilities of the blogosphere and, indeed, the Internet itself as a public sphere are frequently assumed (Papacharissi, 2002). However, simply digitizing content does not necessarily make it more thoughtful or civic minded. While it may be impossible, and even undesirable to mute offensive voices, it would be helpful to identify those voices that are seeking to explain rather than inflame. It is sometimes recommended that interested audience members decide which blog to trust but that seems to be a rather large burden to place on the audience. Instead, it might be helpful to have a mechanism to identify credible blogs and other social media distributing information during a time of crisis. *Global Voices* somewhat serves this role, but a network based in Southeast Asia would likely bring a better understanding of the region. For example, the civic group, *Media Monitor*, based in Bangkok, is already monitoring the Thai watchdogs. In the wake of the protests, it published a report on the ways social media tended to contribute to polarization rather than bridge the divides or bring mutual respect and understanding (Social networks emerge, 2010). Such a media monitoring group could be well positioned to identify and highlight more responsible bloggers.

CONCLUSION

In this study, we sought to understand what the Thailand crisis of spring 2010 could tell us about current events blogging in a non-Western country during a political crisis (as opposed to a natural disaster). The themes that emerged from the analysis both support previous political communication trends in Thailand but also suggest some intriguing new ways of communicating. For example, the partisan lens, which employed exaggerated, one-sided language for talking about the conflict, is not unheard of in Thailand where the media tend to be quite sensational (McCargo, 2001). That said, mainstream news has tended to present the calm surface or what Jackson (2004) calls the "regime of images" that traditionally constructs Thailand for the outside world as a placid, uneventful place.

Obviously, the dramatic events themselves shattered this view but the partisan rhetoric on blogs reinforced the polemical juxtapositioning rather than trying to smooth over the reality. Bloggers did not in fact fall in line and try to bridge the country's divides. Instead, we see that blogging potentially could disrupt traditional, government-run image management by depicting the messy conflicts within internal Thai politics. While many of the blogs examined sought to play down the grievances of the oppositional Red Shirts and naturalize the actions of the current regime, their position was challenged online (though apparently not in mainstream Thai news reports.) This makes blogs more important because they become a source of alternative information apparently unavailable elsewhere. Also, once bloggers are emboldened to critique and take sides, it

becomes difficult to shut down their voices other than through the dramatic moves the government indeed took: censorship and blocking of online news sites. Yet, such moves run the risk of merely raising the outside world's attention. In addition, we see the potential for the development of a pattern in Thailand that has previously been identified in the West: When the mainstream commercial news is not trusted as a source, some news audience members will gravitate toward blogs which they may come to perceive as more credible than traditional news sources (Johnson & Kaye, 2004).

Equally of note were the attempts by some bloggers to serve as rational observers and commentators who could provide background and cultural context, either individually such as by Panuwat on *Tumblerblog* or in collective efforts such as with *New Mandala*, both discussed above. Audiences with an interest in Thai politics could turn to blogs as a viable resource, and could also post comments and participate in the discussions on them, which, particularly in the case of *New Mandala,* often addresses issues left unspoken by the Thai mainstream media. There is a danger, of course, that what is being disseminated is a view skewed toward an elite perspective—and in some cases—an outsider perspective. Still, an ability to step back and provide a dispassionate overview is helpful when a heated political situation is taking place. It also appears that it takes outsiders to enable an objective type of blogging. It is possible that the phenomenon of a dispassionate overview occurred because of the freedom of speech that bloggers enjoy in other countries, a freedom that was smothered in Thailand. For observers outside the vortex of conflict, the distance might have given them the option to see the situation with less emotion.

With the improvised accounts, we mostly see scattered reports that lack nuance. This reminds us that there is a difference between simply a you-are-there photograph or textual account and the more measured voices of the reflective intermediaries who attempt to make sense of what is happening.

Without additional curation to highlight, supplement and challenge the improvised accounts (such as was seen with the *New York Times* careful incorporation of citizen accounts of the Iranian election crisis in summer 2009 on a special blog), the citizen journalist improvisers do not seem to provide more than a traditional mainstream news site would. Indeed, they may be offering less due to the lack of context and additional reportage. A citizen videographer can capture raw footage of a crisis, but the ordinary person cannot account for how widespread the impact, why a country's security services responded in the ways they did, etc. Thus, technology on its own does not bring understanding; added value comes from the creator's own ability to illuminate, reflect, and analyze. Ultimately, we find in the Thai crisis some suggestions that blogging could perhaps enlarge the public sphere, amplifying alternative points of view and voices, but we also see evidence that it could be diverted into parroting discourses already available, serving to reinforce existing social and political structures and distribution of power.

FUTURE RESEARCH DIRECTIONS

The intersection of the attempts by nation states to control media within their own boundaries appear out of touch with current communication patterns. In the case examined here, the Thai law of *lèse majesté* may become increasingly difficult to enforce in a networked world. Crackdowns on the new media behemoths such as Google, Yahoo and Facebook are impossible to carry out undetected. Additional research could identify or track local attempts to shut down or shut up global social media companies and the ultimate consequences of such actions. The U.S. State Department has decided to further assert itself in the Internet arena, claiming it to be a foreign policy priority. For good or bad, this will likely generate even more attention being paid to national communication laws viewed as counter to U.S. or Western standards.

In another area of concern, the omnipresence of social media played an important role in the 2010 Thai crisis. For example, Thaksin, the deposed prime minister, is well known for his Twitter activity. Because mainstream media in the country were forbidden from interviewing him, they frequently turned to his Twitter posts for quotes. Goode (2009) has argued that media scholars need to broaden our definitions of what counts as participation in citizen journalism forms beyond those that privilege original content creation to capture new forms of gatekeeping or as Bruns (2005) puts it, "gatewatching." Clearly, further research on this topic could take a range of social media forms into account. Blogging, then, is but a single iteration of a network of new forms that are re-shaping political communication around the world. Additional study of citizen media would also help to broaden the current body of research on the Thai media landscape, which is almost entirely about mainstream forms and generally has failed to explore alternative voices. The rise and importance of online news sites and political blogs raise important issues about what will constitute mainstream versus alternative news in Thailand's future (Kennix, 2009).

REFERENCES

Allan, S. (2006). *Online news*. Berkshire, UK: Open University Press.

Altheide, D. (1996). *Qualitative media analysis*. Thousand Oaks, CA: Sage.

Amnesty International. (2010a, May 17). *Thailand: Military must halt reckless use of lethal force* [Web log post]. Retrieved January 15, 2011, from http://www.amnesty.org/ en/ for-media/ press-releases/ thailand- military- must- halt- reckless-use- lethal- force- 2010- 05- 17

Amnesty International. (2010b, January 13). *Thailand: Reverse backward slide in freedom of expression* [Web log post]. Retrieved January 15, 2011, from http://www.amnesty.org/ en/ library

Bluhm, A. (2010). *#redhshirt government protest in Bangkok Thailand...social media in action.* Retrieved January 15, 2011, from http://annalisabluhm. posterous. com/ redshirt- government-protest- in- bangkok- thaila

Brooten, L., & Klangnarong, S. (2009). People's media and reform efforts in Thailand. *International Journal of Media and Cultural Politics, 5*(1-2), 103–118. doi:10.1386/macp.5.1-2.103_1

Bruns, A. (2005). *Gatewatching: Collaborative online news production.* New York, NY: Peter Lang.

Carey, J. W. (1992). *Communication as culture: Essays on media and society.* New York, NY: Routledge.

Carlson, M. (2007). Blogs and journalistic authority: The role of blogs in US Election Day 2004 coverage. *Journalism Studies, 8*(2), 264–279. doi:10.1080/14616700601148861

Connors, M. (2008). Thailand: Four elections and a coup. *Australian Journal of International Affairs, 62*(4), 478–496. doi:10.1080/10357710802480717

Corbin, J., & Strauss, A. (2007). *Basics of qualitative research: Techniques and procedures for developing grounded theory.* Thousand Oaks, CA: Sage.

Davis, R. (2008). *Symbiotic relationship between journalists and bloggers* (Discussion Paper Series). Cambridge, MA: Joan Shorenstein Center on the Press, Politics and Public Policy.

Douai, A. (2009). Offline politics in the Arab blogosphere. In Russell, A., & Echchaibi, N. (Eds.), *International blogging: Identity, politics, and networked publics* (pp. 133–150). New York, NY: Peter Lang.

Eveland, W., & Dylko, I. (2007). Reading political blogs during the 2004 election campaign: Correlates and political consequences. In Tremayne, M. (Ed.), *Blogging, citizenship and the future of media* (pp. 105–126). New York, NY: Routledge.

Goode, L. (2009). Social news, citizen journalism and democracy. *New Media & Society, 11*(8), 1287–1305. doi:10.1177/1461444809341393

Gurleyen, P., & Emre, P. O. (2010, April). *Exploring new journalistic platforms: Experiences of Turkish journalist bloggers.* Paper presented at the 11th International Symposium on Online Journalism. Retrieved January 15, 2011, from online. journalism. utexas. edu/ 2010/ papers/ PinarPerrin10.pdf

Ibrahim, Y. (2009). Textual and symbolic resistance: Re-mediating politics through the blogosphere in Singapore. In Russell, A., & Echchaibi, N. (Eds.), *International blogging: Identity, politics, and networked publics* (pp. 173–198). New York, NY: Peter Lang.

Jackson, P. (2004). Thai regime of images. *Sojourn: Journal of Social Issues in Southeast Asia, 19*(2), 181–218.

Johnson, T. J., & Kaye, B. (2004). Wag the blog: How reliance on traditional media and the Internet influence credibility perceptions of weblogs among blog users. *Journalism & Mass Communication Quarterly, 81*(3), 622–642.

Jory, P. (2001). The King and us: Representation of monarchy in Thailand and the case of Anna and the King. *International Journal of Cultural Studies, 4*(2), 201–218. doi:10.1177/136787790100400204

Jotman. (2010, April 15). *Why Thai army raid on protesters failed miserably.* Retrieved January 15, 2011, from http://jotman.blogspot.com/ 2010/ 04/ why- thai- army- raid- on-bangkok.html

Journalists under attack. (2010, May 19). *Reporters without borders*. Retrieved January 15, 2011, from http://en.rsf.org/a-second-journalist-killed-in-19-05-2010,37509.html

Kennix, L. J. (2009). Blogs as alternative. *Journal of Computer-Mediated Communication, 14*, 790–822. doi:10.1111/j.1083-6101.2009.01471.x

Khangthong, T. (2010a, March 24). Barbarians at the gate. *Nation Multimedia*. Retrieved January 15, 2011, from http://blog. nationmultimedia. com/ thanong/ 2010/ 03/ 24/

Khangthong, T. (2010b, March 27). A Buddhist riddle of the four Brahmaviharas. *Nation Multimedia*. Retrieved January 15, 2011, from http://blog. nationmultimedia. com/ thanong/ 2010/ 03/ 27/

Klangnarong, S. (2009). A decade of media reform in Thailand: Running around in circles and walking a tightrope. *Media Development, 1*. Retrieved January 15, 2011, from http://www.waccglobal. org/ images/ stories/ media_development/ 2009-1/ a- decade- of- media-reform- in- thailand.pdf

Kluver, R., & Banerjee, I. (2005). Political culture, regulation, and democratization: The Internet in nine Asian nations. *Information Communication and Society, 8*(1), 1–17.

Lowrey, W., & Latta, J. (2008). The routines of blogging. In Paterson, C., & Domingo, D. (Eds.), *Making online news: The ethnography of media production* (pp. 185–197). New York, NY: Peter Lang.

McCargo, D. (2001). *Politics and the press in Thailand: Media machinations*. London, UK: Routledge.

Media Monitor. (2010). Social networks emerge but with doubts: Survey. Retrieved January 15, 2011, from http://mediamonitor.in.th/ home/ forum/ index.php? topic=277.0

Ministry of Public Health. (2010). *Emergency Medical Institute of Thailand*. Retrieved January 15, 2011, from http://www.niems.go.th

Montesano, M. (2009). Contextualizing the Pattaya summit debacle: Four April days, four Thai pathologies. *Contemporary Southeast Asia, 31*(2), 217–248. doi:10.1355/cs31-2b

Mosco, V. (2005). *The digital sublime: Myth, power, and cyberspace*. Cambridge, MA: MIT Press.

Nakamura, L. (2002). *Cybertypes: Race, ethnicity, and identity on the Internet*. New York, NY: Routledge.

National Electronics and Computer Technology Centre. (2008). *Internet users in Thailand*. Retrieved January 15, 2011, from http:// internet. nectec.or.th/ webstats/ internetuser.iir? Sec= internetuser

National Press Council of Thailand. (2009, July). *Impact of defamation law on freedom of expression law in Thailand*. Retrieved January 15, 2011, from http://www.article19.org/ pdfs/ analysis/ thailand- impact- of- defamation- law- on- freedom- of- expression.pdf

Nguyen, A. (2009). Globalization, citizen journalism and the nation state: A Vietnam perspective. In Allan, S., & Thorsen, E. (Eds.), *Citizen journalism: Global perspectives* (pp. 153–162). New York, NY: Peter Lang.

Nostitz, N. (2009). Red vs. yellow: *Vol. 1. Thailand's crisis of identity*. Bangkok, Thailand: White Lotus.

Panuwat. (2010, April 26). Wassana Nanuam becomes latest victim of Thai media intimidation. *Tumblerblog: A Thai Political and Current Affairs Blog*. Retrieved January 15, 2011, from http://www.tumblerblog.com/ 2010/ 04/ wassana- nanuam- becomes- latest- victim- of- thai-media- intimidation

Panuwat. (n.d.). About. *Tumblerblog: A Thai political and current affairs blog.* Retrieved January 15, 2011, from http://www.tumblerblog.com/about/

Papacharissi, Z. (2002). The virtual sphere: The internet as a public sphere. *New Media & Society, 4*(1), 9–27. doi:10.1177/14614440222226244

Political prisoners in Thailand. (2010, April 9). *Abhisit's dictatorial face* [Web log post]. Retrieved January 15, 2011, from http://thaipoliticalprisoners. wordpress. com/ 2010/ 04/ 09/ pravit-on- abhisits- dictatorial- face/

Preechasilpakul, S., & Streckfuss, D. (2008, January). *Ramification and re-sacralization of the lèse majesté law in Thailand.* Paper presented at the 10th International Conference on Thai Studies, The Thai Khadi Research Institute/Thammasat University, Bangkok, Thailand.

Robinson, S. (2006). The mission of the j-blog: Recapturing journalistic authority online. *Journalism, 7*(1), 65–83..doi:10.1177/1464884906059428

Rojanaphruk, P. (2008, January). *Lese majeste law and mainstream newspapers' self-censorship: The upward spiral effect and its counter reaction.* Paper presented at the 10th International Conference on Thai Studies, The Thai Khadi Research Institute/ Thammasat University, Bangkok, Thailand.

Russell, A. (2009). Introduction. In Russell, A., & Echchaibi, N. (Eds.), *International blogging; Identity, politics, and networked publics* (pp. 1–10). New York, NY: Peter Lang.

Saiyasombut, S. (2010, March 20). Red shirt supporters in Germany. *Saiyasombut.* Retrieved January 15, 2011, from http://saiyasombut. wordpress. com/ 2010/ 03/ 20/ red- shirt- supporters-in- germany

Servaes, J., Malikhao, P., & Pinprayong, T. (2008). Communication rights as human rights for instance in Thailand. *Global Media Journal, 7*(13). Retrieved January 15, 2011, from http:// lass. calumet. purdue.edu/ cca/ gmj/ fa08/ gmj-fa08- servaes- malikhao- pinprayong.htm

Singer, J. B. (2005). The political J-blogger: Normalizing a new media form to fit old forms and practices. *Journalism, 6*(2), 173–210.. doi:10.1177/1464884905051009

Siriyuvasak, U. (2007). *New media for civil society and political censorship in Thailand.* Paper presented at the International Conference on New Media and Civil Society, Nepal.

Slack, J. D., & Wise, J. M. (2002). Cultural studies and new communication technologies. In Lievrouw, L. A., & Livingstone, S. M. (Eds.), *Handbook of new media: Social shaping and social consequences of ICTs* (pp. 142–162). Thousand Oaks, CA: Sage.

Sonwalker, P. (2009). Citizen journalism in India: the politics of recognition. In Allan, S., & Thorsen, E. (Eds.), *Citizen journalism: Global perspectives* (pp. 75–84). New York, NY: Peter Lang.

Thammo, T. (2009). The Internet in Thailand: An alternative means of communication. *Knowledge. Technology & Policy, 22*(2), 125–131.. doi:10.1007/s12130-009-9073-0

The International Telecommunications Union. (2010). *Measuring the information society.* Retrieved January 15, 2011, from http://www.itu. int/ ITU/ ict/ publications/ idi/ 2010/ Material/ MIS_2010_Summary_E.pdf

Ungpakorn, G. (2010). Ji Ungpakorn on current situation; situation in Bangkok very tense. *Political Prisoners in Thailand.* Retrieved January 15, 2011, from http://thaipoliticalprisoners. wordpress.com/ 2010/ 04/ 22/ ji- ungpakorn- on- current- situation/

Wall, M. (2006). Blogging Gulf War II. *Journalism Studies*, *7*(1), 111–126.. doi:10.1080/14616700500450392

Winichakul, T. (2008). Toppling democracy. *Journal of Contemporary Asia*, *38*(1), 11–37. doi:10.1080/00472330701651937

Witulski, F. (2010, April 22). Silom clashes. *Vaitor.com*. Retrieved January 15, 2011, from http://www.vaitor.com/?p=1558

Yoon, S. (2010a, April 18). The yellow shirts are back! *Suthichai Yoon*. Retrieved January 15, 2011, from http://suthichaiyoon. blogspot.com/ 2010/ 04/ yellow- shirts- are- back.html

Yoon, S. (2010b, May 20). Two pictures, two different stories. *Suthichai Yoon*. Retrieved January 15, 2011, from http://suthichaiyoon.blogspot.com/ 2010/ 05/ two- pictures- two- different-stories.html

Zayyan, H., & Carter, C. (2009). Human rights and wrongs: Blogging news of everyday life in Palestine. In Allan, S., & Thorsen, E. (Eds.), *Citizen journalism: Global perspectives* (pp. 85–94). New York, NY: Peter Lang.

ADDITIONAL READING

Allan, S. (2007). Citizen journalism and the rise of 'mass self-communication': Reporting the London bombings. *Global Media Journal* Australian edition. Retrieved January 15, 2011, from http://www.commarts. uws. edu.au/ gmjau/ iss1_2007/ stuart_allan.html

Allan, S. (2009). Histories of citizen journalism. In Allan, S., & Thorsen, E. (Eds.), *Citizen journalism: Global perspectives* (pp. 18–31). New York: Peter Lang.

Allan, S., Sonwalker, P., & Carter, C. (2007). Bearing witness: Citizen journalism and human rights issues. *Globalisation, Societies and Education*, *5*(3), 373–389. doi:10.1080/14767720701662139

Anderson, B. (1983). *Imagined communities: Reflections on the origin and spread of nationalism*. New York: Verso.

Bruns, A. (2008). *Blogs, Wikipedia, Second Life, and beyond: From production to produsage*. New York: Peter Lang.

Cammerts, B., & Carpentier, N. (2009). Challenging the ideological model of war and mainstream journalism? *Observatorio (OBS*) Journal*, *9*, 1-23. Retrieved January 15, 2011, from http://www.obercom.pt/ ojs/ index.php/ obs/ article/ viewArticle/ 276/

Hamilton, A. (2002). The national picture: Thai media and cultural identity. In Ginsburg, F. D., Abu-Lugard, L., & Larkin, B. (Eds.), *Media worlds; Anthropology on new terrain* (pp. 152–170). Berkeley, CA: University of California Press.

Harp, D., & Tremayne, M. (2006). The gendered blogosphere: Examining inequality using network and feminist theory. *Journalism & Mass Communication Quarterly*, *83*(2), 247–264.

Hermida, A. (2009). The blogging BBC: Journalism blogs at 'the world's most trusted news organisation'. *Journalism Practice*, *3*(3), 1–17.. doi:10.1080/17512780902869082

Jenkins, H. (2006). *Convergence culture: Where old and new media collide*. New York: New York University Press.

Johnson, T. J., & Kaye, B. K. (2006). Blog day afternoon: Are blogs stealing audiences away from traditional media sources? In Berenger, R. D. (Ed.), *Cybermedia go to war* (pp. 316–333). Spokane, WA: Marquette Books.

Kaye, B. K., & Johnson, T. J. (2004). Weblogs as a source of information about the 2003 Iraq War. In Berenger, R. D. (Ed.), *Global media goes to war: Role of news and entertainment media during the 2003 Iraq War* (pp. 291–301). Spokane, WA: Marquette Books.

Kim, J. (2007). The spiral of invisibility: Social control in the South Korean blogosphere. MEDIA@LSE Electronic Working Papers. Retrieved January 15, 2011, from http://www.lse.ac.uk/ collections/ media@lse/ mediaWorkingPapers/

Kirdnark, T. (2007). *The portrayal of Muslims in the south of Thailand in Thai newspapers in 2004.* Unpublished Master's thesis, California State University - Northridge, Northridge, CA.

Lewis, G. (2006). *Virtual Thailand: The media and cultural politics in Thailand, Malaysia and Singapore.* New York: Routledge.

Matheson, D., & Allan, S. (2007). Truth in a war zone: The role of warblogs in Iraq. In S. Maltby & R. Keeble (Eds.), *Communicating war: Memory, military and media* (pp. 75-89). Suffolk: Arima Publishing.

Morris, R. C. (2002). A room with a voice: Mediation and mediumship in Thailand's information age. In Ginsburg, F. D., Abu-Lugard, L., & Larkin, B. (Eds.), *Media worlds; Anthropology on new terrain* (pp. 383–397). Berkeley, CA: University of California Press.

Peleggi, M. (2007). *Thailand: The worldly kingdom.* Singapore: Talisman Publishing.

Persaud, W. H. (2005). Gender, race and global modernity: A perspective from Thailand. *Globalizations, 2*(2), 210–227. doi:10.1080/14747730500202214

Reich, Z. (2008). How citizens create news stories: The 'news access' problem reversed. *Journalism Studies, 9*(5), 739–758. doi:10.1080/14616700802207748

Reynolds, C. J. (1998). Globalization and cultural nationalism in modern Thailand. In Kahn, J. S. (Ed.), *Southeast Asian identities: Culture and politics of representation* (pp. 115–145). London: I. B. Tauris.

Reynolds, C. J. (2002). Thai identity in the age of globalization. C. J. Reynolds (Ed.) *National identity and its defenders* (pp. 308-338). Chiang Mai: Silkworm Books.

Singer, J. (2007). Contested autonomy: Professional and popular claims on journalistic norms. *Journalism Studies, 8*(1), 79–95. doi:10.1080/14616700601056866

Van Esterik, P. (2000). *Materializing Thailand.* Oxford: Berg.

Wall, M. (2005). Blogs of war: Weblogs as news. *Journalism, 6*(2), 153–172. doi:10.1177/1464884905051006

Winichakul, T. (1994). *Siam mapped: A history of the geo-body of a nation.* Chiang Mai: Silkworm Books.

KEY TERMS AND DEFINITIONS

Blog: A weblog or an online site that features the most recent post first, often written in an informal, journal-type style incorporating hyperlinks and frequently hosted by a commercial provider such as Blogger, WordPress, etc.

Citizen Media: Media usually produced by non-professional journalists, frequently enabled by new technologies and software.

Freedom of Expression: Ability to communication without censorship or other sorts of limits.

Lèse Majesté: Thai law that criminalizes defaming the country's royal family.

"Red Shirts": Thai political network affiliated with the United Front for Democracy Against Dictatorship that formed when the Thai Prime Minister Thaksin Shinawatra was overthrown by a military coup in 2006. Generally seen as representing the North and Northeast of Thailand though other urban support comes from within Bangkok.

Thailand: Southeast Asian country of 60 million people with a constitutional monarchy form of government.

"Yellow Shirts": An anti-Thaksin Shinawatra political network built around the People's Alliance for Democracy. Generally seen as representing the upper and bureaucratic classes particularly the military, Thai Chinese business owners, conservative royalists and some citizen groups in Central and Southern Thailand.

Chapter 3

Fame, Fantasy, Fanfare and Fun:
The Blossoming of the Chinese Culture of Blogmongering

Zixue Tai
University of Kentucky, USA

ABSTRACT

Phenomenal growth in recent years has made the Chinese blogosphere the largest blogging space in the world. By embedding the blogs against the backdrop of the broad context of the Internet communication environment in China, this chapter offers a panoramic overview of the fast-evolving Chinese blogosphere and critically assesses its social, cultural, and political ramifications. The chapter starts with an examination of landmark developments and milestone events in the historical trajectory of blogging in China in the past decade, followed by an in-depth analysis of major trends, popular practices, and dominant blogger groups. Finally, the chapter evaluates emerging platforms and themes unfolding on the horizon, and discusses their future implications.

INTRODUCTION

Spectacular economic boom in the wake of three-plus decades of economic and political reform in China has ushered in a scale of social transformation unrivaled in the country's history. In particular, the Internet sector, which boasts 384 million users in China as of year-end 2009 (China Internet Network Information Center, 2010) and whose staggering growth shows no signs of slowing down in the years to come, has been a leading area of breakneck growth and a cornerstone in China's state-supported "informatization" strategy (Harwit, 2008; Qiang, 2007; Tai, 2006). Amidst the ongoing ICT revolution is the quick rise of the Chinese blogosphere (Tai, 2009) and

DOI: 10.4018/978-1-60960-744-9.ch003

the mainstreaming of blogs as a socio-cultural phenomenon in China in recent years.

The Chinese blogosphere made its formal debut on August 19, 2002, with the launch of the first blog service provider BlogChina.com.[1] This event marks a fundamental step in three ways: first, it introduced and quickly popularized the term *Boke* as a Chinese term (for both blog sites and bloggers) for netizens in China; second, it promoted the concept and practice of blogging in China through the publication of the "China Blogger Manifesto" in the ensuing month, a widely-circulated milestone document in which blog pioneers Fang Xingdong and Wang Junxiu declared that blogging marks the transition of the Internet from an information distributing technology to a thought sharing culture; third, it set the dominant business model among blog service providers (BSPs)—which mushroomed to hundreds in the next two years on China's Internet—by offering free blog hosting to the blogging community. Since this landmark development in 2002, the Chinese blogosphere has experienced exponential growth in its present-day status as a populist, grassroots cultural phenomenon and the hallmark of Chinese cyberspace.

The diffusion of blogging has injected new dynamics onto China's fast-changing Internet environment and has become a leading force in shaping the landscape of the Chinese cyberculture. This chapter offers an in-depth panoramic overview of the evolving Chinese blogosphere by critically assessing the cultural, social, and to a lesser extent, political ramifications of blogging in China. After reviewing landmark developments and defining moments in the Chinese blogosphere, the chapter analyzes major trends, populist moves and dominant pacesetter groups by embedding them within the particular Chinese socio-political-cultural environment. The chapter ends with an evaluation of the emerging platforms of moblogs and microblogs as well as directions for future development of the Chinese blogosphere.

BACKGROUND

The sheer size of the gargantuan Chinese blogosphere is awe-inspiring: statistics from the China Internet Network Information Center (2009; 2010) indicate that as of June 2009, the blog community (i.e., encompassing those who publish their own blogs) reached 181 million, and that number jumped to 221 million by year-end 2009. Meanwhile, over 50 percent of the Chinese bloggers run multiple blog sites, with an average of 1.82 sites per blogger, while about 44 percent of these bloggers report updating their blog entries weekly or more often. That the blogs play prominent role in Chinese cyber life finds corroboration in the results of the four waves of cross-national "Power to the People" survey of global Internet use from 2006 through 2009 by Universal McCann, a New York-based global media-marketing consultancy firm. In its 4th global survey conducted between November 2008 and March 2009, Universal McCann revealed that Chinese netizens are leading in the blogging experience, with 90 percent of Chinese Internet users reporting reading the blogs and 81 percent of them claiming writing blogs of their own (Universal McCann, 2009). These patterns are highly congruent with the observation that the Chinese Internet population generally displays a higher tendency to rely on user-generated content (UGC) found in bulletin board systems (BBS), online forums, Internet chat rooms, and blogs (Tai, 2006; Yang, 2009). Tai (2006) attributes the skewed dependency of Chinese netizens on UGC to the predominantly controlled nature of the Chinese online environment in which state-sanctioned information dominates major legacy and Internet media outlets, thus channeling user interest to the unconventional, user-generated platforms.

To some extent, developments of the Chinese blogosphere as a multi-faceted, user-empowering platform of public communication have paralleled those in other parts of the world—albeit not without its unique twists and turns. First of all, the blogosphere has established itself globally as a viable public sphere for a wide range of user bases to share information, express opinions, debate issues, and deliberate positions (Barlow, 2008; Rettberg, 2008). Lucas Graves (2007) pinpoints three qualities of blogging's affordances, particularly in regard to news-related blogs—"reader input, fixity, and juxtaposition"—which he elaborates as "finding people with esoteric expertise, affixing articles where anyone can use or critique them, and juxtaposing competing versions for critical analysis" (p. 342). If participatory culture is the hallmark of the current convergence, as Henry Jenkins (2006) claims, then blogging has uplifted user participation to a whole new level largely due to its minimal barriers to entry. Bloggers, therefore, are "produsers," as they become a hybrid of producers/users of information in the brand-new online cultural environment (Bruns, 2008).

The participation of bloggers in the information production process allows for a complementing, competing, and alternative type of "citizen journalism," "participatory journalism" (Barlow, 2008; Gillmor, 2006) or "public's journalism" (Haas, 2005) that would otherwise be denied by the legacy media. In particular, bloggers fill the void of the established media in cases of breaking events, or news sites inaccessible to professional reporters, as amply demonstrated by the 2004 Thailand tsunami, the 2005 London terrorist bombings, or the massive 2008 Wenchuan earthquake in China. Moreover, "blogs are now a 'fifth estate' that keeps watch over the mainstream media" (Drezner & Farrell, 2004, p. 37); bloggers have assumed the role of "watchdog on the watchdog" or "gatewatchers" (Bruns, 2005). Bloggers offer fact-checking and fact-correcting, add in-depth and alternative perspectives, and provide unfiltered eyewitness accounts supplementary to stories carried by the mainstream media; they also serve as a barometer for what issues the conventional media did not, but should, cover. In a related note, the advent of blogs coincides with an era in which the mainstream media in most countries are increasingly

concentrated and commercialized. To offset this trend and to counterbalance the domination of online information production by the global media conglomerates, blogging provides the much-needed low-cost tool for ordinary people to create a kind of grassroots journalism (Gillmor, 2006).

A particular point that bears highlighting in connection to the discussion of blogs and other social media platforms in China is the state controlled media and communication environment in the country. Although economic liberalization and reform since 1978 has shattered the old monolithic and all-penetrative state monopoly of information found in Mao's regime, the Chinese state is still maintaining a formidable presence in the emerging communicative space through development and implementation of a sophisticated multi-tiered and multifaceted technology-centered surveillance system in a sustained effort to reign in the unfettered nature of the Internet era (for a thorough review, see Tai, 2010). Specifically, all Internet sites engaging in any type of content publishing must be licensed by relevant state authorities and must operate within a heavily-regulated environment, which essentially ensures that officially-favored information permeates major Web portals in Chinese cyberspace. Thanks to these structural constraints, user-generated content distributed via new media technology platforms, such as blogs, often serves as viable alternative sources of information (Tai, 2006; Yang, 2009).

THE CHINESE CULTURE OF BLOGMONGERING

For clarification in this context, *blogmongering* is a term used here to refer to the premeditated (and often frivolous) use of blogging to stir up public interest in a particular event or person for a specific end, such as self-promotion. The evolutionary trajectory of the fast-unfolding landscape of the Chinese blogosphere has been indelibly marked with a multitude of high-profile landmark events and eye-catching episodes (Tai, 2009). While many of these trends have become well-entrenched online cultural phenomena, Chinese bloggers also continue to plot a route into new territories. Understanding these historical contours and emerging horizons is critical for deciphering the peculiar nature of blogging in China.

Three distinct stages can be discerned in the development of the Chinese blogosphere.[2] In the take-off stage (2002-2003), blogging belonged to the confined domains of relatively small (for China) proportion of netizens (i.e., half a million in 2003 and 1.6 million in 2004), and content was skewedly limited to the bizarre and the out of ordinary. There were no particular blog groups or organized blog movements, and the sexploitation blogs of Muzimei and Zhuying Qingtong inadvertently publicized the term and practice of "Boke" to the average Chinese Internet surfers at the time. The ensuing three years (2004-2006) witnessed a rapid diffusion of blogs across China, thus forming the next stage of explosive growth in which the blogger base grew from 1.8 million in 2004 to 9.2 million in 2006. Unlike the previous phase in which the blog hosting service was lopsidedly dominated by small start-ups specializing in this niche market, major infotainment Web portals expanded into the blogging business and quickly gained a decisive competitive edge during this stage. The milestone event is the strategic move of Sina Corporation, a leading online media company in China to offer its own blog space—Blog Sina[3]—in September 2005, which made a monumental splash through its Mingren Boke (Celebrity Blogger) campaign in the following month. The current phase, which started in 2007, continues the pattern of exponential growth and marks the full recognition of blogging by the mainstream communication establishment. The status of blogging as a leading social media platform has been solidified by the indispensible role it has played in shaping the course of development in a series of hot-spot events that epitomize the milieu of tremendous dilemma and challenges in Chinese

society. As demonstrated in the following discussion, netizen participation and activism online has found new life in the Chinese blogosphere, while blogs have become a never-failing source of content and story ideas for conventional media.

Bizarre and the Out of Ordinary

In its initial stage of development, a few high-profile incidents accidentally turned "Boke" into a household name for Chinese netizens. It started in June 2003 with Muzimei—the pen name of a 25-year-old Li Li, then a columnist at a Guangzhou-based magazine—who opened an account with the newly-minted blog service provider Blogcn.com. She published her personal diaries titled "Ashes of Love" revealing promiscuous, graphically oriented and eye-rousing "one-night stand" sexual encounters. Her depiction was detailed and direct, and was deemed pornographic by many, running counter to well-established cannons of traditional Confucian values and social mores. What was particularly controversial but effective in attracting eyeballs was her practice of occasionally dropping names in the narrative (and one of the named happened to a well-known local rock star). Muzimei and her blog turned into an Internet craze and her name captivated China's cyberworld so much, that that the server hosting her blog at Blogcn.com required an upgrade to keep up with the heavy traffic (averaging 110,000 visitors a day in the peak month). Her blog became a talk of the day both in the fellow bloggers' journal entries and conventional media headlines. Due to the outpouring of public furor and rising concerns over unwanted impact on young people, Muzimei's blog, the first mass-read online publication in the nascent Chinese blogosphere, was removed from Blogcn.com. A Shanghai publisher, which had scheduled to publish a collection of Muzimei's blog postings as a book, had to cancel the deal out of pressure from the officials.

If 2003 was the year of Muzimei, then 2004 was the year for another like-minded female blogger, Zhuying Qingtong. It was a pseudonym of a 28-year-old college teacher who followed in the footsteps of Muzimei to come into the public spotlight through her mass-read blog hosted on the infotainment portal Tianya.cn.[4] While Zhuying Qingtong continued the sexploitation focus of Muzimei, she added her own nude pictures to the blog subtitled "Becoming a woman of both talent and beauty." The blog again took China's blogosphere by storm, and brought Zhuying Qingtong instant fame—the blog website was so overwhelmed with visitors within the first three days that Tianya.cn's server hosting the blog crashed. Later, Zhuying Qingtong disclosed that she had lost her job "under the pressure of society," and that she would no longer post her pictures, although she would continue to blog. As a matter of fact, her blog stayed popular. To meet the rising demand, she opened a personal website under the title "Nü Dao" (The Feminine Way).[5]

The one who carried on the torch of online sensationalism was Liumang Yan (the pseudonym of Ye Haiyan), who similarly achieved the status of an online celebrity through her blogging on love affairs. She started her blog on Tianya.cn early in 2005, and attracted a large base of regular readers by her blunt talk of personal relationships in combination with her erotic photos. She originally used the domain name of liumangyan.blog.tianya.cn for her blogs, and afterwards continued on a new site at hongchen2006.com (since 2006). Her writing style is congruent with her blatantly defiant motto of "blogging to be myself," while her feminist (and, to many, rebellious) slogan is best manifested in the slogan on her site claiming that, "Men are external things; you [women] don't come to this world with them, nor do you leave the world with them," —obviously borrowing from a popular Chinese saying about the insignificance of money in life. Noticeably, in a departure from Muzimei and Zhuying Qingtong, both of which are elegant-sounding names, this blogger adopted the kitschy and self-derogatory name of Liumang Yan: *Yan* is a popular female

name, and *Liumang* means hooligan or punk in Chinese. The popularity of her writing led to the publication of a book of selective blog entries in 2005 under the title "Summer Flower & Forbidden Fruit" by Hubei People's Press.

While all three of the above bloggers have earned a spot in the initial history of the Chinese blogosphere by ingenuously playing on the eternally popular taste for forbidden fruits of the taboo topics, it turns out that staying in the limelight is much harder than just getting into it. Online public gaze on these sexploitation blogs quickly faded after 2006, and dozens of would-be imitators have been hopelessly enshrouded in obscurity. Although Muzimei, Zhuying Qingtong, and Liumang Yan still maintain a certain level of recognition among Chinese bloggers, their relevance is now largely reduced to what they were in the past, not what they are now. Nonetheless, it is worth noting that these pioneer bloggers, by becoming overnight sensations in Chinese cyberspace, had created a most unexpected source of boost for China's budding blogosphere by attracting public attention and by encouraging more Internet users to jump on the blogging bandwagon.

Fame Mongering

The next waves of eyeball-chasing stunts in the blogosphere that led China's blogosphere to new territories consist of a mind-blowing bazaar of calculated and controversial moves on the part of a small number of individuals by becoming the center of public gaze online. This phenomenon illustrates well what already has become a deeply ingrained trend and well-trodden path of China's Internet culture—*chaozuo*. *Chao* (stir-fry) is a century-old technique in Chinese cuisine, and *chaozuo* is a speculative way to, literally, stir-fry and heat up the story so that it becomes sensationalized, titillating and eye-rousing in order to land online hits and thereby obtain media/public attention. Chaozuo panders to the end-justifies-the-means mindset prevalent in the consumerist culture of Chinese cyberspace. Among the most common techniques of chaozuo are the staging of ferocious events, the use of killing headlines, and the performance of premeditated publicity stunts.

The chaozuo master title undeniably goes to Furong Jiejie, who, aided by the blogs and other social media, became the pacesetter for the art of online attention mongering. Furong Jiejie (Sister Hibiscus or Sister Lotus, as some Western media call her), whose real name is Shi Hengxia and who possesses no particular talent (with the exception of her amazing audacity and perseverance). She started to be known online in the early part of 2005 through her self-portrait postings and video clips with provocative poses—despite mounting ridicule and widespread disdain—which she put on the bulletin board systems of Tsinghua and Peking Universities (China's counterparts to MIT and Harvard), two college campuses she openly admitted admiring but failing to gain entrance into. With her initial success with the BBS bombardments, Shi Hengxia quickly fell in love with the blogs by continuously and tenaciously reinventing herself through daily blog postings on her blog sites at Bokee.com[6] and Blog Sina.[7]

As a matter of fact, Shi Hengxia has gained such a cult status that she has to officially designate her Bokee and Sina sites "the official Furong Jiejie blog" to differentiate them from the numerous other copycat or parody sites. Sister Furong has become such an iconoclastic figure that many prominent media outlets, among them the *Washington Post*,[8] ran stories about her. Skillful in staging media events and in getting into press headlines, Sister Furong made constant public appearances with her typical ineffaceable remarks. Her (in)glorious iconic status as a cyber celebrity led her to star in the 2010 comedy *The Double Life* (directed by Ning Ying and produced by the Zhejiang Golden Globe Picture Co.) which was released in theaters across over 60 Chinese cities on April 29, 2010. As an attestation to her unequivocal popularity, a search using "Furong Jiejie" as the key term in early June 2010 on Baidu.com, the most popular Chinese search engine, landed 18.8 million pages; in another measurement, Furong Jiejie was ranked consistently as No. 1 of the "Top 10 Internet Celebrities" from 2005 to 2008 as reflected in online searches on Baidu. Whether people talk about her out of love, admiration, hate, disgust or for whatever reason, there is no doubt Furong Jiejie has drawn the public attention to herself as she desired.

Another prime example of a quick rise to online fame is the story of Tianxian Meimei (Sister Fairy).[9] *Tianxian Meimei* is the nickname of a young woman in the hinterland of Sichuan Province where China's Qiang nationality resides. Her look of freshness and naivety captivated millions, and she became an overnight sensation on China's Internet when her picture in traditional Qiang costume was posted on the Web in 2005. The picture was taken by Yang Jun, whose hobby of travel and photography led to an accidental meeting with the girl. Yang casually posted the picture with comments on the auto forum of Tom. com, where he was a regular visitor. To his great surprise, Yang found that the photograph attracted tens of thousands of follow-up comments within a few days and became the prime subject of the discussion on a forum typically dominated by auto-related issues. So he went back to take more pictures, which, after being posted on the same forum, attracted the attention of two million visitors within months. Realizing the commercial potential, Yang then teamed up with Tianxian Meimei to amass more publicity. Consequently, Tianxian Meimei started her own blog on Blog Sina,[10] and she became a welcome face on TV programs and newspaper pages. With the explosive fame comes the next natural step of reaping its commercial benefits. Tianxian Meimei starred in a leading role in two award-winning movies—*A Postman of Paradise* (2007, directed by Yu Zhong) and *Er Ma's Wedding* (2007, directed by Han Wanfeng)—and has played leading characters in three teledramas (as of June 2010). In 2009, her biography titled *Sister Tianxian* (penned by Yi Lin and published by Beijing-based Dongfang Publishing House) came out amidst much fanfare. Additionally, she also landed lucrative commercial contracts, which climaxed in advertising deals with Sony Ericsson and Tianfu Online, a premier infotainment portal in Sichuan Province on top of other lucrative deals as a spokesperson for a variety of products in her home region.

The latest successful story of fame mongering is the case of Feng Jie, or Sister Feng. Sister Feng's real name is Luo Yufeng, and is a 4.8-foot 25-year-old young woman with an average appearance. With an associate's degree from a teacher's college in Chongqing that is barely known outside of the region, she left her colorless four-year teaching career in her native town to seek fortune in the cosmopolitan metropolis of Shanghai, where she worked as a cashier in a local Carrefour hypermarket before an occasion guided her to national fame. She came into the public spotlight in November 2009 after an interview with a Shanghai's *Xinmin Evening News* reporter telling him how she hand-distributed 1,300 flyers at a congested subway advertising for a date. Her act would not have been eye-catching if she had not been specifying a list of atrociously stringent conditions for the potential dating candidate, among which were that he must be: a Master of Economics graduate from premiere Peking or Tsinghua universities, between 5.8 to 6 feet tall, between 25 and 28 years old, without a marital history, and residing in an eastern coastal city. The set of requirements later triggered dynamic lines of hilarious cyber debates and analysis, which led to the national consensus among netizens that only 5-6 such candidates can be found throughout China.

As expected, a national excitement broke out in the wake of the *Xinmin* story, whose online presence made it an easy national read. Coupled with the online story was a 20-minute video of the interview that has had millions of views and became fodder for thousands of bloggers. This initial outpouring of online clicks was followed by the release of Sister Feng's official webpage

at fengjiecn.com, which has served as an effective intermediary between her (in terms of latest moves, comments, reflections, responses to comments, calls to the public, etc.) and numerous bloggers. Since the November 2009 media debut, Sister Feng has managed to continuously stay in the public spotlight through a series of shock advertisement type events and sensation-soaked interviews and TV appearances, among them her fleeting encounters with an expanding list of handsome top-notch dates or her plastic surgery. Overflowing with zealous and narcissistic self-confidence, Sister Feng never fails to cause a stir in public, being ferociously chased—celebrity style—by paparazzi and professional as well as amateurish news hunters. In fact, the conventional media are so infatuated with her that she only grants interviews to selective media outlets and that even her mediocre performance was enough to send her to the next round when participating in reality-TV talent shows on popular TV channels. A search in the video archive section of Baidu in June 2010 using the key words "Sister Feng" and "media interviews" yielded 42 videos featuring her being interviewed by the Chinese media. On the official website of *Xinmin Evening News*, the online verson of the newspaper that ran the first news story on her, has more than 2,000 pages mentioning Sister Feng as of June 2010.

The surge of fame-hungry individuals in China has led to the birth of a brand-new profession in Chinese cyberspace, widely known as *wangluo tuishou* (network hand-pusher), or network strategist—an emerging occupation in China that involves identifying for just every imaginable type of talent and then finding creative ways to create and propel the hype to the limits on the Internet (most often for an exorbitant service charge). However, most network hand-pushers prefer to call themselves Internet public relations strategists or online marketers. While these network hand-pushers are responsible for designing the overall strategy and particular tactics for each stage of the online hype manufacturing and puffery engineering, the actual implementation is typically outsourced to the massive, loosely organized swarms of individuals trolling popular Internet sites. These individuals, believed to be in the hundreds of thousands, are commonly known in Chinese cyberspace as *shuijun* (water army) and sometimes pejoratively dubbed as "online mercenaries," because their contracted job is to flood (which is called *guanshui* in Chinese, meaning water-fill) online forums with messages of a predefined tone, thus influencing popular sentiments and swaying public opinion. Water army "soldiers" obtain instructions via instant messaging or emails, and are typically paid in the range of CNY¥0.30-0.50 per blog post.

An investigative report by China's national television network CCTV on December 20, 2009[11] scrutinized this phenomenon and triggered numerous follow-up investigations by other media, the most noteworthy being three in detail stories run by the *People's Daily* in June 2010.[12] The *People's Daily* articles unravel a three-step formula of success for network hand-pushers: first, create an online controversy; second, strive for the attention of conventional media; and, third, harvest commercial benefits.

Although fame mongering shares a lot in common between the previous sexploitation blog writers and the masters of chaozuo already discussed, there is also a substantial difference in the particular approaches and goals of attention-hooking among these types of bloggers. Noticeably, sexploitation blog writers pretty much depend on self-exposure and incur no collaborative scheme with others, whereas behind-the-scene network hand-pushers play a critical role in maneuvering the *chaozuo* celebrities into the never-ending stunts. Moreover, individuals in the latter category have to constantly reinvent themselves by engaging in the escalating eye-rousing activities to remain in the spotlight. Finally, just as Rojek (2001) shrewdly observes, since wealth is the ultimate destination of the "celebrication" process, these self-made Internet celebrities also eye commercial exploitations of their fame.

Spoofing Fun on Blog Pages

Since 2005, a new cultural phenomenon called *e-gao* has quickly taken over Chinese blogosphere as a particular form of individual transgression and self-made grassroots entertainment most typically manifested in audiovisual (re)productions. Playful, subversive and satiric in nature, it parodies a variety of China's mainstream discourses and official ideological postulates propagated by state-sanctioned film, television and print media and their online outlets. Technologically, *e-gao* has been made possible by the mushrooming of sophisticated but widely accessible digital production and editing tools. As a result, hilarious video clips and digital mashups are now spreading virally by many Internet means with blogs as a premier vehicle and destination.

Originating in Japan, *e-gao* soon spread to Taiwan and Hong Kong. It found a permanent place in the Chinese Internet culture after a 20-minute video called *The Bloody Case of the Steamed Bun*. The clip was created by Hu Ge, a sound engineer from Shanghai, as a parody on the prominent Chinese director Chen Kaige's big budget, nationally advertised movie *The Promise* (2005) which suddenly flopped at the box office. Disappointed by the legacy media hype over nothing, Hu borrowed images from the movie for a new wickedly funny storyline for the sake of light-hearted satire, mockery, and criticism in an exaggerated and extremist fashion (Li, 2006). Hu further explained that his aim was to create a multimedia movie review. As a result, in early 2006, when *The Promise* was still on the screens across the country, Hu's satire piece had been viewed by tens of millions of netizens, in much larger numbers than people who actually went to see the movie in the theatre. As a matter of fact, Hu's parody created an unanticipated publicity effect for the movie, as many moviegoers acknowledged that they got interested in the movie only after having seen the parody online. The director Chen Kaige however, was not impressed by the sarcastic tone in Hu's recreation; he told the press repeatedly that he would take Hu to court, but eventually dropped the case.

Hu's piece quickly led to the escalation of *e-gao* into an online cultural phenomenon, spanning a wide spectrum of participants and targets of spoofing. Hu himself gained the status of a household name on China's Internet, avidly sought after by the media for interviews. Now the formats of *e-gao* runs a gamut through text, graphics, photo, audio and video, resulting in virally spread digital productions. Its quality ranges from crude and gross to highly professional. The major targets of *e-gao* have been movies, music releases, different public and popular culture figures, rock stars, with some bloggers even poking fun at themselves, as many *e-gao* artists becoming targets of *e-gao*. As an indisputable indicator of its craze, the authors search using *e-gao* as the key phrase on Blog Sina,[13] the most popular blog provider in China, resulted in over 38 million entries as of mid-June 2010. Most spoof artists post their creations on their blogs, many of which get re-distributed or revised by other bloggers, thus producing some kind of amplification effect. There is even a popular site solely devoted to this practice called E-gao Net[14] where netizens share their works, latest news, and comments.

However, for the Party ideologues and conservatives, online spoofers crossed the line when *The Sparkling Red Star*, a revolutionary classic made in 1974, was parodied in 2006. Pan Dongzi, the teen hero that became a household name in the 1970s, was turned into a contemporary youngster fathered by a real estate millionaire. In the satirical video, Pan wants to enter a singing contest so he can become famous (which is an apparent attempt to mock the popular reality TV shows). For the older generation who grew up watching this undisputable (for them) classic, this was a clear example of rebellious youth turning wild and out of hand. So there have been numerous denunciations and diatribes from the conventional media by educators, moralists, pundits and government officials bemoaning this type of "tasteless,

despicable and pathetic" act. It has led to calls by government officials and legislators to pass laws punishing this kind of behavior. In October 2006, Chongqing became the first metropolis in China to legislate against *e-gao* by passing the Chongqing Municipality Computer Information Systems Security Ordinance, which subjected individuals engaging in "vicious" *e-gao* of others to a fine of CNY¥1,000 to 3,000. Legislation by other municipalities and provinces as well as at the national level, however, has not materialized as of yet amidst mounting dissent and questions about its effectiveness. For now, Bloggers were not prosecuted for creating and posting *e-gao* in their online journals.

E-gao as a seedbed of playful creativity and grassroots entertainment has transformed the Chinese blogosphere on multiple fronts. In discussing the culture phenomenon of *e-gao*, Meng (2009) attributes its subversive potential to three major factors: first, it problematizes the conventional copyright protection framework; second, it disrupts the status quo of the centralized media system in China; and, third, it offers an alternative means for individuals to engage with social political issues in a heavily censored and highly constrained discursive environment (see also Gong & Yang, 2010).

Grassroots Surveillance

Despite decades of market-oriented reform, conventional media in China still operate within a tightly state controlled system, and numerous taboo areas and topics are still off limits to journalists. Therefore, under many circumstances, blogs become viable alternative (and sometimes the sole) sources of information on issues/events of public interest. On some occasions, blogs are the first to break out important stories, which may quickly catch on in the Chinese blogospere and get picked up by the conventional media. In these cases, the Internet acts as a barometer to gauge public sentiments, and conventional media are able to pick significant clues on what stories to follow. Even in cases for which there is an abundance of information from the legacy media, there may still be critical information that the media intentionally or accidentally decide to skip. On such occasions, the blogosphere fills an important niche allowing for netizens to collaborate in uncovering and trading back-alley information regarding cases of misinformation, corruption, mishandling of public funds, human rights violations, or merely judicial injustice.

In one prominent case, on October 12, 2007, the Forestry Bureau of Shaanxi Province released two photos of an allegedly wild-roaming South China tiger taken by local farmer Zhou Zhenglong. Since it belongs to a species that is believed to be extinct in the wild, it made national headlines, including those of the major Chinese news portals. Immediately, there emerged two groups of netizens in response to this story: the so-called "tiger fighters" who challenged the authenticity of the photos and the "tiger protectors" defending it. Each group used the blogs as the chief battlefield to make their case. As more evidence accumulated, especially after the discovery of a poster published years prior to the photos that features an identical picture, it became clear that these photos were digitally doctored. Public uproar triggered by the vigorous online debates led to the involvement of the State Forestry Bureau and other national official agencies in the investigation. Eventually, Zhou Zhenglong was charged with deception and about a dozen officials were disciplined in relation to the incident. In February 2008, deputy director of the Shaanxi Forestry Bureau lost his job, and the Bureau made a public apology for "being too hasty" in rushing the news to the nation. Citizen reporters scored a victory on this occurrence with the help of the blogs as an effective communication platform. Although the whole issue was apolitical, it provided an important opportunity for the Chinese bloggers to participate in a coordinated campaign against government supported misinformation.

In covering the destructive 2008 Sichuan Earthquake, the blogosphere has again demonstrated its potential for public involvement in the news making. In May and June of 2008, a number of netizens reported the misuse of relief funds and profiteering in the disaster area. In particular, embezzlement of relief tents designated for exclusive use by earthquake victims became a symbol of corruption. Bloggers published multiple photo evidence with detailed information, and the traditional media followed up on those cases using the clues offered by blogs. Due to the public fury, officials showed an unprecedented level of timely responsiveness and accountability in investigating these cases and in punishing offenders. However, the Internet coverage of the Sichuan Earthquake also reflected the limitation of blogs in the coverage of politically sensitive news in China. For example, in Sichuan thousands of children may have been killed in collapsed school buildings, with the government suppressing all the related information. Many parents believe that they died as a result of substandard construction. People have persistently demanded that a thorough investigation be conducted and that incriminated corrupted local officials be punished. Such demands and stories exposing the cost cutting practices of the private developers have found their ways online, but have rarely made it to the headlines of the conventional media. The mainstream media customarily ignored peoples' petitions to the government, and the authorities easily suppressed individual protest voices. For example, Huang Qi, a human rights activist and the head of Tianwang Human Rights Center who was previously imprisoned for five years in 2000-2005 for calling to reassess the June 4 Tiananmen massacre of 1989, was arrested again in July 2008 for collecting information from parents regarding the collapsed school buildings in the earthquake-hit areas. As a result, Huang Qi was sentenced in November 2009 to a three year prison term for "divulging state secrets" on the Center's website.[15] So the presence of a dangling sword of state surveillance above the head of each netizen is still very much a fact of life in the Chinese blogosphere, and it forces bloggers to practice self-censorship and be careful in dealing with politically and socially charged topics.

In another story that was widely touted as the "Extravagant Cigarette Incident," Zhou Jiugong, director of the government run Real Estate Bureau in Jiangning District of Nanjing, caused public outrage in the blogosphere in December 2008 for threatening to penalize those private developers who dare to reduce the prices of the apartment units. Zhou made the headline-catching comment to local reporters, which immediately triggered heated debates after the story was picked up by bloggers. Within days, Zhou evolved into a targeted figure of public scrutiny, when individuals volunteered in blogs all types of particular information about him. The critical blow came from an online photo taken by a blogger after a meeting with Zhou featuring him smoking an expensive brand of cigarettes. This photo was subsequently corroborated with a number of pictures of Zhou wearing different high priced name-brand watches on three different occasions. The natural question shifted to how Zhou, as a government functionary, could afford this kind of lifestyle, which culminated in a massive online petition in January 2009 to the local government demanding a thorough investigation. In this event, a number of legacy media decided to follow up on the story, and, in combination with bloggers, created substantial pressure for local officials, who agreed to a criminal investigation on Zhou in early February of 2009. Later, Zhou was found guilty on the charges of corruption, and was sentenced to an eleven-year prison term in October 2009. As demonstrated above, individuals can work effectively online as "smart mobs" (Rheingold, 2003).

The above incidents are by no means isolated happenings, as more and more similar cases emerge regularly due to Chinese netizens nowadays. On such occasions, through concerted collaboration bloggers assume the watchdog role in demanding a certain degree of public accountability from

government officials. This is perfect testimonial to the "many eyeballs" effect that Bruns (2006) has observed in the cases where massive participation online uncovers and addresses public grievances.

Blog Celebrication

In its early years, China's blogosphere was predominantly dominated by the individual bloggers whose names were otherwise unknown in the offline world. A landmark event took place in October 2005, when infotainment portal Sina. com, the leading in China, started its *Mingren Boke* (Celebrity Blogger) movement by inviting social elites (with the noticeable exception of politicians) to open accounts with its blog section Blog Sina as an overall strategy to increase online traffic. The first celebrity to join was the popular writer Yu Hua, quickly followed by hundreds of well-known (in China) names ranging from sports to entertainment to news media to business circles. The star of stars has become the actress Xu Jinglei, who made her fame through movie acting and directing. Her blog recorded nearly 10 million hits within the first 100 days of its existence, making history not only in China but across the world as well. As of June 2010, Xu's blog has landed over 288 million visits, placing her among the top ten Sina.com bloggers. A selection of Xu's blogs resulted in the bestseller *Old Xu's Blogs* (published in 2006 by CITIC Press in Beijing). Interestingly, Xu successfully branded her identity as *Old Xu*, an amicable way to be addressed by peer intimates in the Chinese folk tradition. In no time, Mingren Boke has become a unique cultural formation in cyber China. Each of the entries by these celebrity bloggers is typically followed by comments numbered often in the thousands on the particular blog page, and generates numerous additional discussions and debates throughout the blogosphere.

The popularization of blogging in China has facilitated the birth of a special genre of bloggers, nicknamed *Caogen Boke* (Grassroots Bloggers), who have earned esteem and fame among blog writers and readers solely through their blog sites. Those people, unlike *Mingren Boke*, would otherwise have no way of getting known by the public without the blogosphere. Their eliteness is totally owed to the quality, coupled with the quantity, since those who write little stand a minimal chance of joining the elite league of their blogs. Standing above all grassroots bloggers is Han Han, a young writer from Shanghai, who did not even attend college but has become an undisputable online celebrity through his pungent, blunt and unapologetic blog writings. Many times Han's musing or even comments made big headlines both on and off the blogosphere, and set the agenda of public debates. In fact, Han's blog[16] has continuously made him the No. 1 in the Blog Sina's ranking system. Two other good reads in this category are bloggers *wu2198*[17] and *Acosta*[18]—both nicknames—whose blogs are ranked No. 2 and No. 11 respectively on Sina's blogs with over 772 million and 222 million hits as of mid-June 2010. In contrast with offline celebrities whose life and family background is known to the public in excruciating detail, these grassroots writers gain widespread recognition through the currency of their blogs (i.e., the insightfulness of his (her) timely comments on China's stock market for wu2198 and the beauty and fluency of his writings on personal observations and reflections for Acosta). The other sides of their life are scarcely available, despite their enormous intrigue to many. In fact, "Who is wu2198/Acosta" has been searched (and discussed) so many times in the Chinese blogosphere that both are featured as popular search phrases on search engine Baidu.

Typical of any fast-paced transforming society, today's China is ridden with grinding challenges, mass discontent, and fermenting bitterness among a large number of disenfranchised people throughout the country. Yet the controlled nature of the established news media means that these grievances are rarely addressed in the mainstream discourses. This has led to the formation of a group of bloggers who have risen to the occasion and have taken on the self-imposed mission of advocating and fighting for particular causes in the protection of the public interest. An illustrious example is the case of Lian Yue,[19] a well-known writer who successfully used his blog in 2006 to 2007 as a rally point in organizing concerned citizens to abort a government effort in building a xylene producing chemical plant in the southern city of Xiamen. The stories of seventeen grassroots bloggers who enjoy star status are the focus of the book by Zhai Minglei (2009), in which he coins the term *mengbo* (ferocious or atrocious bloggers) to symbolize the courage, hardship, tenacity and admirableness observable in these online crusaders. The most powerful weapon that these bloggers possess is the keyboard; however, they can summon thousands of fellow bloggers to defend a viable course. Coming from a wide range of educational, professional, and socio-demographic backgrounds, these grassroots bloggers have steadily built a reputation for: (1) their intimate knowledge about how to expose a corrupt official or a shady businessmen; (2) their deep-seated empathy for the commoners living at the lowest echelon of society; and, (3) their natural tendency to speak up for them against what they perceive as evil or injustice in society. Subsequently, the actions of these grassroots bloggers turned them into virtual *Robin Hoods* of the cyberworld.

Over a decade ago, Goldhaber (1997) pointed out that the Internet is an "attention economy"—what becomes scarce is not information but rather attention. The blogging platform, then, is in essence a leveled playing ground. Since attention is guaranteed for nobody, only those with eye-catching posts are destined stand out. But unlike some other bloggers who have to resort to publicity stunts to amass attention, celebrity bloggers discussed in this section rise to popularity heights primarily due to the captivating content that resonates with public sentiments. In the meantime, this new generation of bloggers is navigating in dangerous waters for oftentimes singing out of tune with the state-orchestrated media symphony, and they may become an easy target for a whimsical government crackdown.

FUTURE RESEARCH DIRECTIONS

As mentioned, the highly controlled nature of the Chinese information environment has afforded user-generated content a special place in the eyes and hearts of Chinese netizens. While interactive platforms such as bulletin board systems, online forums, chat rooms, and instant messaging have been extremely popular on China's Internet, the latest blogging revolution has uplifted user participation to a new level. The unfolding public's love affair with the blogs and blogging which we have tried to explicate throughout the chapter will in all likelihood intensify as the China's blogosphere is further ingrained into the everyday life of the society. It constantly adopts new technology tools resulting in innovative productions such as *e-gao*'s. Another two areas that are already promising to significantly reshape the blog landscape in China are moblogs and microblogs.

Moblog (mobile blog) allows users to post and access blog entries on the Web while on the move through a burgeoning set of wireless applications. In mid-2006, China Mobile, the largest wireless phone service operator in the country, started to offer moblog service to its Beijing-based subscribers. Since then, moblog service has been expanded to all major cities in the country among a growing user base. Since text-based moblog has serious limitation due to its length constraints, services have instead diverged in placing more emphasis on audio and video blogs. An important development that has accelerated moblog growth is the latest nationwide implementation of 3G wireless networks, which formally started in January 2009. Within less than a year, mobile Web subscribers exploded by 120 million, creating a wireless Internet user base of 233 million (or close to 61 percent of the overall Internet population) by December 2009

(China Internet Network Information, 2010). As mobile connectivity reaches a new height, recent developments in the moblog subculture are well positioned to reshape the Chinese blogosphere, especially in regard to real-time coverage of breaking events by citizen bloggers.

The unstoppable growth of microblogs (*weibo*) in China's blogosphere is quickly becoming another new trend in blogging. The first native Twitter-type social media platform in China, Fanfou,[20] was founded in May 2007. The name is derived from an abbreviation of the customary Chinese greeting of "Have you eaten yet?" among acquaintances, and is aptly descriptive of the personalized and often trivialized nature of this kind of often-casual exchanges. However, in an unexpected turn of events, Fanfou and a few other popular microblogging services were shut down by the authorities in July 2009, mainly because of their inability for effective self-censoring. This is particularly challenging for the microblog service providers due to the real-time nature of microblogging. However, due to its years of experience as well as its sophisticated technical expertise in information censoring, Sina Corporation set foot in this market in August 2009 with its own service specializing in microblogs[21] and immediately took over as the No. 1 microblog platform in China. How microblogging will affect the Chinese blogosphere will be seen in the coming years.

The need for a domestic version of Twitter (which has blossomed in other parts of the world) is largely due to the structural factors of China's particular information environment, which, as Tai (2010) argues, has placed a great emphasis on state controllability of information flows across the Chinese online networks. As a result, overseas social media applications such as Twitter, Facebook, and YouTube all have been phased out of Chinese cyberspace because of the government's inability to censor information on these platforms. Yet the biggest attraction of blogs and microblogs lies in their user-empowering potential to invite public participation in the information production process. Therefore, how Chinese authorities will incorporate blogs and microblogs into their grand scheme of information censoring will be a matter for global attention in the years ahead.

CONCLUSION

Although the Chinese blogosphere started much later than its counterparts in other countries, phenomenal growth of the Chinese blogosphere in recent years has now rendered it the largest blog space in the world. Alongside this explosive expansion is the critical role the blogs have played in redefining the landscape of the fast-evolving Chinese cyberculture. As pointed out at the start of this chapter, Chinese netizens have an unusual propensity both to contribute and to depend on user-generated content. In that regard, blogs have revolutionized user participation in online information production and consumption in Chinese cyberspace with its unique twists and turns, as manifested in the distinct trends and blogger groups discussed here.

As Drezner and Farrell (2004) observe, "even as the blogosphere continues to expand, only a few blogs are likely to emerge as focal points" (p. 35). The nature of the blogosphere makes it possible for only a limited number of bloggers to make it to the "'A-list' of established, well-known, and often controversial bloggers" (Bruns & Jacobs, 2006, p.1). Two immensely popular groups of A-list bloggers who have established a formidable presence on China's Internet are those so-called *celebrity bloggers* and *grassroots bloggers*, the former being comprised of social elites who already have established popularity in the offline world. Nonetheless, an Internet fame, as measured by blog homepage visits, is guaranteed for no one in the online world; even social elites still have to write in sync with popular resonance to sustain their online celebrity status. Grassroots bloggers, on the other hand, have solely earned their fame through their audacity to speak out on hot-button issues and through their penetrating perspectives on issues of public interest. In functioning as "focal points," these two groups of bloggers are able to successfully grab public attention by setting the agenda for online debates and by creating controversies that less prominent bloggers find convenient to follow up on. Subsequently, big-name bloggers and less renowned ones have developed a symbiotic relationship in sustaining the network chain of information production in the blogosphere. Additionally, news oriented websites and conventional media play the role of an amplifier in constantly turning bloggers into newsmakers serving an ever-increasing audience.

For bloggers who otherwise lack name recognition, the best way to achieve fame and popularity is to publicly stage stunts that are difficult for others to ignore. So, China's blogosphere has to some extent become a mind-boggling bazaar of hype manufacturing by a variety of individuals; whatever their purposes, they are engaged in feeding public curiosity for the sexy, the weird, and the bizarre. For these fame-hungry individuals, the end of an attention-grabber justifies any means imaginable; thus, a new profession emerges called the *network hand-pusher* whose sole service is to calculate the most likely move under a particular circumstance for its shock value. In line with the conventional celebrication process, fame-hunting individuals in this category almost invariably intend to reap commercial benefits from their online attention-garnering success. However, the same ploy is most likely to be spurned by the audience on second use, thereby creating the daunting task for the network hand-pushers to constantly reinvent new gimmicks to engage target audience.

It is important to note that China's blogosphere has provided netizens with the opportunity for collaboration and collective action on events and issues of substantial public interest. In certain situations, individuals can collaborate online with one another to demand public accountability from the officials, stop corruption, and encourage positive societal change. However, censorship and other constraints set by a state apparatus create certain boundaries within which actions of such a nature are solely tolerated. Unlike democratic societies where politics forms a major theme for blogs, the omnipresent state power and heavy-handed official censoring of information in the Chinese blogosphere cause most Chinese bloggers to shy away from politically sensitive and dissident issues and topics. Consequently, most bloggers have opted to focus predominantly on entertainment and amusement as a strategy of self-survival. This peculiar feature of the Chinese blogosphere will be likely to continue to define blogging in China.

REFERENCES

Barlow, A. (2008). *Blogging America: The new public sphere*. Westport, CT: Praeger.

Bruns, A. (2005). *Gatewatching: Collaborative online news production*. New York, NY: Peter Lang Publishing.

Bruns, A. (2006). The practice of news blogging. In Bruns, A., & Jacobs, J. (Eds.), *Uses of blogs* (pp. 11–22). New York, NY: Peter Lang Publishing.

Bruns, A. (2008). *Blogs, Wikipedia, Second Life, and beyond: From production to produsage*. New York, NY: Peter Lang Publishing.

China Internet Network Information Center (CNNIC). (2009). *Research report on China's blog market and blogger behavior: 2008-2009* (in Chinese). Retrieved June 3, 2010, from http://www.cnnic.cn/ uploadfiles/ pdf/ 2009/ 10/ 10/ 105733.pdf

China Internet Network Information Center (CNNIC). (2010). *The 25ᵗʰ statistical report on Internet development in China* (in Chinese). Retrieved May 29, 2010, from http://www.cnnic.org.cn/ uploadfiles/ pdf/ 2010/ 1/ 15/ 101600.pdf

Drezner, D. W., & Farrell, H. (2004). Web of influence. *Foreign Policy, 145*, 32–40. doi:10.2307/4152942

Gillmor, D. (2006). *We the media: Grassroots journalism by the people, for the people*. Sebastopol, CA: O'Reilly.

Goldhaver, M. H. (1997). Attention and the Net. *First Monday, 2*(4). Retrieved February 15, 2011, from http://www.firstmonday.dk/ issues/ issue2_4/ goldhaber/

Gong, H., & Yang, X. (2010). Digitized parody: The politics of *egao* in contemporary China. *China Information, 24*(1), 3–26. doi:10.1177/0920203X09350249

Graves, L. (2007). The affordances of blogging: A case study in culture and technological effects. *The Journal of Communication Inquiry, 31*(4), 331–346. doi:10.1177/0196859907305446

Haas, T. (2005). From public journalism to the public's journalism: Rhetoric and reality in the discourse on weblogs. *Journalism Studies, 6*(3), 387–396. doi:10.1080/14616700500132073

Harwit, E. (2008). *China's telecommunications revolution*. New York, NY: Oxford University Press. doi:10.1093/acprof:oso/9780199233748.001.0001

Jenkins, H. (2006). *Convergence culture: Where old and new media collide*. New York, NY: New York University Press.

Li, J. (2006, March 6). Hu Ge: My heart is filled with fun-making intentions. In Chinese. *China Newsweek, 8*, 22-25.

Meng, B. (2009). Regulating *egao*: Futile efforts of recentralization? In Zhang, Z., & Zheng, Y. (Eds.), *China's information and communications technology revolution: Social changes and state responses* (pp. 52–67). New York, NY: Routledge.

Qiang, C. Z. W. (2007). *China's information revolution: Managing the economic and social transformation*. Washington, DC: The World Bank. doi:10.1596/978-0-8213-6720-9

Rettberg, J. W. (2008). *Blogging*. Malden, MA: Polity.

Rheingold, H. (2003). *Smart mobs: The next social revolution*. Cambridge, MA: Perseus Publishing.

Rojek, C. (2001). *Celebrity*. London, UK: Routledge.

Singer, J. B. (2006). Journalists and news bloggers: Complements, contradictions, and challenges. In Bruns, A., & Jacobs, J. (Eds.), *Uses of blogs* (pp. 21–32). New York, NY: Peter Lang Publishing.

Tai, Z. (2006). *The Internet in China: Cyberspace and civil society*. New York, NY: Routledge.

Tai, Z. (2010). The rise of the Chinese blogosphere. In Dumova, T., & Fiordo, R. (Eds.), *Handbook of research on social interaction technologies and collaboration software: Concepts and trends* (pp. 67–79). Hershey, PA: IGI Global.

Tai (2010). Casting the ubiquitous net of information control: Internet surveillance in China from Golden Shield to Green Dam. *International Journal of Advanced Pervasive and Ubiquitous Computing, 2*(1), 53-70.

Universal McCann. (2009, July 9). *Power to the people: Social media tracker – Wave 4*. Retrieved June 4, 2010, from http://universalmccann.bitecp.com/ wave4/ Wave4.pdf

Yang, G. (2009). *The power of the Internet in China: Citizen activism online*. New York, NY: Columbia University Press.

Zhao, M. (2009). *China's ferocious bloggers: Civil discourse in the new media age*. In Chinese. Hong Kong: Cosmos Books.

ADDITIONAL READING

Calingaert, D. (2010). Authoritarianism vs. the Internet. *Policy Review, 160*, 63–75.

Chung, C. (2009). New media and event: A case study on the power of the Internet. *Knowledge. Technology & Policy, 22*(2), 145–153. doi:10.1007/s12130-009-9078-8

Esarey, A., & Xiao, Q. (2008). Political expression in the Chinese blogosphere. *Asian Survey, 48*(5), 752–772. doi:10.1525/AS.2008.48.5.752

Hearn, K. (2009). The management of China's blogosphere 博客 boke (blog). *Continuum: Journal of Media & Cultural Studies, 23*(6), 887–901. doi:10.1080/10304310903294770

Herold, D., & Marolt, P. W. (Eds.). (2011). *On-line society in China*. London: Routledge.

Liang, B., & Lu, H. (2010). Internet development, censorship, and cyber crimes in China. *Journal of Contemporary Criminal Justice, 26*(1), 103–120. doi:10.1177/1043986209350437

MacKinnon, R. (2008). Blogs and China correspondence: Lessons about global information flows. *Chinese Journal of Communication, 1*(2), 242–257. doi:10.1080/17544750802288081

MacKinnon, R. (2008). Flatter world and thicker walls? Blogs, censorship and civic discourse in China. *Public Choice, 134*(1/2), 31–46.

Mulvenon, J. C., & Chase, M. S. (2006). Breaching the Great Firewall: External challenges to China's Internet controls. *Journal of E-Government, 2*(4), 73–84. doi:10.1300/J399v02n04_05

Paltemaa, L., & Vuori, J. (2009). Regime transition and the Chinese politics of technology: From mass science to the controlled Internet. *Asian Journal of Political Science, 17*(1), 1–23. doi:10.1080/02185370902767557

Shen, F., Wang, N., Guo, Z., & Guo, L. (2009). Online network size, efficacy, and opinion expression: Assessing the impacts of Internet use in China. *International Journal of Public Opinion Research, 21*(4), 451–476. doi:10.1093/ijpor/edp046

Shirk, S. L. (Ed.). (2010). *Changing media, changing China.* New York: Oxford University Press.

Stevenson-Yang, A. (2006). China's online mobs: The new Red Guard? *Far Eastern Economic Review, 169*(8), 53–57.

Wang, S., & Hong, J. (2010). Discourse behind the Forbidden Realm: Internet surveillance and its implications on China's blogosphere. *Telematics and Informatics, 27*(1), 67–78. doi:10.1016/j.tele.2009.03.004

Weber, I., & Lu, J. (2007). Internet and self-regulation in China: The cultural logic of controlled commodification. *Media Culture & Society, 29*(5), 772–789. doi:10.1177/0163443707080536

Wu, W. (2009). The separation of Internet content regulation in the face of the convergence of information and communication technologies: The controversies, challenges and solutions for China. *Canadian Social Science, 5*(1), 24–43.

Yang, K. C. C. (2007). A comparative study of Internet regulatory policies in the Greater China Region: Emerging regulatory models and issues in China, Hong-Kong SAR, and Taiwan. *Telematics and Informatics, 24*(1), 30–40. doi:10.1016/j.tele.2005.12.001

Yu, H. (2007). Blogging everyday life in Chinese Internet culture. *Asian Studies Review, 31*(4), 423–433. doi:10.1080/10357820701710724

Yu. H. (2009). *Media and cultural transformation in China.* London: Routledge.

Zhang, J. G., & Clarke, J. (2008). Blogging in China: A force for social change. *Australian Journalism Review, 30*(1), 3–11.

Zhao, Y. (2010). China's pursuits of indigenous innovations in information technology developments: Hopes, follies and uncertainties. *Chinese Journal of Communication, 3*(3), 266–289. doi:10.1080/17544750.2010.499628

Zhou, X. (2009). The political blogosphere in China: A content analysis of the blogs regarding the dismissal of Shanghai leader Chen Liangyu. *New Media & Society, 11*(6), 1003–1022. doi:10.1177/1461444809336552

KEY TERMS AND DEFINITIONS

Baidu: The most popular Chinese-language search engine on the Internet (www.baidu.com).

Blogmongering: The premeditated (and often frivolous) use of blogging to stir up public interest in a particular event or person for a specific end (e.g., self-promotion).

Boke: The Chinese term for "blog" or "blogger."

Caogen Boke: Chinese term for Grassroots Bloggers. It refers to a particular genre of populist bloggers (otherwise unknown offline) who have earned fame through their poignant, thought-provoking blogs on a variety of topics/issues of public interest.

Chaozuo: It is a way in Chinese cyberspace to create hypes and sensationalize news/events through blogs and other types of online publications in order to pander to the titillating needs of the media and the public for eye-rousing headlines.

E-Gao: Originally comes from the Japanese word *Kuso*, and represents a widespread practice among Chinese netizens to use materials from existing works for derivative creations of satire and parody. This Web-based online spoofing effort often involves movies, teledramas, celebrities, or major news headlines.

Mingren Boke: Celebrity blogger. It is a blogger who already has celebrity status offline. As a Chinese cybercultural phenomenon, it started in 2005 with Sina inviting social elites to create blogs on its blog site at blog.sina.com.cn.

Moblog: Mobile blogs, a late trend of blogging on the move through cell phone and other mobile devices.

Sina: Known as *Xinlang* in Chinese, it is the largest comprehensive portal site in China (via www.sina.com.cn). Among its most popular services are news, entertainment, blogs, games, and a variety of user-centered forums.

Wangluo Tuishou: Network hand-pusher or network strategist. An emerging profession in China that specializes in identifying talent and pushing it to the limits on the Internet through various stunts of unconventional publicity so as to garner public attention and stay in the public spotlight.

ENDNOTES

[1]   See the historic event page of Blog China at http://www.blogchina.com/link/fazhan.htm.

[2]   This portion of the discussion has relied on statistics from China Internet Network Information Center, 2009 & 2010.

[3]   http://blog.sina.com.cn

[4]   http://castle3.blog.tianya.cn

[5]   http://www.ladytoo.com

[6]   http://furongjiejie.bokee.com

[7]   http://blog.sina.com.cn/frjj

[8]   See Edward Cody, "In Chinese Cyberspace, A Blossoming Passion." *Washington Post*, July 17, 2005, P. A15.

[9]   *Tianxian* is a Chinese euphemism for astounding beauty.

[10] http://blog.sina.com.cn/txmm

[11] Summary of the report can be found at http://www.cctv.com/cctvsurvey/special/02/20091221/103378.shtml

[12] The three stories can be accessed at http://news.xinhuanet.com/local/2010-06/09/c_12198379.htm; http://news.xinhuanet.com/fortune/2010-06/07/c_12188523.htm; and http://news.xinhuanet.com/newmedia/2010-06/08/c_12194653.htm.

[13] http://blog.sina.com.cn

[14] http://egaow.com

[15] http://64tianwang.com

[16] http://blog.sina.com.cn/u/1191258123

[17] http://blog.sina.com.cn/u/1216826604

[18] http://blog.sina.com.cn/u/1456252804

[19] http://www.bullock.cn/blogs/lianyue

[20] http://fanfou.com

[21] http://t.sina.com.cn

Chapter 4

The Funhouse Mirror:
The Blogosphere's Reflection of Women's Sports

Marie Hardin
Pennsylvania State University, USA

Bu Zhong
Pennsylvania State University, USA

Thomas F. Corrigan
Pennsylvania State University, USA

ABSTRACT

Depictions of professional sports and athletes in U.S. mainstream media have generally been indicted for reinforcing masculine hegemony and ignoring women's and amateur sports. This study explored the attitudes and values of independent sports bloggers in relationship to gender and, more specifically, to Title IX of the Education Amendments of 1972 prohibiting discrimination on the basis of sex in federally funded institutions. A survey of 200 independent sports bloggers was conducted to determine whether the sports blogosphere provides an alternative to depictions of sports offered through mainstream media coverage. Survey results demonstrate that the sports blogosphere has yet to become a truly alternative, egalitarian space for sports commentary. The analysis suggests that increased participation of female bloggers who are willing to cover female athletes and advocate for women's sports can alleviate the situation. Otherwise, the sports blogosphere will merely replicate old-media values.

DOI: 10.4018/978-1-60960-744-9.ch004

INTRODUCTION

Sports coverage in the United States has been the object of strong criticism over the past several decades for marginalizing female athletes, ignoring women's sports and generally objectifying women. This topic has been the focus of scholarly activity by media and communication scholars, and it is rare that researchers have found exceptions in mainstream media to the prevailing pattern of framing sports as the natural domain of men.

A variety of rationalizations have been used for the failure of mainstream sports journalists and media producers to adopt more progressive lenses. Those explanations have generally integrated an understanding of cultural masculine hegemony with that of gatekeeping processes at the institutional (e.g., newsroom culture, economic structures) and individual (e.g., social identity) levels within media organizations.

One reason for scholars' close attention to gender dynamics in sports is the understanding that such dynamics *matter*; they reflect and influence understandings of gender and, consequently, shared concepts about the roles, opportunities, and rights of men and women in sport and in society. For instance, research has focused on media coverage of women's sports and the framing of Title IX of the Education Amendments of 1972 (hereinafter "Title IX"), which prohibited discriminating on the basis of sex in federally funded institutions (Messner & Solomon, 2007). Since 1973, Title IX has protected the rights of girls and women at educational institutions to participate in sports in equal measure with boys and men. Media researchers have argued that the way women's sports have or have not been covered, along with the way Title IX has been presented through the media, influences public opinion (Hardin & Whiteside, 2009a). Unfavorable public opinion could undermine enforcement of the law and diminish opportunities for female athletes. The sports blogosphere, which has risen in popularity at least in part because of perceptions that it

is an alternative to mainstream media coverage, has also not escaped such critiques; it should be noted, however, that little research has been done to critically assess gender-related dynamics (or others, such as those involving issues of race) in the sports blogosphere (Zirin, 2008).

Sports advocates, though, have also envisioned the blogosphere—and the Internet in general—as a plethora of possibilities for exposure and promotion for women's sports (Maxwell, 2009; Messner, 2002). This vision has been underpinned at least in part by an understanding of the World Wide Web as free of the institutional/economic pressures—"gatekeeping" factors—that constrain mainstream media content. The argument to justify non-coverage of women's sports because they don't "sell," for instance, cannot keep a women's sports fan—or thousands of them—from maintaining blogs that position women's sport as important (and worthy of legal protection). Institutional decisions to marginalize female athletes based on beat-reporting norms also, in theory, dissipate in a blogosphere where individuals can form networks to promote traditionally marginalized sports and athletes; gatekeeping in its traditional sense, then, collapses (Singer, 2006; Williams & Delli Carpini, 2004).

This research explores the attitudes and values of independent sports bloggers in relationship to gender and, more specifically, to Title IX. The influences on decision-making and gatekeeping in mainstream sports media, such as institutional culture and journalistic norms, are often muted in the blogosphere, making social identity and cultural hegemony more salient influences on decision-making about content. Thus, the attitudes and values of sports bloggers are important for understanding the culture of the sports blogosphere and for speculating on its potential as a site for alternatives to mainstream sports media outlets. The authors assess those attitudes and values to better understand the sports blogosphere in relationship to traditional media forms and to speculate on its potential for alternative depictions of sports.

BACKGROUND

Mainstream Media Coverage of Women's Sports and Title IX

Scholars consistently have found that coverage of female athletes—or, more accurately, its lack—reinforces ideology that women are physically and athletically inferior to men (van Sterkenburg & Knoppers, 2004). Women are positioned as less attention-holding and capable athletes than men through both the quantity and quality of coverage; when women's sports and female athletes are covered in the media, they are often trivialized by unfavorable comparisons to men's sports and male athletes that diminish their athleticism (Bernstein, 2002; Billings, Halone, & Denham, 2002; Crosset, 1995; Shugart, 2003).

The lack of attention to girls' and women's sports does not reflect their participation rates, which were bolstered significantly with Title IX enforcement (*Open to all*, 2003; Suggs, 2005). This law was passed by the U.S. Congress in 1972 and stipulates that girls and women receive opportunities equal to those provided for boys and men in any government-funded institution. Since the passage of the statute, girls' participation in high school sports increased 904% and women's participation in collegiate sports increased 456% between 1972 and 2008 (Women's Sports Foundation, 2008). Many professional female athletes credit the law with opening doors to their sports participation and careers.

Even so, the law remains "the most visible gender controversy" in the United States (Suggs, 2005, p. 2). Much of the reason Title IX has remained controversial is the argument of the opponents that it has taken opportunities to compete from boys and men, a position not supported by overall participation numbers (Walton, 2003; Robinson, 2007). Participation opportunities for high school boys are more prevalent than those for girls, and male sports participation in NCAA sports has increased more than 30% since the

early 1980s. Men and boys still practice and play in better facilities and receive more funding at the high school and college levels (Women's Sports Foundation, 2008; Suggs, 2005).

Regardless, Title IX has been blamed for cuts into men's college sports, and some opponents continue to publicly argue that the law should be changed (Suggs, 2005; Messner & Solomon, 2007). Coaches of some men's sports considered a low priority in the fiscal hierarchy (such as gymnastics, wrestling, and diving) have raised the loudest objections to Title IX as those sports have been cut to support ballooning football budgets (Messner & Solomon, 2007; Suggs, 2005). In 2002, the Bush administration formed a Commission on Opportunity in Athletics to explore allegations that gains in women's sports had been paid by losses in men's sports (Messner & Solomon, 2007). Interest groups such as the College Sports Council argued to the Commission that the Title IX regulation should be changed in ways that the law's proponents said would weaken its enforcement. In 2003, the commission produced a report that left Title IX policies open to changes (American Association of University Women, 2007). Overall, mainstream media coverage of Title IX has reinforced the idea that the law is punitive to men and boys. Coverage often frames the public debates either in terms of a "battle of the sexes" or "zero-sum game" implying that either men or women will win since access to resources is limited (Hardin, Simpson, Whiteside, & Garris, 2007; Rosenthal, Morris, & Martinez, 2004; Walton, 2003; Staurowsky, 1998).

Mythology about Title IX in media coverage, combined with the marginalization of women in mainstream sports coverage may continue to influence public sentiment about gender equality and sports in powerful ways. In focus groups with young adults, Hardin and Whiteside (2009a) found that participants questioned the rights of girls and women to pursue sports by reasoning that sports were the natural purview of men. Women were less deserving of legal protection, participants concluded, since they were judged as athletically inferior and their participation had diminished profit potential compared to men's.

Cultural Hegemony, Sport and Media

The idea that sports are the natural purview of men is understood as a key element of a cultural hegemony, which privileges masculinity. Mediated sports serve as an ideological narrative of culture, portraying various ideas on social relations and cultural meanings (Boyle & Haynes, 2000). Perhaps the most potent messages are about gender relations, where men are the center of interest and women are literally along the sidelines in the roles of cheerleaders and spectators (Trujillo, 1991). Scholars have used the term *masculine hegemony*—defined as the "taken-for-granted" system of gendered power relations reinforced by the ideology that men are, and should be, "naturally" at the head of the socio-economic hierarchy—to explain the treatment of women in mediated sports.

Integral to definitions of idealized masculinity, and, thus, to masculine hegemony, is heteronormativity. As Foucault (1978) and others have pointed out, sexuality is tied to gender identities and performance. Compulsory heterosexuality is key to the construction of an idealized masculine identity, and homophobia has become central in that construction (Messner & Sabo, 1994; Plummer, 2006; Whitehead & Barrett, 2001). Because media depictions of sports and athleticism reinforce masculine hegemony, they also create a stronghold for cultural and institutional homophobia (Anderson, 2005). Plummer (2006) argues that a deep, "almost palpable" ambivalence about homophobia in sports persists even though attitudes in U.S. culture have progressed.

For instance, very few professional male athletes have publicly disclosed they are gay. Olympic diver Greg Louganis, figure skater Rudy Galindo, football players Dave Kopay, Jerry Smith and Esera Tuaolo, basketball player John Amaechi,

and baseball players Glenn Burke and Billy Bean came out, but almost all did so after they retired (Amaechi, 2007; Butterworth, 2006). The same is true in women's sports, where homophobia is also common. Although some high-profile female athletes, such as Sheryl Swoopes and Amelie Mauresmo, have come out as lesbian, women's sports advocates suggest that fear of being perceived as a lesbian is a barrier to sports participation for many women and that coaches sometimes harass or shun lesbian athletes (Zirin, 2008). Journalists have generally turned a blind eye to homophobia in locker rooms, accepting it as part of sports culture (Dworkin & Wachs, 1998; Nylund, 2007).

Other Factors in Decision-Making About Media Content

Scholars increasingly consider decision-making behind mainstream media coverage of sports through the lens of cultural hegemony. Such decision-making, or gatekeeping, is the process in which media producers answer the questions: "What will we include or leave out? How will the topic be shaped?" (Shoemaker & Vos, 2009b, p. 75). The consequences of gatekeeping are significant; these decisions "determine what becomes a person's social reality, a particular view of the world" (Shoemaker & Vos, 2009a, p. 3).

Theories about what influences the answers to these questions have evolved since the 1950s. Shoemaker and Vos (2009a) present gatekeeping as occurring at five different levels including cultural hegemony, or what they call the "social-system level." Other levels are: the individual level (influenced by social identity and personal values); the newsroom level (through routines and the adoption of news values, for instance); the organizational level (involving media ownership, for example); and the social institutional level (through the influence of advertisers, for instance).

Research, including that on mediated sports, has focused on all five general levels of influences on the gatekeeping process. A newsroom study published in 2000, for instance, concluded that the emphasis on revenue-producing sports and the reliance on professional sports beats (newsroom-level and organizational-level influences) resulted in male-dominant coverage (Lowes, 2000). Another factor in gatekeeping process is that of media users—or, more accurately, perceptions of users. Expectations of reactions may drive decisions, and media producers may project their values and feelings on users or follow personal judgments in the assumption that users will concur. Journalists may also choose to think about one segment of users, excluding another (Shoemaker, 1991). Such "marketplace considerations" are particularly powerful in the production of sports-related content (Creedon, 1998). For instance, a survey of 175 editors found that even in the face of complaints from readers, they rationalized their choices to downplay women's sports by insisting their readers did not want to see them as much as other sports (Anderson, 1988). A survey almost two decades later (Hardin, 2005) found similar results with one important difference: Female editors were less likely than male editors to assume audiences did not want to read about women's sports.

Individual-Level Influences on Gatekeeping: The Role of Social Identity

In recent years numerous studies have explored the ways social identity (primarily gender) influences media gatekeeping. For instance, Bissell's (2000) analysis of gatekeeping by photo editors found their decisions about coverage reflected the intersection of social identity and cultural hegemony; white, male editors, for instance, made decisions that seemed to support the privilege that comes with that identity. The findings of Bissell and others concerning journalistic decision-making underscore the influence of cultural hegemony on social identity; the two are intertwined in their subsequent influence on content (Len-Rios, Rod-

gers, Thorson, & Yoon, 2005). "Individual" and "social system" level influences (Shoemaker & Vos, 2009a), then, can be understood as virtually inseparable at the nexus of cultural hegemony and gendered or raced identities.

Reporters should be recognized as media gatekeepers (Shoemaker & Vos, 2009a), and studies analyzing sports coverage have found that the gender of reporters can influence content. Lane's (1998) analysis of the *New York Times* and *Washington Post* coverage of Title IX controversy during the early and mid-1970s found that female reporters more often allowed sourcing and data in their stories that presented female athletes negatively. A content analysis of Title IX coverage by Hardin and colleagues found that female reporters were more likely to present the law in affirming terms and to use female sources (Hardin et al., 2007).

Journalists' Attitudes Toward Title IX and Women's Sports

Some research has gone beyond analyses of content to examine the influence of social identity on journalists' attitudes. Several studies examine the values and beliefs of sports journalists in regard to women's sports and Title IX. Phone surveys of journalists in 2005 and 2009 found that about half of sports editors and reporters believed Title IX had "hurt men's sports" (Hardin, 2005; Hardin & Whiteside, 2009b, p. 66). Among reporters, men were far more likely to hold this belief than women. There were also significant differences between men and women on reporters' assessment of their newspaper's coverage of women's sports: Women were more likely to rate the coverage as deficient. Women were also more likely to rate homophobia as a problem in women's sports than were men; when asked about homophobia in men's sports, men and women responded similarly, with most agreeing that it was a problem and that an "out" professional gay male athlete would not be accepted. The results suggested that until more women were hired into the industry, coverage would likely not change in ways that would challenge masculine hegemony in sports (Hardin & Whiteside, 2009b).

RESEARCH QUESTIONS

Traditional media outlets that offer sports coverage have, over the past decade and more acutely in recent years, lost significant ground to fan-based online communities and independent blogs on the Internet. As one observer characterized it, "Sports news is no longer controlled by traditional media... Even the basic function of a sports page—providing accounts of yesterday's games—is threatened" (Lindsay, 2009). Paradoxically, some former newspaper sportswriters, laid off from a struggling industry, have become entrepreneurial bloggers (King, 2009).

Many sports blogs, such as "Sport's Guy World" written by Bill Simmons of ESPN, are affiliated with mainstream media outlets. Other popular sports blogs, however, are not. They are "independent" in the sense that they are enterprises run by individuals or groups of bloggers who update and moderate the sites daily and may or may not generate revenue from advertising. These blogs are highly influential and have, on occasion, broken stories and led the news agenda for mainstream sports media outlets (Mickle, 2006).

A number of studies have been published on the evolution of journalistic practice in the blogosphere, including that of sports journalists. The existing research mostly explores the perspective of mainstream sports media journalists toward blogs or their approach to blogging as part of their professional responsibilities (Schultz & Sheffer, 2007; Wigley & Meirick, 2008). This study, instead, surveys the attitudes and values of independent sports bloggers toward issues relating to gender and sport with the purpose of exploring the influence of social identity in the way bloggers view gender related aspects of

sports and are likely make gatekeeping decisions about content. Those decisions, we suggest, result in contributions to a larger social discourse surrounding the intersection of sport and gender that has implications for public attitudes toward women's sports and Title IX. In this research, the authors also explicitly acknowledge the link between issues of gender and sexuality in sport; as we discussed earlier, heteronormativity is a key element of masculine hegemony. Thus, we propose the following research questions:

RQ1: How does a blogger's gender influence perceptions of Title IX, women's sports and media coverage of women's sports and issues of sexuality in sports?

RQ2: How do the sports (men's or women's) covered by a blogger influence perceptions of Title IX, women's sports and media coverage of women's sports and issues of sexuality in sports?

RQ3: How does assessment of the value of women's sports (e.g., whether spectators might accept them as equally interesting and exciting as men's) by bloggers correlate with their views of Title IX?

METHOD

A survey for independent sports bloggers was designed to address the research questions. Since no comprehensive directory of sports bloggers exists, a list of bloggers' e-mails was generated through a general Web search and close search of the "SB Nation" (short for "SportsBlog Nation") website, which is a popular network of sports blogs and fan communities. In 2010, SB Nation featured about 300 blog sites, many of which featured the work of multiple bloggers; SB Nation was used because it is one of the largest networks of independent blogs on the Web. To make sure the sample included as many women who blog about sports as possible, the blog network "Women Talk

Sports" was also searched for qualifying blogs. "Women Talk Sports" aggregates and highlights the work of more than 100 blogs focused on women's sports; most of the blogs are maintained by women. Only sports blogs—as opposed to fan forums or link aggregators—were included in the compilation. Blogs could not be affiliated with a mainstream sports media outlet (such as a newspaper, broadcast or cable TV, or online news aggregators such as Yahoo!). Furthermore, blogs for this study had to be updated at least once a day and not be maintained by a sport participant (such as an athlete or coach). Sports blogs that were not updated regularly or that were maintained by active, competitive athletes, coaches or others talking about a first-person experience were not included for analysis. Blogs that met the research criteria and included at least one email address were compiled, and a message was sent to each email address, asking the blogger to participate in a phone survey. After email bouncebacks, the list included 783 addresses.

Trained undergraduate students administered the survey by telephone in the spring of 2009 after bloggers were emailed twice and asked to participate. A phone survey was chosen over an online survey for three primary reasons: 1) to confirm and match the identity of a single blogger with multiple online identities and email addresses that a blogger might possess (including vague email addresses, such as "administrator@blogsite"); 2) to replicate the conditions for earlier surveys of sports journalists, from which some of the questions for this study were gleaned (Hardin & Whiteside, 2009b); and 3) to allow the interviewer an opportunity to clarify questions where requested and the blogger an opportunity to clarify answers and to answer questions about the study.

Bloggers who responded to the email with their phone numbers were called at a time they requested. A total of 214 bloggers provided a phone number and then completed the survey for a response rate of 29%. Although this rate is not high, it is acceptable for surveys involving email

solicitation (Sheehan, 2001). Studies of online, non-incentive surveys have shown that response rates typically fall under 30% (Kaplowitz & Hadlock, 2004; Jones & Pitt, 1999).

Bloggers who participated in this survey included those affiliated with top blogs listed on such websites as Sport Media Challenge's "Sports Blog Index," Wikio's "Top Blogs—Sports" and Alexa's list of blogs in its "Top Sites—Sports" category. Several bloggers from high-volume sports websites (such as Deadspin.com) also participated, meaning that the number of blogs represented is lower than the number of bloggers who participated.

Participants

Similar to demographics in the sports-media establishment, male bloggers far outnumbered female bloggers; nine in 10 respondents ($n = 195$, or 91%) were male. Although bloggers under 30 years old made up the single-largest age group ($n = 98$, or 46%), almost 37% ($n = 79$) reported being between 31 and 40 years old. Four percent ($n = 9$) reported being at least 51 years old. Most bloggers ($n = 200$, or 94%) reported being White; no other single racial or ethnic group composed more than 2% of the sample.

Respondents were asked to report their education and any journalistic training or experience. The overwhelming majority reported high education levels. Most—62% ($n = 132$)—reported having completed an undergraduate degree, and another 29% ($n = 61$) report having also completed a graduate degree. Most, however, do not have journalism degrees or professional journalistic experience. Of those who attended college, 18% ($n = 38$) reported majoring in journalism, and slightly more ($n = 46$, or 22%) said they had covered sports for campus media. About 15% ($n = 33$) reported having worked as a sports journalist before starting a blog.

Most bloggers ($n = 176$, or 82%) reported focusing on men's sports in their blogs; another 13%

(n = 28) said they wrote about men and women and only 10 bloggers said they focused solely on women's sports. Most bloggers (n = 141, or 66%) wrote only about professional sports although another 23% (n = 49) said they focused on more than one level—usually professional and college teams. Baseball, football, hockey and basketball were popular topics.

Measurement

The survey contained a series of 5-point Likert-scale questions (1 = strongly disagree; 5 = strongly agree) aimed at the attitudes, values, and beliefs of bloggers. An example of a Likert-scale question used on the survey was, "I believe Title IX has hurt men's sports." The participants' race, gender, age, education (high school diploma, college or graduate degree earned), college major, and sports reporting experience (e.g., reporting campus sports as a college student or working experience as a sports journalist) were used as social-identity variables. The survey also gathered the bloggers' behavioral data (e.g., number of hours spent on blogs each week). Statements were presented to the participants for measuring their perspectives on women's sports, Title IX and homophobia in sports; the statements are presented with the findings for each research question.

RESULTS: GENDER AND VALUES RELATED TO WOMEN'S SPORTS

Significant differences were found among bloggers, based on gender, in their assessment of women's sports and their coverage, Title IX, and issues of sexuality in sports.

Women's Sports and Title IX

Respondents were asked whether they believed women's sports received enough coverage in mainstream sports media outlets; they were also asked whether they believed women's sports had the potential to be considered as exciting or interesting as men's sports to the average sports fan. Overall, 53% (n = 114) of bloggers surveyed said they agreed or strongly agreed that women's sports did not receive adequate coverage, but only 23% (n = 49) reported that they agreed or strongly agreed that women's sports had the potential to be as exciting to fans as men's.

Multivariate analysis of variance (MANOVA) found that female bloggers (M = 4.50, SD = .79) were more likely than men (M = 3.37, SD = 1.06) to believe women's sports were undercovered ($F(1, 203)$ = 19.26, p < .001). Men (M = 2.40, SD = 1.02) were also less likely than women (M = 2.89, SD = 1.15) to believe that women's sports could be perceived as equally interesting and exciting as men's by sports fans ($F(1, 208)$ = 4.55, p < .05). Female bloggers perceived the blogosphere in general as blocking that goal; although 40% of all respondents agreed that sports blogs are "generally quite sexist" (35% disagreed with this assertion, and 19% were neutral), women (M = 3.53, SD = 1.12) were more likely to agree than were men (M = 3.00, SD = 1.07; $F(1, 199)$ = 4.11, p < .05).

Fewer than half of the bloggers indicated that they did not see Title IX as damaging to men's sports. Overall, 48% (n = 102) disagreed or strongly disagreed with that assertion. Most bloggers (75%; n = 140, only 186 answered the question), however, said they did not want to see the law changed. Male bloggers, however, were far more likely to agree (M = 2.74, SD = 1.23) than were female bloggers (M = 1.94, SD = 1.11; $F(1, 194)$ = 6.97, p < .01). When asked if they favored a change to the law, the same pattern emerged, with female bloggers (M = 1.94, SD = 1.11) less supportive of the status quo than men (M = 2.77, SD = 1.12; $F(1, 194)$ = 3.90, p = .05).

Women (M = 4.00, SD = 1.06) were more likely to believe homophobia was an issue that needed to be addressed in women's sports than were their male counterparts (M = 3.33, SD = .91; $F(1, 181)$ = 8.50, p < .01). They did not differ from men, however, on the issue of homophobia in men's sports ($F(1, 198) = 1.91, p = .17$).

Blog Focus as Related to Attitudes and Values

Bloggers were asked to report whether they focused on men's sports, women's sports, or both. Most bloggers ($n = 176$, or 82%) reported covering men's sports. Far smaller numbers covered women's ($n = 10$, or 5%) or both ($n = 28$, or 13%). MANOVA analysis found that those who covered men's, women's sports, or both differed significantly on their views of the impact of Title IX on men's sports ($F(2, 152) = 5.99, p < .01$) and whether the law should be changed ($F(2, 152) = 8.96, p < .001$). Post hoc analyses using the Scheffe post hoc criterion for significance indicated that those who covered women's sports ($M = 1.50$, $SD = .71$) were significantly less likely to view Title IX as hurting men's sports than those covering men's sports ($M = 2.75, SD = 1.25, p < .01$) or both men's and women's sports ($M = 2.61$, $SD = 1.17, p < .05$). Little difference was found between the two latter groups ($p = .76$). Those covering women's sports ($M = 1.40, SD = .70$) were also less likely to advocate changing Title IX than those blogging about men's sports ($M = 2.74, SD = 1.10, p = .001$) or both ($M = 3.07, SD = 1.17, p < .001$).

Bloggers covering women's sports also differed in other key ways from those who focused only on men's sports or on both men's and women's. Women's sports bloggers ($M = 4.90, SD = .32$) were far more likely to believe women's sports were not getting enough coverage in mainstream media than the other groups (men: $M = 3.31, SD = 1.03$; both men and women: $M = 3.96, SD = 1.13$; $F(2, 152) = 15.24, p < .001$). Those who covered women's sports were also more likely to report homophobia as a problem in both women's ($F(2,152) = 7.56$, $p = .001$) and men's sports ($F(2,152) = 3.46, p < .05$) than were bloggers who focused on men's sports or on both sexes.

Valuing Women's Sports as a Predictor of Attitudes Toward Title IX

Most bloggers ($n = 141$, or 67%) estimated that sports fans would never accept women's sports as equally interesting or exciting as men's sports (Remaining participants provided a neutral response or did not answer the question.) Responses to this survey item correlated positively to the responses of bloggers on items asking about Title IX's impact on men's sports ($r = .22, p < .01$) and about whether the law should be changed ($r = .24, p = .001$); responses correlated negatively with responses to the statement asserting that women's sports did not get enough mainstream media coverage ($r = -.24, p < .001$). A multiple regression analysis found that respondents' assessment of women's sports as essentially boring to fans was a good predictor for their agreement that the media did not cover enough women's sports and that Title IX hurts men's sports. As shown in Table 1, those who held the view that women's sports cannot be as interesting as men's were significantly more likely to believe that Title IX hurt men's sports and that women's sports did not need more coverage.

Table 1. Variables predicting the view of women's sports as boring

	B	SE B	B
Step 1			
Constant	2.81	.21	
Title IX hurting men's sports	.30	.07	.35***
Step 2			
Constant	3.58	.40	
Title IX hurting men's sports	.25	.07	.29**
Women's sports not covered enough	-.18	.08	-.19*

Note. $R^2 = .12$ for Step 1; $\Delta R^2 = .11$ for Step 2 ($p < .001$). *$p < .05$, **$p = .001$, ***$p < .001$.

Age as an Intervening Factor

Analyses of other demographic variables, such as age, education or previous journalism experience generated an additional finding that bloggers' responses varied based on their age. The bloggers surveyed were divided into three age groups: those who were under 30 years old ($n = 98$, or 46%), between 31-40 ($n = 79$, or 37%) and 41 and older ($n = 37$, or 17%). Analysis of variance (ANOVA) revealed that the bloggers in the three age groups differed significantly on their attitudes toward women sports ($F(2, 209) = 8.18, p < .001.$) and gay athletes ($F(2, 198) = 3.77, p < .05$). Specifically, as Tukey's HSD Post Hoc tests showed, those who were under 30 ($M = 3.86, SD = .88$) were more likely to agree that "Women's sports will never be considered as interesting or exciting by sports fans as men's sports" compared with older bloggers (for those in 31-40, $M = 2.16, SD = 1.15$, $p < .001$; for those in 41 and older, $M = 3.38, SD = .98, p < .05$). Bloggers in the two older categories (30 to 40, and 40 and older) did not differ. When asked about public acceptance of gay athletes, older participants were more likely to agree that a professional male athlete would be accepted if he came out while active. Tukey's HSD Post Hoc tests showed that those who were 41 and older ($M = 3.00, SD = .98$) were more likely to believe an "out" athlete would be accepted than those who were under 30 ($M = 2.44, SD = .91, p < .05$).

DISCUSSION AND CONCLUSION

Participants in this survey represent only a portion of the scores of bloggers covering and analyzing sports on the Internet. Nevertheless, we suggest that the demographics of the sample—overwhelmingly White and male—is likely representative of the sports blogosphere; it is certainly representative of mainstream sports journalism, where about 90% of news staffs are White men (Lapchick, Little, Matthew, & Zahn, 2008). Media organiza-tions have been criticized for their lack of diverse sports staffs, but in the blogosphere where any fan with an Internet connection can become a sports-writer, the demographics are remarkably similar. This finding indicates that in media organizations, newsroom culture and lack of family-friendly policies (often cited by researchers) may be less a reason than other, more complex factors involving culture and gender norms, for the lack of diversity.

The analysis suggests that such lack of diver-sity among gatekeepers in the blogosphere—in this case, individual bloggers and blogger col-lectives—ensures homogenous content that reinforces old-media patterns. The influence of social identity—namely, gender—on values, beliefs, and attitudes toward women's sports is so pronounced that without more women behind the content, the blogosphere is destined to con-tinue the general pattern of marginalization and stereotyping of women so prevalent in traditional sports coverage. The Internet may be a space of possibilities, but those possibilities are likely to remain unrealized because so few women blog, and men who blog do not see women's sports as interesting or valuable—a pattern similar to that seen in old media (see our discussion, below). The results demonstrate that male bloggers also, in many instances, see Title IX as a problem and do not value legal protection for women's sports.

Most findings of this study are not surprising; for instance, it is apparent why female bloggers would be more likely to see women's sports as having the same potential as men's to be enter-taining and more likely to view women's sports as getting short shrift in coverage. It is also un-derstandable that they would be more supportive of Title IX and less likely to buy into mythology that the law has hurt men's sports. Furthermore, it is not surprising that when bloggers (male or female) cover women's sports, they are more likely to support Title IX. Again, the problem is that more progressive understandings of Title IX and issues, such as homophobia in sport (and the damage it inflicts), are not tied to the majority of bloggers, but only to a sliver.

Assumptions About Media Users as Rationale

Most bloggers said they believed their readers/users would never accept women's sports in the way they have accepted and sought men's sports. As Shoemaker (1991) has suggested, these assumptions have implications; they can be used to rationalize the exclusion of women's sports, and, perhaps, they can also be used to rationalize the objectification of women in sport to make references to female athletes more palatable to their followers. (The fact that much of the sports blogosphere is "sexist" was acknowledged by four in 10 bloggers.)

The view of women's sports as without promise as entertainment is also tied to views of Title IX and whether the law is fair and worth supporting. This finding seems to echo Hardin and Whiteside's (2009a) conversations with young sports fans who see the value of sports in the marketplace—in their ability to entertain spectators. Because of the role sports play in reinforcing masculine hegemony, women's sports will likely always have diminished value for spectators because they contradict traditional gender roles. Our survey findings show the consequences of such a value system: When women's sports are deemed as having less value to spectators as interesting and exciting, support for coverage and for initiatives to protect them diminishes. The history of Title IX demonstrates that the law still has virulent detractors, and the protections it affords—based on the value of sports to educate, build character, teach leadership, and promote fitness, among other things—cannot be taken for granted. This survey suggests that as women's sports are perceived as lacking entertainment value, lack of coverage is justified. A spiraling effect is created, then, when as coverage diminishes, perceptions of the value of women's sports diminishes, and support for the rights of girls and women to pursue the joys of competitive sports becomes even more tenuous.

New Media Mimic Old Media

Although not a focus of this research, it is interesting—and important—to note that according to this survey, young sports fans who blog are not more progressive on issues of gender, sexuality, and sport although they have grown up with Title IX and in a culture where gay-marriage rights are gaining more acceptance. Surprisingly, they were less likely to support women's sports coverage than were older bloggers. Advocates for women's sports and for a more inclusive environment in relationship to sexuality and gender cannot count on a younger generation to carry the mantle of change.

Another key way in which the sports blogosphere, often characterized as part of "new media," mimics "old media" is in the attitudes and values of gatekeepers on issues of gender, sexuality and Title IX. The attitudes of independent sports bloggers on issues of gender and sports in this survey can be compared to those found by Hardin and Whiteside's (2009b) survey of journalists working for traditional media outlets. Results are almost identical in relationship to beliefs about Title IX and about coverage of women's sports. The impact of social identity on the attitudes of male and female bloggers and journalists are also very similar, with women being more sensitive to issues of homophobia and more defensive of Title IX. The blogosphere, for the most part, is not attracting individuals with social attitudes that will allow more progressive ideas about sport to emerge and gain traction; instead, it is attracting more of the same.

Considerations and Limitations

The findings for this study must be considered in light of its limitations. The survey response rate indicates that we cannot claim that the results should be generalized to the entire sports blogosphere, which includes many blogs that are not updated daily and more scores that are written by athletes and coaches. We worked from a convenience sample (a list drawn largely from two blog networks, not a randomly generated list from the entire population of blogs), and the survey results should be understood in that light. Another important consideration is that this survey did not attempt to make a distinction between types of sports blogs, such as those that attempt to strike a more journalistic tone versus those that offer first-person commentary or satirical humor. Furthermore, this survey did not ascertain whether bloggers understood Title IX; some bloggers may have responded to questions about Title IX without being familiar with the law. In addition, agreement by a participant with the statement that Title IX "should be changed" cannot be assumed to mean the intent is to weaken the law (although that is generally how advocates understand arguments to change the law).

It is also important to note the influence of the survey administrator's social identity on responses. Results on two questions were influenced by the gender of the caller, according to t-test results. Among the 214 participants, 131 were surveyed on the phone by a male caller and 83 by a female caller. Analyses revealed that when a male ($M = 3.30$, $SD = 1.11$), rather than a female ($M = 3.76$, $SD = 1.00$), caller conducted the survey, respondents were significantly *less likely* to agree with the assertion that "the mainstream media do not provide enough coverage of women's sports" ($t = -2.98$, df = 203, $p < .01$). Also, when a male ($M = 3.52$, $SD = 1.04$), rather than a female ($M = 3.92$, $SD = .94$), caller conducted the survey, bloggers were significantly less likely to agree that "homophobia in men's sports is an issue that needs to be addressed" ($t = -2.76$, df = 198, $p < .01$). It seems that these results can be explained in one of two ways: by what has been called the "halo effect" in telephone or in-person surveys where respondents seek to provide socially acceptable

answers, and by social attitudes surrounding the definitions of *masculinity* and its relationship to men's sports.

Another limitation of this survey—as with many similar studies—is the lack of context for the findings and the fact that the results raise more questions than they can answer. In this limitation, though, is the opportunity to generate useful ideas for further research.

FUTURE RESEARCH DIRECTIONS

This survey was conducted with the suggestion that the primary "gate" for bloggers in decision-making is at the individual level, which is inextricably tied to the social-system level (cultural hegemony). We have also suggested that assumptions about media users also play a role in the construction of rationales about content by bloggers.

Discussions with bloggers about the decision-making process especially as blogs become more commercialized and even loosely affiliated with large media organizations, however, would be most useful in exploring our assumptions; the process may be more complex and invite other levels of analysis in regard to decision-making. Furthermore, the analysis of decision-making at the individual level needs to be expanded beyond the level of social identity. Other factors, such as bloggers' sports experience or journalism experience, likely influence their decision-making, but we do not know how. The results of this survey would also be better understood in concert with content analyses of sports blogs, especially those that focus on college and high school sports, where issues touching on Title IX are most salient.

Another set of key questions raised by the results of this survey surround the motives of women to venture into the sports blogosphere. As we suggested earlier, we believe the reasons far fewer women than men seek a public forum for sports commentary and analysis—despite their strong participation in sports at almost all levels, thanks to Title IX—are complex and have not been adequately explored. Women who blog about sports are a particularly interesting demographic because of their choice to enter the sports blogosphere as a volunteer endeavor, not necessarily as a career path with its associated institutional barriers and culture. They may be motivated by an activist agenda on behalf of women's sports, seeking to make the most of the Internet as a space of possibilities for women's sport. Their much more protectionist stance on Title IX in this survey may be evidence of their motives: To promote women's sports and protect what they see as hard-fought gains for girls and women. One such example of a women's sports collective of blogs, some with a clearly articulated activist position, is Women Talk Sports (www.womentalksports.com). What motivates these women, how they rationalize their participation in an overwhelmingly male environment, what barriers they face, and what they believe they can accomplish in blogging about sports would be useful for understanding the potential for contesting masculine hegemony in the sports blogosphere.

Independent Women's Sports Blogs

Basketball: http://www.swishappeal.com
General interest: http://becauseiplayedsports.com
Issues of gender/sexuality in sports: http://ittake-sateam.blogspot.com
Research on girls and women in sport: http://tuckercenter.wordpress.com
Title IX: http://title-ix.blogspot.com

REFERENCES

Amaechi, J. (2007, February 26). John Amaechi busts out. *ESPN the Magazine,* 68-74.

American Association of University Women. (2006, May 10). *Title IX: Ensuring equity in education for women and girls.* Retrieved January 7, 2011, from http://www.aauw.org/act/issue_advocacy/ actionpages/ titleix.cfm

Anderson, D. (1988). Changing thrusts in daily newspaper sports reporting. In Bandy, S. J. (Ed.), *Coroebus triumphs* (pp. 175–190). San Diego, CA: San Diego State University Press.

Anderson, E. (2005). *In the game: Gay athletes and the cult of masculinity.* Albany, NY: State University of New York Press.

Bernstein, A. (2002). Is it time for a victory lap? Changes in the media coverage of women in sport. *International Review for the Sociology of Sport, 37*(3/4), 415–428.

Billings, A. C., Halone, K. K., & Denham, B. E. (2002). "Man, that was a pretty shot": An analysis of gendered broadcast commentary surrounding the 2000 men's and women's NCAA Final Four basketball championships. *Mass Communication & Society, 5*(3), 295–315. doi:10.1207/S15327825MCS0503_4

Bissell, K. (2000). Culture and gender as factors in photojournalism gatekeeping. *Visual Communication Quarterly, 7*(2), 9–11.

Boyle, R., & Haynes, R. (2000). *Power play: Sport, the media & popular culture.* New York, NY: Pearson Education.

Butterworth, M. L. (2006). Pitchers and catchers: Mike Piazza and the discourse of gay identity in the national pastime. *Journal of Sport and Social Issues, 30*(2), 138–157. doi:10.1177/0193723506286757

Creedon, P. (1998). Women, sport, and media institutions: Issues in sports journalism and marketing. In Wenner, L. A. (Ed.), *MediaSport* (pp. 88–99). London, UK: Routledge.

Crosset, T. (1995). *Outsiders in the clubhouse: The world of professional women's golf.* Albany, NY: State University of New York Press.

Dworkin, S. L., & Wachs, F. L. (1998). Disciplining the body: HIV-positive male athletes, media surveillance, and the policing of sexuality. *Sociology of Sport Journal, 15,* 1–20.

Foucault, M. (1978). *The history of sexuality.* London, UK: Penguin.

Hardin, M. (2005). Stopped at the gate: Women's sports, reader interest, and decision-making by editors. *Journalism & Mass Communication Quarterly, 82*(1), 62–77.

Hardin, M., Simpson, S., Whiteside, E., & Garris, K. (2007). The gender war in U.S. sport: Winners and losers in news coverage of Title IX. *Mass Communication & Society, 10*(2), 211–233. doi:10.1080/15205430701265737

Hardin, M., & Whiteside, E. (2009a). The power of small stories: Narratives and notions of gender equity in conversations about sport. *Sociology of Sport Journal, 26*(2), 255–276.

Hardin, M., & Whiteside, E. (2009b). Sports reporters divided over concerns about Title IX. *Newspaper Research Journal, 30*(1), 58–71.

Jones, R., & Pitt, N. (1999). Health surveys in the workplace: Comparison of postal, email and World Wide Web methods. *Occupational Medicine, 49*(8), 556–558. doi:10.1093/occmed/49.8.556

Kaplowitz, M. D., Hadlock, T. D., & Levine, R. (2004). A comparison of web and mail survey response rates. *Public Opinion Quarterly, 68*(1), 94–101. doi:10.1093/poq/nfh006

King, B. (2009, July 20). Former newspaper writers keep doing what they love and hope the money will follow. *Sports Business Journal,* 9.

Lane, C. (2005, March 30). High court supports Title IX protection: Law now covers whistleblowers. *The Washington Post,* p. A1.

Lane, J. B. (1998, August). *The framing of Title IX: A textual analysis of the New York Times and the Washington Post, 1971-1975.* Paper presented at Annual Convention of the Association for Education in Journalism and Mass Communication, Baltimore, MD.

Lapchick, R., Little, E., Matthew, R., & Zahn, J. (2008). *The 2008 racial and gender report card of the Associated Press Sports Editors* [Press release]. Retrieved January 7, 2011, from http://www.tidesport.org/ racialgenderreportcard. html

Len-Rios, M. E., Rodgers, S., Thorson, E., & Yoon, D. (2005). Representation of women in news and photos: Comparing content to perceptions. *The Journal of Communication, 55*(1), 152–168.

Lindsay, D. (2009, July 1). *&#$@% Dan Snyder! *Washingtonian.com.* Retrieved January 7, 2011, from http://www.washingtonian.com/ print/ articles/ 6/ 174/ 13044.html

Lowes, M. D. (2000). *Inside the sports pages.* Toronto, Canada: University of Toronto Press.

Maxwell, H. (2009, October 29). *Burden, buzz or both? Reflections on social media & women's sports.* Tucker Center for Research on Girls and Women in Sport. Retrieved November 20, 2009, from http://tuckercenter.wordpress.com/ 2009/ 10/ 28/ social- media- womens- sports- burden- buzz- or- both/

Messner, M. A. (2002). *Taking the field: Women, men, and sports.* Minneapolis, MN: University of Minnesota Press.

Messner, M. A., & Sabo, D. F. (1994). *Sex, violence & power in sports.* Freedom, CA: The Crossing Press.

Messner, M. A., & Solomon, N. M. (2007). Social justice and men's interests: The case of Title IX. *Journal of Sport and Social Issues, 31*(2), 162–178. doi:10.1177/0193723507301048

Mickle, T. (2006, June 19). Blogs that have led the story. *Sports Business Journal, 3.*

National Women's Law Center. (2007, June 19). *Public supports Title IX, but discrimination remains widespread* [Press release]. Retrieved January 7, 2011, from http://www.nwlc.org/ press-release/ public- supports- title- ix- discrimination- against- girls- and- women- remains-widespread- jun

Nylund, D. (2007). *Beer, babes, and balls.* Albany, NY: State University of New York Press.

Open to all: Title IX at thirty. (2003, February 28). The U.S. Secretary of Education's Commission on Opportunity in Athletics report. Retrieved January 7, 2011, from http://www2.ed.gov/ about/ bdscomm/ list/ athletics/ title9report.pdf

Plummer, D. (2006). Sportophobia: Why do some men avoid sport? *Journal of Sport and Social Issues, 30*(2), 122–137. doi:10.1177/0193723505285817

Rosenthal, C. M., Morris, L., & Martinez, J. (2004). Who's on first and what's on second? Assessing interest group strategies on Title IX. *Women in Sport and Physical Activity Journal, 13*(2), 65–86.

Schultz, B., & Sheffer, M. L. (2007). Sports journalists who blog cling to traditional values. *Newspaper Research Journal, 28*(4), 62–76.

Sheehan, K. (2001). E-mail survey response rates: A review. *Journal of Computer-Mediated Communication, 6*(2). Retrieved January 7, 2011, from http://jcmc.indiana.edu/ vol6/ issue2/ sheehan.html

Shoemaker, P. J. (1991). *Gatekeeping.* Newbury Park, CA: Sage.

Shoemaker, P. J., & Vos, T. P. (2009a). *Gatekeeping theory.* New York, NY: Routledge.

Shoemaker, P. J., & Vos, T. P. (2009b). Media gatekeeping. In Stacks, D. W., & Salwen, M. B. (Eds.), *An integrated approach to communication theory and research* (2nd ed., pp. 75–89). New York, NY: Routledge.

Shugart, H. A. (2003). She shoots, she scores: Mediated constructions of contemporary female athletes in coverage of the 1999 US women's soccer team. *Western Journal of Communication, 67*(1), 1–31.

Singer, J. B. (2006). Stepping back from the gate: Online newspaper editors and the co-production of content in campaign 2004. *Journalism & Mass Communication Quarterly, 83*(2), 265–280.

Staurowsky, E. (1998). Critiquing the language of the gender equity debate. *Journal of Sport and Social Issues, 22*(1), 7–26. doi:10.1177/019372398022001002

Suggs, W. (2005). *A place on the team: The triumph and tragedy of Title IX.* Princeton, NJ: Princeton University Press.

Trujillo, N. (1991). Hegemonic masculinity on the mound: Media representations of Nolan Ryan and American sports culture. *Critical Studies in Mass Communication, 8*(3), 280–308. doi:10.1080/15295039109366799

United States Department of Labor. (n.d.). *Title IX, education amendments of 1972.* Retrieved January 7, 2011, from http://www.dol.gov/ oasam/ regs/ statutes/ titleix.htm

van Sterkenburg, J., & Knoppers, A. (2004). Dominant discourses about race/ethnicity and gender in sport practice and performance. *International Review for the Sociology of Sport, 39*(3), 301–321. doi:10.1177/1012690204045598

Walton, T. A. (2003). Title IX: Forced to wrestle up the backside. *Women in Sport and Physical Activity Journal, 12*(2), 5–26.

Wensing, E. H., & Bruce, T. (2003). Bending the rules: Media representations of gender during an international sporting event. *International Review for the Sociology of Sport, 38*(4), 387–396. doi:10.1177/1012690203384001

Whitehead, S. M., & Barrett, F. J. (2001). The sociology of masculinity. In Whitehead, S. M., & Barrett, F. J. (Eds.), *The masculinities reader* (pp. 1–25). Cambridge, UK: Polity.

Wigley, S., & Meirick, P. C. (2008). Interactive media and sports journalists: The impact of interactive media on sports journalists. *The Journal of Sports Medicine, 3*(1), 1–25.

Williams, B. A., & Delli Carpini, M. X. (2004). Monica and Bill environment. *The American Behavioral Scientist, 47*(9), 1208–1230. doi:10.1177/0002764203262344

Women's Sports Foundation. (2008). *2008 statistics — Gender equity in high school and college athletics: Most recent participation & budget statistics*. Retrieved January 7, 2011, from http://www.womenssportsfoundation.org/ Content/ Articles/ Issues/ General/ 123/ 2008-Statistics-- Gender- Equity- in- High- School- and- College- Athletics- Most- Recent- Participation-- Budge. aspx

Zirin, D. (2008). Calling sports sociology off the bench. *Contexts, 7*(3), 28–31. doi:10.1525/ctx.2008.7.3.28

ADDITIONAL READING

Dworkin, S. L., & Messner, M. A. (1999). Just do…what? Sport, bodies, gender. In Ferree, M. M., Lorber, J., & Hess, B. B. (Eds.), *Revisioning Gender* (pp. 341–364). Thousand Oaks, CA: Sage.

Eagleman, A. N., & Pedersen, P. M. (2007, December 31). An analysis of the coverage (and promotion) of females and males in ESPN The Magazine. *Womenssportsfoundation.org*. Retrieved January 7, 2011, from http://www.womenssportsfoundation.org/binary-data/WSF_ARTICLE/pdf_file/1222.pdf

Greer, J. D., Hardin, M., & Homan, C. (2009). 'Naturally' less exciting? Visual production of men's and women's track and field coverage during the 2004 Olympics. *Journal of Broadcasting & Electronic Media, 53*(2), 173–189. doi:10.1080/08838150902907595

Hardin, M., Chance, J., Dodd, J. E., & Hardin, B. (2002). Olympic photo coverage fair to female athletes. *Newspaper Research Journal, 23*(2/3), 64–78.

Hardin, M., Kuhn, K., Jones, H., Genovese, J., & Balaji, M. (2009). 'Have you got game?' Hegemonic masculinity and neo-homophobia in U.S. newspaper sports departments. *Communication, Culture & Critique, 2*(2), 182–200. doi:10.1111/j.1753-9137.2009.01034.x

Higgs, C. T., Weiller, K. H., & Martin, S. B. (2003). Gender bias in the 1996 Olympic games. *Journal of Sport and Social Issues, 27*(1), 52–64.

Hundley, H. L., & Billings, A. C. (Eds.). (2010). *Examining identity in sports media*. Thousand Oaks, CA: Sage.

Kian, E., Mondello, M., & Vincent, J. (2009). ESPN—The women's sports network? A content analysis of Internet coverage of March Madness. *Journal of Broadcasting & Electronic Media, 53*(3), 477–495. doi:10.1080/08838150903102519

Pedersen, P. M. (2002). Investigating interscholastic equity on the sports page: A content analysis of high school athletics newspaper articles. *Sociology of Sport Journal, 19*(4), 419–432.

Turner, P. (1999). Television and Internet convergence: Implications for sports broadcasting. *Sports Marketing Quarterly, 8*(2), 43–49.

KEY TERMS AND DEFINITIONS

Gatekeeping: The process in which media producers decide on what will be covered and how it will be covered to prevent or facilitate certain types of narratives and information reaching media consumers. The gatekeeping process is influenced by a number of factors on different levels.

ESPN: The Entertainment and Sports Programming Network, a popular U.S. cable television network carrying sports programming.

Heteronormativity: A belief system that privileges heterosexuality as normal and desirable.

Independent Sports Blogs: Weblogs produced and maintained by individuals or group of bloggers that are not affiliated with mainstream, traditional, or institutional media outlets.

Levels of Analysis: The division of the social world for analytical purposes along a hierarchal continuum ranging, for instance, from (micro-level) individual processes to broader (macro-level) social and cultural processes.

Marketplace Considerations: The evaluation of goods and services' anticipated consumer demand. According to scholars, the editorial decision-makers' presumptions about the needs and wants of news consumers can be shaped by their own projected feelings and values.

Masculine Hegemony: The dominant/idealized form of masculinity in Western culture and the system of beliefs, values and practices that privilege it.

Title IX: Title IX of the Education Amendments of 1972 is a federal law that prohibits gender-based discrimination in institutions receiving federal financial assistance. It was passed by the U.S. Congress as part of the Education Amendments of 1972 and signed into law on June 23, 1972. The Title IX statute provides, "No person in the United States shall, on the basis of sex, be excluded from participation in, be denied the benefits of, or be subjected to discrimination under any education program or activity receiving Federal financial assistance" (20 U.S.C. § 1681(a)).

SportsBlog Nation (SB Nation): A popular blog network that provides coverage of U.S. professional and college sports.

Women Talk Sports: A popular women's sports blog network (www.womentalksports.com).

Chapter 5
Civility or Censorship?
An Examination of the Reaction to a Proposed Code of Conduct for Bloggers

Gwen L. Shaffer
University of California, USA

ABSTRACT

When two high-profile social media evangelists proposed a code of conduct for bloggers in April of 2007, the idea triggered a heated debate in cyberspace. Critics charged that the draft code contradicted the principles of free speech and expression that make blogs ideal spaces for uncensored discussion. However, proponents of the Internet self-regulation argued that formally adopted rules of conduct are necessary for bloggers to serve as a step towards a virtual civil society. The present analysis, grounded in a civil society theoretical framework and the U.S. tradition of media self-regulation, documents how Web users can routinely take advantage of the Internet's open architecture for self-expression. Rather than attempting to enforce a blanket code of conduct, the author maintains that bloggers' self-moderation based on generally acceptable content policies can foster inclusivity on blog pages and can help move the blogosphere to a virtual civil society.

INTRODUCTION

Constant uncensored social interaction is among the characteristics that distinguish social media from traditional mass media such as print, radio and television. On these platforms of traditional mass media, the conversation is mostly linear. By contrast, social media are uniquely interactive, allowing readers to generate responses nearly simultaneously as they retrieve content. Due to its built-in interactivity, the second generation Internet or Web 2.0 provides a limitless space for people to share diverse opinions and to engage in often-heated discourse. If the ideal virtual civil

DOI: 10.4018/978-1-60960-744-9.ch005

society were to be realized, digital citizens would transcend their own personal interests for the sake of the common good. In reality, however, the anonymous nature of modern cyberculture tempts some Internet users, particularly bloggers, to abandon the rules of civility they typically follow offline. Technology book writer and videogame designer Kathy Sierra, who maintained a blog called *Creating Passionate Users*, learned this through first-hand experience when she began receiving threats and disturbing anonymous comments on her blog. In April 2007, Sierra discovered someone posting to another blog a photoshopped picture of her with a noose (BBC News, 2007; Rawlinson, 2007; Sierra, 2007a). The image was followed by a comment from "Joey," who wrote that "the only thing Kathy has to offer me is that noose in her neck size." These and other similar disturbing images and comments with veiled threats were posted and reposted multiple times in the blogosphere.

As a blogger, Sierra was accustomed to dealing with cyberbullying and *anonymous trolls*—that is, users who post inflammatory anonymous comments in hopes of baiting others into responding (Webopedia, 2007). Still, violent threats and their apparent coordination frightened Sierra enough that she reported online harassment to local police in Boulder, Colorado. Furthermore, subsequent to national and international news media reports of Sierra's ordeal, someone disclosed her home address and social security number online (Schwartz, 2008). In response to harassment, Sierra discontinued her blog and called off public appearances including the 2007 O'Reilly Emerging Technology Conference. In the wake of the online threats, Sierra cancelled all speaking engagements and commented, "I am afraid to leave my yard... I will never be the same"(BBC News, 2007). Consequently, defendants of unrestricted Internet freedoms and proponents of greater personal accountability began debating the limits of free speech on the Internet and the blogosphere.

Two high-profile technologists concluded that this episode of online harassment warranted a far-reaching response. Tim O'Reilly, a technology promoter and publisher credited with coining the term "Web 2.0" (O'Reilly, 2005), and Wikipedia founder Jimmy Wales proposed a 7-point Blogger's Code of Conduct meant to filter abusive and threatening comments that characterize some online discourse. Wales and O'Reilly (2007a) introduced the guidelines this way:

We celebrate the blogosphere because it embraces frank and open conversation. But frankness does not have to mean lack of civility. We present this Blogger Code of Conduct in hopes that it helps create a culture that encourages both personal expression and constructive conversation. One can disagree without being disagreeable.

A primary goal was to convince bloggers that they should not accept behavior "that they wouldn't tolerate in the physical world" (O'Reilly, 2007a). The reaction from the blogosphere was swift and, characteristically, intense. While a small minority of bloggers welcomed the call for respect and common courtesy on the Internet, many more commentators condemned the notion of codifying ethics for bloggers and expressed resentment over the implication that the blogosphere is "broken and misguided" (Furrier, 2007). With 184 million blogs on the Internet (Technorati, 2008) around that time, regulation would have had an impact on billions of online conversations daily.

This chapter explores the inherent tension between preserving the principles of free speech that make blogs ideal forums for deliberation and debate, and the blogosphere's parallel goal of providing a virtual civil society. The study examines reactions to the proposed blogger's code of conduct and, by drawing on civil society and public sphere literature, takes a theoretically grounded approach to analyzing these responses. The author concludes that community moderation and terms of audience engagement established by individual

Figure 1. "Civility Enforced," "Anything Goes," and Creative Commons Badges

bloggers are more appropriate approaches to protecting civil discourse in the blogosphere. For the purpose of this analysis, the term *blogger* refers to both writers and commenters.

BACKGROUND

Heated debate has long been a mainstay of Internet bulletin boards and blogs (Chonin, 2007). As the online population has expanded, the frequency of "flaming"—another common term for "trolling"—has grown along with it. In fact, new social norms are struggling to keep pace with the popularity of blogs. "Netiquette" is not simply the virtual equivalent of eating salad with the proper fork or remembering to say "please." "Netiquette" means abiding by the ethical standards Internet users impose upon their peers for the sake of a peaceful co-existence in cyberspace. As Howard Rheingold noted, the ability to communicate with anyone 24 hours a day is convenient for us as individuals, but it does not always benefit "the collective" (as cited in Chonin, 2007, p. F1). The code of conduct drafted by O'Reilly and Wales was meant to curb what they perceived to be rampant verbal abuse and cyberbullying on blogs. Their stated goal was to strike a balance between institutionalizing civility and preserving free speech in cyberspace (O'Reilly, 2007b). Instead, they sparked what is perhaps one of the most animated dialogues to date regarding online discourse.

The rationale for a bloggers' code of ethics is that the anonymous nature of blog postings tempts some users to make vitriolic comments that they would never repeat face-to-face. As with the Kathy

Sierra case, these messages occasionally cross the line into online harassment and cyberbullying. The guidelines proposed by O'Reilly and Wales call on bloggers to stop posting "unacceptable content" (O'Reilly, 2007b): that is, content characterized as anything that is meant to abuse or threaten others, is libelous or knowingly false, or violates privacy or confidentiality. The code also encouraged blog owners to ban anonymous comments and to respond to any controversial remarks privately via email (O'Reilly, 2007b). Finally, any blogger willing to commit to the code of conduct was asked to post a badge stamped with the phrase "civility enforced." Conversely, blogs that rejected the code were encouraged to post an "anything goes" badge, warning visitors they are entering a free-for-all-zone. O'Reilly likened the badges to the widely recognized Creative Commons tags that indicate specified Web content may be legally shared under certain conditions (see Figure 1).

Flaming: As Old as Electronic Communication Itself

Electronic virtual communities that facilitated social interaction existed more than a decade prior to the appearance of blogging software. In 1979 two Duke University graduate students, Tom Truscott and Jim Ellis, created one of the first computer network communications systems, which later developed into a globally distributed Usenet discussion network. Subscribers accessed Usenet newsgroups using UNIX computers and dial-up modems. Initially, just a few North American universities logged on to the system to trade research articles and ideas. Soon, however, moderated Usenet discussion groups formed on a broad range of topics—politics, science, technology, philosophy, science fiction, literature and music (Usenet, 2007). From the beginning, discussions could be vitriolic in nature. In fact, phrases like "flaming," "spamming" and "trolling" originated on Usenet (Pfaffenberger, 2002). Some newsgroup members reacted by strengthening central control and moderating the conversation. In other instances, members would get fed up with the anti-social behavior and leave to form their own newsgroups (Lampe, 2006). However, Usenet is still used today by millions of people who rely on a set of basic rules and simple conventions for keeping conversations civil and self-enforced.

Designers of CommuniTree, a dial-up bulletin board type discussion system created in 1978, developed an open protocol allowing conversational "branches" to bundle themed messages centered on topics such as religion, philosophy and spirituality without any moderation (Stone, 1993). CommuniTree's programming code prohibited censorship, regardless of a message's content. This presented a problem in 1982 when Apple Computer struck a deal with the U.S. government to supply schools with computer equipment in exchange for tax breaks. Throngs of elementary and high school students began flooding CommuniTree with "obscene and scatological messages" (Stone, 1993). The plug was pulled on the CommuniTree, a unique electronic communications system where deleting or altering posted messages was impossible. Most early electronic newsgroups, however, were moderated. In 1985, Stewart Brand and Larry Brilliant started an online discussion community called The WELL (2010a), an acronym for Whole Earth 'Lectronic Link. This digital town inhabited by residents throughout the world continues to exist today as the self-described birthplace of online community movement. The WELL participants also struggled with whether to formalize rules regarding message content and privacy, and their dilemmas inspired Rheingold (1993) to write his seminal book, *The*

Virtual Community: Homesteading on the Virtual Frontier. The solution was found in abandoning the principle of anonymity. Even if members of The WELL anonymously post to an open or a private forum (conference), they can be easily identified by their real names—a policy that effectively keeps flaming in check (The WELL, 2010a). Thus, the CommuniTree and the Whole Earth 'Lectronic Link systems symbolize some of the major trends in approaching issues of free speech and personal accountability of Internet users.

Two competing online service systems began in the early 1980s. CompuServe enabled subscribers to access email, online conferences and games. The rival GEnie developed "RoundTables," each consisting of a message board, a chat room and a library for permanent text files—features that eventually figured significantly in the virtual community culture (Weyrich, 2010). None of the interactive offerings from CompuServe and GEnie were immune from flamers, of course. Typically, volunteer moderators banished offenders to their own discussion threads, but some censored posts. "CompuServe requires us to delete certain things, such as personal attacks and profanity, libel and scatology," one moderator told *Online Access* magazine (Broadhurst, 1993). America Online (AOL), launched in 1989, relied on volunteer "community leaders" to police chat rooms and message boards. Interestingly enough, the company terminated the program in June 2005, after community leaders filed a class action lawsuit demanding minimum wage for the work they performed (Greenberg, 2010).

Electronic discourse evolved dramatically with the advent of the World Wide Web and online personal diaries, which detailed a person's experiences, observations, social criticisms—and sometimes shocking revelations or commentaries. Claudio Pinhanez's Open Diary is widely considered to be the first online journal. Pinhanez began chronicling his experiences in 1994, while earning a doctorate at the Massachusetts Institute of Technology. In an early post, Pinhanez (1995) characterized his electronic diary as a venue for feelings, ideas and "sensual thoughts" he could not share in-person. Jorn Barger (1997) initially used the term "weblog" on December 17, 1997 to describe the process of "logging the Web" as he surfed. Posting to his personal website some-time around April 1999, Peter Merholz (2002) broke down the phrase "we blog" into the word "weblog"—a name that quickly caught on. Around this same time, free blogging software made online publishing accessible to a broader, less techno-logically savvy population and institutionalized features such as the ability for readers to leave comments, descending chronological order for articles, and trackbacks.

Fostering a Civil Society

The early approaches to emerging electronic virtual communities were grounded in the con-cept of civil society. Adam Ferguson, a leading thinker of the Scottish Enlightenment, introduced the term "civil society" in a sense that it is still used today. In his classic essay on the *History of Civil Society*, Ferguson (1767) asserted that humans develop ethical norms and intellectual abilities only through social relationships. The human capacities to empathize, to see the world through another's eyes, and to be guided by a moral compass are among key components of a civil society. Ferguson (1767) postulated that "innate sociability"—a desire to help one another and foster a sense of community—enables hu-mans to co-exist. A half-century later, Friedrich Hegel's (1820)*Philosophy of Right* advocated for an "ethical order" separate from the state. Hegel believed that property ownership and self-interest failed to satisfactorily explain social bonds or why people are motivated by generosity, altruism and group solidarity. When individuality and freedom converge with moral rules, what emerges is a recognition that each person has a stake in the greater good of the whole. This "ethical life" is, in essence, what binds members of a society (Hegel,

1820). Also in the early 19th century, French so-cial commentator Alexis de Tocqueville (1831) emphasized the importance of autonomous mores and customs in creating a successful democracy. He characterized American democracy as inherent in the attitudes and actions of citizens, rather than something written into laws or imposed by elected officials. De Tocqueville described civil society as more analogous to "a manner of acting than a kind of political system" (Gunnell, 2004, p. 49). Without these guiding principles, participants in the blogosphere would not attempt to find common ground; nor would they find value in opposing points of view.

Similarly, John Stuart Mill (1859) viewed civil society as a balancing act between the prevailing forces of civilization—that is, between the law of the land and the separation dividing the state and society. Mill believed governments should promote autonomy among its citizenry. He ar-gued that it is only through respectful discourse and deliberation that people come to bolster their arguments, and gain the necessary impetus to alter them. Mill's conceptualization of civil society, as a space that required trust and coop-eration, is particularly relevant to a discussion of online discourse. Mill also laid the foundation for public sphere theorists, who envisioned an arena where citizens realize their rights for freedom of expression, open discussion, sincerity and truth (Habermas, 1962). Of course, requirements for the public sphere may be extended to online dialogue—including blogs and other interactive Web applications (Dahlberg, 2001; Gill, 2004; Hacker & Van Dijk, 2000). These new forms of media hold considerable potential to broaden civic engagement and deliberative discourse by drawing in people who may not be motivated to attend an anti-war protest but who will, for ex-ample, add comments to a political blog. Because one's identity may be concealed on the Internet, it is a space where public policy issues may be debated frankly and opinions expressed honestly. Ironically, it is abuse of this same anonymity factor that, in part, compelled O'Reilly and Wales to propose a code of conduct.

While civil society is not synonymous with democracy, contemporary sociologists frequently conflate the two notions. Almond and Verba (1963) defined the ideal democratic way of life as a civic culture in which political engagement is balanced by tradition, a commitment to "parochial values" (p. 32), diversity and consensus. Others have characterized civil society as a "free space" (Barber, 1998, p. 6) where democratic attitudes and behavior are nurtured and where social actors privilege the common good. Barber's conceptualization of civil society also lends itself to the blogosphere, which creates an opportunity for democratic forms of horizontal communication, as opposed to vertical communication among elites who control other mass media platforms. At the same time, Barber (2003) cautions that information-based technologies, such as the Internet, could obstruct the growth of "knowledge" by allowing "unreflected"—and even random biases—into postings with no accountability (p. 43). Uncivil behavior in the off-line world may actually tear at a society's collective conscience, leading to an atmosphere of anger and hostility— and, ultimately, vengeance (Durkheim, 1984). These negative patterns that Durkheim warned about now permeate the virtual world, where flame wars are an accepted aspect of the culture.

Given that 77% of Internet users read blogs (Technorati, 2008), any expectation of reaching consensus on what constitutes acceptable behavior online is unrealistic. In hundreds of comments posted in response to the Blogger's Code of Conduct proposed by O'Reilly and Wales, Internet users debated whether cyberspace should be modeled as a civil society and, if so, who would determine the meaning of the concept itself. The differences in opinion, many of them irreconcilable, explain why the guidelines drafted by O'Reilly and Wales faded into obscurity within weeks of their debut.

METHOD

This study utilized a qualitative analysis of blog posts published in response to the draft of the Blogger's Code of Conduct between April 8, 2007 and May 2, 2007. Comments were submitted on personal and organizational blogs dedicated to a broad range of topics—from arts and culture to public relations and technology. The sample included 50 blog entries and hundreds of comments posted in response to them. While American bloggers were behind the majority of the blogs examined, Irish, Canadian and German bloggers also wrote a handful of entries on the subject. The sample for this analysis also included 350 comments posted directly to the Blogger's Code of Conduct draft on Tim O'Reilly's personal blog, *O'Reilly Radar*, between April 8, 2007 and January 24, 2008. A content analysis of the blog posts was conducted, which entailed multiple readings of each blog entry and related comments with identifying underlying themes in the sentiments expressed by the authors. The underlying themes were categorized and analyzed using the civil society theoretical framework. Emerging themes included: 1) the benefits of anonymity in online discourse; 2) the egalitarian nature of cyberspace; 3) the history of self-regulation on websites; and 4) the unenforceable nature of an online behavior code.

A REVOLT AGAINST RULES

Reinforcing the Right to Free Speech

One principle underlying the decision to draft a code of conduct was to encourage self-examination in the blogging community (O'Reilly, 2007b). Another goal was to convince blog writers they should not feel guilty about deleting insults or banning comments that lack substance. After all, when an intellectual debate slips into a personal mud-slinging match, it loses purpose. Intense anger, or even loathing, does not justify insults or pettiness. In fact, one may argue the opposite is true—negative feelings demand even greater politeness to avoid creating "an easy target for the other side" (Rule, 2005), whether communicating online or offline. This sentiment clearly reflects the philosophy of civil society, suggesting that people are able to co-exist only because they respect one another's ideas and share a common bond (Ferguson, 1767; Hegel, 1820).

But numerous bloggers angrily accused O'Reilly and Wales of threatening the very principles America was founded upon, such as free speech. Some invoked reprehensible episodes in U.S. history—such as McCarthyism and violence against Muslims in the wake of 9/11—and equated these events with the code's perceived attempt to silence bloggers. "Reminds me of some of the things America has done at its worst," wrote a commenter identifying himself as Peter on the *O'Reilly Radar* (2007b) blog. Across the Web, similarly themed posts stressed that transparency is integral to blogs. "We should revel in what they expose, not seek to limit or hide it," blogged Andy Lark (2007). Glenn Reynolds (2007), a University of Tennessee law professor and the author of the Instapundit blog, cautioned that once site moderators begin deleting comments, readers will hold them "more responsible" for comments they choose not to delete. A blogger who commented on *O'Reilly Radar* (2007a) using the name Marcus criticized the idea of creating "community standards" that attempt "to classify and control speech." Marcus mocked O'Reilly and Wales for purporting to know what is best for bloggers and for endeavoring "to save us all from ourselves." Another technology blogger acknowledged personal support for "civility, reasoned discourse, and coherent and respectful discussion in the blogosphere" but scoffed at the idea of imposing these same ideals on others. "I can't tell you how you should be phrasing your sentences or conveying your thoughts, nor would I want to," Dave Taylor (2007) wrote.

These objections reflect the fact that blogs have radically transformed the way people obtain information—whether as gossip, breaking news, or something in between. Blogs empower average citizens to share ideas with strangers from around the globe without interference from traditional media gatekeepers. With no designated editors and obvious biases, interactive blog sites can be sarcastic, cynical and cheeky—all of which make well-written entries entertaining and enlightening to read. If bloggers were to rely on a proscribed set of guidelines for determining what constitutes acceptable content and what is off limits, commenters could lose their ability to trust their own instincts. Instead, effective moderation should be grounded in "habit and practice" (Fukuyama, 1999). Critics of the Blogger's Code of Conduct share de Tocqueville's (1840) conviction that people engaged in debates regarding politics and culture "have scarcely time to attend to the details of etiquette." Anyway, good manners may be beside the point. In their studies of contemporary campaigns, Brooks and Geer (2007) found that even the most negative and uncivil campaign messages did not hamper Americans' level of political engagement. In fact, their study concluded that these types of messages may actually stimulate political interest. Civil society can exist only where all perspectives are valued (Barber, 1998), and even unpopular ideas are expressed.

Comments responding to the draft Code of Conduct pointed out that a major challenge lies in determining exactly who is accountable for "unacceptable" online comments. Lawyer and blogger Ann Althouse (2007) predicted the guidelines crafted by O'Reilly and Wales would lead to an "endless argument about the meaning of the terms in the rules and how the rules apply." New York University journalism professor and writer Jeff Jarvis (2007) expressed concerns that the proposed code "threatens to give back the incredible gift of freedom given to us in Section 230," a provision of the Communication Decency Act asserting that bloggers are not responsible for content created by someone else on their sites. Technologist Tristan Louis (2007) agreed that blog moderators who endorse a code of conduct could increase their chances of being successfully prosecuted for publishing libelous comments on their sites. "By agreeing to delete, they could face a tough battle," Louis (2007) wrote on his blog. Other critics focused on the *lack* of legal weight behind the code. "See, here's the problem: This is a powerless code. It's not able to enforce ****. It's just going to create another silo…and kill off communications with 'outsiders,'" John Welch (2007) wrote on his personal website. Publisher Gerard Van der Leun (2007) accused O'Reilly of possessing a "utopian" mentality disconnected from reality. "O'Reilly's dreamscape unfolds across 'Wouldn't it be nice if….' and rolls to 'Let's make some laws and regulations right away and get people to obey them' in less time than it takes to fry up a tofu burger," Gerard Van der Leun (2007) blogged. These comments highlight the fact that the Internet's open architecture makes it difficult to control or punish the authors of disparaging or vulgar posts.

Perhaps, a more salient question involves whether the author deserves to be rebuked in the first place. Civil society is a balancing act between enforceable rules and the human spirit. It is only through discourse and deliberation that people learn to bolster their arguments (Mill, 1859) and gain exposure to alternative perspectives. Furthermore, each virtual community attracts a unique readership, and individual moderators have their own "tolerance for rude, obnoxious, crude, spammy, obscene, [or] pornographic commenters" (Taylor, 2007). Certainly, participants in the blogosphere are well aware of its unique culture, and the occasional flame war is actually expected in virtual society. Again, this is what distinguishes cyberspace from corporate owned media like TV networks and newspapers. Extreme reactions, even negative and uncivil ones, may actually strengthen the blogosphere because they reinforce the "behavioral expectations" inherent

in online culture (King, 2001, p. 429). Rather than reacting to occasional hateful blog comments with anger and avoidance, virtual community members might be reminded of the moral code that permeates cyberspace the vast majority of the time.

Yet democracy cannot function effectively without rules, a notion acknowledged by Seligman (1992) when he wrote that civil society integrates "the conflicting demands of individual interest and social good" (p. x). Reconciling the ideals of both individualism and the public good often necessitates the creation of limits. Even the most tolerant societies establish boundaries to deter the spread of information that is truly defamatory or false. For instance, many employers frequently enforce speech codes meant to avert offensive language. One may legitimately question why parallel regulations should not also be promulgated in cyberspace. As Sierra's decision to shut down her blog demonstrates, uncivil discourse has a polarizing effect. Unlike-minded bloggers typically refuse to engage with "the other side" (Hwang, Borah, Namkoong & Veenstra, 2008) when group members post hostile messages. If bloggers with opposing points of view stop participating in constructive discussion, democracy as a whole suffers. Substantive debate is a crucial element of a civil society and, when stifled, Habermas' (1962) vision for a lively public sphere is also stifled.

Escaping the Gatekeepers

To many in the blogosphere, discerning what constitutes passionate debate and what crosses the line into harassment is purely subjective. Many blog owners are opposed to a code of conduct imposed on the blogosphere to escape editorial restrictions, relying instead on personal values and judgment to steer their publications. "That may result in some bruised feelings from time to time, but our readers make the decision as to whether we have met their editorial guidelines, and that should be good enough in a free market," wrote Ed Morrissey (2007). Dozens of posts echoed

Gerard Van der Leun's (2007) assertion that blog moderators already have access to "the edit button and the delete button," both of which work sufficiently to squelch vitriol and threats. Other opponents of the code compared it to the "online equivalent of the 'thought police'" (Gonzalez, 2007) and suggested it contradicts the blogosphere's "wild west" (Ingram, 2007) sensibility. Some cynics charged that self-interest motivated O'Reilly and Wales to draft the Blogger's Code of Conduct. These commenters dismissed the proposal as a "linkbait opportunity" intended to attract hits for the *O'Reilly Radar* site. Another blogger speculated that O'Reilly and Wales would open a training company to certify blog "auditors" and charge site owners who adopt their "civility enforced" or "anything goes" logos (Stall the Ball, 2007). A widely read technology blogger feared repercussions if he rejected the guidelines. "Tim O'Reilly is a guy who really can affect one's career online (and off, too)…I feel some pressure just to get on board here and that makes me feel very uneasy," Andy Scoble (2007) wrote.

O'Reilly and Wales argued for limiting anonymous blog comments, yet concerns about negative consequences and retaliation—expressed by Scoble and numerous others—represent a key justification for allowing unidentified bloggers to post comments. In fact, the United States' long tradition of tolerating anonymous speech is essential for preserving both "political and social discourse" (Electronic Frontier Foundation, 2010a). The anonymous comment feature integral to nearly all blogs allows people to challenge authority and to blow the whistle on corruption without fearing retribution. Ideally, the blogosphere is a space for un-coerced discourse, regardless of whether participants share mutual values and convictions, and a space where no one person or entity dictates how views are expressed.

Blog posts that threaten "individual rights" (Papacharissi, 2004) undermine the potential for cyberspace to function as an extension of the public sphere. What must also be stressed,

however, is that the disparaging comments posted online are typically indistinguishable from cruel comments uttered in the corner bar or on the school bus. No code of conduct will modify the sometimes petty and mean-spirited aspects of human nature. Furthermore, research has found that uncivil discourse may even have a positive effect because it exemplifies how actors communicate through a medium that allows them to "test each other's wits" (Weger & Aakhus, 2003, p. 34). The exchanges are valuable when participants support one-liners and jabs with reasoned arguments. Viewed from this perspective, there are intrinsic personal and societal benefits to participating in online discussions, including those that degenerate into flaming. Visitors are exposed to ideas, attitudes and opinions that they are unlikely to encounter elsewhere, and the sense of community cultivated in these virtual spaces contributes to a greater public good (Fernback, 1997; Weger & Aakhus, 2003).

Even if skeptics doubt that these potential benefits outweigh the costs associated with uncivil discourse, they must consider whether mandatory or voluntary regulations are capable of curbing high-tech intimidation. Just as the schoolyard bully cares little about breaking the rules, a code of conduct will not prevent hateful individuals from tormenting others in the blogosphere. An inherent tension lies within "democratic" forms of online communication such as blogs. These powerful tools for sharing information can facilitate both *deliberative* discourse and *destructive* discourse. Establishing how much hateful or ugly language members of civil society are willing to tolerate is far more complicated than throwing down a blanket set of rules. Even if bloggers were to agree upon rules today, new website moderators could feel differently tomorrow. Norms and mores are not stagnant in a culture where "historical forces have shifted and will continue to shift boundaries" (Hall & Trentman, 2010).

A Culture of Self-Regulation

During the 90s, new media was deemed to be maverick and "unregulable" (Calabrese, 2004). This initial perception did not last long, as lawmakers have repeatedly attempted to limit access to certain online information. During the 2005 election season, two Cincinnati, Ohio, candidates—one running for the U.S. House of Representatives and another vying for mayor—claimed they were defamed by bloggers who compared them to Adolf Hitler and accused them of sexual misconduct (Rulon, 2005). As a result of these and similar incidents, some lawmakers contended the federal government should regulate online political speech when it borders on harassment (Rulon, 2005). Although legislators never passed new laws, Section 230 of the Communication Decency Act does apply to bloggers—who are both providers and users of interactive websites. As previously mentioned, the provision states that the owner of a blog may be held liable for defamatory entries posted by blog readers only if he or she "selected" (Electronic Frontier Foundation, 2010b) the third party information. Blog moderators may also be held responsible for any defamatory statements in postings that they substantially edit. This means the instinct to type snide comments along with links to articles could later haunt sardonic bloggers.

In general, the legislative and judicial branches of government have made minimal attempts to facilitate civil discourse in cyberspace. A far more common approach to online discourse depends on *self-regulation*. Soon after the Internet became commercially available, the Clinton-Gore (1997) administration called for self-regulation of online technologies and content. This hands-off approach is typical of American media policy. Powerful U.S. industry organizations like the National Association of Broadcasters and the Motion Picture Association of America—and more recently, the Entertainment Software Ratings Board—have developed their own rating systems for television, film and videogames. By self-imposing rating labels that alert consumers to violent, sexual and profane language or images, these influential industry groups have managed to stave off government efforts to regulate content.

Long before O'Reilly and Wales floated their draft of the Blogger's Code of Conduct, commercial websites began instituting policies to promote civility on their sites. Craigslist and eBay, which host dozens of blogs and discussion forums, are typical of interactive websites that depend on community moderation for policing user-generated content. Specifically, Craigslist (2010) has created an online form for reporting violations, and users may activate a filter that blocks abusive messages. Similarly, a link on eBay (2010) allows users to report violations of the website's "community content policy," which mandates that all messages posted to eBay blogs be "courteous and respectful." A mechanism known as "flagging" represents another attempt at community moderation by popular websites. In the wake of the April 16, 2007, mass shooting at Virginia Institute of Technology, students who attended the university created "I'm OK" pages on Facebook to assure worried friends and family members of their safety (Irvine, 2007). But less civic-minded people used the website to post racist remarks aimed at the gunman, Cho Seung-Hui, and other Asians. Many of the disparaging postings were removed after vigilant Facebook users flagged them—meaning, they reported the messages to Facebook as offensive—but the fact remains that social networking sites have become frequent forums for harassment and cyberbullying. Through a unique system of community moderation, the technology blog Slashdot (2010) allows a pool of registered users to exercise personal judgment to promote or demote comments before publicly posting them. If site visitors choose to read submissions tagged as "flamebait" or authored by an "anonymous coward," that is their prerogative. Other readers, though, may choose to read only posts deemed "informative." Another website that likely could not exist without community moderation is Wikipedia. Although the interactive encyclopedia is frequently criticized for containing inaccuracies and bias (Read, 2006; Blacharski, 2007; BBC News, 2006), at least one study concluded that vigilant community members repair major acts of vandalism in an average of 2 to 3 minutes (Viegas, Wattenberg & Dave, 2004). In addition, Wikipedia hosts "Wikiquette," an electronic bulletin board "where users can report impolite, uncivil or other difficult communications with editors" (Wikipedia, 2010).

In aggregate, these diverse systems for self-regulation demonstrate that communal editing can act as an effective—although not perfect—tool for dealing with the types of insensitive blog posts that O'Reilly and Wales proposed controlling via a code of conduct. The "wisdom of the crowds" (Surowiecki, 2005) and the general expectation of mutual respect are typically powerful enough forces to squash abuse in the blogosphere. As "Ping" commented on *O'Reilly Radar*, "Community is like a garden. The way it grows is defined by the people and norms and social interactions within, not the rules imposed from without" (O'Reilly, 2007b). Perhaps the larger lesson to be learned is that society cannot hold online behavior to a standard higher than that which we expect during face-to-face interactions, phone conversations and postal correspondence. As long as deception and fraud exist in the offline world, they will exist in cyberspace. The Internet, even with its vast potential for deliberative discourse and inclusion, remains an extension of our daily lives. The best we can hope for is that when social norms are violated online, vigilant members of the virtual community will shut out those who choose to make disrespectful and threatening comments. Websites that utilize community moderation remind us that the online public sphere functions as much more than a marketplace of ideas or as a warehouse filled with information. It is actually an important pipeline for generating and distributing culture (Dahlgren, 1995).

The interactive nature of blogs distinguishes them from traditional media platforms in important ways. At the same time, activity on the Internet parallels what is happening in other forms of media—where violent images are increasingly graphic (Media Awareness Network, 2007). Rap music lyrics frequently characterize women as "bitches" and "hos." Local newscasts routinely lead with images of body bags. Primetime television programs feature shootings, rapes and murders. Within this context, it comes as little surprise that some bloggers are desensitized to insults and threats on their websites or that anonymous trolls could post photoshopped images of Kathy Sierra for their own amusement. Civility is subjective and it is, of course, unrealistic to expect consensus in a community as large and diverse as the blogosphere. The goal to codify ethics in the blogosphere, as articulated by O'Reilly and Wales, at least, was not destined for mainstream adoption. However, the author argues that they both performed a valuable service by engaging bloggers in a conversation about the need to reject online behavior that harms others or threatens their rights.

Solutions and Recommendations

Since Internet access became mainstream in the mid-1990s, various ethical and legal concerns about Internet-based communication have emerged. Public fears surrounding online sexual predators and pornography triggered parental alarm and led to the introduction of content filters. The challenge of protecting copyrighted music, movies and books from unauthorized duplication resulted in the creation of digital rights management tools. More recently, consumer advocates campaigned for social networking sites, particularly Facebook, to stop sharing their members' private data with advertisers (Harris, 2010). In light of this pattern, it is fair to question whether anxiety over personal attacks in the blogosphere was simply a fleeting preoccupation for netizens during Spring 2007. Because blogs serve as reliable barometers of online culture, this study concludes that the debate surrounding online civility will remain salient in the long term. In the blogosphere, readers double as editors; conversation is uncontrolled; and the lines between opinion and fact are blurry. Venerable newspapers, such as the *New York Times* and *Washington Post,* rely on blogs to provide readers with up-to-the-minute developments, and allow them to add their own thoughts and reactions to news coverage. Personal blogs provide readers with a sense of community and a genuine connection with the author. When bloggers exhibit uncivil behavior in these virtual spaces, the impacts are hardly inconsequential. The tone bloggers set reverberates across cyberspace. In general, the most effective means of countering abusive speech online is to encourage additional comments, as opposed to cutting off the conversation. Even so, previous research on flaming has found that hurtful and personal online attacks may result in participants quitting the group discussion altogether (Lee, 2005). When this happens, the public sphere is no longer inclusive.

The blogosphere can live up to its potential only when democratic attitudes and behavior are nurtured and when social actors privilege the common good (Barber, 1998). This underscores the need for individual moderators to explicate policies for posting comments on their sites. However, the following recommendations are not meant to stipulate that guidelines mirror the code O'Reilly and Wales proposed, nor do they imply government agencies should step in and police comments. Rather, they are grounded in the Internet's successful reliance on community moderation and in the notion of transparency—both critical elements of a civil society. The parameters for online conduct can be as broad or as narrow as the individual website owner deems fitting. What matters is that visitors clearly understand the rules before they hit the "submit" button to comment. For instance, blog moderators may choose to bar profanity and physical threats, and

delete such comments when they appear. Visitors to those sites who post abusive comments, regardless of the stated rules, will have no room to complain about the consequences. Feminist writer Laurie Penny takes this approach to by stating on the homepage of her personal blog that trolling has forced her to moderate all reader posts. "If your comment isn't blatantly and horrendously misogynist, misandrist, racist, ablist, homophobic, transphobic or xenophobic, and you're not a spambot, it will appear on the site as soon as I get time to approve it. Bullying of any kind will not be tolerated on this blog," the *Penny Red* comments policy states (Penny, 2010). Conversely, blog owners comfortable with rhetoric drifting into territory that includes personal attacks or crass language must make this clear. The WELL's "Weird conference" serves as an example. This online community officially touts itself as a venue for "rabid crackpots" with "twisted minds" (The WELL, 2010b), leaving those who enter the fray no doubt about what to expect. Google's terms of service agreement similarly warns users they may be exposed to online material they find "offensive, indecent or objectionable" (Google, 2010).

While content policies established by individual blog owners vary dramatically, it is critical that they share one tenet—inclusivity. Moderators must strive to treat divergent viewpoints with equal respect, as history demonstrates that civility triumphs when members of a blogging community feel accepted. Fostering a sense of inclusivity is also likely to spur community members to flag unacceptable posts on their own. Who wants to stare at graffiti on their walls or to step over litter in their parks?

FUTURE RESEARCH DIRECTIONS

Civil society is simultaneously harmonious and discordant, a space where citizens perpetually "wobble between allowing difference, and insisting that such difference be bounded" (Hall &

Trentman, 2010). Future research should examine how this duality plays out in the blogosphere. For instance, new media scholars could explore whether reasoned persuasion is an effective tactic for winning over adversaries in the blogosphere or whether heated rhetoric is actually more effective in particular circumstances. In the spirit of the familiar adage, "It's not what you say, but how you say it," another question scholars should examine is whether civility in cyberspace is characterized less by the content of blog posts and, rather, by the tone and tenor of these comments (made obvious by capital letters, exclamation points or emoticons). In light of the fact that many critics of the proposed Blogger's Code of Conduct questioned the meaning of civility, future studies could take up the question of how bloggers establish and perceive "civility norms"—if at all. Finally, new media scholars could employ both qualitative and quantitative methods to assess whether the level of civility in online discourse has increased or decreased since O'Reilly and Wales proposed a code of conduct for the blogosphere in 2007. Both bloggers and policymakers would benefit from a better understanding of current trends in online exchanges.

CONCLUSION

When O'Reilly and Wales floated their idea of a code of conduct for bloggers, they failed to acknowledge the unique and open nature of the blogosphere. Inadvertently, they disregarded the main appeal of blogs—the absence of gatekeepers. A primary function of civil society is to promote social autonomy, as opposed to bringing in officials to negotiate terms or to direct. The egalitarian nature of the blogosphere often leads to more in depth and more substantive debate. Blogging's lack of central control allows an entire community of readers to determine how much space is devoted to an issue, as well as how long a story should stick around. In fact, media gatekeepers

increasingly look to blogs for cues regarding which topics merit coverage in their own media products. Inhibiting virtual conversations could, therefore, create repercussions far beyond the insular blogosphere. Another shortcoming apparent in the draft code is its failure to distinguish between loutish behavior and criminal actions. Despite admirable intentions, O'Reilly and Wales came across as "leveraging" (Althouse, 2007) Kathy Sierra's plight to justify placing limits on free speech in the blogosphere. Perhaps the greatest irony regarding the proposed Blogger's Code of Conduct is the reaction from a person whose negative experience triggered the debate in the first place. In response to the idea proposed by O'Reilly and Wales, Sierra said she is convinced that no set of rules could have prevented anonymous trolls from harassing her. Sierra's own technology blog, *Creating Passionate Users*, had imposed a strict comment policy since the end of 2006 and she deleted inappropriate posts. "But if people are determined to hate, harass, intimidate, or threaten you, it's easy enough to do it on other blogs," Sierra (2007a) wrote. Her observation touches upon an interpretation of civil society that recognizes membership is, of course, purely voluntary (Carothers, 1999).

REFERENCES

Almond, G., & Verba, S. (1963). *The civil culture: Political attitudes and democracy in five nations.* Princeton, NJ: Princeton University Press.

Althouse, A. (2007, April 9). The blogger's code of conduct. *Althouse* blog. Retrieved May 20, 2010, from http://althouse.blogspot.com/ 2007/ 04/ bloggers- code- of- conduct.html

Barber, B. (1998). *A place for us: How to make society civil and democracy strong.* New York, NY: Hill & Wang.

Barber, B. (2003). Which technology and which democracy? In Jenkins, H., & Thorburn, D. (Eds.), *Democracy and new media* (pp. 33–47). Cambridge, MA: M.I.T. Press.

Barger, J. (1997, December 17). *Robot Wisdom* blog. Retrieved April 17, 2007, from http://www.robotwisdom.com/ log1997m12. html

Blacharski, D. (2007, January 29). *Blog insights: The cult of Wikipedia*. ITworld.com. Retrieved April 26, 2007, from http://www.itworld.com/ Tech/5046/nlsblog070131/

Bobs Yer Uncle. (2007). *I dream of Kathy Sierra*. Images and text posted on March 24, 2007, at http/:unclebobism. wordpress.com/ 2007/ 03/ 24/ i- dream- of- kathy- sierra.html (The entire website has since been removed from the Internet)

Broadhurst, J. (1993, June). *Lurkers and flamers: Why they do what they do*. Online Access. Retrieved May 19, 2010, from http://www.polishedprose.com/ lurkers.html

Brooks, D., & Geer, J. (2007). Beyond negativity: The effects of incivility on the electorate. *American Journal of Political Science*, *51*(1), 1–16. doi:10.1111/j.1540-5907.2007.00233.x

Calabrese, A. (2004). Stealth regulation: Moral meltdown and political radicalism at the Federal Communications Commission. *New Media & Society*, *6*(1), 106–113. doi:10.1177/1461444804039902

Chonin, N. (2007, April 22). Going down in flames. *San Francisco Chronicle*, p. F1.

Clinton, W., & Gore, A. (1997). *A framework for global electronic commerce*. Retrieved April 23, 2007, from http://www.w3.org/ TR/ NOTE-framework- 970706.html

Craigslist. (2010). *Terms of use*. Retrieved May 26, 2010, from http://www.craigslist.org/ about/ terms. of. use

Dahlberg, L. (2001). The Internet and democratic discourse: Exploring the prospects of online deliberative forums extending the public sphere. *Information Communication and Society*, *4*(4), 615–633. doi:10.1080/13691180110097030

Dahlgren, P. (1995). *Television and the public sphere: Citizenship, democracy, and the media*. London, UK: Sage.

de Tocqueville, A. (1831). *Democracy in America*. (H. Reeve, Trans.). Retrieved April 20, 2007, from http://www.marxists.org/ reference/ archive/ de- tocqueville/ democracy- america/ ch15.htm

Durkheim, E. (1984). *The division of labour in society*. New York, NY: Free Press.

eBay. (2010). Discussion boards usage policy. Retrieved May 26, 2010, from http://pages.ebay.com/ help/ policies/ everyone- boards.html

Electronic Frontier Foundation. (2010a). *Anonymity*. Retrieved May 24, 2010, from http://www.eff.org/ Privacy/ Anonymity/

Electronic Frontier Foundation. (2010b). *Section 230 protections*. Retrieved June 8, 2010, from http://www.eff.org/ issues/ bloggers/ legal/ liability/ 230

Ferguson, A. (1767). *An essay on the history of civil society*. Retrieved April 20, 2007, from http://socserv.mcmaster.ca/ ~econ/ ugcm/ 3ll3/ ferguson/ civil1

Fernback, J. (1997). The individual within the collective: Virtual ideology and the realization of collective principles. In Jones, S. (Ed.), *Virtual culture: Identity and communication in cybersociety* (pp. 36–54). Thousand Oaks, CA: Sage.

Fukuyama, F. (1999). *Social capital and civil society*. Speech delivered at the IMF Conference on Second Generation Reforms. November 8-9, Washington, DC. Retrieved June 2, 2010, from http://www.imf.org/ external/ pubs/ ft/ seminar/ 1999/ reforms/ fukuyama.htm#V

Furrier, J. (2007, April 9). Tim O'Reilly: Sell out or leadership? *John Furrier's personal blog.* Retrieved May 21, 2010, from http://podtech. wordpress.com/ 2007/ 04/ 09/ tim- oreilly- sell-out- or- leadership/

Gill, K. (2004). *How can we measure the influence of the blogosphere?* Paper presented at the International World Wide Web conference, May 17-22, New York, NY.

Gonzalez, E. (2007, April 12). Blogger code of conduct. *Eric Gonzalez* blog. Retrieved May 21, 2010, from http://ericgonzalez.wordpress.com/ 2007/ 04/ 12/ blogger- code- of- conduct/

Google. (2010). *Terms of service.* Retrieved June 8, 2010, from http://www.google.com/ accounts/ TOS

Greenberg, J. (2010). *AOL minimum wage lawsuit website.* Retrieved May 19, 2010, from http:// www.aolclassaction.com/

Habermas, J. (1962). *Structural transformation of the public sphere* (Burger, T., Trans.). Cambridge, MA: M.I.T. Press.

Hacker, K., & Van Dijk, J. (2000). *Digital democracy: Issues of theory and practice.* London, UK: Sage Publications.

Hall, J., & Trentmann, F. (2004). Contests over civil society: Introductory perspectives. In Hall, J., & Trentmann, F. (Eds.), *Civil society: A reader in history, theory and global politics.* Houndmills, England: Palgrave Macmillan.

Harris, S. (2010, May 21). Facebook privacy concerns heat up. *San Jose Mercury News.* Retrieved May 26, 2010, from http://www.mercurynews. com/ breaking- news/ ci_ 15137969? nclick_ check=1

Hegel, G. (1820). *Philosophy of right.* (H. Reeve, Trans.). Retrieved April 19, 2007, from http:// www.marxists.org/ reference/ archive/ hegel/ index.htm

Hwang, H., Borah, P., Namkoong, K., & Veenstra, A. (2008). *Does civility matter in the blogosphere? Examining the interaction effects of incivility and disagreement on citizen attitudes.* Paper presented at the annual meeting of the International Communication Association, May 22-26, Montreal.

Ingram, M. (2007, April 9). You are your own code of conduct. *Matthewingram* blog. Retrieved May 21, 2010, from http://www.mathewingram. com/ work/ 2007/ 04/ 09/ you- are- your- own-code- of- conduct

Irvine, M. (2007, 17). *Technology: Our coping mechanism.* Associated Press. Retrieved April 22, 2007, from http://news.yahoo.com/ s/ ap/ 20070417/ ap_ on_ re_ us/ virginia_ tech_ virtual_ tragedy

Jarvis, J. (2007, April 9). No twinkie badges here. *Buzz Machine* blog. Retrieved May 21, 2010, from http://www.buzzmachine.com/ 2007/ 04/ 09/ no- twinkie- badges- here

King, A. (2001). Affective dimensions of Internet culture. *Social Science Computer Review, 19*(4), 414–430. doi:10.1177/089443930101900402

Lampe, C. (2009). *Ratings use in an online discussion system: The Slashdot case.* Unpublished dissertation, University of Michigan.

Lark, A. (2007). Why code-of-conducts don't have a role to play. *Andy Lark's Blog.* Retrieved May 20, 2010, from http://andylark.blogs.com/ andylark/ 2007/ 04/ why_ codeofcondu.html

Lee, H. (2005). Behavioral strategies for dealing with flaming in an online forum. *The Sociological Quarterly, 46,* 385–403. doi:10.1111/j.1533-8525.2005.00017.x

Louis, T. (2007, April 9). Blogger's code of conduct: A dissection. *The TNL.net* blog. Retrieved May 20, 2010, from http://www.tnl.net/ blog/ 2007/ 04/ 09/ dissecting- the- proposed- bloggers- code- of- conduct/

Media Awareness Network. (2007). *Violence in media entertainment.* Retrieved April 27, 2007, from http://www.mediaawareness.ca/ english/ issues/ violence/ violence_ entertainment.cfm

Merholz, P. (2002, May 17). Play with your words. *Peterme* blog. Retrieved June 13, 2007, from http:// www.peterme.com/ archives/ 00000205.html

Mill, J. S. (1859). *On liberty.* Retrieved April 22, 2007, from http://www.utilitarianism.com/ ol/ one.html

Morrissey, E. (2007, April 9). Does the blogosphere need a speech code? *Captain's Quarters* blog. Retrieved May 20, 2010, from http://www. captainsquartersblog.com/ mt/ archives/ 009634. php

News, B. B. C. (2007, March 27). Blog death threats spark debate. *BBC News online.* Retrieved May 18, 2010, from http://news.bbc.co.uk/ 2/ hi/ technology/ 6499095.stm

O' Reilly, T. (2005, September 30). What is Web 2.0? Design patterns and business models for the next generation of software. *O'Reilly Radar* blog. Retrieved March 22, 2007, from http://www. oreillynet.com/ pub/ a/ oreilly/ tim/ news/ 2005/ 09/ 30/ what- is- web- 20.html

O'Reilly, T. (2007a). Call for a blogger's code of conduct. *O'Reilly Radar* blog. Retrieved May 17, 2010, from http://radar.oreilly.com/ archives/ 2007/ 03/ call_ for_ a_ blog_ 1.html

O'Reilly, T. (2007b). Code of conduct: Lessons learned so far. *O'Reilly Radar* blog. Retrieved May17, 2010, from http://radar.oreilly.com/ archives/ 2007/ 04/ code_ of_ conduct.html

O'Reilly, T. (2007c). Draft Blogger's code of conduct. *O'Reilly Radar* blog. Retrieved May 17, 2010, from http://radar.oreilly.com/ archives/ 2007/ 04/ draft- bloggers- 1.html

Papacharissi, Z. (2004). Democracy online: Civility, politeness and the democratic potential of online political discussion groups. *New Media & Society,* *6*(2), 259–283. doi:10.1177/1461444804041444

Penny, L. (2010). Comments policy. Retrieved June 7, 2010, from http://pennyred.blogspot.com/

Pfaffenberger, B. (2002). A standing wave in the web of our communications: Usenet and the socio-technical construction of cyberspace values. In Lueg, C., & Fisher, D. (Eds.), *From Usenet to CoWebs: Interacting with social information spaces.* New York: Springer Verlag.

Pinhanez, C. (1994-95). *Open Diary blog.* Retrieved April 16, 2007, from http://www.geocities. com/ pinhanez/ open_diary/ open_diary.htm

Rawlinson, L. (2007, May 29). *Is it time to crack down on the blogosphere?* Retrieved May 18, 2010, from http://edition.cnn.com/ 2007/ TECH/ 05/ 17/ blog.crackdown/

Read, B. (2006, October). 27). Can Wikipedia ever make the grade? *The Chronicle of Higher Education,* 31.

Reynolds, G. (2007, April 9). Proposing a blogger code of conduct. *Instapundit* blog. Retrieved May 19, 2007, from http://instapundit.com/ archives2/004011.php

Rheingold, H. (1993). *The virtual community: Homesteading on the virtual frontier.* Boston, MA: Addison Wesley.

Rule, C. (2005). The role of manners in a divided society. *Colin Rule's Blog.* Retrieved April 19, 2007, from http://cyberlaw.stanford.edu/ blogs/ rule/ archives/ 003592.shtml

Rulon, M. (2005, October 3). Blogs test campaign freedoms. *Cincinnati Enquirer.* Retrieved April 23, 2007, from http://news.enquirer.com/ apps/ pbcs. dll/ article? AID=/ 20051003/ NEWS01/ 510030352

Schwartz, M. (2008, August 3). The trolls among us. *New York Times Magazine*. Retrieved May 18, 2010, from http://www.nytimes.com/ 2008/ 08/ 03/ magazine/ 03trolls-t. html?pagewanted= all

Scoble, R. (2007, April 8). Code of conduct or not? *Scobleizer* blog. Retrieved May 21, 2010, from http://scobleizer.com/ 2007/ 04/ 08/ code- of- conduct- or- not/

Seligman, A. (1992). *The idea of civil society*. New York, NY: Free Press.

Sierra, K. (2007a, March 26). *A very sad day*. Retrieved April 17, 2007, from http://headrush. typepad.com/ whathappened.html

Sierra, K. (2007b). Theoretically going to be in Monday's paper. *Workers Bee blog*. Retrieved April 26, 2007, from http://workerbeesblog. blogspot.com/ 2007/ 04/ theoretically- going- to-be- in- mondays- ny.html

Slashdot. (2010). *Comments and moderation*. Retrieved May 26, 2010, from http://slashdot. org/faq/com-mod.shtml

Stall the Ball. (2007, April 12). *Code of conduct*. Retrieved June 7, 2010, from http://www.stallthe-ball.com/ index.php/ 2007/ 04/ 12/ code_of_con-duct

Stone, A. (1993). *What vampires know: Trans-subjection and transgender in Cyberspace*. Presentation at the In Control: Mensch-Interface-Maschine Symposium, Graz, Austria. Retrieved May 2, 2008, from http://gender.eserver.org/ what- vampires- know.txt

Surowiecki, J. (2005). *The wisdom of crowds*. New York, NY: Random House.

Taylor, D. (2007, June 2). Why I'll never sign up for any blogger code of conduct. *Intuitive Systems* blog. Retrieved June 2, 2007, from http://www. intuitive.com/ blog/ never_ sign_ up_ for_ blog-ger_ code_ of_ conduct.html

Technorati. (2008). *State of the blogosphere 2008: Introduction*. Retrieved May 18, 2010, from http:// technorati.com/ blogging/ article/ state- of- the- blogosphere- introduction/

The, W. E. L. L. (2010a). *What is The WELL?* Retrieved June 7, 2010, from http://www.well.com/

The, W. E. L. L. (2010b). *The Weird Conference*. Retrieved June 5, 2010, from http://www.well. com/ conf/ weird/

Usenet. (2007). *History of Usenet*. Retrieved June 10, 2007, from http://www.usenet.com/ articles/ history_ of_ usenet.htm

Van der Leun. G. (2007, April 9). No stinking badges. *American Digest* blog. Retrieved May 20, 2010, from http://americandigest.org/ mt-archives/ 006559.php

Viegas, F., Wattenberg, M., & Dave, K. (2004). *Studying cooperation and conflict between authors with history flow visualizations*. Paper presented at the Conference on Human Factors in Computing Conference, April 24–29, 2004 in Vienna, Austria.

Webopedia. (2007). *Entry for troll*. Retrieved from http://www.webopedia.com/ TERM/ T/ troll.html

Welch, J. (2007). Tim O'Reilly has lost his mind, and is taking others with him on the trip. *Bynkii.com* blog. Retrieved May 21, 2010, from http://www. bynkii.com/ archives/ 2007/ 04/ tim_ oreilly_ has_ lost_ his_ mind.html

Weyrich, S. (2010). GEnie: 1985-1999. *Apple II history*. Retrieved May 28, 2010, from http:// apple2history.org/ history/ ah22.html

Wikipedia. (2010). *Wikiquette alerts*. Retrieved June 6, 2010, from http://en.wikipedia.org/ wiki/ Wikipedia: Wikiquette_ alerts

KEY TERMS AND DEFINITIONS

Civil Society: A realm, distinct from markets or governments, where citizens respect diverse ideologies and work together for the common good.

Deliberative Discourse: Thoughtful conversation and debate, frequently addressing topics such as religion, politics or culture.

Flaming: The use of derogatory language, verbal harassment or personal insults during an online discussion.

Gatekeeper: An editor who deems which material is most significant to the publication's audience.

Public Sphere: A virtual or physical space where all are invited to exchange ideas, deliberate and voice opinions.

Virtual Community: An online network whose members routinely post and read comments, sometimes forging close personal relationships with one another despite having never met offline.

Section 2
Blogs and Blogging:
Case Studies

Chapter 6
Getting Schooled:
Basketball Blog KnickerBlogger.Net as a Case Study

Anastacia Kurylo
Marymount Manhattan College, USA

Michael Kurylo
KnickerBlogger.Net, USA

ABSTRACT

Although the entrance of blogs into mainstream sports media has not been firmly established, there is evidence that blogs have attained a growing level of credibility particularly as a result of their role in facilitating sports fan communities. Applying the metaphor of a classroom, this chapter discusses how an alternative perspective voiced on a blog can, through the blog's interactive features, create a community and enable the blog's transition into the mainstream. Founded in 2004, KnickerBlogger.Net was designed to fill a niche by providing a viewpoint that was not covered by mainstream sports media. The argument is made that by being a "classroom" for sports fans, KnickerBlogger.Net has created learning opportunities and transitioned from an unknown blog expressing one person's opinion to an affiliate of ESPN.com, a top sports network in the U.S.

INTRODUCTION

The word *blog* derives from logging one's thoughts about the Web (a Web log); it was transformed into its current form when Peter Merholz repositioned the letters from *Web blog* to *We blog* in 1999. In August of that year, Pyra Labs launched Blogger.com, which introduced the term to a larger audience. In 2003 Blogger.com was purchased by Google, and by 2007 it became the 16th most visited domain on the Web. By 2003 there were already four million blogs (Dyrud & Worley, 2005). More recently, specialized search engines and meta-directories like BlogPulse.com or Technorati.com have tracked between 50 and 85 million blogs (Schmidt, 2007, p. 1409).

DOI: 10.4018/978-1-60960-744-9.ch006

Although the entrance of blogs into mainstream sports media has not been firmly established, there is evidence that blogs have attained a growing level of credibility, particularly as a result of their role in facilitating sports fan communities. The purpose of this chapter is to demonstrate that blogs can become more than online journals whose reflection is viewed as idiosyncratic, personal, and unique. Instead, at least in the case of one sports blog, KnickerBlogger.Net, blogs can shift to become virtual learning environments, much like a traditional classroom, allowing alternative viewpoints to transition into the mainstream. The name is derived from the words *Knickerbockers*, the name of the New York National Basketball Association Franchise, and *blogger* the term for someone who blogs.

Blogs, as described by Kelleher and Miller (2006) are characterized by: (1) frequent updating, (2) reverse chronological order, (3) inclusion of personal journal material, (4) ability of readers to comment, and (5) hyperlinks. According to Kelleher and Miller's criteria, KnickerBlogger.Net is a typical blog. In another way, KnickerBlogger.Net is far from a typical blog in that it meets Trammell and Keshelashvili (2005) definition of an "A-list" blog or "a blog that [has] a high readership, resulting in numerous links to the blog... maintained by one person and hyperlinked from at least 100 other blogs, meaning other websites have provided a link to the site, thereby supporting the claim that these blogs are influential" (p. 973). Currently, KnickerBlogger.Net typed into Google's search query produces 56,800 hits.

As a typical and not so typical blog that covers a somewhat innocuous topic and has endured when other blogs remain stagnant or disappear altogether, KnickerBlogger.Net provides a unique opportunity to explore how blogs are able to transcend their use for personal reflection and transition into the mainstream. This case study compares KnickerBlogger.Net to an educational environment through the metaphor of a classroom and its tangible, typical, and traditional features:

classroom, content, instructor, students, class discussion, norms and rules of behavior, and evidence of student learning and satisfaction.

BACKGROUND: KNICKERBLOGGER.NET

In 2004, Mike Kurylo, a mathematician inspired by the work of statistically oriented ESPN writers Rob Neyer and John Hollinger, founded KnickerBlogger.Net because he identified a lack of knowledge related to statistical analysis in most mainstream National Basketball Association's (NBA) sites. Neyer and Hollinger were disciples of Bill James, arguably the grandfather of the modern sports blog, who self-published his revolutionary statistical work on baseball titled *The Bill James Baseball Abstract* (1985). Although statistics had been used in baseball and, to a lesser extent, basketball for decades, they were often misunderstood or applied incorrectly. James, Neyer, and Hollinger sought to provide better insight and newer methods for statistical analysis in sports to replace archaic ones. Kurylo focused his site on basketball statistical analysis.

Mainstream basketball analysts typically used archaic statistics in an effort to explain concepts to readers. For instance one method of evaluating a player is by the percentage of two-point shots made by attempt, also known as *field goal percentage* (fg%). A player that attempts six shots and makes three has a field goal percentage of 50%. Since the 1980 season, the NBA has added the three-point shot, which is a lower percentage shot but with a higher return. Comparing the previous player to one that attempts six three-point shots and makes two is useful. The latter has a lower *field goal percentage* (33%), but scores the same amount of points (six) as the former. Therefore, *field goal percentage* is a poor indicator of a player's scoring efficiency. Efficiency is important because the three-point shot player took fewer shots and produced the same outcome but conserved more energy compared to the person who made more shots. An updated metric exists, *effective field goal percentage* (efg%), which was at one time called *adjusted field goal percentage* (afg%), that gives a 50% bonus for the three-point shot. Using this statistic, both players who scored six points on six shot attempts have an identical effective field goal percentage of 50%.[1]

At the time of KnickerBlogger.Net's inception, nearly all of the mainstream sports media used the flawed field goal percentage instead of the more explanatory effective field goal percentage, but within its first month KnickerBlogger. Net had an article explaining efg% (then called "afg%") and quickly incorporated it into its lexicon (KnickerBlogger.Net, March 9, 2004). Field goal percentage was just one of many faulty metrics used by mainstream basketball analysts in 2004 when KnickerBlogger.Net was created. In 2005, NBA writer Kevin Pelton said, "The blog boom has had its impact on statistical analysis. The premier analytical blog, KnickerBlogger.Net, sprung up last season but really caught stride in 2004-05, leading ESPN.com columnist Eric Neel to term the site 'indispensable'" (Pelton, 2005). In 2009, another NBA blog said, "[KnickerBlogger] has been focusing on [basketball statistics] for a long time now as anyone, and he really knows how to break it all down in (relatively) plain English" (Wade, 2009). Based on the descriptions by Pelton and Wade, KnickerBlogger decided to playfully dub his site, "The NBA's indispensable premier analytical blog." The goal of the site is to educate readers on the better statistics available in sports. In doing so, the blog functions as an educational environment that can impact mainstream viewpoints.

REVIEW OF LITERATURE

Numerous studies have explored how participatory media like blogs can impact mainstream viewpoints such as through facilitating or hinder-ing civic engagement and activism (e.g., Baum & Groeling, 2008; Nah, Veenstra, & Shah, 2006; Trammell, Williams, Postelnicu, & Landreville, 2006; Wojcieszak & Mutz, 2009). Research has discussed the critical role participatory media have played in a variety of crises including natural disasters (Thelwall & Stuart, 2007), personal and sensitive medical issues (e.g., Weisgerber, 2004), and the pet food crisis (Stephens & Malone, 2008). Jansen and Koop (2005) opine on the future of democracy facilitated by the Internet when they note that "the ability of the Internet to allow for citizen interaction that is inexpensive, instantaneous, and not bound by geography opens up possibilities for citizen deliberation" (p. 614). The invitation to participation that alternative media allow particularly facilitates those who are already motivated to voice their views and engage in dialogue and debate on particular issues (Kavanaugh, Kim, Pe´rez-Quinones, Schmitz, & Isenhour, 2008).

As a result of their role in facilitating sports fan communities, blogs have begun to be viewed as credible sources of sports news and information. Particularly, this credence has been achieved when blogs are associated with mainstream sports news organizations or when they are viewed as substitutes for mainstream sports media. Banning and Sweetser (2007) note that "the branding of online content with a trusted source name (such as the *New York Times* or CNN) can increase credibility of content found online" (p. 452). Even without sponsorship by or association with mainstream media, Banning and Sweetser (2007) concluded from their study that "blogs achieved a credibility standing in line with traditional media. This suggests that a person with a computer and knowledge may be able to access the kind of credibility available previously just to traditional media" (p. 462). Several studies have considered the credibility of online news (e.g., Bucy, 2003; Cassidy, 2007; Johnson & Kaye, 2004). Sweetser, Porter, Chung, and Kim (2008) found that both journalists and public relations practitioners "who regularly used blogs for noninteractive research and surveillance purposes found that information more credible" (p. 179).

The credibility afforded to blogs has sparked the interest of instructors. Quible (2005) elaborates on the benefits of using blogs in the classroom noting that they are free to make and read, quick to access, and efficient to provide information to students; they also provide students with practical online experience. As such, their use in pedagogy continues to be explored. Flatley (2005) discusses how his incorporation of blogs into course assignments proved successful especially with regard to facilitating collaboration. He concludes that blogs are functional and not merely a fad stating "their use in politics, marketing, and the classroom indicate they are working, and their potential looks bright" (p. 79). The use of blogs in the classroom has become a fruitful and interesting area of research (e.g., Flatley, 2005; Hewling, 2006; Quible, 2005; Vess, 2005). The current study extends this interest in blogs and pedagogy by discussing how blogs can act as a "classroom."

METHOD

This chapter uses case study methodology to analyze the experience through which a blog, begun as an opportunity to share personal reflection on a specific topic, gains legitimacy. A case study provides the opportunity for in-depth analysis of a single case (Tesch, 1992) and is a useful method for elucidating the particularities of complex and inherently interesting issues relevant in a specific case (Stake, 2000). As indicated, the case study of KnickerBlogger.Net is explored using the metaphor of a classroom to provide a framework from which to understand one blog's successful transitioning into a mainstream sports media outlet.

Since its founding in February of 2004, KnickerBlogger.Net averages 3.4 articles per week, more during the active months of the NBA season. The site is designed such that a hyperlinked title to the newest article appears at the top, with the second newest below it, and so forth. Upon clicking on the link to an article, the reader is brought to a page with the contents of the article. These are written by one of several authors for the site, with the predominant one being the founder of the site Mike Kurylo. Articles sometimes contain a commentary/editorial style of writing. A reader can comment on each article and also see comments from others as well. Often in the article and occasionally in the comments, hyperlinks will be created allowing access to relevant content on other sites.

Because of its typical and atypical character, KnickerBlogger.Net was chosen for this case study. Additionally, two other reasons make the blog appropriate for deeper exploration. First, unlike blogs that speak to political or social issues, KnickerBlogger.Net covers basketball, an American pastime and, as such, a fairly innocuous topic not likely to stir controversy or emotion. Second, KnickerBlogger.Net is an enduring blog in that it has been in regular production since 2004. This contrasts with many blogs that are abandoned and left without updates, stationary but forgotten in cyberspace (Li & Walejko, 2008).

Advice about how blogs become successful abound. For example, one website lists the following "Essential Requirements to Starting a Successful Blog" (About.com, 2010):

- A Subject People are Interested In
- Passion for Your Subject
- Commitment
- Time
- A Desire to Network
- A Desire to Keep Learning
- A Love of Research and Reading
- Creativity
- Patience

However, a successful blog requires more than adhering to a checklist. Although, the unique intricacies and idiosyncrasies of a single case can not be generalized, the case presented in this chapter is suggestive about how other blogs that deal with socially relevant and important issues and which have a motivated and invested audience may transition into the mainstream.

STUDY RESULTS

This case study demonstrates that in addition to the use of blogs as components of class curriculum, a blog can be shown to act as a classroom itself. The metaphor of the classroom is used to provide a viewpoint through which to understand the transition of KnickerBlogger.Net to mainstream sports media. Specifically, KnickerBlogger.Net will be shown to incorporate the tangible components of an educational environment: classroom, content, instructor, students, class discussion, norms and rules of behavior, and evidence of student learning and satisfaction.

Blog as a Classroom

Unlike a traditional classroom environment that occupies real space in real time, KnickerBlogger.Net as a "classroom" for sports fans does not require seats for students, walls, a floor, or a ceiling. Nonetheless, it provides a virtual space for education to take place and as such provides a location like a classroom for people with similar goals to congregate, discuss and share ideas, and read material relevant to the topic about which they want to learn. Some typical classroom elements are included even in this type of virtual classroom. The website itself acts as the blackboard and the location of discussion. Moreover, much like a classroom, the website is accessible to those who wish to learn about a particular topic in depth.

Like a classroom, blogs are locations in which disagreement can spark "a reasonable level of debate" (Jansen & Koop, 2005, p. 630). KnickerBlogger.Net provides a location for alternative viewpoints to be expressed. Comments can be posted by anyone who has registered. KnickerBlogger.Net has approximately 500 people registered. The comment section on his site provides the opportunity for readers to engage with the material, demonstrate their own knowledge, gain clarification, or express dissent. For example, in one statistical study conducted by KnickerBlogger, he showed that players who get only a few minutes on the court have the same per minute production if given more playing time. One poster noted that the study could be strengthened by splitting the group into two random groups and comparing them. Upon that suggestion, KnickerBlogger performed a second analysis showing essentially the same results. Through the comment section of the blog readers debate the merits and values of various topics. For instance in one article the author and readers argue the relative worth of statistics vs. observational methods, and the different types of equations used to gauge a player's worth (KnickerBlogger.Net, June 23, 2007). In another instance, within a four-day span from February 16, 2010 to February 20, 2010, 366 comments were made in response to three different articles on the site expressing opinions regarding the trades the New York Knicks had made. Posters not only debate each other, but at times will question or contradict the poster of the comment as well. Both posters and KnickerBlogger are subject to the same scrutiny by readers.

Content

KnickerBlogger.Net provides virtual space in which people can learn substantive content related to statistical analysis in basketball through course readings made available in a variety of forms including hyperlinks, a basketball statistics page, and a tutorial. Hyperlinks provide relevant links to sources such as other noteworthy Web pages to provide readings related to the content of the blog. The statistics page offers an updated advanced statistical outlook for the current season that acts as a reference for those who want to see original data themselves, provide support for their own arguments, or create their own predictions. The tutorial titled *A Layman's Guide to Advanced NBA Statistics* (KnickerBlogger.Net, October 29, 2007) is included for readers who may not be familiar with the topic of advanced basketball statistical analysis or may need assistance to keep up the pace with the discussion. The tutorial, written in a style that is accessible to the common fan regardless of his or her statistical expertise, is where visitors get a crash course in many of the terms and metrics used on the site.

The primary material for the class remains the blogs themselves. Cumulatively, these articles function as a textbook. These articles range in size from one paragraph up to multiple articles in a series over a period of weeks. For instance in the summer of 2009, KnickerBlogger.Net published 12 articles in a series titled *2009 Report Cards* spanning approximately 2 months. Article titles from 2010 included: *Some Good News for A Change – Projected Cap For 2010-11 To Be $56.1 Million*; *Refs Partly To Blame For Garnett Suspension*; *David Lee – Impending Buyer's Remorse*; *Knicks Draft Prospects*; and *Birth Of A Knick Fan For Life*. Through these articles, KnickerBlogger. Net essentially assigns regular readings related to the substantive content of the site. These readings range from introspective observations, which give the site a subjective viewpoint, to articles weighty with statistics. Additionally, KnickerBlogger.Net occasionally features brief relevant annotated video of actual NBA plays in real time with narrated pop-up boxes applying statistical concepts in basketball and explaining the particular play being showcased.

Despite the transient nature of sports and entertainment news, the substantive content of the site has some consistency from year to year. At the start of the basketball season the site contains season previews. Throughout the season, game previews are posted. At the end of the season, report cards are given for the Knicks players as a way to evaluate their performance. Additionally, some topics that directly or indirectly have implications for the Knicks will always be the basis of blogs as they occur throughout the on and off season: such as trade talks, changes in leadership, and, to a lesser extent, scandals.

Instructor

Mike Kurylo (also known as "KnickerBlogger") serves as the instructor for the site. Unlike a physically present instructor, a virtual instructor does not have the salience of his age, gender, or race to help or hurt his ability to establish authority. The anonymity afforded by the Internet allows bloggers and posters to use pseudonyms to potentially disguise their real identity and create their preferred identity (Qian & Scott, 2007). When he began the site, Mike Kurylo was a thirty year old, unknown, non-sports professional, sports enthusiast; however, this was not made known on the site. This was partially due to the commonality of anonymity in the earlier days of the Internet. Eventually over the years as bloggers in general began to feel more comfortable releasing their identity and as KnickerBlogger.Net grew in popularity and reputation, Mike Kurylo included his name on the site. In lieu of using his name, KnickerBlogger created his identity as an expert and professional through his interactions with others on the site.

Much like an instructor through class lecture, KnickerBlogger establishes his expertise as an instructor through his blogs and their inclusion and discussion of advanced basketball statistics. For example, using three articles within his first month he showed his understanding of possession based team statistics in *The Best & Worst Offenses & Defenses*, Pythagorean expected win percentage in *Lenny Wilkens: Good Or Bad?*, and match up probabilities in *The Next 5 Games*. Like a traditional course instructor, KnickerBlogger engages in considerable course preparation to prepare to discuss relevant content. Also, because of the quick paced nature of the sports field, KnickerBlogger stays up-to-date in the current events in his field by watching each game, reading other writers, attending team events, interacting with other writers and fans, and interviewing coaches and players. In these ways and by publishing consistently over time, he has established and continues to establish his expertise.

Like an instructor adapting his curriculum, KnickerBlogger makes constant efforts to improve the blog's content and format. One way he does this is by updating the design of his website, which is functional and relevant. In July of 2004 the site moved from Blogger.com to KnickerBlogger. Net in order to gain more control over how the site looked and could be maintained. In 2005, he changed the site so that instead of the full articles appearing on the front page one after another, only the titles appeared. This allowed for better mobility between articles, as opposed to scrolling down to find earlier topics. The site's use of a sidebar has also changed over the years. Early on it contained links to different blogs. Later it had links to the most recent comments. In 2009, after affiliation with the True Hoop blog network, a video player was included on the sidebar with videos of current NBA news. To be responsive to suggestions and concerns from those who comment on his blog, features on the site have been added and changed. For example, upon request from readers, a forum for comments was created on the site to enhance the ability of readers to communicate with each other in early of 2009. Three months later as a result of some complaint by readers the forum was removed and the previous format restored because the former had hampered communication unintentionally.

KnickerBlogger effectively manages online discussion much like an instructor keeping class discussion focused on a relevant topic. For example, in both his articles and in his response to comments, KnickerBlogger intentionally does not cover the potentially more popular topics of scandals and celebrity gossip. In 2007 when there was a highly publicized sexual harassment trial concerning MSG (the group that owns the team), Isiah Thomas, and star player Stephon Marbury, KnickerBlogger did not write any articles about it. When a poster commented, "It's weird how much coverage this suit is getting but it's not a topic on KnickerBlogger." KnickerBlogger replied, "I just don't see what this has to do with the season. It's different if Isiah/Marbury is suspended or worse. But until then it's all just speculation. If this wasn't a sex scandal and was an accounting scandal then I don't think it'd be getting a quarter of the attention the media is giving it. What can I say, I'm not a rubbernecker" (KnickerBlogger.Net, September 25, 2007). Once the trial reached a conclusion, KnickerBlogger.Net ran a three-part article linking the trial to the team's failure. Instead of focusing on the tawdry aspects, KnickerBlogger examined the issue by suggesting that it exposed a pattern of contempt the Knicks organization had for others and how this extended into poor decisions for the franchise. In this way, KnickerBlogger kept the blog's content focused responding to comments and posting on relevant, not tangential, topics.

KnickerBlogger acts as an instructor on his site in that he tailors his information to his audience in an accessible way so that it is easier for his readers to digest. This is particularly important considering the potentially intimidating and exclusive nature of advanced basketball statistical analysis. One way he makes his content accessible is with the use of descriptive words along with the statistical analysis he provides. For instance instead of mentioning that Bill Walker's *true shooting percentage* (ts%) is 64.9%, which would be meaningless for someone without intimate understanding of advanced sports statistics, KnickerBlogger said, "Walker's [sic] doesn't average a lot of points (15.4 pts/36 in 2010), but his efficiency (64.9% ts%, 62.5% efg%) is through the roof for a small forward. Only 10 players 6-6 or taller had a true shooting percentage of 60% or better last year, and no one other than Walker was north of 62%" (KnickerBlogger.Net, May 20, 2010). By using descriptive and casual language (such as "doesn't average a lot of points" and "through the roof") and by making comparisons (such as "only 10 players"), KnickerBlogger makes clear that Walker is a medium volume, yet highly efficient, shooter.

Students

KnickerBlogger.Net educates students in a community that encourages learning. Readers of KnickerBlogger.Net are from varied and, more often, unknown backgrounds. Because of the anonymity provided by the Internet, differences between students are neutralized. For example, in online environments, ethnicity becomes irrelevant. Instead, the student identity is defined by their commonality—their desire to gain knowledge on statistical analysis in basketball. In participatory media much like in non-mediated life, "people's social networks are homophilous. Birds of a feather stick together and friends seek out people who are like them" (Boyd, 2008, p. 243).

KnickerBlogger.Net provides an environment for motivated contributors to voice similar opinions through comments posted to the site's discussion board. These comments are usually related to the articles posted on the site or a recent relevant event, such as someone being signed to a contract with the Knicks. Readers, who are often highly motivated repeat visitors, return to the site on a regular basis not because they have paid for a course and are accountable for a grade but because of the value the topic has for them. For example, one regular poster is passionate about European basketball leagues and another is a practicing attorney in New York where networking by engaging in small talk about the Knicks is commonplace.

As a result of the educational environment that KnickerBlogger.Net provides, students develop their knowledge. Some readers, such as *mase* and *Count Zero*, have been around since the blog's inception. Other non-participating readers lurk on the site without ever posting. For example, "bbbb0123" posted a rare Thanksgiving comment

of appreciation, "I read countless debates on this website, I just simply don't post. I'm thankful there's such a smart blog out there, and I'm sure many other people feel that way, even if they never post or talk about it" (KnickerBlogger.Net, November 24, 2010). Other readers post comments more regularly on the discussion board. Some of these return as guest bloggers after years of posting comments on the site.

Engagement in a Discussion

Student participation in the classroom, much like reader participation on the blog, is integral to the educational experience. The most important and frequent form of participation that students engage in is class discussion. KnickerBlogger.Net provides a place for discussion like that which occurs in a classroom. Based on the articles on the site, readers are able to interact with each other through the comments which appear at the bottom of each article. The comments section allows for interaction like a class discussion because each person's comments are viewed publicly. Through this discussion readers demonstrate their willingness to engage in and learn complicated material. The following discussion stemmed from the KnickerBlogger.Net article titled *Jamal Crawford Named Sixth Man*.

Owen says:
April 27, 2010 at 5:44 pm

Yeah, congrats Jamal, why you put up a 57.3% ts% [true shooting percentage] in Atlanta and not in New York is a apbrmetrician's [basketball statistical expert] puzzle, but I am glad he made it happen somewhere…

KnickfaninNJ says:
April 28, 2010 at 6:08 am

Owen,

I don't think it's him being suddenly so much better, just him being in a better situation. He know [sic] has better players around him that the defense may be focusing on, and he may be facing the other teams bench more often than he used to, since he now comes off the bench also.

supernova says:
April 28, 2010 at 7:20 am

KnickfaninNJ,

I agree. Better situation (coming off the bench), surrounded by better players, turned Crawford's play around. In addition, maybe also lower expectations might have helped take some burden off him mentally, which ultimately helped his game.

Owen says:
April 28, 2010 at 10:38 am

KnicksFaninNJ –

Any time a player makes a move to a better team people predict that his efficiency will increase due to playing alongside better teammates. And vice versa for players moving to worse teams. It very rarely happens though. Generally, there is almost no change in efficiency. However, Jamal definitely proved to be an exception to the rule in Atlanta this year. It's interesting, his assist rate fell pretty drastically and his turnover rate declined, which suggests that they used him in more or [sic] a spot up role. However his usage was above his career average. Interesting puzzle...

Crawford finally achieved what we wanted him to, albeit for another team. However, I have to think there were a lot of players more deserving of the

Sixth Man Award, unless it's simply an award for best bench scorer...

(KnickerBlogger.Net, April 27, 2010)

During the discussion, Owen alters his view in light of KnicksfaninNJ's comments. The discussion is collegial using techniques familiar to students and instructors. Specifically, posters on KnickerBlogger.Net in this discussion refer to each other by name, offer evidence in support for each point, are generally polite, and state clearly whether there is agreement or disagreement with a previous point in order to transition from one to another smoothly, such as when KnickfaninNJ says, "I don't think it's him." Although this discussion takes place over a 24-hour period, it resembles the type of discussion that occurs in a classroom setting in real time.

As the above excerpt suggests, discussion on KnickerBlogger.Net is politically passive (Kavanaugh et al, 2008). Despite this, and much like a classroom discussion, KnickerBlogger.Net does not ignore anything that enters discussion in a relevant way. For example, the site recently wrote about the Arizona law viewed by many as racial profiling that adversely affects immigrants because its relevance crossed over into basketball. After being critiqued following a guest blog that made reference to the issue, KnickerBlogger responded.

KnickerBlogger says:
May 5, 2010 at 7:57 am

David approached me about this [aspect of the article] prior, and I gave my OK. Basically this is where a political event has crossed over into sports. So it now enters a area [sic] that is close to him, given his Arizona roots and his field of study. The interesting thing about this law, is that many experts feel it is unconstitutional and will be overturned in court. Also it is being derided by people on both sides of the aisle including (but not limited to) republicans like Jeb Bush,

Connie Mack IV, Marco Rubio, Lindsey Graham and Karl Rove. So I figured this wouldn't be a lightning rod of anger like some other political topics. *(KnickerBlogger.Net, May 4, 2010)*

The discussion on the website and in the specific examples above demonstrates that a community has been created on the site that encourages various viewpoints to be expressed.

Norms and Rules of Behavior

In any educational environment, there are norms and rules for behavior that allow the environment to remain productive for learning. Violations to norms and rules are formally or informally disciplined. Readers of KnickerBlogger.Net, like students in a classroom, are expected to know and abide by these norms and rules.

Knickblogger.Net is an environment with certain norms of behavior. Participants are expected to have some knowledge on the topic, especially with respect to basketball strategy and advanced metrics. When conversing with each other, they can either refer to the username or the comment number (in the style of Twitter). When referencing outside sources, they are expected to use hyperlinks. Additionally, they are expected to act with civility, and personal insults are not tolerated.

In addition to the norms of KnickerBlogger. Net, there are official rules. Today, when someone wants to make a comment on KnickerBlogger.Net, they need to register with a valid email address (there is no fee). When they sign up to register they have to agree to terms that state that they will be respectful of others. The terms designated by KnickerBlogger.Net are an example of the tone of the site overall, which is a tongue-in-cheek sarcastic style with little patience for the obvious, oblivious, or naïve.

"By clicking on the "I Agree" check box below, you agree to the following:

* *You are a human being*
* *You are not here to advertise*
* *You are here to talk about basketball*
* *You will be respectful of others*
* *You will not act like a jerk*
* *You will not act like an Internet Troll*

Failing to do so may require you to appear before me, at a place of my choosing and at your own cost, present me with a sum of money of my choosing, and allow me to give you one swift kick in your rear. You will agree to this kick and promise that I am not liable for any damage to you or your property by this said kick."

Readers of KnickerBlogger.Net are encouraged to participate. If they deviate from the focus on advanced statistics, they are corrected by the article writer or a reader. For instance, an informal example of discipline occurred when someone used a less credible statistic and KnickerBlogger commented, "I just want to point out that per-minute stats are highly reliable and much more consistent that [sic] per-game stats. It's a great way to compare players who play different minutes, and evaluate which players deserve more (or less) playing time" (KnickerBlogger.Net, July 23, 2007). Another example occurred when a reader making a similar correction stated, "However, the one problem I have is the statistical analysis of Hoopshype founder Jorge Sierra and the analyst he cites. He points to fg% instead of more accurate measures of scoring efficiency like efg% and ts%" (KnickerBlogger.Net, February 1, 2010).

At the extreme, people who do not abide by the norms and rules of KnickerBlogger.Net are formally disciplined by being subject to being blocked from contributing to the site or having posts removed from the discussion board. This has occurred approximately 10-20 times since the inception of the blog. One example of a removed comment:

"Well, * you, *!. EVERY SINGLE TIME, I have made my points without personal insults and will not accept * from a little * like you. I have every right to express my views, like everyone else. If you don't like it, don't read it. Be a man and debate with honesty. Branding me a "troll" for expressing views not similar to yours is the stuff of little * like your *, dead *." (KnickerBlogger. Net, December 11, 2009)

In addition to the norms and rules of the educational environment, the instructor has norms and rules that he creates and follows as well (Schmidt, 2007). For the instructor, ethical standards are a priority. This contrasts with stereotypes of sports writers as unethical or morally questionable in their journalism (Oates & Pauley, 2007; Wulfemeyer, 1985-86). Ethics for KnickerBlogger.Net involves assuring the accuracy of the site's content (blogger or reader generated). This focus on accuracy demonstrates the value he places on blogging and contrasts how some sports journalists and newspaper managers view blogging. In a study of these groups by Schultz and Sheffer (2007), one participant summed up their irreverence for blogging, "Editors want three or four people to read something before it gets in the paper, but don't care that no one reads anything before it goes online" (p. 71). For KnickerBlogger, however, accuracy and fact checking is integral to his statistical perspective dedicated to the mission of shifting the mindset of sports enthusiasts and professionals from hunches, superstitions, and basic sports statistics to statistical evidence at an advanced level.

Learning and Satisfaction

Readers can demonstrate their knowledge of basketball statistical analysis in a variety of ways. Regularly, blog readers demonstrate knowledge through comments. For example, at the end of each season KnickerBlogger.Net posts the year-end report cards in which the basketball players are evaluated by KnickerBlogger and guest bloggers. These writers and posters writing in response to these articles are informally assessed on how they respond to these report cards. The discussion board provides posters with the opportunity to discuss and demonstrate their knowledge of advanced basketball statistics. Occasionally readers are provided the opportunity to engage in quizzes or contests in which they can earn prizes or participate in the blog in the form of providing guest blog submissions. One such contest in which readers were encouraged to submit articles was called *Can You Be a KnickerBlogger?* The best articles were selected and appeared on the website.

Evidence of visitor satisfaction can be acquired in various and numerous ways. Blog popularity, for example, can be considered as one measure of satisfaction. Similarly, the number of people that visit, read, and post on a blog is an indicator of satisfaction. KnickerBlogger.Net enjoys a healthy readership (20,000-40,000 readers per month) and averages 38 comments per article. Over time, evidence emerges when readers graduate into becoming regularly contributing guest bloggers. At the time of this writing, there were 10 readers who have ascended into guest blogger status on KnickerBlogger.Net.

The most interesting case is that of "Thomas B." Thomas B. arrived as a poster with no knowledge of advanced metrics. In January of 2008, he commented, "Maybe you and I are not looking at the same stats when it comes to Denver's defense. Denver gives up 104 per game, that is good for 25th place in the NBA, that means only 5 teams give up more points" (KnickerBlogger. Net, January 4, 2008). KnickerBlogger replied that he should check out the article *A Layman's Guide to Advanced NBA Statistics*, and noted that Denver was 6th in the league on defense. Thomas B. replied, "Thanks for sharing that info. So does that mean Denver is actually a good defensive team? What would happen to the Knicks if they played at Denver's pace? Would they give up 110 per because they now give the other team more chances to score?" In this exchange, Knickerblogger seized what some might call a teaching moment or learning opportunity and over the months Thomas B. was able to understand advanced basketball statistics well enough to become an author and published his first article using those statistics and other advanced metrics (KnickerBlogger.Net, November 17, 2008).

The most meaningful indication of learning, however, came from a change in the mainstream view of advanced sports statistics. Lowrey and Mackay (2008) note this possibility when they argue that "awareness of local blogs has an impact on the way journalists practice their profession" (p. 75). Although not, yet, entirely accepted, there is anecdotal evidence of an increase in the popularity of these metrics. For example, recently the *New York Times* published one article using field goal percentage in an attempt to gauge a player's worth (Miller, 2010). In another piece a few months later they used the more accurate effective field goal percentage (Beck, 2010).

DISCUSSION

The role of KnickerBlogger.Net in facilitating the integration of advanced statistics into the mainstream understanding of basketball should not be overlooked. The increased popularity of KnickerBlogger.Net is indicated in the number of hits it receives. Within a year of its inception in 2004, KnickerBlogger.Net averaged approximately 4,000 unique visitors per month. It peaked in July of 2009 with 55,000 unique visitors. By 2009-2010, the blog averaged 30,000 visitors per month, depending on the activity of the team or league.

More notably even than the increased popularity as an indicator of the instructor's ideas being integrated into the mindset of the audience, with the help of others like him, is that KnickerBlogger. Net itself has been accepted into the mainstream. KnickerBlogger.Net has become part of ESPN's

True Hoop Network (THN). THN is an affiliation of independent blogs that work in concert with ESPN to provide complete coverage of each NBA team. Each team is covered by only one blog and KnickerBlogger.Net is the Knicks Blog (True Hoop, January 20, 2009). For KnickerBlogger this meant acceptance, confirmation, and kudos. Additionally, through this affiliation, KnickerBlogger has gained access to benefits that historically have been reserved for mainstream journalists including press credentials to attend basketball games and press conferences, invitations to team events, and interviews of players, coaches and general managers.

KnickerBlogger.Net's ascendance to mainstream in this way coincides with a general trend in large media conglomerates towards incorporating blogs into their websites. As Banning and Sweetser (2007, p. 452) emphasize, "In an effort to keep up with information trends, some news organizations have found themselves competing with sources even more non-traditional than those once labeled such. That is, the emergence of blogs as a citizen journalist device has prompted some news organizations to adopt this commentary, 'diary-like' approach to news and integrate blogs in their online offerings (Gillmor, 2004)." It is notable that of the approximately two dozen Knicks blogs most of which are not statistically slanted, KnickerBlogger.Net was invited to be a part of ESPN's True Hoop blog network.

CONCLUSION

Blogging is a popular topic of research by scholars and of interest to those who are computer savvy enough to follow or write a blog regularly. As varieties of blogs develop into infinite categories and basic topics on blogging research are exhausted, blogs will increasingly be viewed as more than personal journals. This chapter demonstrates that one way to view blogs differently is as a "classroom" in which, without vetting or policing by external agencies, learning is taking place that allows alternative viewpoints to gain legitimacy and transition into the mainstream. The present case study documents the increasing importance and power of blogs as learning environments beyond offering personal opinion.

The metaphor of an educational environment provides a lens through which to view the process whereby one sports blog and its topic, in its short history, gained legitimacy in mainstream sports media. The finding that a successful blog may mirror some of the characteristics of a classroom may resonate with instructors because oftentimes a blogger's goal and an instructor's goal may be similar. Both have as their priority the provision of information and perspectives on a specific topic to their audience in a personal way. A quick online search for "successful blogs" reflects this similarity. Successful blogs are those providing interesting and focused topics, those providing unique experiences, those connecting with their audience, and those demonstrating knowledge of and passion for their topic. The case study discussed in this chapter and its metaphor of a classroom suggests a way to understand the increase in mainstream acceptance of blogs.

This study suggests that blogs can be used not only to disseminate information but also to educate a motivated public about complex and difficult topics and through this educational process make changes in how the topic and/or its advocate are viewed by mainstream media. KnickerBlogger. Net was chosen because in many ways it is a typical blog and as such other blogs may be viewed similarly through the metaphor of the classroom. However, KnickerBlogger.Net is less typical in that it is an enduring A-list blog whose content is fairly innocuous. As a comparatively innocuous blog, it afforded the opportunity to understand the evolution of a blog from personal reflection into the mainstream without the emotional or cognitive baggage that would be involved if a blog on a more controversial topic was studied.

While many blogs are launched and almost as often abandoned or forgotten, bloggers that engage their audiences in ways similar to how an instructor engages students in a classroom may be able to increase their spheres of influence and endure over time. A blogger with a motivated community whose blog may be viewed through the lens of having incorporated features similar to a classroom, content, instructor, students, discussion, norms and rules, and evidence of student satisfaction and learning may be able to transition a blog's viewpoints into the mainstream. However, an unethical blogger, or a blogger with viewpoints that are deviant within a culture, or a blogger motivated towards self-serving ends, may be able to inform and bring about changes in the acceptance of his or her perspectives as quickly as KnickerBlogger.Net was able to do.

REFERENCES

About.com. (2010). *Essential requirements to starting a successful blog*. Retrieved December 1, 2010, from http://weblogs.about.com/od/ starting-ablog/tp/ SuccessfulBlogRequirements.htm

Banning, S. A., & Sweetser, K. D. (2007). How much do they think it affects them and whom do they believe? Comparing the third-person effect and credibility of blogs and traditional media. *Communication Quarterly*, *55*, 451–466. doi:10.1080/01463370701665114

Basketball-Reference.Com. (2000-2010). *Glossary*. Retrieved June 10, 2010, from http://www. basketball-reference.com/ about/glossary.html

Baum, M. A., & Groeling, T. (2008). New media and the polarization of American political discourse. *Political Communication*, *25*, 1–39. doi:10.1080/10584600802426965

Beck, H. (2010, May 8). *NBA Postseason ruled by well-worn maxim: "The game slows down".* Retrieved June 10, 2010, from http://www.nytimes.com/2010/05 /09/sports/basketball/ 09offense.html

Boyd, D. (2008). Can social network sites enable political action? *International Journal of Media and Cultural Politics, 4,* 241–263. doi:10.1386/macp.4.2.241_3

Bucy, E. P. (2003). Media credibility reconsidered: Synergy effects between on-air and online news. *Journalism & Mass Communication Quarterly, 80,* 247–264.

Cassidy, W. P. (2007). Online news credibility: An examination of the perceptions of newspaper journalists. *Journal of Computer-Mediated Communication, 12,* 144–164. doi:10.1111/j.1083-6101.2007.00334.x

Flatley, M. E. (2005). Blogging for enhanced teaching and learning. *Business Communication Quarterly, 68,* 77–80. doi:10.1177/108056990506800111

Hewling, A. (2006). Culture in the online class: Using message analysis to look beyond nationality-based frames of reference. *Journal of Computer-Mediated Communication, 11,* 337–356. doi:10.1111/j.1083-6101.2006.tb00316.x

James, B. (1985). *The Bill James baseball abstract.* Chicago, IL: Free Press.

Jansen, H. J., & Koop, R. (2005). Pundits, ideologues, and ranters: The British Columbia election online. *Canadian Journal of Communication, 30,* 613–632.

Johnson, T. J., & Kaye, B. K. (2004). Wag the blog: How reliance on traditional media and the internet influence credibility perceptions of weblogs among blog users. *Journalism & Mass Communication Quarterly, 81,* 622–642.

Kavanaugh, A., Kim, B. J., Perez-Quinones, M. A., Schmitz, J., & Isenhour, P. (2008). Net gains in political participation: Secondary effects of Internet on community. *Information Communication and Society, 11,* 933–963. doi:10.1080/13691180802108990

Kelleher, T., & Miller, B. M. (2006). Organizational blogs and the human voice: Relational strategies and relational outcomes. *Journal of Computer-Mediated Communication, 11,* 395–414. doi:10.1111/j.1083-6101.2006.00019.x

KnickerBlogger.Net. (2004, March 9). *AFG%.* Retrieved June 10, 2010, from http://www.KnickerBlogger.net/?p=608

KnickerBlogger.Net. (2007, June 23). *Trading David Lee for Kobe Bryant straight-up: Shrewd sabermetrics or laugh test flunkie?* Retrieved June 10, 2010, from http://www.KnickerBlogger.net/?p=561

KnickerBlogger.Net. (2007, September 25). *Knicks 2007 report card (A to Z): Coach Isiah Thomas.* Retrieved December 1, 2010 from http://knickerblogger.net/knicks-2007-report-card-a-to-z-coach-isiah-thomas/

KnickerBlogger.Net. (2007, October 29). *A layman's guide to advanced NBA statistics.* Retrieved June 10, 2010, from http://www.KnickerBlogger.net/?p=608

KnickerBlogger.Net. (2008, January 4). *The poison of 20 and 10.* Retrieved December 1, 2010, from http://knickerblogger.net/ the-poison-of-20-and-10/

KnickerBlogger.Net. (2008, November 17). *Knicks week in advance 11/16/2008.* Retrieved June 10, 2010, from http://www.KnickerBlogger.net/?p=1022

KnickerBlogger.Net. (2009, December 11). *2009 game thread: NYK @ NOH.* Retrieved December 1, 2010, from http://knickerblogger.net/2009-game-thread-nyk-noh/

KnickerBlogger.Net. (2010, February 1). *Does T-Mac make sense for New York?* Retrieved December 1, 2010, from http://knickerblogger.net/does-t-mac-make-sense-for-new-york/

KnickerBlogger.Net. (2010, April 27). *Jamal Crawford named sixth man.* Retrieved June 10, 2010, from http://www.KnickerBlogger.net/?p=3618

KnickerBlogger.Net. (2010, May 4). *Viva Los Suns.* Retrieved June 10, 2010, from http://www.KnickerBlogger.net/ 3653/viva-los-suns.html

KnickerBlogger.Net. (2010, May 20). *2010 report card: Bill Walker.* Retrieved December 1, 2010 from http://knickerblogger.net/ 2010-report-card-bill-walker/

KnickerBlogger.Net. (2010, November 24). *What I, as a Knick fan, am thankful for.* Retrieved December 1, 2010, from http://knickerblogger.net/what-i-as-a-knick-fan-am-thankful-for/

Li, D., & Walejko, G. (2008). Splogs and abandoned blogs: The perils of sampling bloggers and their blogs. *Information Communication and Society, 11,* 279–296. doi:10.1080/13691180801947976

Lowrey, M., & Mackay, J. B. (2008). Journalism and blogging: A test of a model of occupational competition. *Journalism Practice, 2,* 64–81. doi:10.1080/17512780701768527

Miller, S. (2010, February, 20). *After James, the choices aren't easy.* Retrieved June 10, 2010, from http://www.nytimes.com/2010/ 02/21/sports/basketball /21score.html

Nah, S., Veenstra, A. S., & Shah, D. V. (2006). The Internet and anti-war activism: A case study of information, expression, and action. *Journal of Computer-Mediated Communication, 12,* 230–247. doi:10.1111/j.1083-6101.2006.00323.x

Oates, T. P., & Pauly, J. (2007). Sports journalism as moral and ethical discourse. *Journal of Mass Media Ethics, 22,* 332–347. doi:10.1080/08900520701583628

Pelton, K. (2005, July 14). *2004-05: The year in stats.* Retrieved June 10, 2010, from http://www.82games.com/pelton1.htm

Qian, H., & Scott, C. R. (2007). Anonymity and self-disclosure on weblogs. *Journal of Computer-Mediated Communication, 12,* 1428–1451. doi:10.1111/j.1083-6101.2007.00380.x

Quible, Z. K. (2005). Blogging: A natural in business communication courses. *Business Communication Quarterly, 68,* 73–76. doi:10.1177/108056990506800110

Schmidt, J. (2007). Blogging practices: An analytical framework. *Journal of Computer-Mediated Communication, 12,* 1409–1427. doi:10.1111/j.1083-6101.2007.00379.x

Schultz, B., & Sheffer, M. L. (2007). Sports journalists who blog cling to traditional values. *Newspaper Research Journal, 28,* 62–76.

Stake, R. E. (2000). Case studies. In N. K. Denzin & Y. S. Lincoln (Eds.), *Handbook of qualitative research* (2 ed., pp. 435-454). Thousand Oaks, CA: Sage Publications.

Stephens, K. K., & Malone, P. C. (2009). If the organizations won't give us information...: The use of multiple new media for crisis technical translation and dialogue. *Journal of Public Relations Research, 21,* 229–239. doi:10.1080/10627260802557605

Sweetser, K. D., Porter, L. V., Chung, D. S., & Kim, E. (2008). Credibility and the use of blogs among professionals in the communication industry. *Journalism & Mass Communication Quarterly, 85*, 169–185.

Tesch, R. (1990). *Qualitative research: Analysis types and software tools.* New York, NY: Falmer Press.

Thelwall, M., & Stuart, D. (2007). RUOK? Blogging communication technologies during crises. *Journal of Computer-Mediated Communication, 12*, 189–214. doi:10.1111/j.1083-6101.2007.00336.x

Trammell, K. D., & Keshelashvili, A. (2005). Examining the new influencers: A self-presentation study of A-list blogs. *Journalism & Mass Communication Quarterly, 82*, 968–982.

Trammell, K. D., Williams, A. P., Postelnicu, M., & Landreville, K. D. (2006). Evolution of online campaigning: Increasing interactivity in candidate websites and blogs through text and technical features. *Mass Communication & Society, 9*, 21–44. doi:10.1207/s15327825mcs0901_2

TrueHoop. (2009, January 20). *The inauguration of the TrueHoop network.* Retrieved June 10, 2010, from http://espn.go.com/blog/truehoop /post/_/ id/5826/ the-inauguration-of-the- truehoop-network

Vess, D. L. (2005). Scholarship of teaching and learning: Asynchronous discussion and communication patterns in online and hybrid history courses. *Communication Education, 54*, 355–364. doi:10.1080/03634520500442210

Wade, J. (2009, November 30). *Hey everybody – Listen to me talk.* Retrieved June 10, 2010, from http://www.eightpointsnineseconds.com /2009/11/hey-everybody- listen-to-me-talk/

Weisgerber, C. (2004). Turning to the internet for help with sensitive medical problems: A qualitative study of the construction of a sleep disorder through online interaction. *Information Communication and Society, 7*, 554–574. doi:10.1080/1369118042000305647

Wojcieszak1, M. E., & Mutz, D. C. (2009). Online groups and political discourse: Do online discussion spaces facilitate exposure to political disagreement? *Journal of Communication, 59*, 40–56.

Wulfemeyer, K. T. (1985-1986). Ethics in sports journalism: Tightening up the code. *Journal of Mass Media Ethics, 1*, 57–67.

KEY TERMS AND DEFINITIONS

Adjusted Field Goal Percentage (afg%): An early name used for effective field goal percentage.

Blog: Derives from logging one's thoughts about the Web (a Web log), and transformed into its current form when Peter Merholz repositioned the letters from "Web blog" to "We blog" in 1999.

Effective Field Goal Percentage (efg%): Percentage of two-point shots made by attempts to make a shot adjusted to give a 50% bonus for the three-point shot.

Field Goal Percentage (fg%): Percentage of two-point shots made by attempts to make a shot.

Internet Troll: A: person who provokes other online readers in an attempt to elicit an emotional response. The Internet Troll is viewed unfavorably because they often disrupt the normal conversation by steering it towards their own desired goal.

KnickerBlogger: The term is a combination of "Knickerbockers," the name of the New York National Basketball Association Franchise, and "blogger" the term for someone who blogs. Knickerblogger references the creator of Knickerblogger.Net and the main author of articles to the site. It also serves as the nickname for Knickerblogger.Net.

KnickerBlogger.Net: The term is used for the website created by Mike Kurylo in 1994 to discuss advanced basketball statistical analysis.

True Shooting Percentage (ts%): A measure of a player's ability to shoot efficiently. Unlike field goal percentage and effective field goal percentage, true shooting percentage includes free throws.

ENDNOTE

[1]   For more information, see http://www.basketball-reference.com.

Chapter 7
Rebels, Heretics, and Exiles:
Blogging among Estranged and Questioning American Hasidim

Naomi Gold
Samford University, USA

ABSTRACT

The advent of blogging has created a medium in which estranged and disaffected members of religious groups, such as American Hasidim, have written about experiences of alienation from and critical perceptions of their spiritual communities. These blogs have an emancipating function, allowing writers unprecedented freedom of speech and expression. Moreover, such online journals often enjoy a diverse readership beyond the geographical and cultural borders of their respective communities. The present study draws on narrative analysis to explore the ways in which blogging by former and questioning members of Hasidic communities reflects the pursuit of new meaning and direction in their lives. The author contends that blogging among disaffected Hasidim challenges Hasidic communities and offers opportunities for communal self-scrutiny, revitalization, and progress toward engaging difficult and important issues that have been introduced into Orthodox Jewish life by the information and communication revolution.

INTRODUCTION AND BACKGROUND

Blogging can be viewed as a natural extension of conversations that are being conducted via other media, or through conversations that were formerly conducted in more contained and limited venues. Blogging also functions as a public form of journaling, since numerous blogs are spaces in which writers convey observations that were once material for diaries and personal records. One of the medium's most prominent innovations is its provision for exchange between writers and readers. Blogging, therefore, comprises both reflection and conversation taken to electronic lengths. The enormous range of blogs reflects the diversity of human interests and culture, as

DOI: 10.4018/978-1-60960-744-9.ch007

blogging has emerged as an ubiquitous vehicle of self-expression and communication. Blogging has also opened avenues of communication for individuals who were formerly isolated, allowing unprecedented opportunities for exchanging ideas and sharing thoughts and experiences. One of the most interesting examples of this trend involves bloggers belonging to American Hasidic Jewish communities, whose members are adherents of a strictly fundamentalist interpretation of Judaism.[1]

Residents of urban regions of the United States, such as New York and Miami Beach, frequently encounter bearded and black-suited men and boys, as well as women and girls dressed in patently modest attire. Such individuals may be affiliated with any number of Orthodox Jewish communities, all of which adhere to varying standards of dress and demeanor, and significantly, strict codes of behavior and lifestyle that mandate limited contact with the dominant, secular culture. This chapter focuses specifically on Orthodox Jewish communities whose members identify themselves as *Hasidim*, a term derived from the Hebrew word *hesed* that means literally "loving-kindness," and that also has come to signify "pious." As Judith Baumel-Schwartz, professor of Jewish history at Bar-Ilan University in Ramat Gan, Israel, writes,

There is no precise number of Orthodox Jews in the world today, although various studies speak of approximately 12 million Jews worldwide, about 1.5 million of whom are Orthodox. Orthodox Judaism today ranges from Modern Orthodox (MO) to the more right-wing Haredim who are in turn composed of three subgroups: Hassidim, Mitnagdim (also called "Lithuanian" or "Yeshivish") and Sefaradi (Oriental) Haredim. MO and Haredi Jews follow the same basic tradition, but differ in terms of strictness of religious observance of non-halachic issues. These include dress codes, attitude towards language and music, the degree to which they engage or disengage with secular society, the weight each group assigns to Torah study, their attitude towards the State of Israel, the role that they assign women in religious society and their degree of interaction with non-Jews. (2009, p. 2)

To date, there is a paucity of research focused on the relationship between the Internet and Orthodox Judaism, despite the fact that Internet technology dominates and has decisively transformed 21st-century communication practices (Rashi, 2011). In a discussion of Internet forums utilized by Orthodox Jewish women, Baumel-Schwarz (2009) points to a number of methodological issues "… connected with the nature and problems of the Internet in general and virtual communities in particular," citing veracity, representation, and research scope as some of the most essential (p. 6). The question of veracity asks whether the people communicating in the forums and blogs really are who they claim to be. Baumel-Schwarz responds by noting that the "close-knit nature of the Orthodox Jewish world" makes it likely that many of the virtual discussants have some level of personal acquaintance with each other that enhances the level of trust in their online communication. This observation is confirmed by material contained in this chapter, as is her comment that it is not unusual for some bloggers to eventually volunteer personal information online.

The second issue Baumel-Schwartz addresses is representation: to what extent are the founders of and contributors to the Internet forums and blogs representative of their respective communities? An answer to this question can be approached by attending to a small body of research treating the phenomenon of alienation in fundamentalist Jewish communities, which corroborates blog content and confirms the existence of estrangement as a verifiable phenomenon (Margolese, 2005; Winston, 2005). The third methodological issue asks how a "circumscribed study" can avoid becoming merely anecdotal (Baumel-Schwartz, 2009, p. 6. See also Siegel, 2008). Baumel-Schwartz, in particular, responds by acknowledging that her study describes a series of trends and developments.

Such ongoing studies," she affirms "...are not seeking an immediate 'bottom line' but a balanced presentation of an ever-changing dynamic" (2009, p. 7). The same may be said of the current study, which forms one piece of an ongoing academic conversation about the dynamics of physical and virtual identities, and which allows for modest and provisional conclusions as a body of scholarly research slowly develops.

One of the challenges associated with the current topic is linguistic—the myriad vocabulary in Hebrew and Yiddish that peppers the written and spoken communication of Hasidim and other Orthodox Jews. This issue has been raised by Samuel G. Freedman, the author of a regular column on religion in the *New York Times*. In 2010, he wrote an article about the provocative blog "Failed Messiah," whose singular focus is the Orthodox Jewish world. The blog is maintained by Shmarya Rosenberg from St. Paul, Minnesota, a former member of the Chabad Lubavitch Hasidic group. Writing about disparaging remarks that frequently appear in the blog's comments section, Freedman concluded that most readers would require Hebrew and Yiddish glossaries to properly grasp the conflicts expressed in the blog's exchanges (Freedman, 2010). Another challenge is the absence of prior studies targeting Hasidic blogging, although there are a variety of non-academic articles on the subject in Jewish periodical publications such as *The Jewish Daily Forward*, a secular New York based Jewish-American daily, and in publications reflecting an Orthodox perspective, both in print and online.

This chapter explores the ways in which blogging has created avenues of communication and self-expression among formerly isolated members of Hasidic communities, and what these developments may reveal about ways in which Internet technology is impacting the development of American Hasidim. The chapter focuses: (a) on the characteristics of Hasidic culture that make these developments innovative; (b) the needs that blogging fulfills for the disaffected; and (c) recurring themes, such as interpretations of Jewish law and struggles associated with a tradition-bound lifestyle—rigid modes of education, pressure to marry early, warnings about the immorality of the outside world, and the general challenges of transitioning to a non-observant way of life.

THE HASIDIC MOVEMENT AND OTHER TYPES OF JEWISH ORTHODOXY

Although all Hasidic Jews are fundamentalists, not all fundamentalist Jews are Hasidic. Moreover, Jewish Orthodoxy, which entails fundamentalist approaches to Jewish law and tradition, is not homogenous. There are distinctions even among fundamentalist groups that in many ways give every appearance of being almost identical. Within the bounds of certain non-negotiable practices (dietary laws, Sabbath observance, modesty in dress, and educational values), there prevails a diversity of views and practices, particularly in the area of engagement with secular society. Hasidic communities and the people who inhabit those communities, for all their surface uniformity, are likewise not homogenous.

In 2006, the Hasidic population in the U.S. was estimated to be 180,000, or 3 percent of the approximately 6 million Jews in the U.S. (Hoover, 2006).[2] The term *Hasidic* has a number of historical references, the most recognized one belonging to the 18th-century Eastern European Jewish revivalist movement that gave rise to contemporary Hasidism (Ettiner, 1991, p. 227-228). This antiestablishment religious movement drew on strands of the Jewish mystical tradition[3] to advocate the idea that affective experience and ardent prayer were as spiritually significant as scholarship, which had long been established as the normative barometer of prestige and holiness (Dubnow, 1991, p. 27-28; Heilman, 1992, p. 21). The Hasidic communities of Eastern Europe were decimated during the Second World War. Some communities, though, had left Europe and established themselves in the United States and Canada before the war. A number of surviving Hasidic leaders and their followers relocated from Europe to other countries after the war, most notably to Israel, the United States, Canada, and Australia.

Hasidic Jews are distinguished from other Orthodox Jews by connection and loyalty to their respective dynastic leaders, whose origins lay primarily in Eastern Europe; their attention to and focus on mystical aspects of religious texts; and, most conspicuously, in styles of men's dress.[4] There are dozens of large and small Hasidic groups, sometimes referred to as "courts," which are usually named after the Eastern European towns and villages in which their particular communities were founded by charismatic leaders who continue to be deeply revered today. Paradoxically, many Hasidic courts are both firmly situated within urban neighborhoods, and simultaneously deeply insulated (Sharot, 1991). Indeed, Hasidic communities in neighborhoods such as New York's Williamsburg and Boro Park are so removed from mainstream culture that many of their members grow up speaking primarily Yiddish, learning little or no English. [5]

A number of studies of Hasidic culture offer in-depth portraits of its structured and tradition-bound lifestyle that can provide context for the estrangement reported by some community members. These studies include *Holy Days: The World of the Hasidic Family* by Harris (1995); Heilman's *Defenders of the Faith: Inside Ultra-Orthodox Jewry* (1999); Fishkoff's *The Rebbe's Army: Inside the World of Chabad-Lubavitch* (2005); Wellen-Levine's *Mystics, Mavericks and Merrymakers: An Intimate Journey among Hasidic Girls* (2004) and Fader's (2009) *Mitzvah Girls: Bringing Up the Next Generation of Hasidic Jews in Brooklyn.* In addition, there are studies focusing specifically on estrangement in Hasidic and fundamentalist Jewish communities, such as Winston's (2005) *Unchosen: The Hidden Lives of Hasidic Rebels*, and Margolese's (2005) *Off the Derech: Why*

Observant Jews Leave Judaism and How to Respond to the Challenge.[6] Winston's *Unchosen*, for example, began as doctoral research in sociology at the City University of New York, focusing on the Satmar Hasidic community.[7] Winston (2005) had not set out initially to profile disaffected community members, and was surprised to find that the community contacts she established led her to encounter Hasidim who were profoundly unhappy with what they experienced as a deeply restrictive way of life. The resulting study revealed a concealed world hidden behind an already-concealed world: televisions slipped into apartments in garbage bags, clothes changed on the subway during trips into Manhattan, and the creation of double lives.

HASIDIC ATTITUDES TOWARD INTERNET TECHNOLOGY

In the absence of literature specifically directed at the practice of blogging by Hasidim, context can be constructed by examining Hasidic attitudes toward Internet technology, about which there is more documentation. The ubiquity of the Internet presents a serious challenge for many fundamentalist Jews, and more so for those farther to the right of the Orthodox spectrum, such as Hasidim, than for the less strict communities that more readily engage with the secular world. Moreover, the Internet presents a uniquely complex challenge, because while there are no practical aspects of television and movies, the Internet has, at the very least, legitimate business applications. For this reason, it has been difficult to ban Internet technologies outright, although such attempts have been made and continue to be made by some Orthodox Jewish community leaders.

In an article titled "Haredim and the Internet" published by the Center for Religion and Media at New York University, Portnoy (2004) described how, in early 2000, a coalition of prominent Haredi leaders in Israel representing Hasidic, Lithuanian, and Sefardic communities, attempted to issue a ban on Internet use. The rabbis portrayed the Internet as "… a danger 1,000 times greater [than television]…liable to bring ruin and destruction upon all of Israel" (Portnoy, 2004). In November of 2003, the Haredi Jewish communal organization Agudat Israel of America devoted an issue of its publication *The Jewish Observer* to the dangers of the Internet. It declared an explicit warning: "The Internet, with a flick of a button, invades a Jewish home, a Jewish soul, and makes moral disaster." The article cited a speech given by one prominent Hasidic leader at an educational convention: "If your business cannot get along without it, you must create the strictest controls around yourself and your staff…Do not give it free rein! Remember that you are dealing with a force that contains spiritual and moral poison" (Perlow, 2003, p. 9).

On June 24, 2006, the *Washington Post* reported on a blanket prohibition against Internet use instituted in the fundamentalist Jewish community of Lakewood, New Jersey (Diamant, 2006). As was the case in many communities, the ban was not total. The instituted policy made exceptions for home-based businesses, providing that the computers were secured (Diamant, 2006). In 2007, the blog "Failed Messiah" reported that rabbis in Brooklyn had taken up Lakewood's ban. Like the Internet ban that took place in 2000 in Israel, this one was also a collective effort. On December 11, 2009, an Orthodox Jewish online news site, "Yeshiva World News," reported that a group of rabbis promulgated a warning focused explicitly on ultra-Orthodox websites: "The [rabbis] express their fears surrounding the Internet's penetration into the Jewish home, trampling the safeguards of modesty and Jewish life…[they] call on the [congregation] to distance themselves from spiritual danger, as well as to condemn it in every form…" (Spira, 2009).

Based on these reports, it appears that the prevailing aspiration of most rabbinic leaders to the right of the Orthodox Jewish spectrum, including and especially Hasidic leaders, has been to ban the Internet altogether, although there has always been reluctant recognition of its legitimacy in business and commerce. The provisions of rabbinic dispensation for Internet use can vary from group to group, since no form of Judaism is governed by a single religious authority. Therefore, although Hasidic communities have uniformly regarded the Internet with consternation, the various provisions of bans on its use have shown some variance. According to Portnoy (2004), "… it is clear that the…community [ultra-Orthodox] will be as wired as everyone else, if not more." Coming to terms with the inevitability of being "wired" has taken very concrete forms. In July 2008, the Israeli newspaper *Haaretz* ran a story with the headline: "For the First Time, Hasidic Sect Approves Limited Internet Use" (Rotem, 2008). The group in question was the Belz community, which one Orthodox commentator described as being the first to "come out of the closet" by admitting that members of their community utilized the Internet and initiating a search for solutions to make provision for supervised or filtered Internet use. Prior to this, the story states, the subject of Internet use was so charged that it could not even be discussed. Yet at the time of the article's writing, it was asserted, "More than 60 percent of ultra-Orthodox households have computers" (Rotem, 2008).[8] As Portnoy (2004) summarized, "While the internet issue has been condemned from above, the Haredi masses are listening, but not obeying."

It is at this convergence of outright denunciation and tentative acceptance of the Internet that Orthodox Jewish blogs written by estranged and questioning Hasidism begin to emerge, starting in 2003. These blogs display a significant departure from normative community behavior. They also have attracted widespread attention. Samuel Freedman, for example, writing for the *New York Times*, said the following about the author of the blog "Failed Messiah":

... Mr. Rosenberg has had his scoops cited by The Wall Street Journal, Columbia Journalism Review, PR Week and Gawker. The national Jewish newspaper The Forward listed him among the 50 most influential American Jews, and the hip, cheeky magazine Heeb put him in its top 100. (Freedman, 2010)

Although the blogs have been in the main anonymous, some writers chose to eventually identify themselves, as did the authors of the blogs "Hasidic Rebel" and "Failed Messiah." Other bloggers explicitly warn their readers that, as in the case of the blog "A Hasid and A Heretic," they may be "intentionally misguiding" readers to conceal their real identities.

METHOD

The present study draws on narrative analysis to explore the ways in which blogging by disaffected and estranged Hasidic group members reflects a search for new meaning and direction in life. According to Moen (2006), narrative can be viewed as a story that relates an event or series of events that are significant to the speaker or the speaker's audience (p. 4). Narrative research is directed at the ways individuals draw on stories to construct meaningful interpretations of their experiences (p. 5). This study utilizes a narrative research approach with a descriptive focus. The author's goal is echoed in Creswell's (1998) description of the ability of qualitative study to "...fill a void in existing literature, establish a new line of thinking, or assess an issue with an understudied group or population" (p. 94). As a type of qualitative research that explores the stories people tell about their own lives and the ways in which they interpret events, descriptive narrative analysis is particularly compatible with data collection involving diaries, or in the case of this chapter, online blogs.

The current examination involves seven blogs: "Failed Messiah" (2004); "Hasidic Rebel" (2003); "A Hasid and a Heretic" (2004); "Also a Chussid" (2004); "Sitra Achra" ["The Other Side"] (2006); "Formerly Frum" (2010); and "Hasidic Feminist/Culture Shock" (2008). In addition, the analysis integrates material from the online journal titled "Unpious" (2010), which was initiated by the writers of the blogs "Hasidic Rebel" and "A Hasid and a Heretic." The accounts of material recorded in these blogs recreate an impressionistic portrayal of a fluid state of affairs in American Hasidic communities. Validation was established by examining cross-references among blogs, which indicates that bloggers in this genre are aware of and endorse each other's work, and supports authentication of their stated or virtually created identities. The researcher's personal background in the culture of fundamentalist Judaism, and Hasidism in particular, allowed for in-depth analysis of the blogs' content and context, including recurring themes and points of contention, which correspond with the researcher's familiarity with the culture-specific particularities of the Hasidic social and cultural environment.

Methods of research that explore persons in context through self-reported narrative have been a regular feature of social science writing (Josselson, Lieblich, & McAdams, 2003; Labov, 1967). In the social sciences, narrative research works on the principal that personal, self-reported story is the primary vehicle through which people "... make sense of experience, construct the self, and create and communicate meaning" (Chase, 2003, p. 79). Narrative analysis is non-linear, inductive, and personal, engaging the researcher in a process requiring the researcher (himself or herself) to become "...a medium for the discovery and interpretation of meanings" (Josselson, 2003, p. 4). The principal criteria for evaluating scientific research have traditionally rested on objectivity, reliability, replicability, and validity. Researchers in the narrative stream of qualitative research have proposed a refined set of criteria for validation, proposing four categories for evaluating narrative studies (Lieblich, Tuval-Mashiach, & Zilber, 1998). The first criterion is comprehensiveness: the quantity and completeness of content gathered and its adequacy for framing informed interpretation. The second is coherence—how well components of the research fit together to form a meaningful representation of the subject and its context. The third is insightfulness, which encompasses the innovation and originality of the research presentation and analysis. The fourth is parsimony, which evaluates the writer's ability to conceptualize an analysis based on a small quantity of concepts.

Finally, narrative research does not follow a uniform protocol or standardized set of procedures. Within the realm of accepted information-gathering and interpretive and validation methods, the researcher determines procedures based on the demands of the individual study, just as he or she chooses narrative analysis based on the type of data and research question. This study represents an initial step in a larger project that demands, in particular, augmentation of the quantity of material examined to draw out the levels of complexity and nuance inherent in the history and current states of affairs operative in American Hasidic culture, especially as it relates to the phenomenon of its disaffected and alienated members. It does not propose a definitive conclusion, but presents a picture of a developing trend in a deeply religious community whose dynamics are being challenged and transformed by the information and communication revolution.

BLOGGING AMONG DISAFFECTED HASIDIM

There is no authoritative list of Jewish-themed blogs or of blogs written specifically by fundamentalist Jews, although an informal list titled "1000 Frum Blogs," which provides an unofficial, although informative accounting of blogs from across the Orthodox spectrum, is maintained on-line (Ms. SC, 2009). The most effective, though unsystematic way to discover Hasidic blogs is to note the way Hasidic bloggers reference each other by examining lists of thematically-linked blogs included on their respective pages.

The most widely known blog written by an alienated and former Hasidic community member is the previously-mentioned "Failed Messiah." It was initiated in 2004 and is currently maintained, by a former member of the Lubavitch Hasidic group. The subjects of "Failed Messiah" are "... the shortcomings that he sees in the world of Orthodox Judaism..." (Weiss, 2008). Described by *The Jewish Daily Forward* as one of the "essential stops on the Jewish blogosphere," the content of "Failed Messiah," whose title references messianic claims made on behalf of the deceased leader of the Lubavitch Hasidic movement, is regularly updated. It functions as a clearing-house of articles and comments relating the clashes between fundamentalist and secular Jews in Israel, legal cases, news items, and a vast array of issues in the Hasidic world in such areas as education, Jewish law, employment, and women's rights. The extensive comments on the writer's postings are both affirmative and sometimes decidedly reproachful of his critical stance toward the Hasidic world. The author's prominence and controversy as a chronicler of problems in fundamentalist Jewish communities was acknowledged on the pages of the *New York Times*, where the chief historian of the National Museum of American Jewish History, Jonathan Sarna, provided a tale-telling quote highlighting the attitude of the Jewish establishment towards the author of "Failed Messiah," "I know that he is fiercely hated in some Orthodox circles, but he has had many a scoop, and is certainly THE destination for those who want dirt about Orthodoxy exposed to the world" (Freedman, 2010). It is the unremitting regularity and continuity of purpose that sets "Failed Messiah" apart from other blogs written by questioning and former Hasidim.

Of the seven blogs analyzed, "Failed Messiah" is the most explicitly news-focused, and the most trenchantly critical. The writer's early postings in 2004 focused on what he regarded as the failure of the leader of the Lubavitch movement to support action on behalf of Ethiopian Jews (Rosenberg, 2004). The blogger continues to pay particular attention to legal matters (such as incidents of fraud, especially those involving government assistance programs) and the newly-recognized issue of child sexual abuse in Hasidic and other fundamentalist Jewish communities. For example, this blog has been particularly insistent in its coverage of the trial of the former CEO of the Agriprocessors, Inc., the largest kosher slaughterhouse and meatpacking facility in the United States, located in Postville, Iowa. In May, 2008, the owners of this business, who happened to be Lubavitch Hasidim, were found in violation of a wide range of charges, including bank, money and wire fraud, money laundering, abuse of animals, and the use of illegal and underage workers.[9]

The writer of "Failed Messiah" has commented extensively about the consequences he has experienced as a result of his blogging activity, which he describes as nothing less than excommunication that ostracizes him religiously, socially and occupationally (Rosenberg, n.d.). He has remained an observant Jew, and refrains from posting on the Sabbath or Jewish holidays. But in a statement titled "What I Believe," he expresses his ambivalence toward Jewish observance, although he claims to "…believe in God the Creator who many billions of years ago…started the process that brought us – and brings us–into being" (Rosenberg, 2006).

Blogs such as "Failed Messiah" create opportunities for discussion among readers from a variety of religious backgrounds and levels of observance. This aspect is especially evident in blogs that focus primarily on musings about family and community life, and thoughts connected to events in the writers' lives. Among other blogs that appeared in the early 2000s were "Hasidic Rebel" (2003) and "A Hasid and a Heretic" (2004), the writers of which have recently combined their efforts to create a new online journal—"Unpious." The founder of "Hasidic Rebel" recently chose to reveal his identity in a blog post titled "Blogging in Anonymity: A Thing of the Past" and on the pages of "Unpious" in an entry "Anonymous No Longer" (Deen, 2010a; Deen, 2010b). "Hasidic Rebel" writes about a wide variety of topics: religious intolerance (Deen, 2010c), his mother's response to his evidently "shaky" faith (Deen, 2006a), and the impact of the Internet on the formerly insular world of the Haredim (Deen, 2009). It is evident that the author of this blog found an audience almost immediately. On May 5, 2003, he composed a response to some readers' condemnations of his "attacks on the Chassidic community" (Deen, 2003). His justification for blogging demonstrates motives that are grounded in conflict about the simultaneous existence of significant goodness mingled with significant levels of intolerance—attitudes extant in Hasidic communities that have been corroborated by studies documenting Hasidic religious culture (Fader, 2009; Margolese, 2005; Winston, 2005).

Readers of the blog "Hasidic Rebel" can, by searching through the blog's archives, follow the trajectory of this writer's disillusionment, which has led him to leave his community in Rockland County, New York and relocate to the Williamsburg neighborhood of Brooklyn. In a 2006 posting, for example, he wrote candidly about the way his relationship with his community had transformed. He described himself as "…no longer angry… My… participation, practice of ritual, and level of religious stricture is now entirely defined by my comfort level" (Deen, 2006b). Ironically, the Williamsburg neighborhood in which he has settled is the location of one of the largest Hasidic communities in the United States, although in recent years it has become populated by a much wider variety of residents.

By contrast, the author of the blog "A Hasid and a Heretic," who writes under the moniker

"Shtreimel," has always written anonymously. His pseudonym references the Yiddish term for the ceremonial fur hats worn by many Hasidic men. Married with several children, "Shtreimel" continues to maintain a Hasidic lifestyle while blogging privately about his frustrations and internal conflicts. In an interview with *The Jewish Daily Forward*, "Shtreimel" stated that he estimated most of his readers are from religious communities (Grinspan, 2005). "More than anything," commented Hella Winston, who was also interviewed for the *Forward* article, "I've come to think of these blogs as a way for people on the inside to talk to each other. That seems to be one of the biggest functions they're serving: a way for people to connect" (Grinspan, 2005). However, the sense of connection obtained from reading and writing online has its limits. "Shtreimel" writes of his solitude—the uniquely painful isolation that can occur precisely when surrounded by other people: "You sit at the table with your friends, some even childhood friends with whom no secrets were hidden…with nothing to share anymore… you realize that the ones closest and dearest to you share absolutely nothing with what you truly believe in…." (Shtreimel, 2009).

At the start of his blogging, "Shtreimel" wrote that his "secret heretic life is known to only a select few of my closest friends." The statement that follows reveals that those friends were members of his community: "Of course, they try to get me back into the fold…" (Shtreimel, 2004). In a 2007 article for the journal *Sh'ma: A Journal of Jewish Responsibility*, "Shtreimel" described his inability to accept that "…reading and thinking about the core tenets of Judaism is prohibited…" This led him to blogging activity, and "taking a cue" from other Hasidic bloggers, he began to write for a wide audience (Shtreimel, 2007). "Shtreimel" is explicit about what he regards as his "double-life" (Shtreimel, 2008). He also speaks candidly about the need to come to terms with having been born into a community that has deprived him of "normal" life, posing the question "Could it be

possible that I eventually…fall in line with what life dealt me?… I am talking about acceptance of living a life I don't subscribe to" (Shtreimel, 2008). He has expressed frustration about how his community's lack of engagement with the outside world reinforces the notion that "outside" culture was homogenous—comprised entirely of forbidden sexual imagery and violence. It took some time for him to discover, on his own, that all non-Jewish culture was not "Madonna and R-rated action movies" (Shtreimel, 2006).

At one point, "Shtreimel" used the blog as a much-needed emotional outlet during a depressive episode in which he contemplated revealing his identity. He stated: "I now know how my 'outing' is going to happen: in a bout of mania-depression, or during a really bad alcohol or drug induced trip I'm going to post my name and picture on this blog" (Shtreimel, 2007). "Hasidic Rebel" and "Shtreimel" are known to each other, although it is not clear whether they have a personal acquaintance or solely an online one. In a posting formally announcing the creation of "Unpious," "Shtreimel" refers to the writer of "Hasidic Rebel" as "…the fine young man I proudly call my friend" (Shtreimel, 2010). It is also in this posting that readers obtain a hint about the extent of Hasidic Rebel's readership among members of Hasidic communities, when "Shtreimel" refers to his nostalgia for the years when "Hasidic Rebel" postings were fodder for discussion in all the places Hasidic Jews tend to gather: synagogue, ritual bath, and family Sabbath table (Shtreimel, 2010). "Unpious" both replicates and to some extent replaces "Hasidic Rebel" and "A Hasid and a Heretic." The subtitle of "Unpious" is "Voices on the Hasidic Fringe," and it is described as a venue "for those whose roots are in the Chasidic world but have left it in body or spirit." The founders are explicit in their support of unfettered expression (Deen & Shtreimel, 2010). Therefore, "Unpious" represents the next step in the development of communication channels by and about former and questioning members of Hasidic communities, and claims a long list of contributing authors.

Digressing from the self-imposed outcast status of many alienated Hasidic bloggers is the creator of the blog "Also a Chussid." The issues about which he blogs echo themes expressed by "Hasidic Rebel" and "Shtreimel": the absence of secular education in Hasidic schools, especially in the case of boys (Also a Chussid, 2005a); notions about the unique holiness of the Jewish people (Also a Chussid, 2005c); and the burden of Hasidism's insistence on large families (Also a Chussid, 2005b). The author is himself a father of seven children (Also a Chussid, 2007b). This blogger has remained in his community and has not rejected the tenets of Hasidic fundamentalism. He even takes issue with the work of Hella Winston, the author of the book *Unchosen: The Hidden Lives of Hasidic Rebels*, who told the story of the lives of Satmar Hasidic women in Brooklyn. "Shtreimel" accused Winston of stereotyping Hasidic Jews based on a small number of interviewees, extrapolating generalizations about the Satmar community from individual instances of family problems, and propagating outright falsehoods, such as her assertion that a high level of suicide exists in Hasidic communities (Also a Chussid, 2005d). He is one of the few bloggers who has made the explicit decision to negotiate the paradox of adhering to a way of life and a community about which he finds much to criticize.

The blogger "Shtreimel" has, however, been forced to deal with the consequences of his blogging activity. He describes receiving a phone threat from a member of his community belonging to one of the so-called "modesty patrols," in which the caller warned him to cease his blogging activity or risk widespread exposure to the community (Also a Chussid, 2007a). It is clear from this post that while this blogger does not reveal his name in his writing, his identity appears to be known by some. In response, he closed the blog for a time until he was able to determine the identity of the caller. Once this was accomplished, he struck back,

publicly directing a written response directly to his caller in which he affirmed his reputation in the community, financial contributions to charity organizations, and the volunteer work in which he and his wife were involved. "Shtreimel" then emphasized forcefully that he was also a man of means, and promised swift and uncompromising legal action in response to any further threats or acts of exposure (Also a Chussid, 2007a).

While the paths taken by the writers of "Failed Messiah," "Hasidic Rebel," and "A Hasid and a Heretic" reveal these writers' gradual decline of belief, the writer of "Also a Chussid" demonstrates no such developments. In a 2008 posting, he asserted that while he may alter his appearance in minor ways when he ventures outside the community, he "[loves] and will always be proud of" his Hasidic identity (Always a Chussid, 2008). The last blog entry of "Also a Chussid" was January 5, 2009, and it is revealing about the writer's state of mind and the reason he may have ceased writing. Describing the cold, hours-long wait in Times Square New Year's Eve for the ball-dropping ceremony, he contrasted this with the rituals and observances of the Jewish New Year (Also a Chussid, 2009). He concluded that such moments "…reaffirm my fondness for my own culture." In what is to date this blogger's final report about the conflict he recorded over a period of six years, he stated, "I embraced the uniqueness and warmth that emanates from the Jewish New Year's celebrations" (Also a Chussid, 2009).

The Aramaic term *sitra achra* means "the other side" and signifies the forces of evil that are at work in the world. An anonymous Hasidic blog writer has chosen this term to name his blog, which he started in 2006. He describes himself in the blog's subtitle as "physically living the life of a pious and devout Hasid, while intellectually thinking as an atheist, rationalist, and secular humanist" (Baal Devarim, n.d.). Using the pseudonym "Baal Devarim," he describes himself as "as typical [Hasidic] man with my many children and often loving wife" (Baal Devarim, n.d.). Far from typical, the blogger portrays himself as simultaneously "an Atheist in belief and Humanist by conviction," who is able to lead a "happy and fulfilled" Hasidic life. But this happiness and fulfillment are elaborated with irony, when the writer describes that life as "…spent worshiping our one true creator through detailed and meticulous observance of the [commandments] and…associated minutiae…" (Baal Devarim, n.d.).

Subjects addressed by "Baal Devarim" echo those treated by other disaffected Hasidic bloggers, such as the lack of clear and adequate sexual education (Baal Devarim, 2008b), and the overall meagerness of secular, and particularly science education in Hasidic schools (Baal Devarim, 2008c). This writer began his blogging with an entry describing the practice of asking forgiveness of one's friends and family prior to the Jewish Day of Atonement, Yom Kippur (Baal Devarim, 2006). In the exposition that follows, he depicted with bitterness the variety of people outside the community with whom he would never establish sustained or meaningful connections, saying: "Indeed, the pool out of which you can choose your friends is quite shallow" (Baal Devarim, 2006). He described the "uncomfortable" consequence of violating his community's social boundaries and communication taboo, and depicts himself as feeling "trapped" (Baal Devarim, 2006). The consequence of such feelings has led him to maintain an external appearance of piety, while indulging privately in activities and behavior outside the boundaries of community rules and restrictions (Baal Devarim, 2008a). His last post was on March 29, 2009. It is titled "Time," and contains poetic musings that include no references either to Hasidic life or to personal events. It is a cryptic and somewhat peculiar conclusion. Without any statement from him, readers have no way of knowing why this writer stopped blogging or what his current relationship with his community may be.

Two women writers, blogging under the title "Formerly Frum" ("pious"), subtitle their joint blog "Support for Survivors of Ultra-Orthodox Jewish Sects." Both authors are former members of the Lubavitch Hasidic group (Lily and Mimi, 2009a), which they explicitly describe as possessing cult-like qualities (Lily and Mimi, n.d.; Lily and Mimi, 2009a). The blog was initiated in 2009. It appears that as of 2010, the women had been living non-religious lives outside the Lubavitch Hasidic community for only a year. They envision their blog as a meeting place not only for estranged and former members of specifically Hasidic communities, but also for individuals from fundamentalist Jewish communities across the Orthodox spectrum. These communities do not, as the writers acknowledge, all equally display the cult-like features the bloggers describe as having experienced, but a significant motivation for their writing resides in a desire to provide "cult-survivorship literature, advice, and help" (Lily and Mimi, 2009a). Both are unequivocal about the first activity they pursued upon leaving the community—acquiring an education. And they urge readers, especially those "…who are feeling lost, empty or stuck," to do the same. "Educate yourselves, learn a valuable trade, enrich your soul, sharpen your senses, respect the life of your mind and the right to THINK. That is our future" (Lily and Mimi, 2010a). Their struggle to find a way *out* of the Hasidic world was, as they describe it, "…as much a struggle 'in' to self-sufficiency." Readers of "Formerly Frum," therefore, do not follow the writers' process as it unfolds over time, but rather encounter a series of reflections on the culmination of a process of questioning that took place prior to the blog's establishment.

The authors of "Formerly Frum" report that their digression from community standards of belief made them targets of gossip, with some members of their circle going so far as encouraging the husband of one blogger to leave her (Lily and Mimi, 2010b). While they have retained friends from the Hasidic community, they now enjoy the freedom to be selective, and preserve only those friendships in which they feel personally valued apart from religious belief and observance (Lily and Mimi, 2010b). The "Formerly Frum" story of the difficult departure from a Hasidic community appears to have a happy ending. The writers' relationships with their partners are intact. Having obtained educations and established careers for themselves, they write happily about a newfound freedom from fear of community scrutiny (Lily and Mimi, 2009b).

Also writing from a woman's perspective is the creator of the blog "Culture Shock: Reflections of an Ex-Hasid," a blogger who previously wrote for the blog "Hasidic Feminist." This blogger grew up in Brooklyn in the Satmar Hasidic community. Currently a student at Sarah Lawrence College, she relates how, from an early age, she looked for ways to defy the community's insularity. For example, she became an avid, though secret, user of the public library located in the Williamsburg section of Brooklyn (Feldman, 2008c), eventually formulating a plan to use branch libraries in non-Jewish neighborhoods where she would not be recognized. Her blog content echoes familiar themes, in particular, the almost total absence of appropriate sexual education (Feldman, 2008a), and the pressure placed on young people, especially "restless" ones, to marry early (Feldman, 2009). She related that this seemingly incongruous state of affairs produces a peculiar problem in some marriages between spouses in their late teens or early twenties—namely, unconsummated marriages (Feldman, 2008b). It is noteworthy that the bloggers "Shtreimel" and "Baal Devarim" both commented on this posting, demonstrating once again that many of the bloggers in this genre follow each other's work. The blogger also composed her own very individual statement of faith, which she wrote in response to her perception that "people expect me to be Godless" (Feldman, 2010a). On the contrary, she asserts that she maintains a deep and abiding faith, but on her own terms. She refuses to be categorized with other alienated

Hasidic bloggers, who "…pronounced me one of them…quick to assert their own…atheism…" (Feldman, 2010a). The faith she preserves and that preserves her is one that "…does get you everywhere…Belief in the impossible is actually a smart way to live your life" (Feldman, 2010a). It appears that this particular blogger has made a decisive break with the Hasidic world in which she grew up, but refused to be stereotyped either by that community or by outsiders.

CONCLUSION AND FUTURE RESEARCH DIRECTIONS

Electronic communication in the fundamentalist Jewish world is creating a realm of discussion and debate that in its ubiquity and autonomy are difficult to dismiss. Analysis of material written in fundamentalist Jewish newspapers and magazines (some of which are Internet-based) can substantiate the extent to which this development is impacting internal conversations in Hasidic and fundamentalist Jewish communities. A number of prevalent and long-standing issues appear to be receiving the benefits of this enhanced and candid level of communication. Before the advent of blogging, it was very difficult for those "off the path," to use the term employed in fundamentalist Jewish communities, to learn of each others' existence, much less to meet and share ideas. The public and wide-reaching medium of blogging allows both questioning and former community members an unprecedented venue for communicating with each other and with a diverse community of non-Hasidic readers. Blogging has allowed them to connect with like-minded readers: providing a vehicle for communicating thoughts and experiences, offering or receiving support for efforts to leave the community, finding work, and engaging with the non-Hasidic world. Blogging also serves individuals within these communities by providing a communication outlet for those who choose to stay, as well as a communication outlet for those who choose to leave.

One avenue of future research can examine how increased freedom of expression is impacting communities' capacity for self-reflection and change. This area of study would focus on research exploring the possible relationship between the unfettered discussion that takes place in electronic media and the pace and relative openness with which problems (such as sexual abuse) are now acknowledged and addressed in fundamentalist Jewish communities. An important next step, therefore, can encompass an expanded study of blogs coming from disaffected fundamentalist Jewish writers from across the Orthodox spectrum. Another focus of research can comprise a survey of Hasidim who have left their communities in the last 4-6 years, or who are currently trying to leave, in order to determine the extent to which blogs written by alienated community members and former members influenced or is influencing them.

Blogging among disaffected Hasidim both challenges Hasidic communities and offers opportunities for communal self-scrutiny, revitalization, and progress toward engaging difficult and important issues of change produced by the information and communication revolution. There are now dozens of blogs belonging to Hasidim and ex-Hasidim in various stages of questioning, transitioning out of the community, or deliberating the compromises necessary for remaining. Although the type of criticism found on the blogs and described here are far from normative in Hasidic culture, Hasidic communities have many strengths that will not be diminished by unconstrained discourse. More significantly, this opening of more candid discussion can, far from weakening communities, likely provide a constructive foundation for the kind of renewal that is possible even in the most conservative communities. Blogging has truly globalized what was formerly a private world.

CITED BLOGS AND THEIR FOUNDING DATES

Also a Chussid (2004)
http://alsoachussid.blogspot.com/
Culture Shock: Reflections of an Ex-Hasid (formerly Hasidic Feminist) (2010)
http://exhasid.blogspot.com/
Failed Messiah (2004)
http://failedmessiah.typepad.com/failed_messiahcom/
Formerly Frum. Support for Survivors of Ultra-Orthodox Jewish Sects (2009)
http://formerlyfrum.wordpress.com/
A Hasid and a Heretic (2004)
http://hassid.blogspot.com/
Writing under the name Shtreimel
Hasidic-Feminist (2008)
http://hasidic-feminist.blogspot.com/
Hasidic Rebel (2003)
http://hasidicrebel.blogspot.com/
Sholom Deen, now writing on Unpious
Other Side, The (2006)
http://sitra-achra.blogspot.com/
Unpious. News, commentary, and writings by and for Chasidim on the fringe (2010)
http://www.unpious.com/

ADDITIONAL BLOGS

Abandoning Eden: Leaving Orthodox Judaism, and what came after (2007)
http://abandoningeden.blogspot.com/
Destined for Failure. Discussing the Hasidic Community with its Pros and Cons (2008)
http://mikvahneias.blogspot.com/
Frum Follies. Combating foolishness with humor, satire and serious (2009)
http://frumfollies.wordpress.com/
My Frum Side (2008)
http://myfrumside.blogspot.com/
No Longer Frum (2008)
http://shouldistayfrum.blogspot.com/

OTD (Off the Derech) (2008)
> http://offthed.blogspot.com/

Shaigetz, The (2003)
> http://theshaigetz.blogspot.com

Undercover Kofer (2009)
> http://undercoverkofer.blogspot.com/

REFERENCES

Also a Chussid. (2005a, February 10). *Tati ich hob a surprize far deich* [Web log post]. Retrieved February 15, 2010, from http://alsoachussid.blogspot.com/2005/02/tati-ich-hub-suprize-far-deich.html

Also a Chussid. (2005b, February 20). *Hasidim: Machines that love babies* [Web log post]. Retrieved February 15, 2010, from http://alsoachussid.blogspot.com/ 2005/02/hasidim-machines-that-love-babies.html

Also a Chussid. (2005c, February 27). *Anthony!!! It was really nice meeting you* [Web log post]. Retrieved February 15, 2010, from http://alsoachussid.blogspot.com/ 2005/02/anthony-it-was-really- nice-meeting-you.html

Also a Chussid. (2005d, December 1). *I accuse Hella Winston!* Retrieved February 15, 2010, from http://alsoachussid.blogspot.com/2005/12/i-accuse-hella -winston.html

Also a Chussid. (2007a, June 1). והער הכמ רורא ןמא םעה-לכ רמאו רתסב (Cursed be he who smites his neighbor in secret. And all the people shall say 'Amen.') (Deut. 27:24). Retrieved February 15, 2010, from http://alsoachussid.blogspot.com/ 2007_06_01_archive.html

Also a Chussid. (2007b, July 5). *The mitzvah tanz is just around the corner* [Web log post]. Retrieved from http://alsoachussid.blogspot.com /2007/07/mitzveh-tantz-is- just-around-corner.html

Also a Chussid. (2008, April 17). *Some rules should never be broken* [Web log post]. Retrieved February 15, 2010, from http://alsoachussid. blogspot.com/2008/04/some-rules-should-never-ever-be-broken.html

Also a Chussid. (2009, May 5, 2009). *Rosh Hashuneh* [Web log post]. Retrieved February 15, 2010, from http://alsoachussid.blogspot.com/ 2009/01/rosh-hashuneh.html

Ament, J. (2005, February). *American Jewish religious denominations.* New York, NY: United Jewish Communities. Retrieved July 18, 2011 from http://www.jewishdatabank.org/ Archive/ NJPS2000_American_ Jewish_Religious_Denominations.pdf

Anonymous. (2007, February 1). Online diaries: blogging and the Hasidic life. *Sh'ma. A journal of Jewish responsibility.* Retrieved February 15, 2010, from http://www.naomigryn.com/ index_files/February_shma.pdf

Baumel-Schwartz, J. T. (2009). Frum surfing: Orthodox Jewish women's Internet forums as a historical and cultural phenomenon. *Journal of Jewish Identities*, 2(1), 1–30.

Chase, S. (2003). Learning to listen: Narrative principles in a qualitative research methods course. In R. Josselson, A., Lieblich, & D. McAdams (Eds.), *Up close and personal: The teaching and learning of narrative research* (pp. 79-99). Washington, DC: American Psychological Association.

Creswell, J. W. (1998). *Qualitative inquiry and research design: Choosing among five traditions.* Thousand Oaks, CA: Sage.

Deen, S. (2003, May 5). *The truth about Chasidim* [Web log post]. Retrieved February 15, 2010, from http://hasidicrebel.blogspot.com/ 2003/05/truth-about-chasidim- some-readers.html

Deen, S. (2006a, August 21). *My mother on me* [Web log post]. Retrieved February 15, 2010, from http://hasidicrebel.blogspot.com/ 2006/08/my-mother-on-me.html

Deen, S. (2006b, September 2). *The power of choice* [Web log post]. Retrieved February 15, 2010, from http://hasidicrebel.blogspot. com/2006/09/power-of-choice.html

Deen, S. (2009, June 8). *An anthropological disaster* [Web log post]. Retrieved February 15, 2010, from http://hasidicrebel.blogspot.com/ 2009_06_01_archive.html

Deen, S. (2010a, May 16). *Anonymous no longer* [Web log post]. Retrieved February 15, 2010, from http://www.unpious.com/2010/05/ anonymous-no-longer/

Deen, S. (2010b, May 16). *Blogging in anonymity: A thing of the past* [Web log post]. Retrieved February 15, 2010, from http://hasidicrebel. blogspot.com/2010/05/sometimes-it-is-time-to-say-goodbye.html

Deen, S. (2010c, September 10). *Cracking our nuts* [Web log post]. Retrieved February 15, 2010, from http://hasidicrebel.blogspot.com/ 2010/09/cracking-our-nuts.html

Deen, S. (n.d.). Submissions. *Unpious: Voices on the Hasidic fringe.* Retrieved October 7, 2010 from http://www.unpious.com/submissions/

Deen, S., & Shtreimel (2010). About this site. *Unpious: Voices from the Hasidic fringe.* Retrieved February 15, 2010, from http://www.unpious. com/about-2/

Devarim, B. (2006, September 29). *Friends* [Web log post]. Retrieved February 15, 2010, from http:// sitra-achra.blogspot.com/ 2006/09/friends.html

Devarim, B. (2007a, February 12). *Education* [Web log post]. Retrieved February 15, 2010, from http://sitra-achra.blogspot.com/ 2007/02/education.html

Devarim, B. (2007b, June 17). *Administrivia* [Web log post]. Retrieved February 15, 2010, from http://sitra-achra.blogspot.com/ 2007/06/administrativa.html

Devarim, B. (2008a, April 8). *Faking it* [Web log post]. Retrieved February 15, 2010, from http:// sitra-achra.blogspot.com/ 2008/04/faking-it.html

Devarim, B. (2008b, September 17). *Fear, sex and ignorance* [Web log post]. Retrieved February 15, 2010, from http://sitra-achra.blogspot.com/ 2008/09/sex-fear-and-ignorance.html

Devarim, B. (2008c, December 21). *Happy holidays!* [Web log post]. Retrieved February 15, 2010, from http://sitra-achra.blogspot.com/ 2008/12/happy-holidays.html

Devarim, B. (n.d.). *About me* [Web log post]. Retrieved February 15, 2010, from http://www. blogger.com/ profile/30839783

Diamant, J. (2006, June 24). N.J. town's Orthodox Jews sign off the Internet at home. *The Washington Post.* Retrieved February 15, 2010, from http:// www.washingtonpost.com/ wp-dyn/content/article/2006/06 /23/AR2006062301418.html

Dinur, B. (1991). The origins of Hasidism and its social and messianic foundations. In Hundert, G. D. (Ed.), *Essential papers on Hasidism: Origins to present* (pp. 86–208). New York, NY: New York University Press.

Dubnow, S. (1991). The beginnings. The Baal Shem Tov (Besht) and the center in Podolia. In Hundert, G. D. (Ed.), *Essential papers on Hasidism: Origins to present* (pp. 25–57). New York, NY: New York University Press.

Ettinger, S. (1991). The Hasidic movement—reality and ideals. In Hundert, G. D. (Ed.), *Essential papers on Hasidism: Origins to present* (pp. 226–243). New York, NY: New York University Press.

Fader, A. (2009). *Mitzvah girls: Bringing up the next generation of Hasidic Jews in Brooklyn.* Princeton, NJ: Princeton University Press.

Feldman, D. (2008a, December 5). *My vagina monologue* [Web log post]. Retrieved February 15, 2010, from http://hasidic-feminist.blogspot.com/ 2008/12/excerpt-from-essay-on- sexual-repression.html

Feldman, D. (2008b, December 9). *The ghosts of sexual repression* [Web log post]. Retrieved February 15, 2010, from http://hasidic-feminist. blogspot.com/2008/12/ghosts-of- sexual-repression.html

Feldman, D. (2008c, December 14). *Some answers to your questions* [Web log post]. Retrieved February 15, 2010, from http://hasidic-feminist. blogspot.com/ 2008/12/some-answers- to-your-questions.html

Feldman, D. (2009, January 29). *Misplaced trust* [Web log post]. Retrieved February 15, 2010, from http://hasidic-feminist.blogspot.com/ 2009/01/ misplaced-trust.html

Feldman, D. (2010a, June 10). *Still faithful* [Web log post]. Retrieved February 15, 2010, from http:// exhasid.blogspot.com/2010/ 06/still-faithful.html

Feldman, D. (2010b, July 16). *Goyim: Are there different kinds?* [Web log post]. Retrieved February 15, 2010, from http://exhasid.blogspot. com/2010/ 07/goyim-are-there-different- kinds. html

Feldman, D. (n.d.). About me. *Deborah Feldman.* From http://www.deborahfeldman.com/ about-me.php

Fishkoff, S. (2005). *The Rebbe's army: Inside the world of Chabad-Lubavitch.* New York, NY: Schocken.

Freedman, S. A. (2010, January 8). A muckracking blogger focuses on Jews. *The New York Times.* Retrieved from http://www.nytimes.com/2010/ 01/09/us/09religion.html

Grinspan, I. (2005, August 26). Blogs offer glimpse into hidden corners of Orthodox life. *The Jewish Daily Forward.* Retrieved February 15, 2010, from http://www.forward.com/ articles/2669

Heilman, S. (1992). *Defenders of the faith. Inside Ultra-Orthodox Jewry.* Berkeley, CA: University of California Press.

Heilman, S. (2006). *Sliding to the right. The contest for the future of American Jewish orthodoxy.* Berkeley, CA: University of California Press.

Hoover, A. (2006, November 27). As Hasidic population grows, Jewish politics may shift right. *University of Florida News.* Retrieved from http:// news.ufl.edu/2006/11/27/ hasidic-jews

Josselson, R., Lieblich, A., & McAdams, D. (2003). *Up close and personal: The teaching and learning of narrative research.* Washington, DC: American Psychological Association. doi:10.1037/10486-000

Kamen, M. (1985). *Growing up hasidic: Education and socialization in the Bobover Hasidic community.* New York, NY: AMS.

Labov, W., & Waletzky, J. (1967). Narrative analysis: Oral versions of personal experience. In Helm, J. (Ed.), *Essays on the verbal and visual arts* (pp. 12–44). Seattle, WA: University of Washington Press.

Lamm, N. (2002). *Seventy faces: Articles of faith* (*Vol. 1*). Hoboken, NJ: Ktav Publishing.

Levine, S. (2004). *Mystics, mavericks, and merrymakers: An intimate journey among Hasidic girls.* New York, NY: New York University Press.

Lieblich, A., Tuval-Mashiach, R., & Zilber, T. (1998). *Narrative research: Reading, analysis, and interpretation* (*Vol. 47*). Thousand Oaks, CA: Sage Publications.

Lily and Mimi. (2009a, February 23). *Welcome to formerly frum* [Web log post]. Retrieved February 15, 2010, from http://formerlyfrum.wordpress.com/ 2009/02/23/hello-world/

Lily and Mimi. (2009b, December 12). *From frumkeit to freedom: A journey of the soul* [Web log post]. Retrieved February 15, 2010, from http://formerlyfrum.wordpress.com/ 2009/12/12/ from-frumkeit-to- freedom-a-journey-of-the-soul/

Lily and Mimi. (2010a, March 7). *The sweetest thing* [Web log post]. Retrieved February 15, 2010, from http://formerlyfrum.wordpress.com/ 2010/03/07/the-sweetest-thing/

Lily and Mimi. (2010b, July 13). *Conditional acceptance* [Web log post]. Retrieved February 15, 2010, from http://formerlyfrum.wordpress.com/ 2010/07/13/conditional-acceptance/

Lily and Mimi. (n.d.). *About formerly frum* [Web log post]. Retrieved February 15, 2010, from http:// formerlyfrum.wordpress.com /about/

Margolese, F. (2005). *Off the derech: Why observant Jews leave Judaism: How to respond to the challenge*. Israel: Devora Publishing.

Moen, T. (2006). Reflections on the narrative research approach. *International Journal of Qualitative Methods, 5*, 1–11.

Ms. SC. (2009). *1000 frum blogs*. Retrieved February 15, 2010, from http://1000frumblogs. blogspot.com/

O'Shea, W. (2003, July 15). The sharer of secrets. *The Village Voice*. Retrieved February 15, 2010, from http://www.villagevoice.com/ 2003-07-15/ news/ the-sharer-of-secrets/

Perlow, R. Y. (2003, November). Recognizing and dealing with some major moral hazards in contemporary society. *The Jewish Observer*. Retrieved February 15, 2010, from http://www. shemayisrael.com/ jewishobserver/archives/ nov03 /JONov03web.pdf

Polkinghorne, D. E. (1988). *Narrative knowing and the human sciences*. Albany, NY: State University of New York Press.

Portnoy, E. (2004). Haredim and the Internet. *Modiya: Jews, media, religion*. Retrieved February 15, 2010, from http://modiya.nyu.edu/ handle/1964/265

Rashi, T. (2011). Divergent attitudes within Orthodox Jewry toward mass communication. *Review of Communication, 11*(1), 20–38. doi:10.1080/1 5358593.2010.504883

Rosen, C. (2008, February 12). *Standing athwart e-history*. Retrieved February 15, 2010, from http://www.nysun.com/arts/ standing-athwart-e-history/71165/

Rosenberg, S. (2004, October 21). *Ethiopian Jews* [Web log post]. Retrieved February 15, 2010, from http://failedmessiah.typepad.com/ failed_messiahcom/ rabbis-ethiopian-jews.html

Rosenberg, S. (2006, October 24). *What I believe* [Web log post]. Retrieved February 15, 2010, from http://failedmessiah.typepad.com/ failed_messiahcom/2006/10/ what_i_believe.html

Rosenberg, S. (2007, January 18). *Lakewood Internet ban spreads to Brooklyn* [Web log post]. Retrieved February 15, 2010, from http:// failedmessiah.typepad.com/ failed_messiahcom/2007/01/ lakewood_intern.html

Rosenberg, S. (n.d.). *About me* [Web log post]. Retrieved February 15, 2010, from http://failedmessiah.typepad.com/ failed_messiahcom/ about-me.html

Rotem, T. (2008, July 28). For first time, Hasidic sect approves limited internet use. *Haaretz.* Retrieved February 15, 2010, from http://www. haaretz.com/news/ for-first-time-hasidic-sect-approves -limited-internet-use-1.250529

Sharot, S. (1991). Hasidism in modern society. In Hundert, G. D. (Ed.), *Essential papers on Hasidism: Origins to present* (pp. 511–531). New York, NY: New York University Press.

Shtreimel. (2004, October 17). *Pascal's wager* [Web log post]. Retrieved February 15, 2010, from http://hassid.blogspot.com/2004/10 /pascals-wager.html

Shtreimel. (2006, December 12). *King katle* [Web log post]. Retrieved February 15, 2010, from http:// hassid.blogspot.com/2007/10 /king-katle.html

Shtreimel. (2007, November 10). *I've figured it out!* [Web log post]. Retrieved February 15, 2010, from http://hassid.blogspot.com/2007/11 / ive-figured-it-out.html

Shtreimel. (2008, December 18). *Accepting a double life* [Web log post]. Retrieved February 15, 2010, from http://hassid.blogspot.com/2008/12 / accepting-double-life.html

Shtreimel. (2009, May 24). *Allein allein* [Web log post]. Retrieved February 15, 2010, from http:// hassid.blogspot.com/2009/05 /allein-allein.html

Shtreimel. (2010, January 12). *Unpious* [Web log post]. Retrieved February 15, 2010, from http:// hassid.blogspot.com/2010/01 /unpious.html

Siegel, L. (2008). *Against the machine: Being human in the age of the electronic mob.* New York, NY: Spiegel & Grau.

Spira, Y. (2009, December 11). Rabbonim come out strongly against Chareidi Internet. *Yeshiva World News.* Retrieved February 15, 2010, from http://www.theyeshiva-world.com/news /General+News/43219/ Rabbonim+ Come+Out+Strongly+Against +Chareidi+Internet.html

Spira, Y. (2010, January 15). Ban continues: Internet worse than television. *Yeshiva World News.* Retrieved February 15, 2010, from http://www. theyeshivaworld.com /article.php?p=44899

Weiss, A. (2008, July 24). Blogger focuses on Orthodox foibles. *The Jewish Daily Forward.* Retrieved February 15, 2010, from http://www. forward.com /articles/13848/

Winston, H. (2005). *Unchosen: The lives of Hasidic rebels.* Boston, MA: Beacon Press.

ADDITIONAL READING

Bar-Lev, M., & Schaffir, W. (Eds.). (1997). *Leaving religion and religious life.* Greenwich, CT: JAI Press.

Belcove-Shalin, J. (Ed.). (1995). *New world Hasidism: ethnographic studies of Hasidic Jews in America.* Albany, NY: State University of New York Press.

Bromley, D. (Ed.). (1988). *Falling from the faith: Causes and consequences of religious apostasy.* Newbury Park, California: Sage Publications.

Davidman, L. (1991). *Tradition in a rootless world: women turn to Orthodox Judaism.* Berkeley and Los Angeles, CA: University of California Press.

Deutsch, N. (2009). The forbidden fork, the cell phone holocaust, and other Haredi encounters with technology. *Contemporary Jewry, 29,* 3–19. doi:10.1007/s12397-008-9002-7

Goldschmidt, H. (2006). *Race and religion among the chosen people of crown heights.* Rutgers, NJ: Rutgers University Press.

Heilman, Samuel C., & Cohen, S. (1989). *Cosmopolitans and parochials: Modern Orthodox Jews in America.* Chicago, IL: University of Chicago Press.

Kamen, M. (1986). *Growing up Hasidic: Education and socialization in the Bobover Hasidic community.* New York: AMS.

Kaufman, D. R. (1991). *Rachel's daughters: Newly Orthodox Jewish women.* New Brunswick, NJ: Rutgers University Press.

Landau, D. (1993). *Piety and power: the world of Jewish fundamentalism.* London: Secker and Warburg.

Mintz, J. (1992). *Hasidic people. A place in the new world.* Cambridge, MA: Harvard University Press.

Rubin, I. (1997). *Satmar: Two generations of an urban island.* New York: Peter Lang.

KEY TERMS AND DEFINITIONS

Chabad Lubavitch: The world's largest Hasidic group, with members and activity centers (known as "Chabad Houses") all over the world. Chabad Lubavitch has become famous for its outreach to non-religious and unaffiliated Jews, which also makes it unique among Hasidic groups.

Derech: The Hebrew word for way, or path. When used by Orthodox Jews in the expression "off the derech," it refers to a person who has partially or completely abandoned Orthodox Jewish observance.

Frum: A Yiddish word describing an Orthodox Jew committed to strict observance of Jewish law as elaborated in the Talmud and other Rabbinic texts.

Halakhah: Jewish law based on the written Torah—the first five books of the Bible—and rabbinic scholarship and tradition. At the core of Halakhah, therefore, are the 613 positive and negative commandments, or mitzvot (plural of mitzvah) found in the Bible, and the many layers of discussion and elaboration of these commandments in the Talmud and other Rabbinic writings. Halakhah prescribes every aspect of life for Orthodox Jews.

Haredim (plural of Haredi): The most conservative element of Orthodox Jewry. The term is derived from a Hebrew word meaning "anxiety" or "fear," and signifies "those who tremble before God." Haredim regard themselves as the most authentic custodians of Jewish religious law and tradition which, in their opinion, is binding and unchangeable. They consider all other expressions of Judaism, including Modern Orthodoxy, as deviations from God's laws. There are two primary divisions of haredim, consisting of Hasidim and non-Hasidim. The non-Hasidic haredim tend to have their communal roots in the particular style of orthodoxy that flourished in pre-war Lithuania. Non-Hasidic haredim, therefore, are sometimes colloquially referred to as "Litvish." There is, in addition, a haredi movement among Sephardic Jews, who originated in Spain and North Africa.

Hasid (also Chassid, or Chosid): A member of a Hasidic (Chasidic) Haredi religious community (derived from Hebrew the "pious ones"). Hasidim are known for their strict observance of the Jewish law, or Halakhah, which they adhere to in minute detail.

Hasidim (plural of Hasid): Members of a Hasidic Haredi group centered on a charismatic spiritual leader (the rebbe) and his descendents. Hasidic groups are named after the places in which their leaders originated, or in which their rebbe was born or resided. The most well-known Hasidic communities are as follows: Belz (from Beltz, Ukraine), Bobov (from Bobowa, Poland), Breslov (from Bratslav, Ukraine), Chabad Lubavitch (from Lyubavichi, Russia), Ger (from Góra Kalwaria, Poland), Satmar (from Szatmárnémeti, Hungary), and Vizhnitz (from Vyzhnytsia, Ukraine).

Judaism: As a religion and a comprehensive way of life, contemporary American Judaism is represented by a broad mix of ideologies, institutions, movements, and groups. Among the main branches are Orthodox, Conservative, Reform, and Reconstructionist.

Kofer: A term of Hebrew origin designating a non-believer who has rejected Orthodox Jewish belief and practice.

Modern Orthodox Judaism: A stream within the diverse spectrum of the Orthodox branch of Judaism. It is represented by a loose association of movements and groups, and is based on the idea of combining participatory and contributing membership in the dominant, secular society with a strict observance of Halakhah, or Jewish law. Modern Orthodoxy Jewry is especially notable for its support for the State of Israel.

Shaigetz (masculine; Shiksa, feminine): A Yiddish term for a non-Jewish man, or in the case of "shiksa," a non-Jewish woman. Both terms have a derogatory connotation, and are often used in a pejorative sense to identify a Jewish man or woman who is not conforming to the norms and standards of his or her Orthodox Jewish community.

Shtreimel: A fur hat worn on the Sabbath and Jewish holidays by married men in many Hasidic communities.

ENDNOTES

[1] The vocabulary employed to refer to various expressions of Jewish fundamentalism is problematic. The term "ultra-Orthodox" is used in many genres of writing to describe the most insular communities of Orthodox Jews. For some writers, the term *haredi,* which is derived from the Hebrew term for "tremble," and denotes "the ones who tremble before God," is preferable (Lamm, 2002, p. 1; also see Heilman, 1992, p. 12).

[2] A study by Ament (2005) stated that the Orthodox Jewish population of the United States stood at approximately 567,000.

[3] Specifically, Hasidic teachings in their formative stage were "...closely tied to principles of mysticism as elaborated in Lurianic Kabbalah" (Heilman, 1992, p. 21).

[4] While the modest conventions of dress for Hasidic women and girls are clearly evident, it is men's dress that is most conspicuous in the urban areas populated by Hasidic communities.

[5] There are both formal and informal gathering spaces and support groups for Hasidic young people and adults seeking an outlet from community pressures. One formal venue is called "Footsteps," founded by a former member of the Lubavitch Hasidic sect named Malkie Schwartz (www.footsteps.org).

[6] There are, in addition, novelized accounts of alienation from fundamentalist Jewish communities, such as the novels of Pearl Abraham, Naomi Alderman, Reva Mann, and Naomi Ragen.

[7] The term "Satmar" is derived from the name of the Hungarian town in which this particular group was founded.

[8] The introduction of various types of filtering software, both general and specifically "Jewish" filtering software, has provided some reassurance for many users.

[9] In 2000, eight years before the unfolding of the "Rubashkin scandal," University of Iowa professor Stephen Bloom published a study titled *Postville: A clash of cultures in heartland America,* describing the conflicts that developed in the Iowa town of Postville between the local residents and members of the Lubavitch Hasidic group.

Chapter 8
The Status of Blogging in the Republic of Ireland:
A Case Study

Lori F. Brost
Central Michigan University, USA

Carol McGinnis
Central Michigan University, USA

ABSTRACT

This chapter examines the phenomenon and the status of blogging in the Republic of Ireland. It focuses on the social, cultural, political, technological, and legal factors that have influenced the existence and functioning of the Irish blogosphere and seeks to ascertain whether it is in good health, in decline, or in transition. To date, there is no research on the history and evolution of Irish blogging, and there are no assessments of the status of the blogging practice in the Republic of Ireland. This case study scrutinizes the history of blogging in Ireland, traces its evolution, and draws conclusions about the state of Irish blogging. Data collection for the study involved an extensive review of Irish blogs as well as e-mail and phone interviews with Irish bloggers. The authors conclude that the Irish blogosphere is vibrant, diverse, and evolving; additionally, they offer directions for future research.

INTRODUCTION

Four men carried a large Styrofoam coffin on their shoulders into a room decorated with tombstones. "The Funeral March of a Marionette," popularly known as the theme song from the Alfred Hitch-cock television series of the 1960s played in the background, while fog flowed from a machine usually used for Halloween festivities. The mock funeral procession kicked off the 5th annual Irish Blog Awards held in March 2010 in Galway's Radisson Blu Hotel. The theme, "Blogging is Dead," was inspired by press coverage that had

DOI: 10.4018/978-1-60960-744-9.ch008

declared Irish blogging was dying—or at least in significant decline.

Journalist John Burns asked in the London-based *Sunday Times* in December 2009, "Where have all the Irish bloggers gone?" Burns estimated there were a mere 4,000 Irish blogs, the same number as in 2008, and quoted experts who believed that the adoption of newer social media applications, especially Twitter, was slowing the growth of the Irish blogosphere. Trevor Butterworth of *Forbes* magazine also weighed in on the topic in January 2010, as did several Irish bloggers. In addition to the influence of microblogging and social networking sites, Burns and Butterworth suggested additional factors in the decline of Irish blogging: (1) connectivity concerns, i.e., lack of broadband access in rural parts of Ireland; (2) legal issues, in particular Ireland's strict libel and blasphemy laws; and, (3) demographic issues, such as Ireland's relatively small population. Although most of Irish bloggers contested the idea that blogging in Ireland was in decline, some agreed and blamed Irish bloggers themselves, declaring their posts poorly researched and written and not worth following. Butterworth (2010) asked, "Is Ireland, then, a new-media Galapagos, weirdly unique—or is it a leading indicator for a broader trend of what the *Guardian*'s Charles Arthur calls blogging's 'long-tail' decline?"

Arthur's (2009) speculation about blogging's "long-tail" decline is a reference to Anderson's (2006) theory which posits that by providing a limitless number of choices, the Internet ended the era of blockbusters and opened the era of an infinite number of niche products—music, books, movies, and more—and triggered the fragmentation of the consumer and media market. This infinite choice is often referred to as the "long tail." Pointing to anecdotal evidence and surveys conducted by Technorati, the leading authority in blog search and tracking, Arthur (2009) argued that the popularity of blogs is fading as bloggers switch to new social media platforms, such as Twitter and Facebook. He referred to this phenomenon as the demise of

blogging. Butterworth (2010) further argued that Ireland might be leading in the "long-tail" decline of blogging. Therefore, researchers wondered: Is the Irish blogosphere shrinking, as Butterworth suggests? Or, as many Irish bloggers claim, is the Irish blogosphere merely changing?

In this chapter the authors examine the status of blogging in Ireland focusing on the social, cultural, political, technological, and legal factors that influence the existence and functioning of the Irish blogosphere. This largely descriptive case study summarizes the history of blogging in Ireland, traces its evolution, draws conclusions about the current state of Irish blogging, and offers directions for future research.

BACKGROUND AND LITERATURE

The Republic of Ireland is a small country of 4.2 million people located on the island of Ireland. It shares the island with Northern Ireland, which is a part of the United Kingdom and occupies a smaller part of the island. The Republic of Ireland, often referred to as Ireland, had for generations a largely traditional, homogeneous tight-knit community culture where everyone knew everyone and where the oral tradition of storytelling was particularly revered. The country's news media traditionally were partisan, and in the dawn of the 20th century, were fiercely engaged in nation building. The picture changed dramatically, however, from the 1990s into the 2000s with the emergence of Ireland as a prosperous, dynamic modern European economy, nicknamed "the Celtic Tiger." This was the time when Irish blogging emerged as a social phenomenon and a popular Internet practice.

Research on Irish blogging has focused on a number of topics: (1) a blogger's behavior and motivations (Loftus, 2006); (2) the uses and perceptions of blogs in Irish society (Cochrane, 2009); (3) blog writing for purposes of self-reflection and self-expression in educational settings (Murray,

Hourigan, & Jeanneau, 2007); (4) the uses and perceptions of library blogs by Irish librarians (Lee and Bates, 2007); and, (5) the use of reflective blogs to support newly qualified teachers (Killeavy & Maloney, 2010). There has been a lack of research on the history and evolution of Irish blogging; the effect of social, cultural, legal, and other factors on blogging; and there have been no scholarly assessments of the status of blogging in the Republic of Ireland.

Just what is meant by an "Irish" blog? Do only individuals who were born and reared and who currently reside in Ireland create Irish blogs? Is a blog considered Irish if its writer is someone living in Ireland, regardless of citizenship or heritage? Is a blog written by an Irish expatriate, regardless of geographic location, considered Irish? Or is a blog's content—focusing on Irish concerns and issues—the characteristic that defines its Irishness?

Previous country-specific studies of blogs (De Vries, 2009; Pedersen & Macafee, 2006) have selected blogs for analysis based on the country of residence of the blog's writer. Sinead Cochrane (2009), who looked at uses and perceptions of blogs in Irish society, limited her research to "Irish (or living in Ireland) participants" (p. 19). This criterion for defining Irish blogs was echoed by bloggers interviewed by the authors of this chapter. Although there were some variations in their definitions, most used nationality or geographic location, rather than the content of the blog, to define Irish blogs. Dr. John Breslin, one of the first Irish bloggers, described an Irish blog as one "written by someone who is Irish (either at home or abroad) or someone living in Ireland long term" (personal communication, June 8, 2010).

Similarly, blogger Gav Reilly defined an Irish blog as one that is written by an Irish native or someone living in Ireland, rather than one that discusses Irish topics: "The blog of an Irishman writing about Ireland is obviously an Irish blog, but an Irishman writing about a foreign topic or niche … is also still an Irish blog" (personal communication, June 2, 2010). Reilly used Arseblog, an award winning fan blog of the English football club Arsenal, as an example of a popular blog produced by Irish people on a non-Irish topic. Although early Irish bloggers were criticized for writing "about Iraq, the U.S. and anything except Ireland" (O'Brien-Lynch, 2005), many bloggers then and today point to the diversity of topics as a strength of Irish blogging and not something that should define it.

RESEARCH QUESTIONS AND METHODOLOGY

The case study methodology is frequently employed in the social sciences when research questions require an extensive, in-depth examination of social phenomena. This method "allows investigators to retain the holistic and meaningful characteristics of real-life events" conducting data collection and analysis simultaneously (Yin, 2009, p. 4). There are three major types of case studies: exploratory, descriptive, and explanatory. A descriptive case study method is utilized when researchers aim to investigate an observable phenomenon in a real-life context (Gerring, 2007; Swanborn, 2010; Yin, 2009).

The case study methodology provides a useful framework for the analysis of Irish blogging from its beginnings to the present. Using the case study method, the authors of this chapter seek to address the following questions: When did blogging emerge as a practice in the Republic of Ireland? What are the social, cultural, legal, technological, and political factors that have influenced blogging? Finally, what is the status of blogging in Ireland today?

Primary research for this study involved interviewing a convenience sample of Irish bloggers, some of whom are also journalists or academics, by e-mail and phone. Open-ended questions asked bloggers about their knowledge of the history and social and cultural factors of blogging in Ireland, how they define an Irish blog, their opinion about the current state of the Irish blogosphere, their personal experiences with blogging, and their opinion about the most influential bloggers in Ireland.

Interviewees were selected based on their geographic location and length of time in practicing blogging, with preference given to those who had been blogging in the Republic of Ireland for a number of years. Additionally, the blogger's apparent influence and popularity with other Irish bloggers, based on the frequency with which they were listed on blogrolls, was a factor in the selection process. Further, several bloggers whom researchers had initially e-mailed recommended additional Irish bloggers to contact.

Secondary research for this study relied on the Internet for access to articles in databases, particularly Communication & Mass Media Complete by EBSCO Publishing and LexisNexis Academic. The researchers used the Internet to immerse themselves in the Irish blogosphere during the spring of 2010, reading and analyzing the content of Irish blogs and following links on blogrolls to get a sense of the interconnections. Finally, the present examination of blogs is limited to those written by bloggers in the Republic of Ireland; the researchers omitted blogs written in the Gaelic language.

THE IRISH BLOGOSPHERE

The blogosphere, the term used to describe a space of interconnected blogs, is virtually created by bloggers linking their blogs to others and commenting about individual blog posts (Marlow, 2004; Schmidt, 2007). Cochrane (2009) observes that networks of blogs often are linked to a centralized location online. These centralized locations include blog aggregators and directories. Aggregators often profile recent blog posts and offer readers the ability to search through the variety of blogs, while directories categorize blogs and provide links to the blog homepages. Three aggregators and two directories were located that focus predominantly on Irish blogs. Two earlier directories ceased to exist: iLoggers by Tony Ayres and Tom Cosgrave (Cosgrave, 2006) and Planet of the Blogs by John Breslin (J. Breslin, personal communication, June 8, 2010).

Irishblogs.ie aggregates more than 470,000 blog posts from about 4,000 blogs (Cochrane, 2009); among its offerings are the most recent blog and microblog posts on its homepage and links to popular topics discussed in blogs (Irishblogs.ie). Two additional Irish aggregators follow specialized topics. Politics in Ireland, located at http://www.politicsin-ireland.com/, is an aggregator for blog posts about Irish political life. This nonpartisan blog aggregator was established in June 2005 and is searchable via political parties, constituencies, current TDs (*Teachta Daile*, the Gaelic term for a member of the Irish Parliament), and former TDs. Food and Drink in Ireland (foodfight.ie) aggregates blog posts about culinary issues and offers original content, including recipes, by some of Ireland's most notable food bloggers. It was established in June 2006.

The aggregator Irishblogs.ie offers a separate Irish blog directory, located at http://www.irish-blogdirectory.com/. According to its homepage, the directory is open to anyone in the world with a blog of Irish interest. Although most of the nearly 300 featured blog writers self-report that they are located in Ireland, the directory also includes approximately 200 blogs from other parts of Europe, as well as from Africa, Asia, North America, and South America. Some of the links, however, are not functional or lead to blogs that have not been updated in two or more years. A similar number of Irish blogs, some of them also outdated, can be found on Globe of Blogs, a directory located at http://globeofblogs.com/.

A BRIEF HISTORY OF IRISH BLOGGING

Although many Irish bloggers say they do not know who was the first to start blogging in Ireland (Mulley, 2006), they say that blogs began appearing in Ireland in the late 1990s. This was prior to the introduction of specialized blogging software such as Pitas and Blogger in 1999 (Barlow, 2007; Blood, 2000). John Breslin dates his blog to 1997 although, he noted, "Back then, blogs didn't have commenting systems or RSS feeds, so maybe they weren't blogs per se but rather outlets for one's personal articles" (personal communication, June 8, 2010). Breslin also cited John Cormac's Hack Watch News as an early blog, going back to at least 1998. Tom Cosgrave (2006) listed the blog titled "Whatever... the Musings of an Eccentric Insomniac" by Dee in 1998 as another early blog. According to Kirstie McDermott many of the early bloggers were "techies (a lot of them men)" who had viewed blogging "as their turf" (personal communication, June 16, 2010).

The majority of Irish blogs were started after the turn of the 21st century, due in part to the ease of use of the new generation of blogging software. Blogs in this timeframe included Maura McHugh's Babbleogue, started in 2000; Bernie Goldbach's Irish Eyes, 2001; and, Tom Raftery's Tom Raftery's IT Views (J. Breslin, personal communication, June 8, 2010). The first Irish technical blog was most likely Mersault Thinking by Vincent O'Keefe's started in 2001 (Cosgrave, 2006). Gavin Sheridan's Gavin's Blog, 2002, and Damien Mulley's self-titled Damien Mulley, 2003, were other early blogs (G. Reilly, personal communication, June 2, 2010). In January 2002 iLoggers listed 41 "personal Irish websites and weblogs" (Cosgrave and Ayres, 2002). John Breslin (as cited in Reid, 2006) noted that there were about 100 Irish blogs in 2005 and more than 1,000 by 2006.

Although there are divergent views as to precisely when blogging matured in Ireland, the consensus is that blogging in Ireland lagged behind other countries, particularly the United States. "Blogging started here in earnest around 2004/2005 though there were people blogging before that," said Kirstie McDermott of the award-winning Beaut.ie: The Irish Beauty Blog (personal communication, June 16, 2010). In 2004 Karlin Lillington in an *Irish Times* article noted, "Blogging is coming of age in Ireland, too. At first, just a small, scattered community of bloggers tapped their way about the Internet..." She listed Dervala: A Love Letter, Irish Eyes by Bernie Goldbach, and the Babbleogue blog among her favorites. Twenty Major, an award-winning blogger, started blogging in September 2004 under that pseudonym (personal communication, June 16, 2010).

In 2005, blogs were beginning to increase in number, but according to O'Brien-Lynch (2005), the Irish blogosphere suffered from two problems: "its infancy and audience." Many blogs had started only in the previous year, and bloggers were a close-knit community, largely interacting with one another—frequently reading and commenting on one another's posts and linking to each other. O'Brien-Lynch called this "backslapping between internet buddies."

Sarah Carey points to 2005 as the year in which "there was a lot of buzz" about blogging (personal communication, June 12, 2010). Good blogs were "personal, quirky, provocative," and involved "regular posts and intimate community," she says. Carey notes that the earliest bloggers included: Karlin Lillington; Damien Mulley, "an activist in relation to the government's telecommunications policy"; Gavin Sheridan, "one of the few who ever broke into the mainstream media in terms of news breaking"; and, Twenty Major, "who was funny and outrageous and used appalling language."

Alexia Golez and Una Mullally both began blogging in 2005. The first bloggers, Golez notes (personal communication, June 15, 2010), were Gavin Sheridan (2002), Bernie Goldbach, an American based in Ireland (2001), and Damien Mulley (2003). Like other bloggers, Darragh

Doyle (personal communication, June 11, 2010) points to 2006 as the year in which blogging became popular.

Blogorrah, a New York-based site, was launched by Irish publisher John Ryan in April 2006 (Hancock, 2006). A satirical blog that poked fun at Irish public figures and Irish culture, journalist Shane Hegarty from the *Irish Times* declared it "brilliant and witty" (2006). Reilly noted that it helped to publicize the potential of blogging in Ireland (personal communication, June 2, 2010).

In 2006-2007, blogging in Ireland received a boost due to the expansion of broadband and high-speed Internet services. Reilly noted:

I believe the movement to critical mass in the blogging platform was fuelled by Ireland largely catching up with the rest of Western Europe in terms of broadband Internet penetration. Vast swathes of rural Ireland were—and still are—inaccessible to always-on broadband (being restricted either to internet carried over mobile telephone networks or to dial-up services) but medium- and small-sized rural towns were generally connected to the national broadband grid at around 2006/2007. Thus the freedom to publish at will was only truly extended to the population-at-large at around that time and it is this freedom that fuels blogging. (personal communication, June 2, 2010)

Haydn Shaughnessy (2007) noted that blogging was still taking hold in Ireland in 2007, a time when it already had peaked elsewhere. He cited freelance journalist Fergus Cassidy as having concluded that blogging in Ireland was still in its infancy and did not challenge the mainstream media or the political system as bloggers had done even in the early days of American blogging. Kennedy (2008) noted that between 2005 and 2008 there was a 300% growth in the number of people participating in the Irish blogging community, with an excess of 3,000 people blogging on everything from technology and politics to beauty and wine.

By 2009 the number of Irish blogs reported in the *Sunday Times* was approximately 4,000, the same number as the previous year (Burns, 2009). However, the numbers may have been much higher. For example, Amarach Research, a Dublin-based marketing research agency that has tracked Irish Internet usage since 1998, indicated in a 2009 study that 5% of all Irish Internet users were keeping blogs. The Amarach study also found that 67% of the 4.2 million population of Ireland were using the Internet as of February 2009. This means there could have been closer to 140,700 blogs in the Republic of Ireland. If one includes blogs written by Irish expatriates and blogs written throughout the world about Irish topics, the total would increase, further casting doubt on Burns' (2009) contention that the number of blogs in Ireland remained steady at about 4,000 and that blogging in Ireland was dying.

MOTIVATIONS FOR BLOGGING

Blogging serves various needs in Ireland. Most bloggers report a need to belong, to give expression to their thoughts and opinions, or to share news and information among their reasons to blog. Only a few have made money out of blogging, and the mainstream media were slow to embrace blogging by their professional journalists. Although there are many bloggers in the mainstream media today, in 2008 there were only five (McGuinness, 2008), most notably Jim Carroll, Conor Pope, and Shane Hegarty of the *Irish Times*.

Blogging resembles "the coffeehouses of the 18th century where debate and exchange of ideas took place," and it also parallels "going down to the pub and having a few drinks and discussing Bertie's [former Prime Minister Bertie Ahern's] latest shenanigans with friends, only cheaper!" (McGuinness, 2008). Irish bloggers point to blogging as a way "to post shorter, more immediate thoughts" (McGarr, 2007); as a way to express what's on their minds (Collison, 2009); to communicate news, views and opinions (Carroll, 2010); and even for its therapeutic value, "keeping lots of people out of John-of-Gods [a psychiatric hospital in Dublin]," according to Richard Delevan (as cited in Breathnach, 2005a).

Professionals cite other reasons for maintaining a personal blog. Phil Mac Giolla Bhain notes, "Blogging gave me my own opinion column—freed from editors and sub-editors. It was, of course, liberating!" (personal communication, June 24, 2010). One of the country's prominent bloggers is Dr. Ferdinand von Prondzynski, President of Dublin City University, who started his personal blog, Diary of a University President in 2008. In it, he discusses everything from "his battle with lumbago to the supposed 'modernisation' of higher education" (Flynn, 2008).

Social, political, and economic issues have provided the motivation for many in Ireland to begin blogging. Carey stated that the war in Iraq and the political alignment between U.S. President Bush and Great Britain's Prime Minister Blair "drove a lot of people online to vent their frustration" (personal communication, June 12, 2010). Others, she explained, have gotten involved to discuss politics and the economy. In her first blog entry, Foodie Mummy (2009) gave thanks to the economic recession and "a pretty decent redundancy package from [her] soon to be ex employer" for giving her the opportunity to become a stay-at-home mother.

Although bloggers have been critiqued for the "peercasting" type of communication (Carroll, 2010), Irish bloggers do far more than indulge in diary-like musings and sharing opinions with each other. Bloggers, for example, are credited with being the first to report the Dublin riots in 2006 (Burns, 2009), and they continue from time to time to break important news. Suzy Byrne, who blogs as Maman Poulet, has scooped the mainstream media on a number of stories, and according to Aisling McDermott (2008) became "one of the best news and current affairs bloggers in Ireland." Her scoops have included Sarah Palin's reported

visit to Ireland as nothing more than a stopover at Shannon Airport. "The story was taken up by the Huffington Post and my site traffic just went through the roof," noted Byrne (2009). She has been credited with playing "a part in setting the news agenda" (Adi, 2010) and helping to teach the mainstream media how to report on the case of a fraudulent solicitor (lawyer) Michael Lynn, according to a blog post by Will Knott (as cited in Weckler, 2008). McDermott (2008) notes, "Revelations on Maman Poulet have tripped up the high and mighty on occasion, ensuring that politicians and members of the legal profession keep a close eye on her blog."

Other blogs such as Gaelick, aimed at making lesbian issues in Ireland more visible (McDermott, 2008), serve an important social and political purpose. Irish Autism Action blog attempts to raise awareness of issues surrounding the illness and provide support and resources to families. Redmum chronicles the "life and perils of a single mother" (McDermott, 2008). Beaut.ie, a blog started in 2006 by sisters Kirstie and Aisling McDermott and which gets around 200,000 hits a day (Burns, 2009), is a beauty blog that grew out of "a sense of deep personal chagrin [at not being able to buy certain beauty products in Ireland] and selfless public service" (McDermott, 2008). In her first post for her blog, The Waiting Game, Fiona McPhillips (2005) explained that her desire was to chronicle her struggles to conceive "so that crazy ladies the world over can find some symptoms, some patterns and some comfort in the TT [test tube] endeavors of others." Others like Thrifty Mammy offer ways to economize during the economic downturn, and the blogger Lidl Treats shares recipes and information about the cut-price supermarket Lidl.

Bloggers endeavor to entertain and inform others about a variety of topics: such as design and technology (Sabrina Dent), literature (Sinead Gleeson), music (Nialler9), and food (Donal Skehan). A number of businesses have started blogs to improve their marketing and public relations efforts. Kieran Murphy, co-founder with his brother Sean, of Murphy's Ice Cream, said he "started blogging to offer recipes to our customers and create an online forum for feedback on ideas and flavours" (as cited in Gleeson, 2008).

When Irish bloggers give up writing, it is usually because of time constraints, relocation or career change, they simply no longer enjoy it, or because the cause over which they started the blog is no longer relevant. For example, long-time and highly respected Irish blogger Gavin Sheridan (Gavin's Blog) quit blogging when he moved to Dublin and started working for Storyful, a website focused on collaborative news stories from around the world told by individuals involved in the events. Una Mullally (2009) gave up her highly regarded Una Rocks blog in February 2009 because, she said, "I want to feel what it's like not to be a blogger … I'm sort of sick of the obligations and constraints I feel about it." Rick O'Shea (2010) admitted in his last post, "The fire I once had for blogging is long since gone." In her final blog post in June 2010, Irish Mammy on the Run (2010b) explained, "I don't think the blog is an adequate outlet for my expression any more."

IRISH BLOG AWARDS

A well-known Irish blogger, Damien Mulley, suggested in his October 8, 2005, blog post that it was time to set up an annual Irish Blog Awards since the Irish blogosphere "is now maturing a bit and becoming a real community." He acknowledged that it was not a unique idea, since the Freedom Institute sponsored its own Irish blog awards, called the Liberty Blog Awards, in February 2005, but, he said "it would be good for the citizens of the blogger/boggersphere [*sic*] to nominate bloggers and posts and have them line up shoulder to shoulder and be recognized as the cream of the crop." The awards were open to bloggers in the Republic of Ireland and Northern Ireland.

Alexia Golez pointed to the first Irish Blog Awards ceremony, which took place in Dublin on March 11, 2006, as a milestone in the history of Irish blogging (personal communication, June 15, 2010). In an *Irish Times* interview, published the day before the awards, Mulley, the organizer of the event, said the small blogging community "outputs a considerable amount of work that is consistently of very high quality" and that Irish blogging "is marked by its quality and diversity" (as cited in Ihle, 2006). The first awards featured 13 categories, including politics, humor, photo, technology, arts and culture, Irish language, personal, and group blogs. One hundred and sixty Irish bloggers attended the event. Winners had been decided in an online poll after 1,700 votes were cast, not all by bloggers (Goldbach, 2006).

Ihle (2006) identified the star bloggers among the nominees as Sarah Carey and Northern Ireland's Mick Fealty, who ran the political blog Slugger O'Toole. Fealty said the first phase of blogging in Ireland was over "because it is now popular" (as cited in Ihle, 2006). Mulley predicted that bloggers would now move away "from personal commentary to more subject-specific blogs emerging from companies, political parties and other institutions" (as cited in Ihle, 2006).

Indeed, the following year saw a number of additional blog awards categories, including news and current affairs, music, sport and recreation, business, and specialist blogs, added to reflect the growing number of individuals and organizations in the blogosphere. One hundred blogs competed against each other in the second annual Irish Blog Awards in 2007. The following year, 750 blogs were nominated across 22 categories. Each year new categories of blogs have been added to represent the evolving blogosphere. In 2008, the new categories included blogs on crafts, food and drink, pop culture, and blog posts from a journalist; in 2009, fashion became a new category; and in 2010, politicians' and youth blogs were among the new topic areas. The Irish Blog Awards has grown from 13 categories in 2006 to 22 categories and hundreds of nominees in 2010. Growth in the Irish Blog Awards has paralleled growth in the blogging community.

Golez explained that the Irish Blog Awards were from the start, and continue to be, "an important part of the blogging calendar" (personal communication, June 15, 2010). She added, "If the popularity of blogging can be seen anywhere, it's in the dedication of bloggers to travel from different parts of the country or *indeed* from different parts of the world to come to the annual event."

THE IMPORTANCE OF CONTEXT

Russell (2009) cautions scholars studying blogging to consider context when evaluating blogs throughout the world. Demographic, social-cultural, political, technological, legal, and economic factors influence—and provide context for—blogging in Ireland and everywhere else. As noted previously, Ireland has a population of 4.2 million, roughly half of the population of New York City. There are fewer blogs in Ireland than in many other countries because there are fewer people, but the small population may influence blogging in other ways.

Blogger John Fay noted that the Irish blogosphere was less polarized than that of the United States. "Maybe because the country's so small people are more wary of offending someone they might know or who might know their family or whatever," he said (as cited in Breathnach, 2005b). Although Shaughnessy (2007) praised "its diversity of viewpoints" as one of Irish blogging's "exceptional traits," he also pointed to the weakness caused by a lack of collective strength among voices on the Web. In Ireland, a debate is likely "to begin wide and remain so," rather than polarizing along party lines as in the United States and United Kingdom. As such, it is unlikely to have a great impact on political policy.

Dr. Niall O'Dochartaigh, a political scientist at the National University of Ireland Galway, hypothesized that Irish bloggers might never attain the political influence of bloggers in the United States because of the country's small population. Politics in Ireland is very much about face-to-face contact, since political candidates can more easily campaign in the smaller electoral districts. "A candidate for the Dail [Irish Parliament] can reasonably expect to personally canvass a good proportion of the electorate," O'Dochartaigh said. "That's an absolute impossibility in the U.S. so voters can be much more reliant on the Internet for information" (as cited in Reid, 2006).

According to Jim Carroll, politicians today use online media as an "add-on," not as part of their main strategy. "Irish politics is about slogging around, going to funerals; it's old fashioned" (personal communication, June 14, 2010). Reid (2006) also noted that unlike the United States, political blogs remained "on the fringes of political life" in Ireland, something that some Irish bloggers wanted to change. One effort to bring about such change was a "Blogging the Election" conference, organized in October 2006 in Dublin, by IrishElection.com. The purpose of the conference was to discuss how blogging could help "influence the very traditional political process in Ireland" (Irishelection.com, 2006).

Blogs in Ireland continue to be important in giving a platform and voice for people to highlight issues of concern, particularly when people cannot make personal presentation, for whatever reason, to a member of parliament. "It was through this humble blog that the PACUB [Protest Against Child Unfriendly Budget] campaign started last year and gave over 16,000 families a voice to vent their frustrations (via a petition) at plans to cut child benefit" (Irish Mammy on the Run, 2010a). Sometimes, however, writing a blog post about an issue may seem pointless. "When constituents have a grievance they can address it to their TD [member of parliament] in person at his or her weekly surgery [constituency office]," notes

McGuinness (2008). "Why, then, bother writing a blog when you can shove your finger at Bertie's [Prime Minister Bertie Ahern's] nose?"

As important as blogs about political issues may be in Ireland, some think that political blogging detracts from political activity. McGuinness (2008) noted:

DIT [Dublin Institute of Technology] media lecturer Harry Browne argues that political blogging is a distraction from the real business of marching in the streets and going to branch meetings. According to Browne, if the people are pouring their energies into reading and spreading information while sitting at home, those in power can rest easy. Traditional collective action is more effective, says Browne, at bringing about political change.

THE PRACTICE OF LIVE BLOGGING

While traditional forms of political action still may be important in Ireland, there is no denying that technology is changing the way people get involved to bring about political change. One of the most recent trends in blogging is the practice of live blogging, which, according to Golez (personal communication, June, 15, 2010), has become increasingly popular in Ireland. With the help of live blogging, an ongoing event may be covered by posting regular updates to a blog. Twitter messages that use a specific *hashtag* (or a particular individual's tweets) may also be incorporated into a blog. Event photos and videos can be added as well through a smart phone.

Golez explained that over the past two years or so, she and Suzy Byrne, known as Maman Poulet, set up a number of live blogging events:

on the Irish budgets and speeches on the budgets in the Dáil (Irish Parliament), liveblogs on the Rose of Tralee TV programme (a famous beauty meets talent contest), the counts and results of the Local (council) and European elections in 2009.

Reporting in the Local and European election counts was particularly successful as contributors went to their local count centres and liveblogged. We reported numbers and results before the mainstream media—which is incredibly powerful ... I ... got to interview politicians before and after they lost their seats. (personal communication, June 15, 2010)

Byrne added that during the 2009 election for local government, "National broadcasters went to bed, but live bloggers stayed up and did the job. Nobody got paid. Some of them took holiday to do it" (personal communication, June 21, 2010). People from around the country sent text messages if they had no Internet access; it was a collaborative effort. "The really great thing about liveblogs is that they belong to the people that contribute to them, not to the people that start them or the people that just publish them on blogs" (personal communication, June 15, 2010).

Simon McGarr (2010) argues that live blogging has not yet reached its potential. In addition to participating with Golez and Carey, he set up a website, liveblog.ie, which currently houses five live blog projects conducted from December 2009 to January 2010. McGarr believes that reporting events through live blogging helps citizens stay informed about the issues their communities are facing, and allows them to make informed decisions about the direction they should take. If newspapers in Ireland ever collapse, he believes live blogging could fill the need of informing citizens about their communities. "When (or if, should you wish to remain cheery), I am correct and newspapers shut their doors we will have built a safety net."

TECHNOLOGICAL FACTORS

The transformation of Ireland's economy from one of the poorest in Europe to one of the most prosperous was prompted in part by foreign investment from high-tech companies, such as Dell, Intel, Google, and Microsoft. Yet despite its flourishing high-tech economy, Ireland's Internet penetration rates—and especially access to high-speed Internet connections—lagged behind those of the United States and much of Europe. By 2006, roughly half of all Irish households had Internet access, but only 13% of Irish households had a broadband connection (Central Statistics Office, 2006). By comparison, broadband penetration rates during the same timeframe were the highest in Denmark and the Netherlands at 29%; they were 22% in Canada, 19% in the United Kingdom, and 18% in the United States.

By December 2009, the number of broadband subscribers in Ireland had reached almost 20% (Organisation for Economic Cooperation and Development, 2010), up from 15% in June 2007 (Kanellos, 2008). Although improving, Ireland's broadband penetration rate is still behind 21 other Asian, European, and North American countries; these countries include the United Kingdom, the United States, and Japan (Organisation for Economic Co-operation and Development, 2010). The lack of broadband access is often blamed for the relatively low number of people blogging in Ireland (Cochrane, 2009; McGuinness, 2008). As blogger John Fay, an American expatriate living in Ireland, explained in a 2005 interview, "Truth is, I'd probably have done this years ago, but couldn't afford all the requisite online time. I started blogging when I could get a free, always-on Internet connection" (as cited in Breathnach, 2005b). A lack of high-speed Internet access has negatively influenced blog adoption in Ireland, but so, too, have other factors.

THE POTENTIAL CHILLING EFFECT OF IRISH DEFAMATION LAW

Irish bloggers—like other types of media writers—need to understand defamation law. As of January 2010, there was only one "known case

of a libel award based on content in an Irish blog" (Ryan, 2010). The case stemmed from a December 1, 2006, post in which a blogger, who calls himself Ardmayle, wrote about the sale of a collection of James Joyce papers by Laura Barnes, an American book dealer, to the Irish state. One year later Barnes began a relationship with an assistant secretary in the Department of Arts, Sports and Tourism. Ardmayle's post, titled "Barnes and Noble," commented on both the sale and the couple. After a legal complaint, Ardmayle took down the post in February 2007 and posted an apology. The couple still pressed charges, and a €100,000 (approximately $139,000 U.S.) settlement was reached in late 2009 (Burns, 2010).

The case is predicted to have "a chilling effect on the Irish blogosphere" (Burns, 2010), especially given the fact that Ardmayle's blog was not a popular one (Ryan, 2010). Mark Coughlan, (as cited in Ryan, 2010), said the blog was so "obscure that Google finds zero—repeat zero—inward links." In other words, no one had linked to the blog post. T.J. McIntyre, a law lecturer at University College Dublin said bloggers "could protect themselves from large [libel] awards by ensuring they keep server logs, showing just how widely particular posts have been read" (as cited in Ryan, 2010).

Ireland's libel law became stricter with the Defamation Act of 2009, which went into effect on January 1, 2010. The act also includes the crime of blasphemy, which is defined by Irish Statute as: "grossly abusive or insulting in relation to matters held sacred by any religion, thereby causing outrage among a substantial number of the adherents of that religion" (Defamation Act 2009). About 30 minutes after the new law took effect, a group of Irish atheists published 25 blasphemous statements on the blog Blasphemy.ie (Mackey, 2010). Published by Atheist Ireland, the blog is part of a campaign to repeal the blasphemy law (Nugent, 2009).

THE INFLUENCE OF TWITTER AND FACEBOOK

Observers of the Irish blogosphere have noted the controversial influence of new social media tools and applications, such as Twitter and Facebook, on traditional blogging. Mulley (as cited in Burns, 2009) explained, "Blogging has definitely slowed down as all these other tools that allow us to communicate have come along." In part, that's because "the reasons people blogged could be served by other platforms," noted Carey, who added that she loves Facebook "because everyone is friends – no more rows!" (personal communication, June 12, 2010). Carey (as cited in Butterworth, 2010), said she believes the Irish are moving to closed networks like Facebook to protect themselves against incivility and possible repercussions from Irish libel law.

Facebook, a social networking site, has had explosive growth in Ireland. The number of Irish Facebook accounts doubled from about 200,000 users in January 2008 to about 400,000 users a year later (Mulley, 2009a) and then more than doubled again to about 906,000 in August 2009 (Mulley, 2009b). Twitter, a popular microblogging service, had nearly 8,000 Irish accounts by February 2009, up from less than 100 at the end of 2006 ("Twitter Uptake Statistics," 2009). Twitter allows users to send and receive messages, known as *tweets*, which are limited in size to 140 characters.

Breslin (personal communication, June 8, 2010) and Reilly noted that Twitter is being used for short updates, and blogging is used for detailed articles. Reilly said blogging is the best medium for "content which simply cannot be adequately shared within a curtailed character limit" (personal communication, June 2, 2010). Mullally (2010) said blogging in Ireland isn't over, but Twitter is being used for "short form thoughts, linking, news, titbits [*sic*], whereas blogging will increasingly be about longer form pieces." She, herself, claims to be "quite addicted to" Twitter (personal communication, July 27, 2010). Doyle noted, "If you can say something in 140 characters or less, why say it in any more?" (personal communication, June 11, 2010).

However, other bloggers claim that new and emerging social media platforms are revitalizing blogging. Twenty Major argued that Twitter has made blogs more accessible to people by giving them an opportunity to build relationships with each other. "They're engaged with people now far more than they were when they blogged," he said (personal communication, June 16, 2010). Breslin explained that bloggers use social media tools to "augment their blogging with status updates and pointers to new blog posts, thereby reinforcing each other – getting feedback for posts, posting updates that would not warrant a full blog post, and disseminating new blog posts amongst a wider network than was previously possible through RSS subscriptions, blog aggregators or blog roll links/trackbacks" (personal communication, June 8, 2010).

NICHE BLOGGING

Golez says that niche groups have started blogging in areas such as human rights (Human Rights in Ireland, a group academic blog) and the Irish economy (The Irish Economy). "Without blogging becoming popular, I don't think that these area experts would have jumped on the blogging bus" (personal communication, June 15, 2010). Money—or the lack of it—became a major story in Ireland, as in the rest of the world, in 2009. In Ireland, mainstream media had to explain international capital markets and their impact on Ireland after the international financial crisis of 2008. Many turned to the blog The Irish Economy. Described by journalist Proinsias O'Mahony (as cited in Price, 2009) as "a must-read for anyone with an interest in the Irish economy and the international financial crisis," the blog extended beyond national boundaries and "gained a global influence in its first year of existence." The blog's readers include influential figures in the International Monetary Fund, the European Commission and the World Bank. "In other words," noted Price (2009), "it is read by institutions that have active interests in the Irish economy or may have in the future."

Started in 2009 by Philip Lane, professor of macroeconomics at Trinity College Dublin and a Harvard graduate, The Irish Economy blog gets about 3,000 hits a day. The site influences mainstream media coverage with information written by "respected academics and professional economists who fathom the complexities of Ireland's fiscal crisis and debate a wide range of remedies" (Price, 2009). According to Carey (as cited in Burns, 2009), "Irish Economy took off because it acted as a resource for facts. It gave us the stats, charts, papers and the economics behind the spin rather than simply expressing opinion. It's a success because we desperately needed it." Butterworth (2010) noted that the Irish Economy blog represented a new media way of tackling the financial crisis.

Blogs cover other niche areas including sports, politics, film, fashion, technology, parenting, and food. Bord Bia (the Irish Food Board) sponsored the Irish Food Bloggers Event in May 2010 in which "30 people—some strangers in the flesh, yet already intimate online—gathered for a day of food demonstrations, discussions, and attempts at matching faces to personalities" (Hennessy, 2010). During the event, Irish blogging expert Damien Mulley gave an informational presentation on blogging, and Eoin Purcell, publishing industry analyst, spoke about the Irish boutique publishing industry.

BLOGGING AS A CAREER LAUNCH PAD

Many Irish bloggers have landed mainstream media jobs as a result of their blogging. Sarah Carey, for example, got a column in the *Sunday Times* and later in the *Irish Times*. Bernie Goldbach landed a

weekly column in the *Examiner*. Damien Mulley wrote for the now-defunct *Electric News* and later for the *Sunday Tribune,* as does former blogger Una Mullally. Other bloggers-turned-mainstream media writers include: Adrian Weckler, whose column "Your Tech Stuff" appears in the *Sunday Business Post*; Karlin Lillington, *Irish Times* tech writer who has written for the *Sunday Times*, the *Guardian*, *Wired News*, the *San Jose Mercury News*, and other publications; Donal Skehan, *Irish Independent*; Sinead Gleeson, *Irish Times*; Kirstie and Aisling McDermott of the blog Beaut.ie who now have radio gigs as well as a column in the *Evening Herald*; and, Gavin Sheridan, formerly a production journalist on the *Irish Examiner* and now working at Storyful with Mark Little. Sarah Carey (in Butterworth, 2010) noted that when she landed her column in the mainstream media, her blog readers were delighted. "They saw it as an endorsement," she said.

Just as many bloggers have obtained mainstream media employment, many, too, have landed book deals. Several high-profile bloggers around the world landed deals "before the concept of bloggers as published writers hit Ireland" (Gleeson, 2008). Among the Irish bloggers to have gotten book deals are: Aisling McDermott of the blog Beaut.ie with *The Beaut.ie Guide to Gorgeous* (Gill & Macmillan, 2009); Fiona McPhillips of The Waiting Game blog with *Trying to Conceive* (Liberties Press, 2008); Sean and Kieran Murphy of the Ice Cream Ireland blog with *Murphy's Ice Cream Book of Sweet Things* (Mercier Press, 2006); Richard O'Connor of the Head Rambles blog with *Head Rambles* (Mercier Press, 2009); Donal Skehan of the GoodMoodFood blog with *Good Mood Food* (Mercier Press, 2009); and, Twenty Major, with *The Order of the Phoenix Park* (2008) and *Absinthe Makes the Heart Grow Fonder* (Hachette Books, 2009).

Twenty Majors' book, *The Order of the Phoenix Park*, featured characters from his blog, which had 1,500 hits a day. Ciara Dooley, Twenty Majors' editor at Hachette Books Ireland, said the author's anonymity was not a problem for sales. "Obviously he doesn't do publicity in person but he's very open to being interviewed by phone or e-mail," she said about the author who never has revealed his real name. "The blog's existing success means there is already huge awareness of Twenty Major and his humour" (as cited in Coyle, 2008). Richard O'Connor, who has the persona of Grandad on his blog, Head Rambles, wrote a book on themes similar to those of his blogs, for example, the complaints of older people about aging, politics, their neighbors, and television. In April of 2007 Kieran Murphy was contacted by a representative from Mercier Press who liked his blog, and the book deal was completed that June (personal communication, June 14, 2010). Gleeson (2008) suggested that book deals are major accomplishments for bloggers

in a small country like Ireland.... Long accused of amateurish soapboxing, there is no doubt that the quality of Irish blogs varies, and the ultimate validation of a book deal reinforces the idea of separating the online wheat from the chaff.

CONCLUSION

Although mainstream journalists and bloggers alike have debated whether blogging in Ireland is withering out with the advent of Twitter and Facebook, our findings indicate that this is not the case. Some bloggers quit, while others continue to blog. New forms such as live blogging, as well as microblogging and social networking, may be influencing blogging practices, but as blogger Twenty Major notes, "change is natural" (personal communication, June 16, 2010).

The total number of blogs in Ireland may be rather low in comparison with other countries, but it is not unexpected, given the size of Ireland's population. Although the pioneers of Irish blogging mostly were males with technology expertise or interests, people from a cross section of Irish

society now blog. Technological advances such as the easy use of blogging software and more widespread distribution of broadband, along with lower costs of Internet access have made it possible for more people in Ireland to go online. Reilly comments on the state of blogging in Ireland, "I think the medium is in a state of evolution, moving from something practiced by a hardcore circle of dedicated people to something that becomes accessible by a greater critical mass" (personal communication, June 2, 2010).

Additionally, the topics covered in Irish blogs today reflect a broad range of social, political and cultural interests, concerns, and activities. Byrne notes that there is a variety of blogs and that the blogging scene is "lively" (personal communication, June 21, 2010). Doyle observes that the Irish blogosphere is "hugely vibrant, growing continuously and with passion ... filled with interesting ideas and innovation and has never been as varied" (personal communication, June 11, 2010).

The Irish blogosphere continues to evolve and change. While the Defamation Act of 2009 has yet to severely impact blogging practices, it remains to be seen how it might influence blogging in the future. Communication technologies, of course, will continue to change. So, too, will social, cultural, economic, political, and other aspects of Irish life that influence blogging as a social phenomenon and communicative practice. One cannot even imagine the challenges and opportunities of the future. However, despite speculation about the demise of Irish blogging, the authors have found that such reports have been greatly exaggerated. Blogging is alive and well in Ireland.

LIMITATIONS AND FUTURE RESEARCH DIRECTIONS

This case study has certain limitations, among them the constraints of the researchers working only in the English language, thereby omitting Gaelic blogs. Further, limiting the study to bloggers in the Republic of Ireland is problematic, since an identity of "Irishness" may extend beyond geographic borders. Methodologically, by using a convenience sampling, researchers might have overlooked some Irish bloggers who may have provided valuable data for the study. Despite the limitations, this study focuses on the social, cultural, political, technological, and legal aspects of Irish blogging, which have not been previously examined by scholars. Irish blogging is a topic rife with opportunities for future research.

As live blogging becomes more commonplace, its influence on Irish politics and on journalistic practice and norms should be explored in more detail. Examining the influence of different social media applications on traditional blogging could shed light on new and emerging trends. A longitudinal study of a particular Irish blog or several blogs could help media scholars understand continuity and change in blogging practices in Ireland. Other opportunities for research include comparative studies of blogging in countries similar to Ireland with comparable populations and technological infrastructure.

Gender differences among bloggers, including differences in how women and men use blogging as a communication tool, their levels of personal satisfaction, and their motivations also are worthy of research. Additionally, researchers may explore whether gender inequality exists in the popularity rankings of male and female bloggers in Ireland. An examination of gender and multicultural identity expressed through blogging is another topic of study.

In the educational realm, an exploration of how educators in Ireland are using blogs to enhance communication with their students or of how blogs facilitate learning in the classroom would be valuable. Further, a study of business blogs in Ireland could be undertaken from a strategic or integrated marketing communications perspective. Researchers could also explore niche blogs, such as those related to faith, parenting, health, arts

and entertainment, consumerism, human rights, and other topics as they emerge.

NOTABLE IRISH BLOGS/BLOGGERS

Alexia Golez
http://golez.net/
Ardmayle
http://ardmayle.blogspot.com/
Arseblog
http://arseblog.com/
Beaut.ie – Kirstie McDermott and Aisling McDermott
http://beaut.ie/blog/
Bibliocook: All About Food
http://www.bibliocook.com/
Damien Mulley
http://www.mulley.net/
A University Blog: Diary of life and strategy inside and outside the university – Ferdinand von Prondzynski
http://universitydiary.wordpress.com/
Eoin Purcell's Blog
http://eoinpurcellsblog.com/
FoodieMummy
http://foodiemummy.blogspot.com/
Gaelick
http://www.gaelick.com/
Gav Reilly: Thinking Out Loud
http://gavreilly.com/
The Good Mood Food Blog – Donal Skehan
http://www.thegoodmoodfoodblog.com/
HeadRambles: Rambles Around the Head of an Irish Grandad – Richard O'Connor
http://www.headrambles.com/
Holy Shmoly! – Donncha O Caoimh
http://ocaoimh.ie/
Human Rights in Ireland
http://www.humanrights.ie/
Ice Cream Ireland – Kieran Murphy, director of Murphy's Ice Cream
http://www.icecreamireland.com/

Inside View from Ireland – Bernie "topgold" Goldbach
http://irish.typepad.com/irisheyes/
Irish Autism Action
http://irishautismaction.blogspot.com/
The Irish Economy
http://www.irisheconomy.ie/
Irish Election
http://www.irishelection.com/
John Breslin
http://www.johnbreslin.com/blog
Liveblog.ie – Simon McGarr
http://liveblog.ie/blog/
Maman Poulet – Suzy Byrne
http://www.mamanpoulet.com/
Nialler9 – Niall Byrne
http://www.nialler9.com/
On the Record – Jim Carroll, *Irish Times*
http://www.irishtimes.com/blogs/ontherecord/
Phil Mac Giolla Bhain
http://www.philmacgiollabhain.com/
Piaras Kelly PR – Public Relations Ireland
http://www.pkellypr.com/blog/
Red Mum: The Times and Perils of a Single Parent
http://www.redmum.ie
Rick O'Shea (The pointy adventures of Jean-Claude Supremo)
http://rickoshea.wordpress.com/
Sabrina Dent
http://www.sabrinadent.com/category/blog/
Sinead Cochrane
http://www.sineadcochrane.com/
This is What I Did – Darragh Doyle
http://darraghdoyle.blogspot.com/
Thrifty Mammy
http://www.thriftymammy.com/
Trust Tommy – Tommy Collison
http://trusttommy.com/
Tuppenceworth – Simon McGarr
http://www.tuppenceworth.ie/blog/
Twenty Major
http://twentymajor.net/
The Waiting Game – Fiona McPhillips

http://makingbabies.ie/wordpress/
Your Tech Stuff – Adrian Weckler, *Sunday Business Post*
http://yourtechstuff.com/

ACKNOWLEDGMENT

The authors would like to thank the following Irish bloggers for their responses to our inquiries about blogging: John Breslin; Suzy Byrne (Maman Poulet); Sarah Carey; Jim Carroll; Sinead Cochrane; Darragh Doyle; Alexia Golez; Phil Mac Giolla Bhain; Kirstie McDermott; Una Mullally; Kieran Murphy; Gavan Reilly; and Twenty Major. Thanks to their helpful insights, we were able to bring rich detail to our exploration of blogging in Ireland.

REFERENCES

Adi. (2010, January 12). Omphaloskepsis for the nation [Web log comment]. *Irish Times*. Retrieved from http://www.irishtimes.com/blogs/ontherecord/category/blog-stuff/

Amarach Research. (2009). *Life online 2009: Amarach*. Retrieved from http://www.amarach.com/assets /files/Life%20Online %202009.pdf

Anderson, C. (2006). *The long tail: Why the future of business is selling less of more*. New York, NY: Hyperion.

Arthur, C. (2009, June 24). The long tail of blogging is dying. *The Guardian*. Retrieved from http://www.guardian.co.uk/ technology/2009/jun/24/charles-arthur-blogging-twitter

Barlow, A. (2007). *The rise of the blogosphere*. Westport, CT: Praeger Publishers.

Blood, R. (2000, September 7). *Weblogs: A history and perspective*. Retrieved from http://www.rebeccablood.net/ essays/weblog_history.html

Breathnach, K. (2005a, September 29). *Interview #1: Richard Delevan* [Web log post]. Retrieved from http://disillusionedlefty.blogspot.com /2005/09/interview-1- richard-delevan.html

Breathnach, K. (2005b, November 3). *Interview #6: John Fay* [Web log post]. Retrieved from http://disillusionedlefty.blogspot.com /2005/11/interview-6-john-fay.html

Breathnach, K. (2006, January 26). *Interview #16: Damien Mulley* [Web log post]. Retrieved from http://disillusionedlefty.blogspot.com /2006/01/interview- 16-damien-mulley.html

Burns, J. (2009, December 20). Where have all the Irish bloggers gone? *The Sunday Times*. Retrieved from LexisNexis Academic Database.

Burns, J. (2010, January 31). Blogger must pay €100,000 for libel. *The Times*. Retrieved from http://www.timesoline.co.uk/tol /news/world/ Ireland/ article7009820.ece

Butterworth, T. (2010, January 27). Erin go blog. Forbes.com. Retrieved from http://www.forbes.com/ 2010/01/26/ireland-blogs -twitter-media-opinions-columnists -trevor-butterworth.html

Byrne, S. (2009, December 3). My decade. *Irish Times*. Retrieved from LexisNexis Academic Database.

Carroll, J. (2010, January 12). Omphaloskepsis for the nation. *Irish Times*. Retrieved from http://www.irishtimes.com/blogs /ontherecord/category/blog-stuff/

Central Statistics Office. (2006, November 8). *Information society statistics: First results 2006*. Dublin, Ireland. Retrieved from http://www.cso.ie/releasespublications /documents/industry/2006/iss_firstresults2006.pdf

Cochrane, S. (2009). *Blogs: A study into current uses and perceptions in Irish society*. Unpublished Master's thesis, Dun Laoghaire Institute of Art, Design and Technology, Dun Laoghaire, Ireland.

Collison, T. (2009, August 9). My week. *Sunday Times*. Retrieved from http://www.timesonline.co.uk/tol/news/world/ireland/article6788575.ece

Cosgrave, T. (2006, February 6). *Who was Ireland's first blogger* [Web log comment]. Retrieved from http://www.mulley.net/2006/ 02/06/who-was-irelands- first-blogger/comment-page-1/

Cosgrave, T., & Ayers, T. (2002, January 15). *iLoggers site list*. Retrieved from http://web.archive.org/web/ 20020115045344/ http://www.nofusion.com/ ilog/sites.jsp

Coyle, C. (2008, March 23). Blogger fails to click as novelist: Twenty Major has minor sales. *The Sunday Times*. Retrieved from LexisNexis Academic Database.

De Vries, K. (2009). Bridges or breaches? Thoughts on how people use blogs in China. In Russell, A., & Echchaibi, N. (Eds.), *International blogging: Identity, politics, and networked publics* (pp. 47–64). New York, NY: Peter Lang Publishing Inc.

Defamation Act. (2009). *Irish statute book*. Retrieved from http://www.irishstatutebook.ie/2009/en/act/pub/0031/ sec0036.html#sec36

Flynn, S. (2008, June 13). DCU president enters the blogosphere. *Irish Times*. Retrieved from LexisNexis Academic Database.

Foodie Mummy. (2009, December 9). *Thank you recession* [Web log post]. Retrieved from http://foodiemummy.blogspot.com/ 2009/12/thank-you-recession.html

Gerring, J. (2007). *Case study research: Principles and practices*. New York, NY: Cambridge University Press.

Gleeson, S. (2008, February 29). Misfits no longer, Irish bloggers are snapping up book deals; It's Friday! Books. *Daily Mail*. Retrieved from LexisNexis Academic Database.

Goldbach, B. (2006, March 13). Twenty Major in *Irish Times* [Web log post]. Retrieved from http://www.insideview.ie/ irisheyes/2006/03/ twenty_major_in.html

Hancock, C. (2006, June 25). From dogs to blogs. *The Sunday Times*. Retrieved from LexisNexis Academic Database.

Hegarty, S. (2006, December 2). Can blogs beat papers to a pulp? *Irish Times*. Retrieved from LexisNexis Academic Database.

Hennessy, C. (2010, May 21). *Pork and bloggers* [Web log post]. Retrieved from http://www. bibliocook.com/ 2010/05/ pigging-out-wit.html

Ihle, J. (2006, March 10). Bloggers line up for first Irish awards. *Irish Times*. Retrieved from LexisNexis Academic Database.

Irish Blogs.ie. (n.d.). *Website*. Retrieved from http://www.irishblogs.ie

Irish Mammy on the Run. (2010a, March 16). *Is Irish blogging over?* [Web log post]. Retrieved from http://irish-mammy.blogspot.com/ 2010/03/ is-irish- blogging-over.html

Irish Mammy on the Run. (2010b, June 7). *So this is goodbye* [Web log post]. Retrieved from http:// irish-mammy.blogspot.com/

Irishblogs.ie. (2009, February 9). *Twitter uptake statistics - explosive growth in2009*. Retrieved from http://blog.irishblogs.ie/ 2009/02/10/twitter-uptake- statistics-explosive-growth- in-2009/

Irishelection.com. (2006, October 7). *Announcement: "Blogging the Election" Conference Oct 7th 2006* [Web log post]. Retrieved from http:// www.irishelection.com/ 2006/09/announcement-blogging-the -election-conference-oct-7th-2006/

Kanellos, M. (2008, March 3). Why blogging isn't big in Ireland. *CNET News*. Retrieved from http:// news.cnet.com/ 8301-10784_3- 9884266-7.html

Kennedy, J. (2008, February 27). *Brace yourselves - The bloggers are growing up!* Retrieved from http://www.siliconrepublic.com /news/news. nv?storyid =single10382

Killeavy, M., & Maloney, A. (2010, May). Reflection in a social space: Can blogging support reflective practice for beginning teachers? *Teaching and Teacher Education, 26,* 1070–1076. doi:10.1016/j. tate.2009.11.002

Lee, C. M., & Bates, J. A. (2007). Mapping the Irish biblioblogosphere: Use and perceptions of library weblogs by Irish librarians. *The Electronic Library, 25,* 648–663. doi:10.1108/02640470710837092

Lillington, K. (2004, October 29). Blogging is a labour of love but it can also be hard work. *Irish Times*. Retrieved from LexisNexis Academic Database.

Loftus, M. (2006). *The Irish blogosphere: Who is blogging and what motivates them to do so?* Unpublished master's dissertation, Dublin City University, Dublin, Ireland.

Mackey, R. (2010, January 4). Attempt to break new Irish blasphemy law. *New York Times*. Retrieved from http://thelede.blogs.nytimes.com/ 2010/01/04/new-irish- blasphemy-law-broken/

Marlow, C. (2005, May). *Audience, structure and authority in the weblog community*. Paper presented at the meeting of the International Communication Association Conference, New Orleans, LA.

McDermott, A. (2008, September 13). Blog her. *Irish Times*. Retrieved from LexisNexis Academic Database.

McGarr, S. (2007, June 8). *Politics and blogging - My answers* [Web log post]. Retrieved from http://www.tuppencworth.ie/blog /2007/06/08/ politics- and-blogging-my-answers/

McGarr, S. (2010, February 10). *My liveblogged year, part one* [Web log post]. Retrieved from http://www.tuppenceworth.ie/blog /2010/02/10/ my-liveblogged -year-part-one/

McGuinness, M. (2008, February 12). *On talking shite. The Dubliner.* Retrieved from http://thedubliner.typepad.com/the_dubliner_magazine /2008/02/talking-shite.html

McPhillips, F. (2005, September 26). *Freebie - 1 DPO* [Web log post]. Retrieved from http://makingbabies.ie/wordpress/2005/09/26/ feebee-1-dpo/

Mullally, U. (2009, February 23). *I kill her* [Web log post]. Retrieved from http://unarocks.blogspot.com/

Mullally, U. (2010, January 5). *On Irish blogging being over* [Web log post]. Retrieved from http://twentymajor.net/2010/01 /05/on-irish-blogging -being-over/

Mulley, D. (2005, October 8). *Irish blog (and podcast) awards 2005* [Web log post]. Retrieved from http://www.mulley.net/2005 /10/08/irish-blog-and -podcast-awards-2005/

Mulley, D. (2006, February 6). *Who was Ireland's first blogger?* [Web log post]. Retrieved from http://www.mulley.net/2006 /02/06/who-was-irelands- first-blogger/comment-page-1/

Mulley, D. (2008, July 26). *Zzzzz, it's boring* [Web log comment]. Retrieved from http://twentymajor.net/2008 /07/26/zzzzz-its-boring/

Mulley, D. (2009a, January 4). *Facebook doubles in size in Ireland in 12 months – 400k in January 09* [Web log post]. Retrieved from http://mulley.ie/blog/2009/01/ facebook-doubles-in-size-in-ireland -in-12-months-400k-in-january-09/

Mulley, D. (2009b, August 1). *Facebook hits 900k in Ireland* [Web log post]. Retrieved from http://mulley.ie/blog/2009/ 08/facebook-hits-900k-in-ireland/

Murray, L., Hourigan, T., & Jeanneau, C. (2007). Blog writing integration for academic language learning purposes: Towards an assessment framework. *Iberica, 14,* 9–32.

Nugent, M. (2009, May 8). *Atheist Ireland publishes 25 blasphemous quotes.* Retrieved from http://blasphemy.ie/

O'Brien-Lynch, R. (2005, February 11). Lots of blogs but few talking about Irish matters. *Irish Times.* Retrieved from LexisNexis Academic Database.

O'Shea, R. (2010, January 4). *Out of business* [Web log post]. Retrieved from http://rickoshea. wordpress.com/

Organisation for Economic Co-operation and Development. (2010). *OECD broadband portal.* Retrieved from http://www.oecd.org/document/54 /0,3343,en_2649_34225_38690102_1_1_1_1,00. html

Pedersen, S., & Macafee, C. (2006, June). The practices and popularity of British bloggers. In B. Martens, & M. Dobreva (Eds.), *Proceedings of the 10th International Conference on Electronic Publishing* (pp. 155-164). Retrieved from http:// elpub.scix.net/data/works /att/213_elpub2006. content.pdf

Price, S. (2009, December 20). Many blogs are simply rants by opinionated amateurs but one stands out from the masses. The Irish Economy is written by experts and its influence extends across the globe. *The Sunday Times.* Retrieved from LexisNexis Academic Database.

Purcell, E. (2006, June 29). *Blogs, Begorrah and Ireland* [Web log post]. Retrieved from http://eo-inpurcellsblog.com/ 2006/06/29/blogs- begorrah-and-ireland/

Reid, L. (2006, March 21). Prepare for the power of the blog. *Irish Times.* Retrieved from LexisNexis Academic Database.

Russell, A. (2009). Introduction. In Russell, A., & Echchaibi, N. (Eds.), *International blogging: Identity, politics, and networked publics* (pp. 1–10). New York, NY: Peter Lang Publishing Inc.

Ryan, L. (2010, February 5). *The libel laws and Irish bloggers*. Retrieved from http://journalist.ie/2010/02/ libel-and-irish-bloggers/

Schmidt, J. (2007). Blogging practices: An analytical framework. *Journal of Computer-Mediated Communication, 12*, 1409–1427. doi:10.1111/j.1083-6101.2007.00379.x

Shaughnessy, H. (2007, March 2). Should you blog in or blog off? *Irish Times*. Retrieved from LexisNexis Academic Database.

Sullivan, D. (2008, July 29). *Zzzzz, it's boring* [Web log comment]. Retrieved from http://twentymajor.net/2008/ 07/26/zzzzz-its-boring/

Swanborn, P. G. (2010). *Case study research: What, why and how?* London, UK: Sage Publications.

Twenty Major. (2008, August 26). *Zzzzz, it's boring* [Web log post]. Retrieved from http://twentymajor.net/2008/ 07/26/zzzzz-its-boring/

Weckler, A. (2008, July 25). Are Irish blogs just crap? *TechWire*. Retrieved from http://www.yourtechstuff.com/ techwire/2008/07/ are-irish-blogs.html

Yin, R. K. (2009). *The case study research* (4th ed.). Thousands Oaks, CA: Sage Publications.

KEY TERMS AND DEFINITIONS

Blog Aggregator: A website that assembles information from or links to other websites; it does not offer original content. Some aggregators focus on a certain topic. Aggregators often link to specific stories within a website and may offer keyword searches.

Blogosphere: The total number of blogs and their connections via such practices as links within posts (articles) or blogrolls.

Blogroll: A list of blogs recommended by the writer of a particular blog. These links are often displayed on the first page of a blog in a list on the right or left side of the page.

Broadband Access: Though different criteria are used to define broadband access, it usually means a high-speed connection to the Internet, one that is faster than dial-up access via telephone lines.

Hashtag: A convention used to mark keywords or topics in a Twitter message.

Inward Link (or Backlink): A link from one website to another. Also known as an inbound link, an inward link brings traffic into a website. The total number of inward links to any one page or site is one way to gauge the popularity of that Web page or site.

Live Blogging: The practice of posting information on a blog about an event as it happens.

Chapter 9
Blogging for Sovereignty:
An Analysis of Palestinian Blogs

Justin D. Martin
The University of Maine, USA

Sherine El-Toukhy
The University of North Carolina at Chapel Hill, USA

ABSTRACT

Blogs addressing political issues are often viewed as highly polarized online discussion spaces. To test the universality of this assumption, the authors evaluated 127 Palestinian blogs written in both Arabic and English languages. Blogs authored by Palestinians living in the Palestinian Territories and the State of Israel, members of the Palestinian Diaspora, and Palestinian advocates of other nationalities were analyzed in terms of the prevalence of political content, perceptions of the State of Israel, and differences in content due to language, nationality, and geographical location. Results of the analysis indicate that blogs in the sample were primarily political and that most blogs were critical of the State of Israel and its policies. The tone of discourse regarding the State of Israel, however, was not as reflexively visceral as one might have anticipated, particularly among blogs written in English and those authored by Palestinian advocates.

INTRODUCTION

While a considerable amount of research has been conducted in recent years on blogs as a global phenomenon, most of the inquiries have focused on the Western blogosphere. Overlooked in much of the scholarly investigations are many blogging

communities including Palestinian. A blog can be easily turned into a weapon of information warfare as favorable public opinion becomes a valuable commodity in international conflict zones. This might trigger "the struggle for influence on public opinion in addition to territory and sovereign power, and so new online activity captures the imagination and headlines every day" (Whitaker & Varghese, 2009, p. 1). In an attempt to extend

DOI: 10.4018/978-1-60960-744-9.ch009

the scholarly understanding of international blogging and explore the role of online discourse in international conflict resolution as well as its potential for peace building, the authors of the current study focused on blogs from the Palestinian segment of the Arabic blogosphere.

Blogs that dwell on politics are habitually assumed to be toxic, partisan and polarized discussion spaces. *Forbes* magazine once ran a cover story revealing the controversial nature of blogging, in which Daniel Lyons (2006) described blogs as "the prized platform of an online lynch mob spouting liberty but spewing lies, libel and invective." To test the universality of this assumption, 127 blogs written in both Arabic and English were examined and content-analyzed. Blogs in the sample were authored by Palestinians living in the Palestinian Territories and the State of Israel, members of the Palestinian Diaspora, as well as Palestinian advocates of other nationalities.

The present study aimed to determine whether Palestinian blogs were predominantly political in nature and how partisan bloggers were while reflecting on political issues. For these purposes some of the overarching characteristics of blogs were identified, including authorship, language, nationality, as well as blog content and tone. Additionally, the study explored general sentiments and attitudes that bloggers projected toward the State of Israel and its policies regarding the Palestinian issue. Overall, this chapter probes the role of online discourse in international conflict resolution and adds to the scholarly understanding of international blogging and the temper of online discourse in the political blogosphere. The chapter is organized into the following sections: background on online information consumption and blogging in the Arab world, review of the pertinent literature, description of the methodology, discussion of the findings, and implications for further research.

BACKGROUND

Arab countries in the Middle East and North Africa including Palestinian Authority are lagging behind the rest of the world, having only a 29.8% Internet penetration rate compared to other regions (Internet World Statistics, 2009). Despite that, the International Telecommunications Union quotes an impressive number of 64 million Arab netizens that surfed the Internet as of 2009 (International Telecommunications Union, 2010). The distribution of Internet users varies greatly within the Arab nations. Bahrain, for example, has the Internet penetration rate of 88% whereas Libya has only 5.5% (Internet World Statistics, 2009). The comparatively late adoption of new communication technologies and the fluctuation of penetration rates among Arab countries can be traced back to a host of reasons including Internet connection costs, a high adult illiteracy rate, the dominance of English language on the early World Wide Web, and a reluctance to loosen state controls over the flow of information (Hofheinz, 2007; Warf & Vincent, 2007). This explains why blogging is a relatively novel phenomenon for the Arabic Internet.

Abdallah Al-Miheiri, a blogger from Abu Dhabi, is credited with the Arabic translation of the word *blog*, "al-mudawwana" (Hofheinz, 2005). Arabic Network for Human Rights Information counted near 40,000 Arabic blogs (as cited in Hamdy, 2009). A more detailed tally identified close to 45,000 Arabic-language blogs and blogs with mixed use of Arabic, English and French (Etling, Kelly, Faris, & Palfrey, 2009).

New communication technologies have brought down many barriers to intellectual dissemination and have drastically altered the media landscapes in Arab countries previously controlled tightly by the governments. "[I]n spite of government attempts to censor and police the network[s], individual citizens manage to work around the state," stresses Wheeler (2009, p. 305). As Wheeler goes on to say, "The cumulative, long-term effects of these subversions will alter the ways in which people live their lives in the region, but may not on their own transform authoritarian states." Across the Arab world, people can now share their thoughts and opinions online, a medium much more difficult for governments to control. A cafe owner in Algiers, a student in Mauritania, or a farmer in Syria can all freely project their thoughts to the whole world, simply given the availability of an Internet connection. In a real-life example, a 29-year-old architect from Baghdad Salam al-Janabi started to blog in 2003 as *Salam Pax* (which means "peace" in Arabic and Latin) about his life during and after the Iraq War.[1] His English-speaking blog attracted global attention and was published as a book (Salam Pax, 2003).

Blogging has offered Arab women an unprecedented opportunity for empowerment in the mostly male-dominated social and political environment. *Baghdad Burning*,[2] a blog written by a young Iraqi woman in 2003-2007, is an example of expanding pluralism and a reflection of the bravery and activism of women in the Arab world. Writing under the nom de plume *Riverbend*, the blogger provided daily accounts of life in Iraq after the occupation by a multinational force led by the United States. Her blog was disseminated as a book in several languages with the publisher touting the blogger as "a daring and uncensored voice from embattled Iraq" (Riverbend, 2005).

Demonstrating an unprecedented pluralism of opinion, blogs are diversifying the political scene in the Arab world. "Middle Eastern Web logs," reported the *Columbia Journalism Review* (Beckerman, 2007), "expose a hidden trove of multiple perspectives in a world that the West often imagines as having only one perspective," (p.16). Currently, Arab bloggers use the Web not only for information gathering, sharing and discussing political and human rights issues, but also for arranging public protests and rallies which, although often short lived, would have been difficult to organize otherwise (Ambah, 2006).

Blogs have expanded the access of Arab citizens to unbiased sources of news and political information that are free from governmental censorship. The *Columbia Journalism Review* notes that political opposition in the Middle East has been more likely to voice disapproval of leaders through blogs than in other media (Beckerman, 2007). Jordanians blogging in English, for example, may criticize King Abdullah II in a way that would have drawn severe consequences had the writings appeared in print. In blogs, Syrian critics of President Bashar Al-Assad can question his directives in a tone previously unheard in Damascus. Even in war-torn Iraq, blogs are multiplying; a phenomenon bolstered by the harsh security realities that make blogging from one's home more appealing than traditional reporting from the streets.

In the Palestinian Territories, bloggers frequently float criticism of governmental officials and the leaders of Fatah and Hamas that was previously impermissible in print or broadcast media. Rugh (2004) argues that the Palestinian Territories are home to a "loyalist" press, where journalists are frequently punished for any reporting that does not exhibit support for leading political groups. He states that Palestinian reporters, fearful of reprisal, mainly support factions in power, despite the fact that most media outlets are privately owned. Other researchers confirm that the media regime of the Palestinian Authority provides limited support for the freedom of expression despite the existence of several pertinent clauses in the Palestinian Basic Law (Jamal, 2005). Therefore, blogs filled the niche by responding to the demand of ordinary Palestinians in unfiltered news and nonpartisan political commentary. However, digital divide creates a formidable barrier to the widespread adoption of blogging since only 14.2% of the households in the Palestinian Territories have Internet access (Internet World Statistics, 2009). That explains the prevalence of international voices in the Palestinian blogosphere.

Certainly, blogging in the Arab world does not represent or guarantee full freedom of self-expression due to the ever-present governmental control and constant oversight over traditional and new media. While bloggers in Arab countries are frequently enjoying more freedoms than their print counterparts, many Arab governments attempt to keep a tight lid on online discourse. Syrian, Jordanian and Egyptian bloggers, for instance, are increasingly being put on trial and often get convicted. In February 2007, Egyptian courts convicted 22 year-old blogger Abdel Kareem Nabil of defaming Egyptian President Hosni Mubarak, sentencing him to four years in prison (Abou Al-Majd, 2007). Human rights watchdog Amnesty International lamented the decision, claiming that it imposed a chilling effect of self-censorship on bloggers throughout the Middle East. According to Reporters Without Borders (2010), Egypt has become one of the world's twelve "Enemies of the Internet" after three bloggers were imprisoned during the state crackdown on online political activism in 2008 (Fahmy, 2010).

Whatever impediments to Internet communication in the Arab world do exist, blogs constitute an emboldening development for citizens of all Arab nations with historically loyalist press systems. Blogging can level many barriers of entry to free speech and self-expression, and Arab citizens in growing numbers are taking advantage of Internet-based communication technologies and articulate their political views and opinions with newfound fervor.

LITERATURE REVIEW

Scholarly research of the Arabic blogosphere is still in its infancy. A search resulted in studies that are either commentary in nature (e.g., Hamdy, 2009; Lynch, 2007; Talaat, 2006) or unpublished (Fahmy, 2010; The Ethical Blogger, 2009). The only systematic and comprehensive study of the Arabic blogosphere at the time of this writing was conducted by the Berkman Center for Internet and Society at Harvard University (Etling, Kelly, Faris, & Palfrey, 2009). Researchers explored both the structure and content of the Arabic blogosphere using sophisticated computational social network mapping along with computer-assisted content analysis. They also employed advanced link and term frequency analysis to reveal the most connected blogs and hand-coded 4,370 individual blogs to study them in-depth.

As a result of such an exemplary large-scale social network analysis, an interactive map of the Arabic blogosphere was created. The Berkman Center study found that it is mostly populated by bloggers from Egypt, Saudi Arabia, Kuwait, Levant (Lebanon, Palestine, Jordan, Syria), and Maghreb (Morocco, Tunisia, Algeria). 75% of all bloggers are largely young (under the age of 35), with 45% in this category being in the 25-35 year old range, and mostly males (60%). The biggest percentage of female bloggers was found in Egypt among the youth sub-category. Results of a computational text and metadata analysis combined with human-coded content analysis demonstrate that the majority of Arab bloggers tend to write mostly about personal matters, discuss local news and politics, cultural and religious events, with much less emphasis on international issues, including the wars in Iraq and Afghanistan. It is important to note that the Berkman Center study found that the Palestinian issue came to be the only common political theme to transcends across the whole Arabic blogosphere (Etling, Kelly, Faris, & Palfrey, 2009).

As the Berkman Center researchers wrote,

...it is hard to imagine any issue or perspective in the Arab world for which we did not find at least an advocate or two, including a sympathetic view of Israel's struggle with Hamas (though this was indeed rare). We found Islamists, secularists, and avowed atheists. ... Among secularists there were Western-leaning democrats, anti-Western Socialists and Communists, and a healthy dose of

Feminists. Some topics of concern, like women's rights and the Israeli/Palestinian struggle, are discussed by large numbers of bloggers across the map. Other topics, like disputes between Sunni and Shi'a, corrupt royals, or parliamentary politics, were more active in national contexts. Still other topics, like gay rights and atheism, appear to have their niches. (2009, p. 9)

The Berkman Center scholars dispelled some widespread myths including, "a view of the Internet as primarily a vehicle for radicalization," as they found "very little support for terrorism or violent jihad in the Arabic blogosphere and quite a lot of criticism" (p. 10).

Of politics in Palestine, renowned Palestinian poet Mourid Barghouti (2000) wrote the following in his autobiographical book *I Saw Ramallah*: "…talk of politics—and trying to guess what will happen next—never ends. It will remain thus for a long time. Politics have entered into the miniature details of the souls of our men and our women" (p. 118). Barghouti's observation comments on one of the most essential aspects of Palestinian life—its strong political pulse; and, this study sought to determine whether or not such a preoccupation with politics is a basic characteristic of an online discourse in Palestinian blogs.

STUDY METHODOLOGY

The present study explored the nature of the Palestinian cluster of the Arabic blogosphere by examining some of its pertinent features. Content analysis was chosen as the primary research method of inquiry as it has become increasingly recognized as a tool for scholarly examination of blogs (Herring, Scheidt, Kouper, & Wright, 2007; Papacharissi, 2007; Trammell, Tarkowski, Hofmokl, & Sapp, 2006; Wei, 2004). As one of the first studies of Palestinian blogs, the present investigation aimed to contribute to the knowledge base of international blogging in conflict zones

and thus lead to the better understanding of the role of online discourse in international conflict resolution.

Research Questions

RQ1: Are Palestinian blogs predominantly political, as opposed to apolitical, or social, in nature?

Research Question 1 examined to which degree the "talk of politics" exists in the Palestinian blogosphere. For many Palestinians and Palestinian advocates, blogging provides ample opportunities to disseminate their aspirations towards Palestinian statehood. Research Question 1 examined the prevalence of political content in blogs under the examination.

RQ2: What is the tone of discourse regarding the State of Israel in Palestinian blogs?

One can assume that Palestinian bloggers talk about the State of Israel, its policies and military actions in the Palestinian Territories. Therefore, Research Question 2 specifically examined the prevalence of such content as well as its tone.

RQ3: Is there a relationship between the geographical location and origin of the authors of Palestinian blogs and the tone of the discussion of the State of Israel?

Research Question 3 takes the essence of the previous two questions and relates them to bloggers' nationality and geographical location. It examines the differences in political discourse and discussion of the State of Israel among bloggers living within Palestinian Territories, the State of Israel, and outside. Presumably, bloggers living inside the Palestinian Territories may be more antagonistic in their attitudes toward the State of Israel than bloggers living elsewhere.

RQ4: Are there differences between English and Arabic language blogs in terms of their nature and tone regarding the State of Israel?

Research Question 4 attends to the nuances of political discourse and the treatment of the State of Israel. It explores the differences between Arabic language blogs and those written in English. Prior research (Rugh, 2004) claims that Middle Eastern publications written in English often enjoy more latitude to publish political opinions than those in Arabic, since Arab governments recognize that most of their citizens will not read them due to the lack of the Internet access. The study examined whether or not blogs in English were more or less partisan than those in Arabic.

Taken together, these four research questions engage the basic attributes of Palestinian blogs and match them with blog content.

Sampling

Blogs (*n* = 127) examined in this study were selected among those listed on the *Palestine Blogs* website.[3] The site advertises itself as: "Aggregator and directory of Palestinian blogs, dedicated to pro-Palestine advocacy through the presentation of news and views." A score of blogs centered on the Palestinian cause is featured on this site. Many blogs were written in English, although a significant number were composed partly or entirely in Arabic. A point of contention was how to define a "Palestinian" blog. The study applied a broad definition that encompassed not only Palestinian-Arab blogs, but also blogs devoted to the Palestinian cause but written by international authors. Blogs of Palestinian advocates from outside of the Palestinian Authority were included because they play an important agenda-setting function and perform a bridging role with the larger English-speaking blogosphere. The *Palestine Blogs* aggregator website provides links to contributing bloggers registered with the site. Except for a handful of blogs that were neither authored by Palestinians nor focused on Palestinian issues, all other blogs of registered users were included in the sample, compiling a total of 127 blogs.

Content Classification and Coding

A codesheet with appropriate categories was developed for the purpose of this study. To examine a given blog, the coders accessed the codesheet online and entered coding decisions that were automatically registered in an online database and later exported into statistical analysis software. The codesheet contained basic categories such as those identifying the coder and provided a Web address for a given blog. Among the major content classification categories on the codesheet were:

Author Identity. Coders were asked to decide whether or not the blogger could be identified as a Palestinian native. If not, coders were asked to identify the nationality of the blogger when possible.

Author's Geographical Location. Coders indicated the geographical location of the blog's author, noting whether or not the blogger lives in the Palestinian Territories. If not, coders recorded the actual location of the bloggers when that information was available.

Political vs. Social Nature. This category dealt with whether the blog served as a political venue or as a personal, or social outlet, such as an online diary discussing the blogger's daily activities, hobbies, sports, etc. In cases where a blog seemed to be both political and social (which was fairly infrequent), coders were provided with an option to reflect that.

Captivating Quote. When coders indicated that a particular blog was more political in nature than social, they were asked to provide a quote from the blog demonstrating the tone of political writing. Similarly, coders also provided quotes from apolitical blogs.

Soliciting Action. Coders were asked to determine whether or not a particular blogger asked readers to get politically involved by joining a certain listserv, donating money to the Palestinian cause, writing to the U.S. Congress Representatives, etc. This was a criterion coders used to determine if a given blog tended to be more political than social, or vice versa.

Linking to Other Palestinian Blogs. In many cases, bloggers advocating a certain cause would link to other blogs in an attempt to initiate political grassroots efforts. For this reason, coders were asked to indicate whether blogs were linked to other Palestinian blogs.

Discussing News Stories/Videos. Cooper (2006) has argued that bloggers frequently act as a watchdog on mainstream media, and this is a part of their role. Here coders indicated whether bloggers discussed news and linked to news stories or videos from the media outlets covering current political events.

Mentioning the State of Israel. Coders recorded whether or not a given blog mentioned the State of Israel.

Overall Tone of Discussion of the State of Israel. Coders were asked to establish whether the tone of the coverage was positive, neutral, or negative toward the State of Israel.

Scale of the Tone. More precisely, coders rated the tone toward the State of Israel on a scale of 1-10, with 1 being the most favorable and 10 the most negative. In cases where the State of Israel was mentioned, coders were asked to provide what seemed to them to be the most interesting quote.

Three trained coders coded the sample. Any disagreements that arose during the coding process were resolved by consensus. A pilot study testing the reliability of the coding protocol was conducted on a subsample ($n = 20$). A coder, fluent in Arabic, coded blogs that were either written entirely or partially in Arabic language. Coders achieved an average agreement of .89 across classification categories in accordance with Holsti's

(1969) formula. To answer Research Question 4, an independent samples t-test was conducted.

STUDY RESULTS

The present study analyzed the content of 127 Palestinian blogs written both in Arabic and English languages. A little less than a third of blogs in the sample were written partly or entirely in Arabic (29%), all others were composed in English. In terms of authorship, three-fourths of the sample (75.3%) were authored by Palestinians and one-fourth by non-Palestinians. Males authored approximately half or 52% of all blogs in the sample. Median age for those bloggers who disclosed it (about 40% of authors in the sample) was 25.

Political Content

Research Question 1 asked whether blogs examined in the sample tended to be political, as opposed to apolitical, or social. Results revealed that the majority of blogs in the sample were politically oriented. Approximately two thirds (66.1%) of all blogs in the sample were political in nature. Another 20.5% were social, while 13.4% of the sample were found both political and social. About one third (34%) of blogs in the sample encouraged readers to get involved in Palestinian advocacy. A majority of blogs or 67% discussed political news and provided links to news items. Eighty percent of blogs identified as political contained either discussion or a hyperlink to news items.

Perceptions of the State of Israel

Research Question 2 analyzed the extent to which Palestinian blogs in the sample made reference to the State of Israel, which a sizeable majority did. Eighty-seven percent of blogs in the sample made at least one reference to the State of Israel with some blogs seemed to exist for the sole purpose of commenting on its policies.

The study found that much of the discussion of the State of Israel contained negative reviews and comments. Overall, 73% of the examined blogs mentioned the State of Israel negatively, while 23% were neutral. Not a single blog was completely favorable toward the State of Israel. Using a less discrete measure, coders were also asked to indicate bloggers' tone on a 10-point scale, with zero being most favorable to State of Israel and ten the most negative ($M = 6.8$, $SD = 1.77$). Using the standard deviation acquired from this distribution, about 65% of blogs fell between 5 and 8.5. This means that approximately one-third (or 32%) of blogs in the sample were just below or around the median of the scale.

Nationality, Geographical Location and Language

Research Question 3 dealt with blog authors in terms of their nationality and geographical location. In many cases, bloggers chose not to disclose their nationality (46%). Otherwise, they indicated a wide variety of national backgrounds. Of those that identified themselves, 75% were Palestinians, 11% Americans, and another 14% hailed from Israel, Jordan, the UK, Ireland, Sweden and France.

In terms of bloggers' geographical location, not all blog authors wrote from the country of origin. Bloggers in the sample examined live in 15 different countries. Sixty percent of bloggers who disclosed their whereabouts live within the Palestinian Territories. Fifteen percent live in the United States, eight percent in Jordan and five percent in the UK. One blogger lives in each of the following 11 countries: Egypt, Syria, Jordan, Kuwait, Morocco, Bahrain, Tunisia, Australia, Austria, Canada, Italy, and South Africa.

Research Question 4 involved a difference in perceptions of the State of Israel in Arabic versus English language blogs, as well as differences among bloggers living inside and outside Palestinian Territories. Blogs in Arabic ($M = 7.3$ on a 10-point scale, $SD = 1.64$) were more critical

of the State of Israel than those in English ($M = 6.46$, $SD = 1.68$). An independent samples *t*-test indicates that this difference borders on statistical significance $t(96) = 1.87$, $p = .06$ (two-tailed). There was no significant difference between blogs originating from the Palestinian Territories and those in other localities in terms of the tone toward the State of Israel $t(68) = -.117$, $p = .907$. When entered into a least-squares regression model as a dummy variable, geographical location still did not affect sentiments toward the State of Israel, even after controlling for nationality.

On the other hand, nationality, not location, seemed to be a much better predictor of the tone of the discussion of the State of Israel. Bloggers hailing from the Palestinian Territories ($M = 7.22$, $SD = 1.73$) were considerably more critical of the State of Israel and its policies than bloggers of other nationalities ($M = 5.93$, $SD = 1.49$). The difference between these two means is significant $t(57) = -2.52$, $p = .015$. Entered into a least squares regression model as a dummy variable, nationality is still predictive of the tone toward the State of Israel when gender and geographical location of blogger were controlled. This relationship disappears, however, when controlled for language, indicating that authors in the sample were more likely than other bloggers to express criticism of the State of Israel only when writing in Arabic.

DISCUSSION

True to the statement by Mourid Barghouti that Palestinian "talk of politics—and trying to guess what will happen next—never ends" (2000, p.118), Palestinian blogs examined in the sample revealed the prevalence of political content and were highly discussant of political events. A significant number of blogs tried to encourage their readers to get involved with the Palestinian cause. In most cases, and on the grand scale, this predilection implicated the Palestinian statehood—freeing the Palestinian Territories from the State of the Israel control—and the discussion on how to achieve it through peaceful means.

In addition to the criticism of the State of Israel, bloggers were also critical of the Arab governments in general, and the Palestinian Authority in particular. "I often find myself caught between anti-Arab racism and Arab reactionary politics, both of which threaten to gag me," wrote one young Palestinian blogger. "I'm raising my voice against both, hoping in the process to contribute an improvised note to a progressive Arab blogosphere." Taking a direct aim at the Palestinian Authority, one blogger who identified himself as *Zaytoun* (Arabic for "olives") argued that the government of the Palestinian Authority is collectively punishing the Palestinian people.

Regardless of whether bloggers discussed the politics of Palestinian self-determination or criticized Arab governments for inaction and indifference to the suffering of the Palestinian people, most authors seemed to use their blog writing as a conduit for catharsis—a venue to vent their frustrations that they could not release through any other outlet. In one instance, a non-native English speaker and resident of Gaza, while knowingly communicating in broken prose, felt strongly that the world needed to hear her story. "I am one of the least angry residents of Gaza," she wrote. "But this very little anger is forcing me to scream through these electronic pages I am creating, hoping it can reach anyone… Forgive the poor language; forgive the unprofessional writing and designing. Try to read this anger and this love to life." Another young woman described her blog *My Occupied Territory* as "an idealistic 22-year old's attempts to vent feelings and rationalize happenings in this world through this space."

As with many other blogs in the sample, the author of the above cited online journal treats her blog as a highly personal space that helps her sort through emotions that reflect the condition of her community and her own life. However, the writings produced by bloggers' inner tensions tend to be more political, then personal. Perhaps we might expect Palestinians to use the medium of blogging in this way. In a hypothetical project examining Chechen, Tibetan, or Kurdish blogosphere one might similarly expect the highly political and at the time emotional discourse centered on independence. This is evident in the case of blogs devoted to the Palestinian cause. Palestinian bloggers appear to use their online journals as both vehicles of catharsis and persuasion—against the backdrop of unhurried political progress towards the Palestinian statehood.

This is not to say that apolitical content was not found in the sample. For example, musing on the nature of physical beauty one blogger writes, "I've always believed that beauty has no rules, limits, or standards. Beauty, I strongly believe, is a matter of taste. There are no such things as "beauty idols," or "steps to beauty," or anything of the kind." Hashem (2009) found in a study of young adults in the Middle East that respondents engaged in plenty of online apolitical activities such as nonpolitical information seeking and entertainment gratifications. Still, a majority of blogs in the sample focused on the political aspects of Palestinian life, both in terms of political persuasion as well as emotional release. "Why do I write?" one young Palestinian asked a rhetorical question. "I write because I can," he answered himself. "If I couldn't, then I wouldn't be who I am. I write for freedom, I write about the girl, I write about peace."

A great deal of the political release was directed at the State of Israel and its policies in the Palestinian Territories. The majority of blogs in the sample exhibited negative attitudes toward the State of Israel, a minority was neutral, and none were completely positive. This, however, may be a bit misleading, for what is perhaps the more revealing finding of this study is how restrained the perceptions of the State of Israel were found in the sample. Consider, for example, the fact that the mean score of the sentiments toward the State of Israel for all blogs in the sample was 6.8 on a 10-point scale, with 10 being the most negative.

The median, however, is 5.5, which means that about 32% of the sample (one standard deviation below 6.8) were at or above the median of the scale. This measure suggests that perception of the State of Israel in Palestinian blogs in the sample was not as highly polarized as one might suspect. It is true that the State of Israel and its policies were a focal point in blogs examined in this study, but this focus did not assume as caustic a tone as one might expect.

Several acrimonious statements boosted the mean of the overall tone measurement closer toward ten, but not all treatment of the State of Israel was nearly universally acerbic. One author stated, "I know a few Jews who I really like, and I am glad for each and everyone. I refuse to believe that all Jews are evil." In a blog titled *From Gaza, With Love*, one author described her daughter's reaction to "seeing Israeli soldiers so close for the first time. My daughter's comment was 'some of them are nice'. Yes that is true." Another blogger posting under the name *Imaan on Ice* described with great restrain his disappointment in not attaining a travel permit from the Israeli military that he had been hoping for. "My permit was not approved by the Israelis," he wrote, "So I unpacked my suitcase."

Milder statements like these, expressing genuine frustration but not devolving into an *ad hominim diatribe*, are quite uncharacteristic of a political blogosphere typically rife with malice. While some Palestinian blogs examined in the sample certainly spew highly emotional rhetoric, there are far too many blogs treating the topic of Israeli-Palestinian relations moderately to support a generalization on the grand scale like Lyons' (2006). Criticism of the State of Israel was severe at times, but not uniform across the sample, and the authors of this chapter consider it as the most striking finding. The current study confirms the conclusions of the Berkman Center at Harvard University: "Perhaps the most interesting thing was the way in which, as we see in the U.S. blogosphere, the identities and attitudes of real people regularly fail to conform to stereotypical expectations" (Etling, Kelly, Faris, & Palfrey, 2009, p. 9).

Bloggers in the sample hailed from the Palestinian Territories and a number of other countries. While most authors identified themselves as Palestinians, 25% of bloggers in the sample claimed American, Swedish, Jordanian, French, and a handful of other national backgrounds. Nationality was highly predictive of tone toward the State of Israel. Regardless of whether they lived inside the Palestinian Territories or not, Palestinians were far more critical of the State of Israel than were Palestinian advocates of other nationalities. This may be what one might expect since the former were directly experiencing the inability of the international community to aid in solving the long-standing issue of the Palestinian statehood. One might anticipate that bloggers with Palestinian roots and, perhaps, with displaced family members living outside the Palestinian Territories would demonstrate more visceral disapproval of the State of Israel. However, this was only the case for Palestinian authors blogging in Arabic.

When language is controlled, the effect of nationality on attitude and tone regarding the State of Israel is no longer significant. This may say something about Palestinians who are educated in Western languages and values. Or, it could be due instead to the fact that Palestinians writing in Arabic and, therefore not writing for a Western audience feel that they have more expressive latitude to criticize the State of Israel.

CONCLUSION

Taken together, what do the findings listed above indicated? What generalizations can be made about the Palestinian blogosphere that may serve as a stepping-stone for further research? Results indicate that the content of blogs in the sample was mostly political, as opposed to apolitical, or social, and that most bloggers were critical in their perceptions of the State of Israel and its policies. The authors can note that blogs in the sample tend to be far more political than personal, and dealing less with social, cultural and religious issues.

Results of the present study attest to the reasons why Palestinians blog and propel their voices into cyberspace. Further, the authors of this study tested a widespread assumption about the acrimonious and incendiary nature of online discourse in the political blogosphere. They found that the overall tone of the Palestinian blogs regarding the State of Israel was not reflexively derisive and belligerent, as one might have anticipated. This is noteworthy, given that online discourse in the political blogosphere is often conceptualized as dividing not a unifying. Additionally, voices of the Palestinian bloggers were not uniform and monolithically mordant toward the State of Israel as is commonly assumed. Perhaps it is a flaw of outside spectators in perceiving international conflict as being extremely pungent and beyond hope of a peaceful resolution.

In the case of the Palestinian blogosphere, it appears that there are blog authors whose writings are not based solely on contemptuous partisan preferences, who are trying to reach to the other side and demonstrate empathy and kindness. While some bloggers—mainly those of Palestinian descent and writing in Arabic—do frequently criticize the State of Israel and its policies in the Palestinian Territories, many eschew invective and vituperative style and embrace a calmer self-restrained tone. Such sentiments observed in a number of blogs testify to the fact that some bloggers are convinced that the Israeli–Palestinian conflict in the Middle East is not actually intractable.

The above findings fall in line with the general conclusion of the Berkman Center study of the Arabic blogosphere, which points to the fact, "that Arabic language blogs are not to any significant degree used to support extremism, preach hate, or organize terrorist activities" (Etling, Kelly, Faris, & Palfrey, 2009, p. 48). The authors of the cur-

rent study share the view of the Berkman Center researchers that:

...academic studies and media reports that focus exclusively on terrorist uses of the Web can leave the impression that this is a dominant form of discourse in the Arabic language Internet, and could lead to ill-informed policy responses, which could unintentionally limit the diverse, open, and often civically minded political, cultural, and religious discussions that take place in blogs and other open Internet spaces. (p. 48)

Future research of the Palestinian blogosphere may incorporate a larger amount of blogs from a number of different outlets to conduct similar or dissimilarly constructed analyses. Different theoretical approaches, such as agenda setting, framing, or uses and gratifications (see, for example, the examination of Polish blogs by Trammell, Tarkowski, Hofmokl, and Sapp (2006) or a study of Egyptian blogs by Fahmy, 2010) can be incorporated into future research models.

REFERENCES

Abdulla, R. (2007). *The Internet in the Arab World: Egypt and beyond.* New York, NY: Peter Lang.

Abou Al-Majd, N. (2007, February 22). Blogger gets four years for insulting Islam. *The San Francisco Chronicle.*

Ambah, F. S. (2006, November 12). New clicks in the Arab world: Bloggers challenge longtime cultural, political restrictions. *The Washington Post,* A13.

Barghouti, M. (2000). *I saw Ramallah.* Cairo, Egypt: The American University in Cairo Press.

Beckerman, G. (2007, February). The new Arab conversation. *Columbia Journalism Review,* 16–19.

Cooper, S. D. (2006). *Watching the watchdog: Bloggers as the fifth estate*. Milwaukee, WI: Marquette Books.

Enemies of the Internet. (2010, March). *Annual report from Reporters without borders*. Retrieved October 8, 2010, from http://www.rsf.org/IMG/ pdf/ Internet_enemies.pdf

Etling, B., Kelly, J., Faris, R., & Palfrey, J. (2009). *Mapping the Arabic blogosphere: Politics, culture, and dissent* (Internet & Democracy Case Study Series, Berkman Center Research Publication No. 2009-06). Retrieved December 15, 2010, from http://cyber.law.harvard.edu/sites/ cyber. law.harvard.edu/files/ Mapping_the_Arabic_ Blogosphere_0.pdf

Fahmy, N. (2010). *Revealing the agenda-cutting through Egyptian blogs: An empirical study*. Retrieved December 15, 2010, from http://online. journalism.utexas.edu/2010/papers/Fahmy10.pdf

Hamdy, N. (2009). Arab citizen journalism in action: Challenging mainstream media, authorities and media laws. *Westminster Papers in Communication and Culture*, 6(1), 92–112.

Hashem, M. E. (2009). Impact and implications of new information technology on Middle Eastern youth. *Global Media Journal, 8*(14).

Herring, S. C., Scheidt, L. A., Kouper, I., & Wright, E. (2006). Longitudinal content analysis of blogs: 2003-2004. In Tremayne, M. (Ed.), *Blogging, citizenship and the future of media* (pp. 3–20). New York, NY: Routledge.

Hofheinz, A. (2005). The Internet in the Arab world: Playground for political liberalization. *International Politics and Society*, 3, 78–96.

Hofheinz, A. (2007). Arab Internet use: Popular trends and public impact. In Sakr, N. (Ed.), *Arab media and political renewal: Community, legitimacy and public life* (pp. 56–79). London, UK: I. B. Tauris.

Holsti, O. R. (1969). *Content analysis for the social sciences and humanities*. Upper Saddle River, NJ: Addison-Wesley.

International Telecommunications Union. (2010). *Home page*. Retrieved from http://www.itu.int/en/ pages/ default.aspx

Internet World Statistics. (n.d.). *Home page*. Retrieved from http://www.internetworldstats.com

Jamal, A. (2005). *Media politics and democracy in Palestine: Political culture, pluralism, and the Palestinian Authority. Portland, OR*. Sussex: Academic Press.

Johnson, T. J., & Kaye, B. K. (2004). Wag the blog: How reliance on traditional media and the Internet influence credibility perceptions of Weblogs among blog users. *Journalism & Mass Communication Quarterly, 81*(3), 622–642.

Kerbel, M. R., & Bloom, J. D. (2005). Blog for America and civil involvement. *The Harvard International Journal of Press/Politics, 10*(4), 3–27. doi:10.1177/1081180X05281395

Lynch, M. (2007, February). Blogging the new Arab public. *Arab Media & Society*. Retrieved December 15, 2010, from http://www.arabmediasociety.com/ articles/downloads/20070312155027 _AMS1_Marc_Lynch.pdf

Lyons, D. (2006, November 14). Attack of the blogs. *Forbes*. Retrieved December 15, 2010, from http://www.forbes.com/forbes/ 2005/1114/128. html

Papacharissi, Z. (2007). Audiences as media producers: Content analysis of 260 blogs. In Tremayne, M. (Ed.), *Blogging, citizenship, and the future of media* (pp. 21–38). New York, NY: Routledge.

Riverbend. (2005). *Baghdad burning: Girl blog from Iraq*. New York, NY: The Feminist Press.

Rugh, W. (2004). *Mass media in the Arab world.* Westport, CT: Praeger.

Salam Pax. (2003). *Salam Pax: The clandestine diary of an ordinary Iraqi.* New York, NY: Grove Press.

Schleiffer, Y. (2005, April 18). Blogging for a new Middle East. *The Jerusalem Report*, 19-21.

Talaat, S. (2006). *Bloggers or journalists: New perspective in the Arab media.* Paper presented at the International Association for Mass Communication Research, Cairo, Egypt.

The Ethical Blogger. (2009, March 10). *Free spaces: Arab women blogging.* [Web log post]. Retrieved from http://ethicalbloggerproject. blogspot.com/2009/03/free-spaces-arab-women-blogging.html

Trammell, K. D., Tarkowski, A., Hofmokl, J., & Sapp, A. M. (2006). Rzeczpospolita blogów [Republic of Blog]: Examining Polish bloggers through content analysis. *Journal of Computer Mediated Communication, 11*(3). Retrieved December 15, 2010, from http://jcmc.indiana.edu/vol11/issue3/trammell.html

Warf, B., & Vincent, P. (2007). Multiple geographies of the Arab Internet. *Area, 39*(1), 83–96. doi:10.1111/j.1475-4762.2007.00717.x

Wei, C. (2004). *Formation of norms in a blog community.* Into the Blogosphere. Retrieved December 15, 2010, from http://blog.lib.umn.edu/blogosphere/formation_of_norms.html

Wheeler, D. L. (2009). Working around the state: Internet use and political identity in the Arab world. In Chadwick, A. (Ed.), *Routledge handbook of internet politics* (pp. 305–320). New York, NY: Routledge.

Whitaker, J., & Varghese, A. (2009). *Online discourse in the Arab world: Dispelling the myths.* Washington, DC: United States Institute of Peace. Retrieved December 15, 2010, from http://www.usip.org/files/resources /arab_world_online_pb.pdf

KEY TERMS AND DEFINITIONS

Arab World: Arabic language speaking countries in North Africa and the Middle East including the Palestinian Authority.

Blog Tone: The style, intonations and manners in which bloggers express their thoughts, emotions and attitudes.

Palestinian Blog: A blog either written by a person of Palestinian origin or by an individual writing about the Palestinian issue.

Palestinian Cause (Issue): A Palestinian claim for statehood, a central matter in Middle East politics since the Israeli declaration of independence in 1948.

Political Blog: A blog devoted to political issues and/or particular governmental policies and actions.

Social Blog: A blog used for purposes other than political commentary and political advocacy.

ENDNOTES

[1] http://salampax.wordpress.com
[2] http://riverbendblog.blogspot.com
[3] http://palestineblogs.net (formerly http://palestineblogs.org)

Chapter 10
Blogging as a Means of Grieving

Jocelyn M. DeGroot
Southern Illinois University, USA

Heather J. Carmack
Missouri State University, USA

ABSTRACT

People are increasingly turning to the Internet to grieve and manage the traumatic experience of losing a loved one and to cope with emotional pain after the loss. Many bereaved individuals establish personal blogs following the death of a parent, spouse or partner, sibling, close family member, or child. For some, blogging about the death of someone special serves as a form of therapy, healing, and emotional release; for others, it serves as a public way to cope with grief. This chapter zeroes in on the communicative experiences of grief bloggers and examines the role of computer-mediated communication in the process of grieving. It starts with a discussion of the stages of grief, explicates the positive and negative impact of blogging on the grieving process, and outlines practical and ethical dilemmas presented by grief blogs and blogging.

INTRODUCTION

As people experience the loss of someone special to them, they are often overcome with grief. As bereft individuals mourn their losses, they engage in "grief work": that is, a process in which they attempt to make sense of the loss and reorient themselves to the world without the deceased (Attig, 2001). One way in which individuals may perform grief work is through the means of blog-

DOI: 10.4018/978-1-60960-744-9.ch010

ging. Blogging about the death of a loved one can serve as a public way to cope with grief. Sharing emotional events with others (for example, blog readers) may be useful during one's grief, since social support is critical for successfully coping with the death of someone special.

An important element of the grieving process is the ability to talk about the grief and loss. Bereaved individuals have to determine how much to communicate about their loss with others. This communication influences how the individual is able to mourn the loss and craft a new identity in the absence of the deceased. A variety of grief models exist to explain the multifaceted nature of mourning. Several common threads that run across these models include: an appreciation of the chaos and disorder caused by the loss, recognition of the loss, and the reorganization of life (Corr & Corr, 2007). Grief blogs chronicle individuals' unique journeys through the grief process, document the highs and lows of mourning, and allow individuals to comment on the process.

Following the loss of someone, people encounter feelings of shock and numbness, yearning and searching, disorganization and despair, and reorganization and recovery. Although people have encountered these feelings from the beginning of humankind, the specific ways in which individuals communicate these feelings have changed over time, with many in contemporary times turning to the Internet to articulate the uncertainty and confusion associated with death (deVries & Roberts, 2004). Grief blogs showcase an overarching tension in the grieving process: a desire to hold on to the deceased while simultaneously letting go (Moss, 2004).

Blogs chronicling someone's journey through the grieving process have increasingly become a widespread phenomenon. This chapter focuses on the communicative experiences of grief bloggers and examines the role of computer-mediated communication in the process of grieving. It starts with a discussion of the stages of grief, discusses the positive and negative effects of blogging on the grieving process, identifies benefits for bloggers and blog readers, and outlines practical and ethical dilemmas presented by grief blogs.

BACKGROUND: GRIEVING PROCESS

Although research has identified various phases of grief, scholars tend to agree on three broadly defined stages, including (1) shock, (2) acknowledgement, and (3) reconstruction (Bowlby, 1980a,

DeVaul, Zisook, & Faschingbauer, 1979; Harvey, 1996; Kübler-Ross, 1969). These phases might overlap, but the first two stages generally precede the reconstruction phase (Shuchter & Zisook, 1993; Weiss, 1993). We find Parkes (1970b, 1972) and Bowlby's (1961, 1969, 1972, 1980a) conceptualizations of the stages of grieving to be most useful for discussing this topic. Their interpretation of grieving is clear and comprehensively acknowledges all of the challenges that someone might encounter during the course of grieving. The phases may overlap with one another. In some cases, the phases of grief may be accompanied by prolonged depression or by acute and episodic "pangs" (Parkes, 1972, p. 39). A grieving person might also experience several overlapping phases at the same time or may swing between phases (Parkes, 1970a).

Shock and Numbness

Feelings of shock and numbness are evident in the initial phase of grieving. Survivors cannot believe that a death has occurred, and they struggle to comprehend their loss (Bowlby, 1980a). The influence of loss is overbearing, and the individual might feel "overloaded" and unable to take in external stimuli or might feel "numb" (Parkes, 1970a, 1970b). These feelings can last from a few hours to a week (Parkes, 1970b). Often, those who are in this phase seek to understand why something happened (Pennebaker, 1997a).

After the loss of a loved one, support from others within the social network is especially important in the days following the death (Stylianos & Vachon, 1993). An important communicative experience, social support provides the bereaved an opportunity to talk about her or his loss in a safe environment (Hoover, Hastings, & Musambira, 2009). Grieving people often say that talking with friends and verbalizing their emotional experiences is beneficial (Pennebaker, Zech, & Rimè, 2001). Pennebaker and colleagues (2001) noted that sharing emotions might perform cognitive, psychological, and social functions. Interviews with bereaved people revealed that it was beneficial for them to have another person listen, accept grief, offer support or encouragement, handle practical matters, or simply keep them company (Frantz, Trolley, & Farrell, 1998).

Yearning and Searching

In the yearning and searching phase, survivors are unable to accept the loss, and consequently suffer from separation anxiety (Parkes, 1972). Lasting anywhere from a few months to several years, mourners are preoccupied with thoughts of the deceased person, constantly scanning their environment for indications that their loved one is present (Bowlby, 1980a; Parkes, 1970b, 1972). When working through grief, the bereaved individual's feelings might vary between the two extremes of longing for reminders of the deceased to avoiding reminders altogether (Bowlby, 1980b). Saving the deceased's items and keeping them around all of the time are examples of separation anxiety and longing to be with the deceased (Parkes, 1972).

In the same period, people might also choose to "protest" the death by ignoring what happened. They do this by avoiding places, which the deceased had visited, or by occupying their time with an activity (Bowlby & Parkes, 1970). People often "keep busy" so that they do not necessarily have to comprehend the death of a loved one (Frantz et al., 1998). Anger is also common during this phase, but it is only typical during the first few weeks following the loss (Parkes, 1972). Sometimes grieving people in this stage do not want to grieve with others, and they might get irritated if others try to talk with them (Attig, 2001).

Disorganization and Despair

In this phase of grieving people are easily distracted, and they might experience difficulty concentrating. This is a natural occurrence, as people are beginning to cope with life events as a

person without his or her significant one. Identities might be compromised, as survivors might question how they now define themselves in the absence of a loved one (Attig, 2001; Bowlby, 1980b; Parkes & Weiss, 1983). In this phase, the bereaved might start to have an interest in returning to some semblance of a "normal" life. While the bereaved individuals often cannot yet wholly manage trying to return to normalcy, this sign of interest in the future with attempts to plan for it are part of the recovery process (Parkes, 1972).

Reorganization and Recovery

When survivors begin to restructure their lives, they demonstrate behaviors from the reorganization and recovery phase. As people grieve, they manage their sorrow and "relearn" how the world functions without the deceased (Attig, 2001). The final step in managing a significant loss lies in the need to redefine aspects of one's sense of self (Davis, 2001). People develop an identity where the deceased is now part of the past self and not the present self (Davis, Nolen-Hoeksema, & Larson, 1998).

Talking about the death with others is also a helpful way for the survivor to begin developing his or her new identity where the deceased is now in a new role (Harvey, Carlson, Huff, & Green, 2001). When people avoid sharing their emotions regarding a traumatic experience such as the death of a loved one, they risk developing detrimental cognitive side effects. Talking with others helps grieving persons organize their thoughts and confront their experience (Pennebaker et al., 2001). Communicating grief with others allows the bereaved to restructure his or her worldview. Additionally, by exchanging, discussing, and exploring memories or thoughts of the deceased, people extend their own memories and reconnect with the deceased's life (Attig, 2001).

BLOGGING ABOUT LOSS AND GRIEF

People create personal blogs for numerous reasons (Blood, 2002). Some grief bloggers start their blogs almost immediately after the loss. Others begin blogging after finding out that a loved one has a terminal illness; they also use blogging to grieve in an anticipatory way. Both categories use the blog as an outlet for their emotions. Generally, grief blogs are similar to other personal diaries. The bloggers post pictures and links, share stories, and write about personal experiences. The main difference between grief blogs and other types of blogs is the blog's purpose. One grief blog author explained why she created her blog following the deaths of her two young children:

This blog will be my story as I attempt to find some purpose and reason for living after my devastating loss. It may not be something anyone else wants to read, which is fine. Maybe it will help me. Maybe it won't. Maybe it will give me an outlet for the crazy spectrum of emotions I experience on an hourly basis. Maybe people will read it. Maybe their comments will help me and something I write will be meaningful to them. Maybe I'll find other parents in my situation who understand. I have no idea. (Ambrusko, 2010)

In a different blog, *A Widow for One Year*, the blogger describes the purpose of her blog: "This is my journey through grief and single parenthood and all that goes with it. It's not always pretty, but I refuse to be defined by my grief" (Duffy, 2010). Another blogger noted that he hoped that writing a blog would alleviate his grief following the death of his partner and perhaps alleviate the pain of others who are grieving. He wrote, "It is my hope that all of this will serve a purpose, if not for me, then for just one person who one day stumbles upon this blog" (Cano, 2010). Another widower wrote, "I started this blog as a way to

get out my thoughts, with no real intentions of sharing it. And I think for my own sanity I need to continue. And will. Soon" (Sven, 2010).

Grief-Related Blogging as a Form of Computer-Mediated Communication

Grief blogs have the potential to change the ways in which people communicate about death and loss online and offline. However, grief blogs, just like many other forms of computer-mediated communication (CMC), also have the potential to impede people's ability to talk about death and how they grieve over the loss. Various characteristics of computer-mediated communication have an effect on grief-related blogging. For example, less interpersonal risks exist for those sharing emotional information online. As a result, bloggers might be less apprehensive when disclosing sensitive information because they are not as concerned with a negative response to their ideas (McKenna & Bargh, 2000).

Anonymity was listed as a potential advantage to discussions of grief online (Weinberg, Schmale, Uken, & Wessel, 1996). Some grief bloggers voluntarily self-identify themselves by providing first and last names. Others use only first names or create screen names to avoid identification. Although many bloggers are easily identifiable by information provided on their blogs (Viégas, 2005), a degree of anonymity still exists because the bloggers do not directly face their audience, nor are they seen by it. This degree of anonymity in the blogosphere increases the blogger's online disinhibition (Joinson, 2001).

Online, people often feel dissociated from their offline identity. Separating their actions online from their offline actions makes people feel less vulnerable about their self-disclosure (Suler, 2004). Although many grief bloggers' identities are made known on the blogs, they still feel "physically invisible," which strengthens the online disinhibition effect, giving people the courage to write about sensitive issues (p. 322). Suler continued to explain that people do not need to be concerned with how they look when they utter a particular message because "text communication offers a built-in opportunity to keep one's eye averted" (p. 322). For example, on her grief blog, Jimenez (2010) touched upon a sensitive matter for her topic of intimacy after her husband died. She warned her readers:

I have debated writing this entry a long time.
My family reads my blog.
Roger's family read my blog.
But so do other widows.
So do other widows who are new to the "club".
So fair warning... this may be TMI.

In early blog entries, another grief blogger asserted that she would be honest and uncensored. A few months later, she admitted that she was becoming more careful and critical of what she wrote because she knew that what she writes could make others worry about her (Ambrusko, 2010).

Asynchronicity is another aspect of CMC that affects communication on blogs. On blogs, communication is *asynchronous*, meaning that the blogger does not interact with his or her readers in real time. Comments can be posted minutes, hours, or days after the initial blog is posted. This asynchronicity can add to feelings of perceived anonymity online and the disinhibition effect, which can allow people to feel safer when discussing emotional issues online. Suler (2004) explained asynchronicity in this way: "Some people may even experience asynchronous communication as 'running away' after posting a message that is personal, emotional, or hostile. It feels safe putting it 'out there' where it can be left behind" (p. 323).

Therapeutic Value of Grief Blogging

Grief-related blogging can be beneficial to both the blogger and his or her audience. The actual act of writing is therapeutic for the blogger, and the social support given to the blogger from the reading audience also helps the author. Reading grief blogs helps the blog's audience in two ways. It allows the audience to understand the process of grieving and become a part of the grieving experience.

Writing Benefits the Blogger

Writing or expressing grief in a blog can provide a means of catharsis for the bereaved (Sofka, 1997). While it can be difficult on a personal level, people often discuss their loss in one context or another to cope with the intense grief experienced following a death. Communicating about death is a natural act that we engage in to express ourselves (Pennebaker, 1997a). Writing about an emotional experience helps individuals both mentally and physically, as emotional responses to memories become less intense when one constantly writes about or addresses a traumatic event (Pennebaker, 1997a). People who share their harrowing incidences with others experience consistent and significant health improvements (Pennebaker, 1997b). Additionally, disclosing emotional issues results in lower ratings of hopelessness and depression (Segal, Bogaards, Becker, & Chatman, 1999).

The act of writing about an emotional incident is a way to externalize that traumatic experience. Pennebaker (1997a) believed that because the distressing event has been written down and "preserved," individuals were less likely continuously and mentally to rehearse the event. Those most likely to benefit from revealing emotional experiences are those who might not typically talk to others about their experiences (Pennebaker et al., 2001). It is not accidental that Ambrusko (2010) revealed the importance of her grief blog to her grieving process. She wrote, "So there. I said it, it's out there and hopefully getting it out will make it feel a little more bearable."

Blogging Provides Space for Identity Renegotiation

Individuals have multiple social identities that converge and conflict with each other in everyday interaction (Baxter, 2004); that is, individuals can simultaneously be parents, spouses, relational partners, siblings, and friends. The death of a loved one ultimately means that one or more of these identities changes or comes to an end. Parents who lose their only child are no longer able to enact the traditional role of parent (Toller, 2008); spouses who lose husbands, wives, or partners are no longer able to enact the role of spouse (Cadell & Marshall, 2007; Lopata, 2000). Part of the grieving process is renegotiating identities and being able to communicate about the frustrations of loss. As Hastings (2000) pointed out, "Opportunities for some healthy disclosures are necessary for healing a fractured identity" (p. 359). Grief blogs serve this particular function; they provide space for individuals to talk about the loss and work through the changes to their identities.

One benefit of grief blogs is that readers (and the bloggers themselves) are able to see the progression of identity renegotiation that might not be apparent offline. Ambrusko's (2010) blog shows her journey as she wrestles with moving from being a divorced mother to a single childless woman. Readers are able to read about her first vacation after her children's deaths, where she talks about how it is sad to be alone on the trip. A remarkable element of grief blogs is how bloggers communicate their struggles to make sense of the meaning in their lives since the death of their loved one. A sense of meaning is important to identity construction (Attig, 2001), and bloggers often talk about how a death opens a door to question that meaning behind life and death. DeCabooter (2008) wrestles with this in her blog after the death of her sons:

My heart aches for them and my mind questions constantly "WHY, Why did this happen?" Yet, I have no answers...will I ever get the answer I so badly need? Even if I do get the answer, will I ever agree with why the boys were taken from me? Is there a reason that my husband and I are forced to live and suffer without them?

Several blogs discuss the difficulties associated with trying not to engage in activities that would define who they were before the death. Behaviors often help to define an individual's identity and ability or inability to do these activities makes it difficult for a mourner to define who they are after the death of a loved one (Corr & Corr, 2007). In some cases, bloggers talk about how they have to take on an additional role or activities not expected. *Split-Second Single Father* (2010) wrote about his Mother's Day experience after the death of his wife. He mentioned that he is "the mom by default," and his daughter makes the Mother's Day crafts in school for him now. In this blog, the father does not only have to negotiate his new identity as a widower, but also the new role of father *and* mother.

Social Support From the Reading Audience Helps the Blogger

According to Viégas (2005), 92% of the bloggers surveyed said that their audiences have the option to leave comments on the blog. The comments left on the blog can create a conversation between the blogger and his or her audience. This conversation can have a positive effect on people who are grieving.

When readers respond to a blog through comments or e-mails, the audience essentially validates the blogger's grief-related experiences. Blogging as a sort of validation of feelings and experiences is not necessarily available through face-to-face communication (Sofka, 1997). The presence of people willing to listen positively affects that individual's grieving, as bereaved people need social support to get them through this traumatic time (Davidson, 1984; Frantz et al., 1998).

In her blog, Ambrusko (2010) noted that she was thankful for the hundreds of people online who had supported and helped her following the traumatic loss of her two children. Her blog read, "When I truly did not have the strength or energy to cope another day, all of you 'internet strangers' and 'virtual friends' have carried me. Thank you, thank you, thank you to all of you!" In the comments section of Duffy's (2010) blog, someone wrote, "Please know that there are strangers, sort of, out here in the wide world sending good wishes towards you and your beautiful kids." Another commenter posted: "Just know, Star, you have an army behind you on your battle with August [the month the blogger's husband died]. Many like myself don't even know you, but we are here" (Jimenez, 2010).

As Ambrusko's (2010) blog and comments on Duffy's (2010) blog indicated, strangers supported the bereaved bloggers. These strangers might also be known as "emotional rubberneckers" (De-Groot, 2009), discussed later in this chapter. It is not uncommon for strangers to feel connected to a deceased person or bereaved individual whom they have never met. Jorgenson-Earp and Lanzilotti (1998) argued that, in the midst of the numerous television reports of death, some tragedies will "break through the feeling of mediated unreality"; and "under such conditions, the deaths of strangers can seem more real than deaths in the local community" (pp. 156-157). In the wake of some tragedies, a sense of community is formed (Jorgenson-Earp & Lanzilotti, 1998). Many of the blog authors posed death-related questions to their readers. Ambrusko (2010) asked her readers what they thought happens when people die. Later in the blog, she revisited this question and explained that the readers' responses helped her make sense of death itself. The presence of Ambrusko's blog, and other grief blogs, creates an online support system where grieving individuals feel comfortable talking about issues of death and the afterlife.

Reading the Grieving Blogs Helps the Audience

Blogs about loss can create a shared space for families and friends to come together and grieve. When people who also knew the deceased read a blog explaining another's view of the loss, they are, in a sense, congregating in a common space to grieve. Often following a death, people seek emotional support from people who have also suffered a loss. Morgan, Carder, and Neal (1997) found that widows preferred to associate with other widows in face-to-face instances because they shared a common tragedy in the loss of a husband. The bloggers demonstrated evidence of desiring to associate online with others who are grieving and tended to follow other bereaved people's blogs. In a sense, they formed a network of grieving individuals. The bloggers posted others' grief blogs as "related blogs" on their blog, and they also commented on each other's various blog entries. One blogger discussed how her offline friends rarely comment when she discusses her deceased husband, but other blogging widows comment on her blog entries frequently (Supa Dupa Fresh, 2010).

Sometimes the social support comes from reading about others' experiences with death. Sofka (1997) argued that reading others' stories about their experiences with grief can decrease feelings of isolation. Recognizing that there is a shared experience can cause a sense of relief, as many people might believe they are the only ones who feel as they do about the loss of a loved one (Yalom, 1970). Reading about others' reactions to grief can help people recognize "normal" reactions to loss. Ambrusko (2010) indicated that she hoped others would benefit from her blog: "[This blog] will also hopefully help others to understand what grief is like[...]while someone is going through it[...]not in retrospect." She noted that she received feedback indicating that her blog helped her readers. In the comments section of another grief blog, a reader wrote:

I just came across your blog and wanted to let you know that I too have lost the love of my life and father of my 3 young children a year ago. He lost his battle with stage IV lung cancer after only 4 months.

So I guess your words and stories have great meaning to me. A year out and I still struggle with the waves of grief.

Your blog gives me some comfort and perhaps a way for me too to express myself. Look for my blog some day. (Duffy, 2010)

This reader, like the blogger, was suffering the loss of her husband. As evident in her comment, it appears that she is grateful to be able to connect with someone who has also endured a similar loss.

The author of the blog *Split-Second Single Father* described how his family handled Mother's Day following the loss of his wife. One reader commented:

I also really appreciate reading the detailed explanations of how grief continues to hit you and your daughter, as you get farther out from your wife's death. I know many widows, but few widowers my age ... and it really helps me to hear both the commonalities and the potential differences because of gender. (Split Second Single Father, 2010)

Many of the bloggers intend for their blogs to help others in their grief, and many of the readers read the blogs because they are helpful to them. Although the blogs can help both the blogger and the readers, there can be problems associated with blogging about such a sensitive topic.

Dilemmas of Blogging One's Grief

It is evident that blogging one's grief can be beneficial to the blogger and the audiences. However, numerous problems can plague the sharing of an emotional topic, such as death online. In some instances, *emotional rubberneckers*, or people who did not personally know the deceased but read the blog, can reduce the therapeutic effects of grief blogging. Online disinhibition, present in all online contexts, can lead to audience members leaving inappropriate comments on blogs. Blogging also blurs the line between public and private issues, which might be precarious to the blogger if too much personal information is disclosed.

Emotional Rubberneckers Might Be Present

While bloggers generally write a blog with the intention that it will be read by people who knew the deceased, blogs that discuss emotionally sensitive topics might invite a large number of readers whose sole intent is to gawk at other people's grief. *Emotional rubberneckers* are people who did not personally know the deceased or the bereaved individuals in an intimate capacity yet chose to visit online memorial websites and grief blogs to read about the death and others' responses to it (DeGroot, 2009). Some rubberneckers lurk on such sites simply to watch others respond to a traumatic experience, and others write comments to the blogger. Such behavior can be beneficial to the rubberneckers. As discussed earlier, people can learn a lot about grieving and death by reading others' reactions to it. Rubbernecking can become problematic if it causes the blogger and his or her supportive audience to be apprehensive about sharing genuine feelings.

Some strangers might search out grief blogs to read, while others come across the blogs by chance, become interested in the blog, and continue to check back. In the comments section of *A Widow for One Year*, a reader wrote, "I stumbled upon your blog accidentally" (Duffy, 2010). In another blog's comment section, someone wrote, "I have no words, I stumbled across your page and I am in tears! Stay strong sweetie. Keep up the positivity! I know you don't know me, but just know,

I'm praying for you!" (Jimenez, 2010). Another person commented, "We have never met. I am a CFL Nestie that has been following your blog, but have never commented" on another entry of the same blog. Although these people have never met the bereaved person, they offer their positive thoughts to the blogger. One blogger even wrote a message to her rubberneckers:

To all the strangers who have reached out to me through prayer, emails and cards with sympathy for our loss and stories about their own loss. These stories have help[ed] us to realize that we are not alone in our grief and that while at times the grief seems more than we can bare, we will survive and find our own "new normal." (DeCabooter, 2008)

People do not always comment positively, however. Sometimes limitations of computer-mediated communication can result in people posting comments that are rude or inappropriate (DeGroot, 2009). This type of emotional rubbernecking may be difficult to document since bloggers are able to remove any offensive or hurtful comments.

Online Disinhibition Can Lead to Inappropriate Comments Left on the Blog

The anonymity and asynchronicity afforded by online communication creates the online disinhibition effect. The *online disinhibition effect* refers to bloggers and readers feeling less interpersonal risk in disclosing private information online than in face-to-face situations. Although anonymity can be very positive in allowing bloggers to share personal issues online, it can also lead to inappropriate behaviors and messages (Suler, 2004). Because people do not have to face each other when communicating online (for instance, visiting websites, message boards, and chat rooms), they can integrate language that they might not use otherwise (Suler, 2004). They can leave hostile

messages and "run away" from them without having to see the emotional repercussions of their messages. One anonymous reader of the *A Widow for One Year* blog left the following comment in response to a tongue-in-cheek advice column posted by Duffy (2010):

If only we could all be as perfect as you... Were you this judgmental before your husband died, or did becoming a widow intensify your bitchiness? My advice to you? Take a good look in the mirror and try to figure out what it is that drives you to be so critical and nasty to other people!

Because bloggers have the administrative rights to delete rude or inappropriate blog comments, many of these comments are no longer publicly available. On the same blog, Duffy (2010) did remove some entries. This was evident by the "Comment deleted. This post has been removed by the author" message that now stands in place of the original comment.

Blogging Online Blurs the Public and Private Communication Boundaries

In general, the online readership is often comprised of diverse people and multiple audiences (Schlosser, 2005). Because many blogs are not password protected, they are open for anyone to read. Although blogging can be helpful to the blogger and his or her readers, making one's private experiences publicly accessible through blogs can also be risky. Although Serfaty (2004) likened blogs to online diaries, Nardi, Schiano, and Gumbrecht (2004) warned bloggers against viewing blogs as private spaces. The researchers indicated that blogs should not be thought of as private diaries; rather, they should be characterized as social activities.

Bloggers can overlook the fact that their blogs are public (depending on privacy settings), and the audience can react to the blog entries in various ways. Viégas (2005) explained:

If bloggers experience the authoring environment as an intimate, secluded space – and the evidence suggests that many do view it as "their" space – it may not occur to them that, once their thoughts are published on the Web, they automatically become part of the most public, fragmented environment in existence today. (paragraph 6)

The bloggers mentioned that they had difficulty navigating privacy boundaries in certain situations. Bloggers do realize that it is not necessarily safe (or advisable) to disclose private information in their blogs, yet they continue to write about sensitive topics (Viégas, 2005).

Self-disclosure on blogs can provoke others to reject ideas, thereby placing the blogger in a vulnerable position (Pennebaker, 1989). In a survey conducted by Qian and Scott (2007), bloggers indicated that unlimited self-disclosure could create problems in the blogger's offline life. Because some of the information on the grief blogs is so emotionally based, the readers sometimes mentioned that they felt intrusive reading some of the posts. One person, who also lost a spouse, commented on the Widow for One Year blog, "I am going to look through your blog. I hope you don't mind" (Duffy, 2010).

Ethical Dilemmas of Researching Grief Blogs

Researchers who study grief blogs are presented with a variety of ethical challenges and dilemmas. First of all, those who wish to study grief blogs need to decide how to approach the information published online. Is the Internet akin to an open public forum, where social scientists can do naturalistic observations? Or, is the Internet more like a private living room, where one needs to ask for permissions from the people inside? For grief blogs, this is an extremely important issue to consider because scholars are dealing not only with the bloggers, but also with people's memories about the deceased. The authors of this

chapter approached discourse on blogs as information published in newspaper letter columns (Hudson & Bruckman, 2004). Although we did not ask permission to examine the discourse, we provided citations of the blogs and gave credit to the bloggers.

The caveat of providing citations means that researchers interested in studying grief blogs have to wrestle with issues of privacy and anonymity. Should researchers include the actual names of bloggers and the names of the deceased? Should blog titles be included in the reference list? Does this violate the privacy of the bloggers? A partial answer may be that if researchers approach blog discourse as public, it would be appropriate to use bloggers' names (Hoover, et al., 2009). However, when private blog discourse is analyzed, researchers need to get approval from the blogger.

Solutions and Recommendations

Writing, reading, and studying grief blogs present a number of issues for bloggers, readers, and researchers. Given the increasing number of grief blogs, several of these issues require specific recommendations. First, bloggers and blog readers need to pay attention to negative emotional rubbernecking. Bloggers could monitor the comments section to remove any malicious remarks. If it becomes a problem to have strangers reading and commenting negatively on blog pages, bloggers can utilize password protection. This can help the bloggers avoid negative rubberneckers altogether, but it can also discourage others from reading the blog and providing positive social support through comments.

Researchers who study grief blogs need be mindful of many of the specific issues raised above. Researchers must determine how to approach blogs: Are blogs considered public or private? Do researchers need to get bloggers' approval before using blog comments? Part of this confusion may be alleviated by creating a clear set of Institutional Review Board (IRB) guidelines to determine if IRB approval is needed. Some academic institutions have determined that research projects dealing with blogs should be exempt from IRB approval if data collection involves online spaces accessible by anyone. In other forms of quantitative and qualitative research, there are specific guidelines that help researchers determine whether their study needs IRB approval. The scholarly community needs to decide how to methodologically approach grief blog research to ensure that ethical standards for the protection of human subjects have been met.

CONCLUSION AND FUTURE RESEARCH DIRECTIONS

Research on online grief communication continues to grow and offers many different points for future investigations. The communication discipline has begun to delve into issues of death and grief expressed online, but has yet to explore in depth the communicative impact and functions of grief blogs. The research that has been conducted to date on grief Internet postings suggests that the posts serve several functions, including empowerment, overcoming grief, identity renegotiation, and privacy boundary management (Hoover et al., 2009). Although this research focuses primarily on online bulletin boards and online support groups, the same functionality may be present in grief blogging. Scholars need to explore the discursive nature of grief blogs to determine whether there are specific communication typologies of grief blogging. Moreover, this chapter alludes to other communication issues that are unique to grief blogs, such as the role of social support from people who read and post on blogs. How are mourning and grief complicated by the fact that we can be comforted by individuals whom we do not know?

As discussed in the earlier sections of this chapter, grief blogs problematize issues of public and private expressions of grief. In the age of the Internet, grief is no longer a private experience. Blogging about grief transforms grief to a public experience that can be experienced by people around the globe. Grief blogs serve as an example of how Internet discourses are simultaneously "publicly private" and "privately public" (Waskul & Douglas, 1996). McCullagh (2008) argues that bloggers actively choose to blur public and private as a way to make sense of experiences. This problematization of grief as both private and public challenges our cultural understanding of death and grief experiences. Do grief blogs highlight a cultural change in discussing death? Are there "appropriate" and "inappropriate" online grief responses that are similar to and different from offline grief responses? Researchers need to continue to explore how grief blogs demonstrate a shift in communication about death and grief.

Grief blogs examined in this chapter are written by individuals living in Western culture. However, blogging is not a solely Western activity. As we become more globally connected, research needs to move beyond Western cultural norms to explore issues of death and grief. Since it has been established that different cultures approach death and grief differently (Rosenblatt, 2007), it stands to reason that different cultures may approach the idea of grief blogging in different ways. Do other cultures find it appropriate to grieve online? If so, are their expressions of online grief experiences similar to the online expressions of Western grief experiences? Do the grief models we use help to explain death and grief to other cultures?

The presence of emotional rubberneckers in dramatic situations serves as another point of interest. There appears to be a tension between conflicting emotional needs as the rubberneckers choose to identify with or to distance themselves from the deceased. Continued grief-related research would benefit from further examination of emotional rubbernecking. While much communication research on blogs uses discourse or rhetorical methodologies, scholars interested in exploring the phenomenon of grief blogs could move beyond what is posted on blogs and interview or survey grief bloggers to examine the reasons behind why they decided to create a grief blog. Moreover, specific case studies of grief blogs are needed to exemplify the unique ways in which individuals communicate grief. Research on grief blogs needs to begin to generalize and create typologies as well as explore the individual narratives of mourners.

Overall, grief blogs provide a space for individuals to communicate their feelings and experiences as they mourn the loss of their loved ones. Blogging about death serves as a public way to cope with grief, recover from losses, and retain productive lives. In this chapter, the authors have examined the discursive phenomenon of grief blogging, combining theoretical concepts in thanatology and communication to underscore the distinctive nature of this phenomenon. Grief blogs highlight the contradictory nature of the Internet, emphasizing how bloggers communicate normally private information in a public forum as a way to recover from loss. The discussion of positive and negative effects of grief blogging introduces some unique communicative issues, such as the emotional rubbernecking of bloggers' experiences. Finally, grief blogging presents researchers with a host of ethical dilemmas that must be considered. As grief blogs become more common, more research is needed to understand the functions and impact of grief blogs on the perceptions of death and grief.

GRIEF BLOGS

A widow for one year. Sandi Duffy, http://stduffy.blogspot.com/

Sandi discusses life after the loss of her husband who died of pancreatic cancer. She is raising their two children by herself.

And you may ask yourself – well…how did I get here? Star Jimenez, http://sumstarles.blogspot.com

The author of this blog records her thoughts about grief in a stanza. Star discusses her life following the death of her husband who died in a car accident less than one year after they were married.

Callapitter. Amy Ambrusko, http://callapitter46.blogspot.com

This blog chronicles the life of a divorcee following the deaths of her two young children who died in a car accident.

Dan, in real time. Dan Cano, http://www.blogcatalog.com/blog/dan-in-real-time

In this blog, Dan grieves the death of his husband, Michael. Michael died of a brain tumor.

Emails to my dead wife. Sven, http://journey-to-forever.blogspot.com/

This blog contains emails that Sven writes to his now-deceased wife who died after a long battle with cancer.

Fresh widow. Supa Dupa Fresh, http://fresh-widow.blogspot.com/

The author of this blog lost her husband to a lengthy fight with cancer. She has since remarried and takes care of her daughter.

Our boys. Melissa DeCabooter, http://decabooter-macksboys.blogspot.com/

In this blog, Melissa discusses the loss of her twin boys, who died several days after birth after being born 3 months premature.

Split-second single father. Split-Second Single Father, http://widowedsinglefather.blogspot.com

This blogger discusses how he grieves and attempts to continue living after the death of his wife who died after a lengthy illness. He is raising their 6-year-old daughter.

REFERENCES

Attig, T. (2001). Relearning the world: Making and finding meanings. In Neimeyer, R. A. (Ed.), *Meaning reconstruction & the experience of loss* (pp. 33–53). Washington, DC: American Psychological Association. doi:10.1037/10397-002

Baxter, L. A. (2004). Relationships as dialogues. *Personal Relationships*, *11*, 1–22. doi:10.1111/j.1475-6811.2004.00068.x

Blood, R. (2002). *The weblog handbook*. Cambridge, MA: Perseus.

Bowlby, J. (1961). Processes of mourning. *The International Journal of Psycho-Analysis*, *42*, 317–340.

Bowlby, J. (1969). Attachment and loss: *Vol. 1. Attachment*. New York, NY: Basic Books.

Bowlby, J. (1972). Attachment and loss: *Vol. 2. Separation*. New York, NY: Basic Books.

Bowlby, J. (1980a). Attachment and loss: *Vol. 3. Loss, sadness and depression*. New York, NY: Basic Books.

Bowlby, J. (1980b). *Loss: Sadness and depression*. New York, NY: Basic Books.

Bowlby, J., & Parkes, C. M. (1970). Separation and loss. In E. J. Anthony & C. Koupernik (Eds.), *International yearbook for child psychiatry and allied disciplines, vol. 1: The child in his family*. New York, NY: Wiley-Interscience.

Cadell, S., & Marshall, S. (2007). The (re)construction of self after the death of a partner to HIV/AIDS. *Death Studies*, *31*(6), 537–548. doi:10.1080/07481180701356886

Corr, C. A., & Corr, D. M. (2007). Historical and contemporary perspectives on loss, grief, and mourning. In Balk, D., Worgin, C., Thorton, G., & Meagher, D. (Eds.), *Handbook of thanatology: The essential body of knowledge for the study of death, dying, and bereavement* (pp. 131–142). Florence, KY: Association for Death Education and Counseling.

Davidson, G. W. (1984). *Understanding mourning: A guide for those who grieve*. Minneapolis, MN: Augsburg Fortress.

Davis, C. G. (2001). The tormented and the transformed: Understanding responses to loss and trauma. In Neimeyer, R. A. (Ed.), *Meaning reconstruction & the experience of loss* (pp. 137–155). Washington, DC: American Psychological Association. doi:10.1037/10397-007

Davis, C. G., Nolen-Hoeksema, S., & Larson, J. (1998). Making sense of loss and benefiting from the experience: Two constructs of meaning. *Journal of Personality and Social Psychology*, *75*, 561–574. doi:10.1037/0022-3514.75.2.561

Davis, C. G., Wortman, C. B., Lehman, D. R., & Silver, R. C. (2000). Searching for meaning in loss: Are clinical assumptions correct? *Death Studies*, *24*, 497–540. doi:10.1080/07481180050121471

DeGroot, J. M. (2009). *Reconnecting with the dead via Facebook: Examining trancorporeal communication as a way to maintain relationships*. Unpublished doctoral dissertation, Ohio University, Athens, OH.

DeVaul, R. A., Zisook, S., & Faschingbauer, T. R. (1979). Clinical aspects of grief and bereavement. *Primary Care*, *6*, 391–402.

deVries, B., & Roberts, P. (2004). Introduction. *Omega*, *49*(1), 1–3. doi:10.2190/XR23-NDBN-UUM8-FALQ

Frantz, T. T., Trolley, B. C., & Farrell, M. M. (1998). Positive aspects of grief. *Pastoral Psychology*, *47*, 3–17. doi:10.1023/A:1022988612298

Harvey, J. H. (1996). *Embracing their memory: Loss and the social psychology of storytelling*. Needham Heights, MA: Allyn & Bacon.

Harvey, J. H., Carlson, H. R., Huff, T. M., & Green, M. A. (2001). Embracing their memory: The construction of accounts. In Neimeyer, R. A. (Ed.), *Meaning reconstruction and the experience of loss* (pp. 213–230). Washington, DC: American Psychological Association. doi:10.1037/10397-012

Hastings, S. O. (2000). Self-disclosure and identity management by bereaved parents. *Communication Studies, 51*(4), 352–371.

Hoover, J. D., Hastings, S. O., & Musambira, G. W. (2009). Opening a gap in culture: Women's uses of the Compassionate Friends website. *Women & Language, 32*(1), 82–90.

Hudson, J. M., & Bruckman, A. (2004). "Go away": Participant objections to being studied and the ethics of chatroom research. *The Information Society, 20*, 127–139. doi:10.1080/01972240490423030

Joinson, A. N. (2001). Self-disclosure in computer-mediated communication: The role of self-awareness and visual anonymity. *European Journal of Social Psychology, 31*(2), 177–192. doi:10.1002/ejsp.36

Jorgensen-Earp, C. R., & Lanzilotti, L. A. (1998). Public memory and private grief: The construction of shrines at the sites of public tragedy. *The Quarterly Journal of Speech, 84*, 150–170. doi:10.1080/00335639809384211

Kübler-Ross, E. (1969). *On death and dying*. New York, NY: Macmillan.

Lopata, H. Z. (2000). Widowhood construction of self-concept and identities. *Studies in Symbolic Interaction, 23*, 261–275. doi:10.1016/S0163-2396(00)80041-1

McCullagh, K. (2008). Blogging: Self presentation and privacy. *Information & Communications Technology Law, 17*(1), 3–23. doi:10.1080/13600830801886984

McKenna, K. Y. A., & Bargh, J. A. (2000). Plan 9 from cyberspace: The implications of the Internet for personality and social psychology. *Personality and Social Psychology Review, 4*(1), 57–75. doi:10.1207/S15327957PSPR0401_6

Morgan, D., Carder, P., & Neal, M. (1997). Are some relationships more useful than others? The value of similar others in the networks of recent widows. *Journal of Social and Personal Relationships, 14*, 745–759. doi:10.1177/0265407597146002

Moss, M. (2004). Grief on the Web. *Omega, 49*(1), 77–81. doi:10.2190/CQTK-GF27-TN42-3CW3

Nardi, B. A., Schiano, D. J., & Gumbrecht, M. (2004). Blogging as social activity, or, would you let 900 million people read your diary? *Proceedings of the 2004 ACM Conference on Computer Supported Cooperative Work* (pp. 222-231). Chicago, IL: ACM.

Parkes, C. M. (1970a). The first year of bereavement. *Psychiatry, 33*, 444–467.

Parkes, C. M. (1970b). Seeking and finding a lost object: Evidence from recent studies of reaction to bereavement. *Social Science & Medicine, 4*, 187–201. doi:10.1016/0037-7856(70)90115-0

Parkes, C. M. (1972). *Bereavement: Studies of grief in adult life*. New York, NY: International Universities Press.

Parkes, C. M., & Weiss, R. S. (1983). *Recovery from bereavement*. New York, NY: Basic Books.

Pennebaker, J. W. (1989). Confession, inhibition, and disease. In Berkowitz, L. (Ed.), *Advances in experimental social psychology* (pp. 211–244). New York, NY: Academic Press.

Pennebaker, J. W. (1997a). *Opening up: The healing power of expressing emotions*. New York, NY: Guilford Press.

Pennebaker, J. W. (1997b). Writing about emotional experiences as a therapeutic process. *Psychological Science, 8*(3), 162–166. doi:10.1111/j.1467-9280.1997.tb00403.x

Pennebaker, J. W., Zech, E., & Rimè, B. (2001). Disclosing and sharing emotion: Psychological, social, and health consequences. In Stroebe, M. S., Hansson, R. O., Stroebe, W., & Schut, H. (Eds.), *Handbook of bereavement research* (pp. 431–448). Washington, DC: American Psychological Association.

Qian, H., & Scott, C. R. (2007). Anonymity and self-disclosure on weblogs. *Journal of Computer-Mediated Communication*, *12*, 1428–1451. doi:10.1111/j.1083-6101.2007.00380.x

Rosenblatt, P. C. (1996). Grief that does not end. In Klass, D., Silverman, P. R., & Nickman, S. L. (Eds.), *Continuing bonds: New understandings of grief* (pp. 45–58). Washington, DC: Taylor & Francis.

Rosenblatt, P. C. (2007). Culture, socialization, and loss, grief, and mourning. In Balk, D., Worgin, C., Thorton, G., & Meagher, D. (Eds.), *Handbook of thanatology: The essential body of knowledge for the study of death, dying, and bereavement* (pp. 115–119). Florence, KY: Association for Death Education and Counseling.

Schlosser, A. E. (2005). Posting versus lurking: Communicating in a multiple audience context. *The Journal of Consumer Research*, *32*, 260–265. doi:10.1086/432235

Segal, D. L., Bogaards, J. A., Becker, L. A., & Chatman, C. (1999). Effects of emotional expression on adjustment to spousal loss among older adults. *Journal of Mental Health and Aging*, *5*, 297–310.

Serfaty, V. (2004). *The mirror and the veil: An overview of American online diaries and blogs*. New York, NY: Rodopi.

Shuchter, S. R., & Zisook, S. (1993). The course of normal grief. In Stroebe, M. S., Stroebe, W., & Hansson, R. O. (Eds.), *Handbook of bereavement: Theory, research, and intervention* (pp. 102–111). New York, NY: Cambridge University Press. doi:10.1017/CBO9780511664076.003

Sofka, C. J. (1997). Social support internetworks, caskets for sale, and more: Thanatology and the information superhighway. *Death Studies*, *21*, 553–574. doi:10.1080/074811897201778

Stroebe, M. S., & Schut, H. (2001). Meaning making in the dual process model of coping with death bereavement. In Neimeyer, R. A. (Ed.), *Meaning reconstruction & the experience of loss* (pp. 55–73). Washington, DC: American Psychological Association. doi:10.1037/10397-003

Stylianos, S. K., & Vachon, M. L. S. (1993). The role of social support in bereavement. In Stroebe, M. S., Stroebe, W., & Hansson, R. O. (Eds.), *Handbook of bereavement: Theory, research, and intervention* (pp. 102–111). New York, NY: Cambridge University Press. doi:10.1017/CBO9780511664076.027

Suler, J. (2004). The online disinhibition effect. *Cyberpsychology & Behavior*, *7*(3), 321–326. doi:10.1089/1094931041291295

Toller, P. W. (2008). Bereaved parents' negotiation of identity following the death of a child. *Communication Studies*, *59*(4), 306–321. doi:10.1080/10510970802467379

Viégas, F. B. (2005). Bloggers' expectations of privacy and accountability: An initial survey. *Journal of Computer-Mediated Communication*, *10*(3). Retrieved from http://www.jcmc.indiana.edu/vol10/issue3/viegas.html.

Waskul, D., & Douglas, M. (1996). Considering the electronic participant: Some polemical observations on the ethics of online research. *The Information Society*, *12*(2), 129–139. doi:10.1080/713856142

Weinberg, N., Schmale, J., Uken, J., & Wessel, K. (1996). Online help: Cancer patients participate in a computer-mediated group. *Health & Social Work*, *21*, 24–29.

Weiss, R. S. (1993). Loss and recovery. In Stroebe, M. S., Stroebe, W., & Hansson, R. O. (Eds.), *Handbook of bereavement: Theory, research, and intervention* (pp. 102–111). New York, NY: Cambridge University Press. doi:10.1017/CBO9780511664076.019

Yalom, I. (1970). *The theory and practice of group psychotherapy*. New York, NY: Basic Books.

ADDITIONAL READING

Blando, J., Graves-Ferrick, K., & Goecke, J. (2004). Relationship differences in AIDS memorials. *Omega, 49*, 27–42. doi:10.2190/A6DJ-5EVH-56D3-VLAR

Bosticco, C., & Thompson, T. (2005). The role of communication and story telling in the family grieving system. *Journal of Family Communication, 5*(4), 255–278. doi:10.1207/s15327698jfc0504_2

Bosticco, C., & Thompson, T. L. (2005). An examination of the role of narratives and storytelling in bereavement. In Harter, L. M., Japp, P. M., & Beck, C. S. (Eds.), *Narratives, health, and healing: Communication theory, research, and practice* (pp. 391–411). Mahwah, NJ: Lawrence Erlbaum Associates.

Capps, L., & Bonanno, G. A. (2000). Narrating bereavement: Thematic and grammatical predictors of adjustment to loss. *Discourse Processes, 30*(1), 1–25. doi:10.1207/S15326950dp3001_01

Child, J. T., Pearson, J. C., & Petronio, S. (2009). Blogging, communication, and privacy management: Development of the blogging privacy management measure. *Journal of the American Society for Information Science and Technology, 60*, 2079–2094. doi:10.1002/asi.21122

deVries, B., & Rutherford, J. (2004). Memorializing loved ones on the World Wide Web. *Omega, 49*(1), 5–26. doi:10.2190/DR46-RU57-UY6P-NEWM

Dyer, K., & Thompson, C. D. (2000). The Internet use for web-education on the overlooked areas of grief and loss. *Cyberpsychology & Behavior, 3*(2), 255–270. doi:10.1089/109493100316111

Foot, K., Warnick, B., & Schneider, S. M. (2006). Web-based memorializing after September 11: Toward a conceptual framework. *Journal of Computer-Mediated Communication, 11*, 72–96. doi:10.1111/j.1083-6101.2006.tb00304.x

Golish, T. D., & Powell, K. A. (2003). 'Ambiguous loss': Managing the dialectics of grief associated with premature birth. *Journal of Social and Personal Relationships, 20*(3), 309–334. doi:10.1177/0265407503020003003

Hastings, S. O., Hoover, J. D., & Musambira, G. W. (2005). 'In my heart for eternity': Normalizing messages to the deceased. *Storytelling, Self, Society, 1*, 11–25.

Hastings, S. O., Musambira, G. W., & Hoover, J. D. (2007). Community as a key to healing after the death of a child. *Communication & Medicine, 4*(2), 153–163. doi:10.1515/CAM.2007.019

Hollander, E. M. (2001). Cyber community in valley of the shadow of death. *Journal of Loss and Trauma, 6*, 135–146. doi:10.1080/108114401753198007

Musaambira, G. W., Hastings, S. O., & Hoover, J. D. (2006-2007). Bereavement, gender, and cyberspace: A content analysis of parents' memorials to their children. *Omega, 54*(4), 263–279. doi:10.2190/R865-85X7-15J0-0713

Nager, E. A., & deVries, B. (2004). Memorializing on the World Wide Web: Patterns of grief and attachment in adult daughters of deceased mothers. *Omega, 49*(1), 43–56. doi:10.2190/WA9E-AK5L-2P2G-1QP1

Parkes, C. M. (1995). Guidelines for conducting ethical bereavement research. *Death Studies, 19,* 171–181. doi:10.1080/07481189508252723

Riches, G., & Dawson, P. (1996). 'An intimate loneliness': Evaluating the impact of a child's death on parental self-identity and marital relationships. *Journal of Family Therapy, 18,* 1–22. doi:10.1111/j.1467-6427.1996.tb00031.x

Roberts, P., & Vidal, L. A. (2000). Perpetual care in cyberspace: A portrait of memorials on the web. *Omega, 40,* 159–171.

Roberts, P., & Vidal, L. A. (2004). The living and the dead: Community in the virtual cemetery. *Omega, 49*(1), 57–76. doi:10.2190/D41T-YFNN-109K-WR4C

Toller, P. W. (2005). Negotiation of dialectical contradictions by parents who have experienced the death of a child. *Journal of Applied Communication Research, 33*(1), 46–66. doi:10.1080/0090988042000318512

Toller, P. W., & Braithwaite, D. O. (2009). Grieving together and apart: Bereaved parents' contradictions of martial interaction. *Journal of Applied Communication Research, 37*(3), 257–277. doi:10.1080/00909880903025887

KEY TERMS AND DEFINITIONS

Bereavement: The objective situation of individuals who have experienced a loss of some person or thing that they valued.

Emotional Rubberneckers: People who did not know the deceased or the bereaved individuals in an intimate capacity but visit online memorials, blogs, or funeral home guestbooks to read about the death and others' responses to it.

Grief: One's reactions to loss.

Grief Blog: An online weblog that gives an account of a person's experience with grief.

Grief Work: Process of coping with loss and grief.

Online Disinhibition Effect: Occurs when people feel less interpersonal risks disclosing information online than they feel in face-to-face situations.

Social Support: Physical and emotional aid provided by friends and family.

Section 3
Analyzing Blogs:
Approaches and Perspectives

Chapter 11
U.S. Political Blogs:
What Aspects of Blog Design Correlate with Popularity?

Lynne M. Webb
University of Arkansas, USA

Tiffany E. Fields
University of Arkansas, USA

Sitthivorada Boupha
University of Arkansas, USA

Matthew N. Stell
University of Arkansas, USA

ABSTRACT

Previous studies of successful political blogs have focused primarily on their content. However, a closer look at a blog website can reveal an array of channel characteristics that can be associated with blog popularity. To provide a holistic assessment of the popularity of political blogs, the authors of this chapter examined the formal features of blog homepages in a sample of 100 top political blogs in the U.S. The purpose of the study was to determine whether blog channel characteristics (such as complexity, interactivity, user-friendliness, and navigability) were associated with blog popularity. Ideological orientation was included among the variables to account for any differences associated with channel characteristics across the political spectrum. The analysis indicated that blog complexity, interactivity, user-friendliness, navigability, and political ideology were directly related to blog popularity. The authors argue that these results allow researchers to distinguish between blog popularity based on blog content and blog channel characteristics. The results also may permit blog developers to develop the formal features of the blogs to maximize popularity.

DOI: 10.4018/978-1-60960-744-9.ch011

INTRODUCTION

According to the Pew Internet and the American Life Project researchers, by 2004 blogs and blogging became a vital part of the American online culture. At that time 27% of all Internet users in the United States were writing, commenting on, or reading blogs (Pew Research, 2005). In a six-year period, 1998-2004, blog readership increased by 297,000 views, demonstrating steady growth (Johnson & Kaye, 2004). By the end of 2004, 8 million American Internet users had created blogs; 32 million Americans adults read blogs; almost 9% of U.S. Internet users infrequently accessed political blogs during election season for political news updates, and 4% reported doing so regularly (Pew Research, 2005). By 2008, 42% of Internet users in the United States had read someone else's blog and 12% said they had created or worked on their own blog; approximately 5% of American Internet users blog on any given day (Smith, 2008).

Blogs exist on a variety of topics, as they can fulfill various information and communication needs of the audience. Political blogs in the United States have become a widely read and cited source for news and opinions on public issues, as 'well as a recognized form of political participation and public deliberation. Many Internet users rely heavily on political blogs to follow domestic and world political events (McKenna, 2007). Many users perceive blogs as more credible sources of political news and commentary than traditional media outlets or other online news sources (Johnson, Kaye, Bichard, & Wong, 2008).

Researchers, journalists and lay-people alike may be particularly interested in the popularity of political blogs because of their potential to influence elections, public policy, and government actions. We elected to study political blogs due to their enormous communication potential in a democratic society. Political blogs in the U.S. are plentiful and diverse—in short, obvious targets for analysis in the examination of blog channel characteristics.

Perlmutter (2008) described the political blog, as "a personal commentary on nonpersonal events, issues, ideas; a site for interaction; a spawning ground for activism; a vessel of wrath" (p. 11). Blogs devoted to politics provide the opportunity for bloggers to express their views and for readers to post their responses. While blogs do not always have the power to directly influence the political process, scholars (Williams, Trammell, Postelnicu, Landreville, & Martin, 2005) have noted that U.S. Senate Majority Leader Trent Lott "lost his job because bloggers would not allow the story of his inappropriate racial remarks … to go away" (p. 178). Similarly, Rogers (2005) posited that the blogosphere often attends to poignant issues ignored by traditional mass media.

U.S. presidential and other candidates running for office now routinely maintain blogs as online campaigning tools (Sweetster, 2007). Internet audiences actively contribute to the political blogosphere by posting responses to messages from candidates, pundits, and fellow bloggers.

A remarkable feature of the so-called Web 2.0 movement with its tremendous growth of user-generated content is the rise of weblogs, or blogs. Gordon (2006) defined the blog as "an online journal or log" (p. 32). Blogs provide Web users with an interactive content-sharing platform that allows bloggers to reflect on literally anything and that allows blog readers to respond. Research on blogging after one of the most devastating natural disasters in the United States history, Hurricane Katrina in New Orleans in 2005, documented that blogs fulfilled at least four major functions for the affected communities: communication, political, information, and helping (Macias, Hilyard, & Freimuth, 2009). During the time of crisis and afterwards, blogs established a critical line of communication, provided social support and help, distributed valuable information, and encouraged political participation by discussing federal and local governments' responses to the crisis.

Perlmutter differentiated "bloggers" from "*uber*-bloggers," the latter describing writers of "the elite [blogs] with large audiences, heavily linked by other bloggers, and whose pronouncements tend to attract mainstream media attention" (p. xxii). While communication researchers have begun to investigate *uber*-bloggers (e.g., Ekdale, Kang, Fung, & Perlmutter, 2010) and the content of *uber*-blog posts (Liu, 2010), we could locate no previous examination of the formal features of the so-called *uber*-blogs. Therefore, one may ask, what blog channel characteristics distinguish regular political blogs from *uber*-blogs? To answer this question, we reviewed previous studies on political blogs and conducted an original research project. In the data collection phase of the project, we identified and coded channel characteristics of political blogs displayed by blog homepages, including complexity, interactivity, user-friendliness, and navigability on both *uber*-popular and "simply-popular" political blogs. We included ideological orientation among blog attributes to identify variations in formal features across the political and partisan spectrum. As Goren observed, U. S. "citizens rely heavily on partisanship and core principles to construct their policy preferences, to guide their evaluations of public officials and to inform their votes" (2005, p. 881). If citizens rely on partisanship, then partisan political blogs may be more popular than nonpartisan political blogs.

The purpose of this chapter is (a) to review the existing research as well as (b) to report the results of an original study that provides a holistic assessment of the channel characteristics associated with popular U.S. political blogs. To these ends, this chapter includes a review of the existing research followed by a report of the study methods, results, and interpretation of the findings.

LITERATURE REVIEW

Our review of literature begins with a general examination of research on political blogs, advances to blog popularity, and culminates in an in-depth review of the research on blog channel characteristics, such as complexity, interactivity, user-friendliness, and navigability. Virtually all research on blog popularity has examined political blogs.

A review of previous studies on blogs reveals that researchers tend to: (a) survey bloggers (e.g., Guadagno, Okdie, & Eno, 2008) or blog readers (Kaye, 2005) to discover their perceptions and motivations; (b) analyze the content of the blogs *per se*, typically to assess particular aspects of posts, such as the use of certain words (Thelwall & Stuart, 2007); or (c) assess outcomes, such as the influence of blog use on political engagement (DeZuniga, Puig-I-Abril, & Rojas, 2009).

What kinds of blogs do researchers tend to examine? Researchers have examined a variety of blogs, ranging from organizational blogs (e.g., Kelleher & Miller, 2006) to teenage diaries (e.g., Huffaker & Calvert, 2005) or even "mommy" blogs (blogs written by women who primarily discuss their families using a diary or journal format; e.g., Lopez, 2009)—but the vast majority of blogging research examines political blogs (e.g., Johnson, Kaye, Bichard, & Wong, 2008).

Research on Political Blogs

Because political blogs provide an inexpensive means of talking to, with, and about the government, many scholars view blogging as a "vehicle of democracy because it fosters decentralized citizen control as opposed to hierarchical, elite control" (Meraz, 2009, p. 682). Perhaps because blogs also function as a form of social media, "political blogs are used to make opinion statements far more often than they are used to mobilize political action, to request feedback from readers, or to pass along information produced by others" (Wallsten, 2007, p.19). In sum, political blogs allow users to comment on government and politics in a format where such comments can simultaneously function as responses to and prompts for on-going political dialog.

Much of the research on political blogs compares them to traditional news media on issues such as credibility (Johnson & Kaye, 2004), non-partisanship (Reese, Rutigliano, Hyun, & Jeong, 2007; Singer, 2005), issue coverage (Xenos, 2008), crisis coverage (Liu, 2010), and depth of analysis (Kenix, 2009). Researchers have examined how political bloggers view mainstream media (Tomaszeski, Proffitt, & McClung, 2009) and how mainstream media depict political blogs (Jones & Himelboim, 2010).

Studies of political blogs have focused primarily on content, examining various issues, such as gender disparity in dominant beliefs (e.g., Harp & Tremayne, 2006). A focus on blog content appears rationale, given that users can be drawn to blogs based on content. We believe that channel characteristics also may influence blog popularity, as we suspect that users prefer blogs that are interactive (allow them to readily comment) and easy to navigate (number of tabs). However, only a few previous studies have examined blog popularity (e.g., Schmidt, 2007; Trammel, Williams, Postelnicu, & Landreville, 2006).

Blog and Website Popularity

Popularity is important for all websites, including those featuring user-generated content such as blogs, because it "reflects the importance of a page in the world of Web users" (Garofalakis, Kappos, & Makris, 2002, p. 45). However, there is a paucity of research on blog popularity (e.g., Benkler & Shaw, 2010; Hargittal, Gallo, & Kane, 2008).

Popularity has been assessed in a variety of ways, including the number of references or links to a given page. Google's PageRank system has provided the first widely available link-based ranking system. Other methods include Technorati Links, Alexa Rank, and Quantcast Rank ranking services. Link-based ranking algorithm is based on an idea that "a link from a page p to a page q means that the creator of page p recommends the page q as important" (Brin & Page, 1998, p. 47). However, according to Garofalakis et al. (2002), a website with few links pointing to it also can be popular if the links have a high page ranking. Previous examinations of popular political blogs have tended to focus on specific characteristics of blogs, such as linking patterns (Reese et al., 2007; Sinha & Pan, 2006), frequency of updates, or content of postings (Hargittai, Gallo, & Kane, 2008). The present study extends this line of research by examining multiple blog channel characteristics to discover which, if any, are associated with blog popularity. Consistent with previous analyses (Anderson, 2006; Lu & Hsiao, 2007), we elected to assess popularity by the number of "hits" or page views the blog received.

Hevern (2004) used qualitative analytic strategies to group blog characteristics, such as graphic content, that promote interaction. Interactivity elements must be easy to use and user-friendly to increase popularity (Hassan & Li, 2005). Marlow (2004) further studied postings and their influence on interaction on blogs, and concluded that the most basic form of blog social interaction was the comment. Comments served as "a simple and effective way for webloggers to interact with their readership" (p. 3). However, there are limits to interactivity as a measure of blog success and popularity. The present analysis integrated the number of comments as a second measure of blog popularity.

Channel Characteristics of Blogs

Like all websites, blogs exhibit channel characteristics within the parameters of current technology. Blog developers have the option to include or exclude certain elements (e.g., provide or nor provide links to mainstream media websites) as well as emphasize certain characteristics that may change the character of the blogging experience (e.g., provide numerous navigational tabs allowing easy movement among and between threads). While many bloggers use templates as they create and maintain blogs, they have choices among and within templates for the number of tabs, comment opportunities, and so forth. Thus, blog developers who employ original designs as well as those employing templates typically control the blog channel characteristics: namely, complexity, interactivity, user-friendliness, and navigability.

Complexity

Multiple studies have documented that website complexity influences popularity (Bucy, Lang, Potter, & Grabe, 1999) and user satisfaction (Nadkarni & Gupta, 2007). Complexity is comprised of several attributes that include the number of links, length of the homepage, and number of graphics (Bucy et al., 1999; Geissler, Zinkhan & Watson, 2006; Nadkarni & Gupta, 2007) as well as the percentage of white space, number of words, and the mean number of colors (Nadkarni & Gupta, 2007; Bucy, Lang, Potter, & Grabe, 1999). These channel characteristics can function together as a measure of complexity; they also can individually influence the users' behavior. For example, a trustmark graphic can trigger perceptions of safety and security (Endeshaw, 2001).

Several studies on website complexity reference Berlyne's (1960) stimulus complexity theory; this theory posited that complexity is partially objective and partially subjective. While the properties of an object remain stable, the perceived complexity of the object can vary between subjects. Berlyne (1960) defined complexity as "the amount of variety or diversity in a stimulus pattern" (p. 8). In many of his studies, Berlyne created patterns, and then determined their complexity based on the number of elements within them (Pandir & Knight, 2006). Berlyne's theory suggests that websites or blogs that are moderately complex will be the most effective in attracting viewers.

Early research argued that the more complex the website, the more viewers the website attracted. Bucy, Lang, Potter, and Grabe (1999) conducted

a content analysis of 496 websites, drawn from a sample of top 5,000 most visited sites generated by 100Hot.com search engine[1] to examine the formal features and the relationship between website complexity and website traffic. The researchers coded ten formal features including graphical elements, dynamic elements, interactive elements, and colors, and compared their assessments to the number of visits the website received according to 100Hot's InSite Pro Web ranking service. Complexity and traffic were positively related; however, in regard to homepage length the "average" page was 2.4 screens in length and contained 4.2 graphical elements (p. 1254). With advances in technology in the following years, contemporary websites may contain more graphic elements—and perhaps occasionally too many graphics.

Geissler et al. (2006) argued that users respond more positively to websites that are moderately complex. Their 360 respondents evaluated multiple versions of a homepage using seven-point semantic differential scales to assess complexity, interactivity, amount of attention given to the page, and attitude toward the page, among other factors. Complexity was influenced by the length of the homepage, the number of graphics, and the number of links. The authors concluded that homepages "must go beyond some minimal range of complexity" and "present enough information and graphics, but not too much of either" (p. 75). This balance allows a website to retain the attention of the viewer as well as attract other viewers. The present study examined whether or not political blogs functioned in a similar manner.

Interactivity

Hassan and Li (2005) defined *interactivity* as the "features in a Web site that facilitate a two-way communication between users and site owners or other pre-assigned personnel" (p. 53). Because encouraging feedback is one of the purposes of a blog, political blogs may offer multiple opportunities to communicate: responding to an entry, beginning a conversation, (or thread) or by completing posted surveys. Interactivity is particularly enhanced when images accompany text (Coyle, Mendelson, & Kim, 2008), such as when bloggers display their pictures with their comments.

For example, Cozma's (2009) research with health blogs suggests that credibility is more influential in changing beliefs than the interactivity of blogs; the same may be true with political blogs. More recent research on interactivity focuses on psychological variables. Results suggest that users may view interactivity as entertainment (Chang & Wang, 2008) but that blog dialog can increase relational trust between users (Yang & Lim, 2009). The present study examined interactivity to assess its relationship with blog popularity.

User-Friendliness

Many channel characteristics of a political blog can work together to attract viewers; perhaps most widely known of these characteristics is usability or user-friendliness. Shakel and Richardson (1991) defined usability as the "users' ability to utilize the [website's] functions" (p. 22). Nielsen (1993) separated utility from usability. Utility is whether the system does what is needed, while "usability relates to the question of how well users can use the functionality" (Hassan & Li, 2005, p. 48). Lu and Yeung (1998) developed a Web-based model of usability, and defined *usability* as the "users' ease-of-browsing, ease-of-reading, and satisfaction" (p. 168).

Hassan and Li (2005) identified 57 criteria of Web usability through content analysis of the relevant literature and organized these criteria into seven categories including accessibility, navigation, and interactivity—three of the variable categories assessed in our study. The most basic way to attract as many visitors as possible to a website is "to ensure that the site is accessible" (Hassan & Li, 2005, p. 52).

Search engines employ several methods to index websites. How easily various search engines access a website can affect its popularity. Garofalakis et al. (2002) explained that websites attempt to increase website traffic by maximizing homepage accessibility, including restructuring to fulfill specific search engines' criteria. For example, in Google's PageRank system, accessibility can be improved by increasing the number of links pointing to a website. Meta-search engines sort and rank search results by relevance. A way to improve accessibility for these engines is to increase relevance. For example, "many times multiple words are written in Web pages with the same color as the background's, making the excessive words invisible to the human eye but visible to the search engine" (p. 45). By increasing external accessibility, the number of views increase, and thus popularity increases.

User-friendliness and complexity not only affect website popularity, they affect each other as well. Tisinger, Stoud, Meltzer, Mueller, and Gans (2005) conducted four experiments on political websites to discover how complexity and usability were related. The 478 participants viewed one of four types of political websites and then answered nine questions about usability and complexity. Researchers found that when given a choice between a simpler versus more complex format that presents the same information, users preferred the simpler format. Therefore, a high level of complexity can negatively impact the level of user-friendliness. The present study measured both user-friendliness and complexity to assess their potential influence on the popularity of political blogs.

Website Internal Accessibility

Often considered part of user-friendliness, internal accessibility allows users to easily "get a full and complete understanding of the information contained there, as well as have full and complete ability to interact with the site" (Williams,

Rattray, & Grimes, 2007, p. 157). To gain traffic and thus potential popularity, website content must be universally accessible, including to users with disabilities and users who speak languages other than the default language of the site. The HTML validation software *Bobby*[2] developed by the Center for Applied Special Technology (CAST) evaluates 16 characteristics that the World Wide Web Consortium (W3C), and its Web Accessibility Initiative (WAI) included in its Web Content Accessibility Guidelines (WCAG). The principles included checkpoints: the inclusion of a text equivalent for every non-text element, all information conveyed with color also available in black and white, and use of the clearest language appropriate for content. We assumed that political blogs that adhere to the same W3C and WAI standards would be more readable and therefore more popular than those that did not.

Navigability

"Navigation is the key to making the [blog] experience enjoyable and efficient" (Hassan & Li, 2005, p. 52). The more enjoyable the experience, the more likely a user will return and tell others about the blog. Good navigation entails "proper grouping of contents and use of navigational tools on all pages." In short, "users know where they are, where they have been, and where they can go from their current position" (Hassan & Li, 2005, p. 52). Cooke (2008) documented that users preferred navigational menus organized by past users, when they identified with the intended users, rather than organized by topic.

Kline, Morrison, and St. John (2004) evaluated user-friendliness of Indiana Bed and Breakfast websites including those factors that provide navigability (e.g., website search capability, home button, and tabs). Kline et al. (2004) found that easily navigable websites enabled users to "freely click in and out of pages without causing confusion" (p. 256), contained a home button that "ma[d]e it easy to get information without get-

ting lost" (p. 256), and displayed "buttons [that] enable[d] the user to click from page to page" (p. 256) without difficulty. They concluded that "the more user-friendly a website, the more likely a user would continue to view the information" (p. 256). Similarly, our study assessed navigability to explore its potential association with the popularity of political blogs.

Hyperlinking

Sometimes described as "external navigability," hyperlinking enables users to move from one blog to another with ease. A number of studies have examined the influence of hyperlinking, since links serve multiple functions for blogs including enhancing visibility, publicizing content, organizing information, and optimizing individual blog entries (Luzon, 2009). While links can be inserted anywhere in blogs, users appear most likely to follow and recall links embedded in text; they also are more likely to access links at the bottom of the page rather than on sidebars (Chu, Paul, & Ruel, 2009). Nonetheless, one study documented that very few users (4.17%) clicked on links (Chu et al., 2009). Another study found that the interconnectedness of political blogs by links tends to decrease over time (Herring, Scheidt, Kouper, & Wright, 2007).

The vast majority of links on political blogs reference other blogs (Tremayne, Zheng, Lee, & Jeong, 2006) or mainstream media reports (Leccese, 2009), and about half of the links to media sites are non-partisan (Reese et al., 2007). The more users access a blog, the more they "cite back" or link to it (Gonzalez-Bailon, 2009). Thus, highly trafficked blogs may garner even more page views as users post links back to the blog.

Ideological Orientation

Political blogs offer a diversity of political viewpoints on their subject matter. An indicator for this characteristic could be the ideological orientation of political blogs (i.e., liberal, moderate, or conservative) and the evident ideological bias of the posted responses that is referenced in the present study as *political ideology*. Although blog users practice selective exposure when seeking on-line discussions of politics (Johnson, Bichard, & Wei, 2009), few studies have examined the blog political ideology as a variable, especially in conjunction with blog channel characteristics. Bichard (2006) documented differences in the content of presidential candidate blogs in the U.S. presidential election in 2004 and reported that John Kerry used blogs more extensively than George Bush, perhaps implying that the political blogosphere was inhabited more by those leaning left than by conservatives.

Hargittai et al. (2008) concluded that both liberal and conservative blogs tend to provide links to websites that espouse consistent views; however, the content of their posts often directly addresses the major arguments from the other side of the political spectrum. Other studies of link analyses reported few differences between right versus left political blogs (Adamic & Glance, 2005; Benkler, 2006; Hindman, 2008). Most recently, Benkler and Shaw (2010) documented important differences in the channel characteristics of popular left versus right political blogs, including adoption of innovative technologies. Given the mixed results of past research, we elected to assess whether blog popularity or channel characteristics differed by political ideology of the blog.

METHODS

The present study continued the main threads of scholarship on political blogs outlined above by sampling popular U.S. political blogs and documenting their homepage channel characteristics. By evaluating political blogs on their channel characteristics, rather than content, the current analysis contributes insights into the type of blogs that users find most appealing. We believe that the

study's results may prove equally useful to blog researchers and blog developers. Blog researchers may distinguish between blog popularity based on blog content and blog channel features; blog developers may exercise more control over the channel characteristics of their blogs. Research in this direction also may help blog developers learn more about the strategies of increasing the number of views their blog receives, as well as the number of comments.

Research Questions

The purpose of this study was to provide a holistic assessment of the channel characteristics associated with popular U.S. political blogs. To this end, we posed three research questions:

RQ1: To what extent do popular political blogs employ specific channel characteristics (i.e., complexity, interactivity, user-friendliness, navigability, and political ideology) to facilitate communication from and among users?

RQ2: What channel characteristics of political blogs (i.e., complexity, interactivity, user-friendliness, navigability, and political ideology) are associated with their popularity?

RQ3: Do uber-popular political blogs differ from popular political blogs across channel characteristics (i.e., complexity, interactivity, user-friendliness, navigability, and political ideology)?

Sample

We developed the sampling frame by using the Truth Laid Bear (TTLB) blog directory[3] which provides traffic and link rankings for registered blogs. Developed by Neppell in 2002 as one of the first blog-tracking sites, the TTLB Blogosphere Ecosystem soon became a popular clearinghouse of American blogs. It utilized software applications, which daily scanned blogs registered with the directory and generated a list of blogs based on a two-prong system of popularity measurement: number of front page views and the count of incoming links, excluding inline trackbacks, organized into ranking categories. Unlike Technocrati, which indexes all pages, the TTLB Blogosphere Ecosystem system indexes only front pages. We looked at every blog in the listing on October 30, 2007, beginning with the most popular, and discarding sites unless the majority of the content was political, until a list of 100 top political blogs was generated. Afterwards we collected the front pages of 30 high-ranked and 30 low-ranked political blogs from the list. Although the sampling frame represented only a small portion of the U.S. political blogosphere, we believe that the purposive, yet diverse sample was appropriate for a study of popular political blogs. Because blog channel characteristics affect the users' overall perceptions, set expectations, and influence whether or not readers decide to return (Pandir & Knight, 2006), we assumed that there might be a difference between high-ranked and low-ranked blogs on the list.

Measurement

The study examined the relative influence of a variety of channel characteristics on the popularity of political blogs. We considered for inclusion in the assessment the previously discussed channel characteristics, as reviewed above, and assessed them as described below.

Popularity. Two indicators of popularity were employed in the study: (a) the number of "hits" or views the blog received, using the TTLB Blogosphere Ecosystem rankings; and, (b) the number of comments, as counted by the researchers.

Complexity. By counting the number of links and number of graphics on the blog homepage as well as noting the length of the homepage, complexity was assessed. Like numerous researchers before us (e.g., Nadkarni & Gupta, 2007; Xifra & Huertas, 2008), we assessed the

number of links by taking into the account the number of incoming links from other websites or blogs. While the length of blog home pages is moving toward standardization (Jones, 2007), a cursory glance at political blog websites revealed continued diversity.

Consistent with the above-cited research, we measured the length of the homepage by determining the number of frames (8 by 10 inches with a 1 inch margin) the page covered. We assessed the number of graphics by counting how many images appear on the homepage, exclusive of advertisements. We omitted advertisements in coding for multiple reasons including our belief that users do not perceive advertisements as part of the blog's homepage and that bloggers exercise less control over the graphics within advertisements versus other graphics on the homepage such as pictures they themselves post.

Interactivity. Marlow (2004) defined *interactivity* as a massive distribution of social connections covering multiple topics of interest. To assess such connections and thus measure interactivity, we counted the number of opportunities for readers to comment. Comment opportunities typically occurred at the end of blog posts, but were counted anywhere they occurred on the homepage, including the opportunity to begin new treads and post additional links.

User-friendliness. The study employed multiple indicators of user-friendliness including three of Hassan and Li's (2005) 57 criteria—accessibility, navigation, and interactivity. We focused on internal accessibility measured it in the same manner as Williams et al. (2007), using the HTML validation software, *Bobby*. In short, the level of internal accessibility was determined by the number of compliances the software found.

Navigability. Kline et al. (2004) measured navigability by whether or not a website offered a website search function, a home button, and navigation tools. We assessed navigability in a similar manner; however, instead of simply answering *yes* or *no* regarding whether a blog homepage had navigation tools, or tabs, the number of tabs was counted on each homepage.

Political Ideology. Blog's political ideology was assessed on a 3-point scale, assigning a score of 1 for conservative, 2 for moderate, and 3 for liberal political views, as determined by the title of each blog. In cases where titles did not provide an adequate basis for judgment, the coders analyzed headlines from the blog; the intercoder agreement for this measure was 90%.

Procedures

The pilot analysis produced the desired level of reliability for each of the measures. After the pilot analysis, three independent coders (one female and two males) assessed each indicator (e.g., number of links) across the 60 blog homepages in the final sample. All coders were in their early 20s and M.A. students in Communication. To assess intercoder reliability, six homepages or 10% of the sample were randomly selected (Lombard, Snyder-Duch, & Bracken, 2002), including three among the high-ranked blogs and three among low-ranked blogs. The six blogs then were re-coded by a randomly assigned second coder from among the original three coders. Intercoder agreement for political ideology was 90%. Intercoder agreement for all other measures was 93%. Disagreements were settled amicably through discussion.

STUDY RESULTS

An examination of the frequency distributions revealed that several measures of interest displayed non-normal distributions (see skew and kurtosis scores in Table 1). Therefore, we calculated non-parametric statistics for subsequent analyses at the standard alpha level of .05 and employed two-tailed alpha tests to answer the research questions.

Research Question 1 asked: To what extent do popular political blogs employ specific channel characteristics (i.e., complexity, interactivity,

user-friendliness, navigability, and political ideology) to facilitate communication from and among users? Overall, the blogs selected for the analysis represented a wide variety of political perspectives along the U.S. partisan spectrum and included both single and multi-authored blogs. Some blogs received as few as 1,150 and as many as 469,000 views per day. Homepages ranged from 3 to 73 frames (8 by 10 inch) in length and included as few as one graphic and no links, to as many as 31 graphics and 286 links. The blogs contained from 0 to 50 advertisements, comprising 0 to 63.25% of the homepages. The number of comment opportunities ranged from zero to 38; the number of comments ranged from zero to 7,738 comments.

Research Question 2 asked: What channel characteristics of political blogs (i.e., complexity, interactivity, user-friendliness, navigability, and political ideology) are associated with their popularity? We calculated Spearman *rho* across the nine measures of interest. The Spearman *rho* or rank correlation coefficient is the most appropriate of the nonparametric tests of association when both the independent and dependent variables are assessed at the ordinal level or above, as is the case with our data. The Spearman *rho* serves as a useful alternative to the Pearson product-moment correlation coefficient *r* when normal distributions cannot be assumed. Siegel (1956), a pioneer in application of inferential statistical methods in behavioral sciences, reported the power efficiency of the Spearman rank correlation as 91% compared to the parallel parametric correlational analysis, the Pearson *r*. The analysis revealed ten significant correlations (see Table 2). The next logical step, path analysis, was not appropriate, given the non-normal distributions of the measures. Figure 1 provides a visual representation of the confirmed relationships. Results concerning individual variables are discussed below in Table 2.

Table 1. Channel characteristics of U. S. political blogs

characteristic	operationalization	M	Mdn	Mode(s)	SD	Range	Kurtosis	Skew
1. complexity	home page length	15.72	12.00	5, 16	13.83	3-73	6.50	2.41
	No. of graphs	8.30	7.50	2.00	6.94	0-31	1.43	1.20
2. interactivity	No. of comment opportunities	13.78	14.50	0	10.82	0-38	-0.84	0.33
3. user-friendliness	internal accessibility (No. of compliances)	11.58	12.00	13, 14	2.81	5-15	8.43	2.81
4. navigability	No. of tabs	8.50	7.00	5.00	5.36	0-28	1.35	0.98
	No. of links	49.28	29.50	0	59.96	18-286	4.33	1.86
5. political ideology	political slant in blog's title	2.13	2.00	3.00	0.91	1-3	-1.77	-0.27
6. popularity	No. of comments	667.37	138.00	0	1464.87	9-7738	13.02	3.55
	No. of hits	40752.05	13213.50	43170.00	72040.33	1150-469172	21.28	4.08

Note: N = 60 political blogs.

Complexity and Navigability

Early researchers, such as Bucy et al. (1999), believed that the more complex the website, the more users the website would attract. Later, Geissler et al. (2006) concluded that moderate complexity is more desired by viewers. The results appear to confirm Geissler et al.'s 2006 findings; as complexity (number of links, number of pages, and number of graphics) increased, popularity of the website decreased. Consistent with Tisinger et al.'s (2005) results, our results indicate that the more complex the blogs, the less user-friendly (accessibility, navigability, and interactivity) they tended to be. Finally, consistent with Gonzalez-Bailon (2009), our results indicated that the sample of *uber*-blogs had significantly more links than the popular blogs, as discussed further below.

Interactivity

Hassan and Li (2005) included interactivity in their seven categories of Web usability. Marlow (2004) described comments as a simple means of communication, and found that blogs that were less trafficked offered fewer opportunities for comment, and thus displayed fewer comments. Our results indicated that the more opportunities a blog provided to comment, the greater the number of comments.

User-Friendliness

Kline et al. (2004) evaluated user-friendliness by examining multiple aspects of a website's channel characteristics including navigational tabs. They found that the more user-friendly the website, the more users the website potentially

Table 2. Spearman Rho correlations across the measures of interest

Blog channel characteristic		1	2	3	4	5	6	7	8	9
1. home page length	*rho*	1.000								
	p	.								
2. comment opportunities	*rho*	.289*	1.000							
	p	.025	.							
3. internal accessibility	*rho*	-.190	.086	1.000						
	p	.146	.514	.						
4. number of tabs	*rho*	-.123	-.146	.506* 8140	1.000					
	p	.349	.264	.000	.					
5. number of links	*rho*	.224	.120	.377*	.193	1.000				
	p	.085	.360	.003	.140	.				
6. number of graphics	*rho*	.151	-.142	-.350*	-.002	-.120	1.000			
	p	.251	.280	.006	.988	.362	.			
7. political ideology	*rho*	-.104	.039	.005	-.143	.156	-.017	1.000		
	p	.428	.766	.967	.274	.233	.898	.		
8. number of comments	*rho*	.197	.774*	.253	-.140	.219	-.209	.142	1.000	
	p	.131	.000	.051	.285	.092	.110	.278	.	
9. number of hits	*rho*	-.138	.085	.274*	.015	.486*	.471*	-.323*	.913*	1.000
	p	.291	.518	.034	.906	.000	.000	.012	.000	.

Note:N = 60. * Correlation is significant at the 0.05 level or below, 2-tailed alpha.

attracted. Among our sample, the more tabs a blog contained, the more popular the blog. Similarly, the more links displayed on the blog's homepage, the more popular the blog. Hassan and Li (2005) argued that a major indicator of user-friendliness, internal accessibility, is the most basic way to ensure website popularity. The current results were consistent with their claim; in our sample of political blogs, as internal accessibility increased, blog popularity increased.

Political Ideology

Political ideology was not a direct indicator of a blog's popularity. We found, as expected, that liberals, conservatives, and moderates alike employ blogs to disseminate information and to

Figure 1. Confirmed relationships

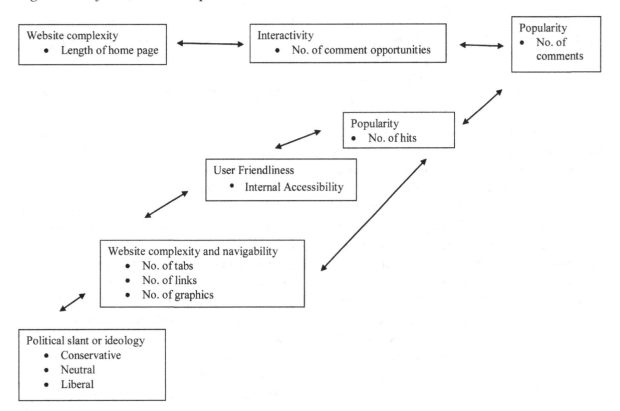

initiate public discussion. Previous research (e.g., Benkler & Shaw, 2010) indicated that channel features and political orientation of blogs could be related. Therefore, a one-way analysis of variance (ANOVA) was used to assess potential differences between conservative, moderate, and liberal blogs across the nine measures of interest. Siegel (1956) recommended the Kruskal-Wallis test as a powerful nonparametric test parallel to the parametric F test. The analysis revealed only one significant difference between groups in terms of political ideology, i.e., a difference in the number of links on the homepage, X^2 (df = 2) = 7.18, p =.03. Liberal blogs (n = 29, M = 60.69, SD = 59.13) and conservative blogs (n = 21, M = 47.29, SD = 65.41) displayed more links than moderate blogs (n = 10, M = 20.40, SD = 42.72). Thus, the complexity of the blogs varied by ideology. Blogs expressing liberal viewpoints were most likely to incorporate links; conservative

blogs were the next most likely; and moderate blogs were the least likely to include links. Perhaps blogs representing definitive viewpoints were more likely to be included in networks and thus more likely to offer links to additional blogs within these networks that espouse similar viewpoints. Such an explanation is consistent with an earlier finding that political websites—both liberal and conservative—may provide links to likeminded websites (Hargittai et al., 2008).

Research Question 3 asked: Do *uber*-popular political blogs differ from popular political blogs across channel characteristics (i.e., complexity, interactivity, user-friendliness, navigability, and political ideology)? A series of Mann-Whitney U tests were conducted to assess how the two sets of political blogs (high-ranked versus low-ranked) differed across the same nine variables. The analysis revealed three significant differences between the *uber*-blogs versus the popular blogs. The *uber*-blogs displayed: 1) more links ($U = 195.50$, $\alpha = .00$; $M_{uber\text{-}blogs} = 77.47$, $SD = 68.78$; $M_{popular\,blogs} = 21.10$, $SD = 30.65$); 2) more tabs ($U = 164.50$, $\alpha = .00$; $M_{uber\text{-}blogs} = 10.93$, $SD = 4.09$; $M_{popular\,blogs} = 6.07$, $SD = 5.42$); and 3) more internal accessibility ($U = 25.00$, $\alpha = .00$; $M_{uber\text{-}blogs} = 13.63$, $SD = 1.07$; $M_{popular\,blogs} = 9.53$, $SD = 2.50$).

The results documented that *uber*-blogs differed from popular blogs in three ways: they provided more internal accessibility, had more links, and more tabs. Further, website complexity of blogs in the sample differed by political orientation of the blog. Website complexity and navigability, in turn, co-varied with internal accessibility and number of hits. As displayed in Figure 1, the results depict two paths to increase the blog's popularity: (a) one path dealing with length of the homepage and opportunities to interact; and (b) another path that addresses the website characteristics of complexity, navigability, and accessibility.

DISCUSSION AND CONCLUSION

The purpose of this study was to provide a holistic assessment of the channel characteristics associated with popular U.S. political blogs. The study documented that three blog characteristics are correlated directly with popularity as measured by the number of "hits" or page views; they are interactivity as measured by number of comments, user-friendliness as measured by internal accessibility, and navigability as measured by number of tabs, links, and graphics. Additionally, the results revealed two blog characteristics that are *indirectly* correlated with popularity: complexity as measured by the length of the homepage and political ideology. We further found that the number of views and number of opportunities for comments—the two measures of popularity—were directly correlated; they also appeared to be directly related to alternative sets of website characteristics. *Uber*-blogs contained navigation

aids (more tabs and links) and offered greater user-friendliness (greater internal accessibility). In short, *uber*-blogs are easier to use and navigate than popular blogs.

A Holistic, Systematic Perspective

One advantage of assessing multiple channel characteristics simultaneously is that the findings provide a holistic picture of the characteristics' relative contributions to blog popularity. While previous studies examined the influence of one, two or occasionally three variables on the popularity of various types of websites, no previous study has examined the simultaneous influence of such a large number of channel characteristics on blogs generally nor political blogs specifically. The analysis reveals two paths to popularity, perhaps illuminating two systemic methods to popularity as a political blog.

The first path depicted in Figure1 may be of particular interest to bloggers who desire a forum-style blog perhaps with nonpartisan content along with in-depth discussion of political issues. Given the positive association between length of home page and number of comment opportunities, and ultimately number of comments, blog developers need not limit the length of the home page and may want to provide multiple opportunities for comments on the homepage. Thus, this first path to popularity depicts a political blog, perhaps with a fairly lengthy homepage, with frequent opportunities for users to comment. More opportunities to comment are associated with the forum atmosphere so prized for serious political debate.

The second path depicted in Figure 1 may be more applicable to those developing political blogs with a distinctly conservative or liberal slant. Such blogs tend to display more links, a feature directly associated with number of hits. Further, the results revealed a positive association between number of tabs and number of hits. Thus, the results encourage partisan blog developers to add as many tabs and links to their blogs as they can reasonably use. Conversely, the results indicate blog designers may want to limit the number of graphics on the homepage, perhaps to the sample mode of two, as results revealed a negative association between number of graphics and number of hits. When it comes to graphics on the homepages of political blogs, it appears that less is more. Further, partisan political blogs may be expensive to develop, as popularity is associated with internal accessibility—a relatively expensive channel feature to develop and not typically on the blogging templates readily available to anyone with Internet access.

Thus, while the results can articulate a set of channel characteristics associated with popularity (i.e., more tabs and links, greater internal accessibility, fewer graphics), blog developers may have financial limitations that, in turn, limit their ability to develop blogs with the characteristics that facilitate popularity. To address such a situation, blog developers might add features as they become affordable over time. As their blogs become more popular, developers may purchase more and more popularity-facilitating features with the increased ad revenue generated by the number of hits their blog receives. Finally, our holistic and systemic examination of multiple channel characteristics is based on an examination of political blogs. Would a sample of popular blogs with non-political content yield the same results? The answer is unknown but the question provides direction for future research.

Blog developers more readily exercise control over the channel characteristics of their blog than the content because users' posts often provide the bulk of the blog content. The results here presented may help blog developers learn ways to increase the number of hits their blogs attract, as well as the number of comments they provoke via their choices in channel characteristics. Finally, analysis of channel characteristics provides insights into the type of blog that users find most appealing: blogs with more tabs, more links, greater internal accessibility, and fewer graphics.

Limitations and Suggestions for Future Research

This study examined only popular political blogs rather than offering an examination of blogs that receive very few page views per day. While we examined only U.S. political blogs, political blogs in other countries and cultures can function quite differently, as documented by recent research on political blogging in Taiwan (Chen, 2010) and Singapore (Lee & Kan, 2009). Additionally, we examined only political blogs and not blogs addressing additional or alternative subject matter. Further, aside from a general assessment of political ideology, we employed no measures of blog content. Additional aspects of the content, including for example quality of the comments, also may influence blog popularity. Finally, the methods of measurement, while standard in many ways, presented its own set of limitations: that is, we employed number of hits to assess popularity, while number of unique visitors offers an alternative perspective on popularity. Using number of comments to assess popularity also can be questioned, as polarized topics often attract more comments; thus, blogs with extreme views that present issues in polarizing terms may receive inflated popularity scores.

Despite these limitations, the present study contributes to the knowledge base in several ways: First, the data presented in Table 1 offer a first glimpse of multiple channel characteristics of popular U.S. political blogs. Second, the results of the correlational analyses provide preliminary evidence of the characteristics of political blogs that are associated directly and indirectly with their popularity, among one sample of political blogs drawn during the early 2008 U.S. presidential primary season. Third, as depicted in Figure 1, the findings of the study offer two potential paths to increase blog popularity. Further, the results of the current study offer a first glimpse at how *uber*-blogs differ from popular political blogs: namely, they have more tabs, more links, and greater internal accessibility.

REFERENCES

Adamic, L., & Glance, N. (2005). *The political blogosphere and the 2004 U.S. election: Divided they blog.* Retrieved October 6, 2010, from http://www.blogpulse.com/papers/ 2005/Adamic-GlanceBlogWWW.pdf

Anderson, C. (2006). *The long tail: Why the future of business is selling less of more.* New York, NY: Hyperion.

Benkler, Y. (2006). *The wealth of networks: How social production transforms markets and freedom.* New Haven, CT: Yale University Press.

Benkler, Y., & Shaw, A. (2010). *A tale of two blogospheres: Discursive practices on the left and right.* Berkman Center for Internet & Society at Harvard University. (Research Publication No. 2010-6). Retrieved October 6, 2010, from http://ssrn.com/abstract=1611312

Berlyne, D. E. (1960). *Conflict, arousal, and curiosity.* London, UK: McGraw-Hill. doi:10.1037/11164-000

Bichard, S. L. (2006). Building blogs: A multidimensional analysis of the distribution of frames on the 2004 presidential candidate web sites. *The American Behavioral Scientist, 50,* 1255–1263.

Brin, S., & Page, L. (1998). The anatomy of a large-scale hypertextual web search engine. *Computer Networks and ISDN Systems, 30,* 107–117. doi:10.1016/S0169-7552(98)00110-X

Bucy, E. P., Lang, A., Potter, R. F., & Grabe, M. E. (1999). Formal features of cyberspace: Relationships between web page complexity and site traffic. *Journal of the American Society for Information Science American Society for Information Science, 50,* 1246–1256. doi:10.1002/(SICI)1097-4571(1999)50:13<1246::AID-ASI10>3.0.CO;2-E

Chang, H. H., & Wang, I. C. (2008). An investigation of user communication behavior in computer-mediated environments. *Computers in Human Behavior, 24,* 2336–2356. doi:10.1016/j.chb.2008.01.001

Chen, Y. K. (2010). Examining the presentation of self in popular blogs: A cultural perspective. *Chinese Journal of Communication, 3,* 28–41. doi:10.1080/17544750903528773

Chu, S., Paul, N., & Ruel, L. (2009). Using eye tracking technology to examine the effectiveness of design elements on news websites. *Information Design Journal, 17,* 31–43. doi:10.1075/idj.17.1.04chu

Cooke, L. (2008). How do users search web home pages? An eye-tracking study of multiple navigation menus. *Technical Communication, 55,* 176–194.

Coyle, J. R., Mendelson, A., & Kim, H. (2008). The effects of interactive images and goal-seeking behavior on telepresence and sire ease of use. *Journal of Website Promotion, 3,* 39–61. doi:10.1080/15533610802052639

Cozma, R. (2009). Online health communication: Source or eliminator of health myths? *Southwestern Mass Communication Journal, 25,* 69–80.

DeZuniga, H. G., Puig-I-Abril, E., & Rojas, H. (2009). Weblogs, traditional sources online and political participation: An assessment of how the political environment. *New Media & Society, 11,* 553–574. doi:10.1177/1461444809102960

Ekdale, B., Kang, N., Fung, T. K. F., & Perlmutter, D. D. (2010). Why blog? (then and now): Exploring the motivations for blogging by popular American political bloggers. *New Media & Society, 12,* 217–234. doi:10.1177/1461444809341440

Endeshaw, A. (2001). The legal significance of trustmarks. *Information & Communications Technology Law, 10*, 203–230. doi:10.1080/13600830120074690

Garofalakis, J., Kappos, P., & Makris, C. (2002). Improving the performance of Web access by bridging global ranking with local page popularity metrics. *Internet Research, 12*, 43–54. doi:10.1108/10662240210415817

Geissler, G. L., Zinkhan, G. M., & Watson, R. T. (2006). The influence of home page complexity on consumer attention, attitudes, and purchase intent. *Journal of Advertising, 35*(2), 69–80.

Gonzalez-Bailon, S. (2009). Traps on the web. *Information Communication and Society, 12*, 1149–1173. doi:10.1080/13691180902767265

Gordon, S. (2006). Rise of the blog. *IEE Review, 52*, 32–35. doi:10.1049/ir:20060301

Goren, P. (2005). Party identification and core political values. *American Journal of Political Science, 49*, 881–896. doi:10.1111/j.1540-5907.2005.00161.x

Guadagno, R. E., Okdie, B. M., & Eno, C. A. (2008). Who blogs: Personality predictors of blogging. *Computers in Human Behavior, 24*, 1993–2004. doi:10.1016/j.chb.2007.09.001

Hargittai, E., Gallo, J., & Kane, M. (2008). Cross-ideological discussions among conservative and liberal bloggers. *Public Choice, 134*, 67–86. doi:10.1007/s11127-007-9201-x

Harp, D., & Tremayne, M. (2006). The gendered blogosphere: Examining inequality using network and feminist theory. *Journalism & Mass Communication Quarterly, 83*, 247–264.

Hassan, S., & Li, F. (2005). Evaluating the usability and content of usefulness of web sites: A benchmarking approach. *Journal of Electronic Commerce in Organizations, 3*(2), 46–67. doi:10.4018/jeco.2005040104

Herring, S. C., Scheidt, L. A., Kouper, I., & Wright, E. (2007). Longitudinal content analysis of blogs: 2003-2004. In Tremayne, M. (Ed.), *Blogging, citizenship, and the future of media* (pp. 3–20). New York, NY: Routledge.

Hevern, V. W. (2004). Threaded identity in cyberspace: Weblogs & positioning in the dialogical self. *Identity: An International Journal of Theory and Research, 4*(4), 321–335.

Hindman, M. (2008). *The myth of digital democracy*. Princeton, NJ: Princeton University Press.

Huffaker, D. A., & Calvert, S. L. (2005). Gender, identity, and language use in teenage blogs. *Journal of Computer-Mediated Communication, 10*. Retrieved September 10, 2008, from http://www3.interscience.wiley.com/ cgi-bin/ fulltext/120837938 /HTMLSTART

Johnson, T. J., Bichard, S. L., & Wei, Z. W. (2009). Communication communities or cyberghettos? A path analysis model examining factors that explain selective exposure to blogs. *Journal of Computer-Mediated Communication, 15*, 60–82. doi:10.1111/j.1083-6101.2009.01492.x

Johnson, T. J., & Kaye, B. K. (2004). Wag the blog: How reliance on traditional media and the internet influence credibility perceptions of weblogs among blog users. *Journalism & Mass Communication Quarterly, 81*, 622–642.

Johnson, T. J., Kaye, B. K., Bichard, S. L., & Wong, W. J. (2008). Every blog has its day: Politically-interested internet users' perceptions of blog credibility. *Journal of Computer-Mediated Communication, 13*, 100–122. doi:10.1111/j.1083-6101.2007.00388.x

Jones, J., & Himelboim, I. (2010). Just a guy in pajamas? Framing the blogs in mainstream US newspaper coverage (1999-2005). *Mass Media & Society, 12*, 271–288.

Jones, S. L. (2007). Evolution of corporate homepages 1996 to 2006. *Journal of Business Communication*, *44*, 236–257. doi:10.1177/0021943607301348

Juang, W. T. (2001). Learning from popularity. *Econometrica*, *69*, 735–747. doi:10.1111/1468-0262.00211

Kaye, B. K. (2005). It's a blog, blog, blog world. *Atlantic Journal of Communication*, *13*(2), 73–95. doi:10.1207/s15456889ajc1302_2

Kelleher, T., & Miller, B. M. (2006). Organizational blogs and the human voice: Relational strategies and relational outcomes. *Journal of Computer-Mediated Communication*, *11*, 395–414. doi:10.1111/j.1083-6101.2006.00019.x

Kenix, L. J. (2009). Blogs as alternative. *Journal of Computer-Mediated Communication*, *14*, 790–822. doi:10.1111/j.1083-6101.2009.01471.x

Kline, S. F., Morrison, A. M., & St. John, A. (2004). Exploring bed & breakfast websites: A balanced scorecard approach. *Journal of Travel & Tourism Marketing*, *17*, 253–267. doi:10.1300/J073v17n02_19

Leccese, M. (2009). Online information sources of political blogs. *Journalism & Mass Communication Quarterly*, *86*, 578–593.

Lee, T., & Kan, C. (2009). Blogospheric pressures in Singapore: Internet discourses and the 2006 general election. *Continuum: Journal of Media and Cultural Studies*, *23*, 871–886. doi:10.1080/10304310903294804

Liu, B. F. (2010). Distinguishing how elite newspapers and A-list blogs cover crises: Insights for managing crises online. *Public Relations Review*, *36*, 28–34. doi:10.1016/j.pubrev.2009.10.006

Lombard, M., Snyder-Duch, J., & Bracken, C. C. (2002). Content analysis in mass communication: Assessment and reporting of intercoder reliability. *Human Communication Research*, *28*, 587–604. doi:10.1111/j.1468-2958.2002.tb00826.x

Lopez, L. K. (2009). The radical act of mommy blogging: Redefining motherhood through the blogosphere. *New Media & Society*, *11*, 729–747. doi:10.1177/1461444809105349

Lu, H. P., & Hsiao, K. L. (2007). Understanding intention to continuously share information on weblogs. *Internet Research*, *17*, 345–361. doi:10.1108/10662240710828030

Lu, M. T., & Yeong, W. L. (1998). A framework for effective commercial Web application development. *Internet Research: Electronic Networking Applications and Policy*, *8*, 166–173. doi:10.1108/10662249810211638

Luzon, M. J. (2009). Scholarly hyperwriting: The function of links in academic weblogs. *Journal of the American Society for Information Science and Technology*, *60*, 75–89. doi:10.1002/asi.20937

Macias, W., Hilyard, K., & Freimuth, V. (2009). Blog functions as risk and crisis communication during Hurricane Katrina. *Journal of Computer-Mediated Communication*, *15*, 1–31. doi:10.1111/j.1083-6101.2009.01490.x

Marlow, C. (2004, May). *Audience, structure and authority in the weblog community*. Paper presented at the meeting of the International Communication Association, New Orleans, LA. Retrieved on October 5, 2007, from http://rockngo.org/archives /ICA2004.pdf

McKenna, L. (2007). Getting the word out: Policy bloggers use their soap box to make change. *Review of Policy Research*, *24*, 209–229. doi:10.1111/j.1541-1338.2007.00278.x

Meraz, S. (2009). Is there an elite hold? Traditional media to social media addenda setting influence in blog networks. *Journal of Computer-Mediated Communication, 14,* 682–707. doi:10.1111/j.1083-6101.2009.01458.x

Nadkarni, S., & Gupta, R. (2007). A task-based model of perceived website complexity. *Management Information Systems Quarterly, 31,* 501–524.

Nielsen, J. (1993). *Usability engineering.* San Francisco, CA: Morgan Kaufmann.

Pandir, M., & Knight, J. (2006). Homepage aesthetics: The search for preference factors and the challenges of subjectivity. *Interacting with Computers, 18,* 1351–1370. doi:10.1016/j.intcom.2006.03.007

Perlmutter, D. D. (2008). *Blogwars: The new political battleground.* New York, NY: Oxford University Press.

Pew Research Center. (2005). *The state of blogging.* Retrieved September 30, 2007, from http://www.pewinternet.org/PPF /r/144/report_display.asp

Reese, S. D., Rutigliano, L., Hyun, K., & Jeong, J. (2007). Mapping the blogosphere: Professional and citizen-based media in the global news arena. *Journalism, 8,* 235–261. doi:10.1177/1464884907076459

Rogers, R. (2005). Poignancy in the U.S. political blogosphere. *ASLIB Proceedings: New Information Perspectives, 57,* 356–368.

Schmidt, J. (2007). Blogging practices: An analytical framework. *Journal of Computer-Mediated Communication, 12,* 1409–1427. doi:10.1111/j.1083-6101.2007.00379.x

Shakel, B., & Richardson, S. (Eds.). (1991). *Human factors for informatics usability.* New York, NY: Cambridge University Press.

Siegel, S. (1956). *Nonparametric statistics for the behavioral sciences.* New York, NY: McGraw-Hill.

Singer, J. B. (2005). The political j-blogger: Normalizing a new media form to fit old norms and practices. *Journalism, 6,* 173–198. doi:10.1177/1464884905051009

Smith, A. (2008). *New numbers for blogging and blog readership.* Retrieved June 15, 2010, from http://www.pewinternet.org/ Commentary/2008/July/ New-numbers-for-blogging-and- blog-readership.aspx# Sweeter, K. D. (2007). Blog bias: Reports, inferences, and judgments of credentialed bloggers at the 2004 nominating conventions. *Public Relations Review, 33,* 426-428.

Sweetser Trammell, K. D. (2007). Candidate campaign blogs: Directly reaching out to the youth vote. *The American Behavioral Scientist, 50,* 1255–1263. doi:10.1177/0002764207300052

Thelwall, M., & Stuart, D. (2007). RUOK? Blogging communication technologies during crises. *Journal of Computer-Mediated Communication, 12,* 523–548. doi:10.1111/j.1083-6101.2007.00336.x

Tisinger, R., Stroud, N., Meltzer, K., Mueller, B., & Gans, R. (2005). Creating political websites: Balancing complexity & usability. *Knowledge, Technology, &. Policy, 18,* 41–51.

Tomaszeski, M., Proffitt, J. M., & McClung, S. (2009). Exploring the political blogosphere: Perceptions of political bloggers about their sphere. *Atlantic Journal of Communication, 17,* 72–87. doi:10.1080/15456870802701352

Trammel, K. D., Williams, A. P., Postelnicu, M., & Landreville, K. D. (2006). Evolution of online campaigning: Increasing interactivity in candidate Web sites and blogs through text and technical features. *Mass Communication & Society, 9,* 21–44. doi:10.1207/s15327825mcs0901_2

Tremayne, M., Zheng, N., Lee, J. K., & Jeong, J. (2006). Issue publics on the web: Applying network theory to the war blogosphere. *Journal of Computer-Mediated Communication, 12,* 290–310. doi:10.1111/j.1083-6101.2006.00326.x

Wallsten, K. (2007). Political blogs: Transmission belts, soapboxes, mobilizers, or conversation starters? *Journal of Information Technology & Politics, 4*(3), 19–40. doi:10.1080/19331680801915033

Williams, A. P., Trammell, K. P., Postelnicu, M., Landreville, K. D., & Martin, J. D. (2005). Blogging and hyperlinking: Use of the web to enhance viability during the 2004 US campaign. *Journalism Studies, 6,* 177–186. doi:10.1080/14616700500057262

Williams, R., Rattray, R., & Grimes, A. (2007). Online accessibility and information needs of disabled tourists: A three country hotel sector analysis. *Journal of Electronic Commerce Research, 8,* 157–171.

Xenos, M. (2008). New mediated deliberation: Blog and press coverage of the Alito nomination. *Journal of Computer-Mediated Communication, 13,* 485–503. doi:10.1111/j.1083-6101.2008.00406.x

Xifra, J., & Huertas, A. (2008). Blogging PR: An exploratory analysis of public relations weblogs. *Public Relations Review, 34,* 269–275. doi:10.1016/j.pubrev.2008.03.022

Yang, S. U., & Lim, J. S. (2009). The effects of blog-mediated public relations (BMPR) on relational trust. *Journal of Public Relations Research, 21,* 341–359. doi:10.1080/10627260802640773

ADDITIONAL READING

Baker, F. W. (2009). *Political campaigns and political advertising: A media literacy guide.* New York: Greenwood.

Barlow, A. (2008). *Blogging America: The new public sphere (New directions in media).* Westport, CT: Praeger.

Davis, R. (2009). *Typing politics: The role of blogs in American politics. New York.* USA: Oxford University Press.

Keren, M. (2006). *Blogosphere: The new political arena.* Plymouth, UK: Lexington Books.

Panagopoulos, C. (2009). *Politicking online: The transformation of election campaign communications.* New Brunswick, NJ: Rutgers University Press.

Pasqua, M. (2009). [*I am correct and you know it: Notes and blogs from the political universe.* Maryland, VA: iUniverse.]. *MFP, 3,* 16.

Perlmutter, D. D. (2008). *Blogwars.* New York: Oxford University Press USA.

Pole, A. (2009). *Blogging the political: Politics and participation in a networked society.* New York: Routledge.

KEY TERMS AND DEFINITIONS

Complexity: "The amount of variety or diversity in a stimulus pattern" (Berlyne, 1960, p. 8).

External Accessibility: The likelihood of search engines extracting a particular website.

Interactivity: "Features in a Web site that facilitate a two-way communication between users and site owners or other pre-assigned personnel" (Hassan & Li, 2005, p. 53); Marlow (2004) defined *interactivity* as a massive distribution of social connections covering multiple topics of interest.

Internal Accessibility: The extent to which users can readily access a website's content.

Mommy Blogs: Blogs written by women who primarily discuss their families using a diary or journal format.

Navigation: "Proper grouping of contents and use of navigational tools on all pages [of the website], [so that] users know where they are, where they have been, and where they can go from their current position" (Hassan & Li, 2005, p. 52).

Political Blog: "A personal commentary on nonpersonal events, issues, ideas; a site for interaction; a spawning ground for activism; a vessel of wrath" (Perlmutter, 2008, p. 11).

Political Ideology: A set of ideas and perspectives through which public policy events are interpreted in a blog.

Popularity: The extent to which an individual duplicates or follows the trend of what others are doing (Juang, 2001).

Uber-**Blogs:** "The elite [blogs] with large audiences, heavily linked by other bloggers, and whose pronouncements tend to attract mainstream media attention" (Perlmutter, 2008, p. xxii).

Usability: "Users' ability to utilize the [website's] functions" (Shakel & Richardson, 1991, p. 22).

ENDNOTES

[1] http://www.100hot.com

[2] http://bobby.watchfire.com

[3] http://truthlaidbear.com

Chapter 12
Blogging Motivations for Latin American Bloggers:
A Uses and Gratifications Approach

Jenny Bronstein
Bar-Ilan University, Israel

ABSTRACT

The author of this chapter investigated the motivations that drive bloggers in Spanish-speaking Latin American countries to write personal blogs. The conceptual framework drew on the uses and gratifications theoretical perspective as a means for exploring such motivation. Different types of motivation for blogging were analyzed. The motivations included self-documentation, improving writing skills, self-expression, information sharing, passing time, and socialization. An online survey was designed, and 90 bloggers from six Latin American countries participated in the study. Results of both quantitative and qualitative analyses indicate that the three most-cited reasons for blogging were the opportunity that blogs provided for participants to freely express their thoughts and feelings, the facility for publishing information in their areas of interest, and the chance to practice their writing skills.

INTRODUCTION

Weblogs or blogs, frequently updated Web pages in which dated entries are listed in reversed chronological order, are one of the most popular forms of communication on the World Wide Web. Blogging in its current form began around 1997

DOI: 10.4018/978-1-60960-744-9.ch012

with Dave Winer's scripting news, an online record of Winer's reflections on a wide range of topics (Nardi, Schiano, & Gumbrecht, 2004). At the beginning, personal blogs resembled the online journals that had emerged in the mid-1990s (Flynn, 2003). These online journals focused on personal content and were regularly updated. The first blogs presented a mixture of links to a wide variety of sites, commentary, and posts. They can be viewed as being directly descended from the hotlists of "what's new?" or "cool links" (Blood, 2002). In this initial stage there were only a handful of blogs because their publication required users to have an extensive knowledge of HTML code. The emergence of free publishing platforms, such as Blogger.com in 1999, allowed users with no knowledge of HTML to publish a blog. With the creation of easy and free publishing tools the number of blogs grew exponentially and new and original types of blogs emerged, so that today's variety of blogs is as diverse as the human interests they represent (Thelwall, 2006).

Blogs and bloggers have been at the forefront of new media research in the United States, Canada, and Europe. Because early research on the emergent blogosphere focused on blog classification, several categorizations of blogs were proposed. Blogs were classified in the following ways: according to their purpose (journalistic, educational or business oriented) (e.g., Mernit, 2003); by authorship (single, group or communal) (e.g., Bar-Ilan, 2005; Herring, Scheidt, Bonus, & Wright, 2004) or by type of content (personal or topic-oriented) (e.g., Bar-Ilan, 2005; Dearstyne, 2005). The Pew Research Center's Internet & American Life Project blogger survey (Lenhart & Fox, 2006) found that the American (USA) blogosphere is dominated by those who use blogs as personal journals, citing 37% of participants as reporting that one of their main writing topics was "my life and experiences" (p. ii). Yet, few studies have focused on the state of the blogosphere in Latin America (Jeffrey Group, 2008), despite the growing size of the bloggers' population among Internet users in this region. According to Internet World Statistics, there were an estimated 175 million Internet users in Latin America in 2009, approximately 8.4% of the world's Internet users' population. Furthermore, there are an estimated 9.1 million bloggers in Latin America that represent 7.2% of that region's Internet users (Jeffrey

Group, 2008). Given the predominance of personal blogs in the Latin American blogosphere (State of the Hispanic Blogosphere, 2009; Yu, 2007), the present study investigated the motivations that drive bloggers in Spanish-speaking Latin American countries to write individually authored, personal journals.

MOTIVATIONS FOR BLOGGING

The concept of motivation has been described as "a directing force over behavior and that motivation can act to begin the behavior as well as influence its continuation" (Brady, 2006, p. 4). The reasons and motivations for authoring a blog have been at the center of blog research in recent years and different motivations for blogging have been found. Individually authored blogs give their authors a personal space on the Web by allowing them to publish their subjective views, feelings and statements easily and for free. Self-expression in a free and unrestricted environment has been revealed as an important motivation for blogging (Lenhart & Fox, 2006; Nardi et al., 2004; Trammell et al., 2006; Yu, 2007). Blogs have also been described as "protected spaces" that allow bloggers to share the feelings that they would not share otherwise and tell their story or relate their thoughts without interruption (Gumbrecht, 2004).

Several studies have indicated that the need to socialize along with the need to create and maintain social ties produces a strong motivation to blog because "by identifying, formulating, and discussing problems and interests, a socially shared view can evolve through the interaction of others" (Mosel, 2005, p. 4). When using a blog as a socialization tool, bloggers' motivations can either be intrinsic (that is, a blog is started to contact the people on the Internet) or extrinsic (that is, a blog is started to maintain relationships formed elsewhere) (Walker, 2000). Self-expression and the creation and improvement of social relationships have been found to be strong reasons for bloggers to continue writing rather than abandon their blog (Miura & Yamashita, 2007). In addition, bloggers appeared to be motivated to share information with others; they seemed motivated because blogs are inexpensive. Blogs also make it easy to create, maintain and provide a means of collecting and organizing fresh insights and opinions; besides, through blogs, it is easy to spark creativity and cooperation (Dearstyne, 2005; Jones & Alony, 2008; Lenhart & Fox, 2006; Trammell et al., 2006). Moreover, bloggers might be motivated to continue to share information through their blog because they expect a reward or a change of image (Lu & Hsiao, 2007). Bloggers might also feel motivated to blog by the need for entertainment, passing time and professional advancement (Trammell et al., 2006).

Two earlier studies on bloggers' motivations were based on the uses and gratifications theory that provides a theoretical framework for this study. Using ethnographic interviews, Nardi et al. (2004) concluded that blogging students had five main motivations: to document their life experiences, to provide commentary and opinions, to express deeply felt emotions, to articulate ideas through writing, and to form and maintain community forums. In a later study, Huang, Shen, Lin, and Chang, (2007) developed Nardi et al.'s (2004) approach by seeking to build a model that addressed the relationships among blogging motivations and behaviors. They argued that "interaction by blogging is driven by motivations of self-expression, life documenting and commenting...while content gathering by blogging is found to be driven by the motivations of commenting, forum participation and information seeking" (p. 480). Understanding the motivation or reasons why people blog may add to the understanding of blogs as a communication medium enhancing knowledge of the development of patterns of social behavior and contributing to innovations in information and communication technology.

Research Questions

The present study investigated the following research questions:

RQ1: What motivates bloggers to write a personal blog?

RQ2: Is there a correlation between gender, age and education levels of the bloggers and their motivations for blogging?

THEORETICAL PERSPECTIVE

The study utilized the uses and gratifications approach to explore the reasons that lead bloggers in Latin American countries to create and maintain personal blogs. The uses and gratifications approach focuses on the needs that a particular mass medium fulfills for its users (Katz, Blumler, & Gurevitch, 1974). The primary strength of the uses and gratifications theory is its ability to permit researchers to investigate "mediated communication situations via a single or multiple sets of psychological needs, psychological motives, communication channels, communication content, and psychological gratifications within a particular or cross-cultural context" (Lin, 1996, p. 574). The main objectives of the this type of inquiry are to explain how people use media to gratify their needs, to understand motives for media behavior, and to identify functions or consequences that follow from needs, motives and behavior (Katz, Blumler, & Gurevitch, 1974).

Rubin (2002) proposed five assumptions intrinsic to the uses and gratifications approach: (a) people's communication behavior is functional and goal directed, which implies individual and social consequences; (b) people select and use specific communication vehicles to satisfy their unique needs or desires; (c) expectations about the media and media content are shaped by individual social and psychological factors, such as personalities, social environment, interpersonal interactions, and communication channel availability; (d) the extent to which people's motives are satisfied by certain media is determined by the media attributes as well as individual's social and psychological circumstances; and (e) an individual's media use and subsequent media effects are mainly (though not completely) a function of the individual's reasons for using the media. To summarize, the uses and gratifications theoretical framework is built on the supposition that individuals use different media for specific reasons or motives as well as for social and psychological characteristics. Therefore, this theoretical perspective can greatly aid in understanding why bloggers invest their time and efforts in creating and maintaining a personal blog.

The uses and gratifications approach has served as a theoretical framework in a large number of studies that investigated users' use of and interactions with different types of media, such as: radio listening (Mendelsohn, 1964), utility of videocassette recorders (Rubin & Bantz, 1989), television viewing (Rubin, 1981), computer and video games (Funk & Buchman, 1996), website design (Eighmey & McCord, 1998; Paparachisi, 2004), online gaming (Sun, Zhong, & Zhang, 2006), and the use of the Internet for communication purposes (Newhagen & Rafaeli, 1996). Similarly, the uses and gratifications approach also has been used to investigate the motivations behind blog creation (Huang, 2007; Li, 2005; Nardi et al., 2004; Papacharissi, 2004; Trammell, 2004).

STUDY METHODOLOGY

This study examined the motivations that drive bloggers in Spanish-speaking Latin American countries to write personal blogs. An online survey was utilized to collect personal data about the bloggers as well as descriptive data regarding their most prevalent motivations for writing a personal blog. The findings presented in the study are based

on the results of an online survey conducted for one month (January 15 to February 15, 2010). Although the survey was developed specifically for the study, it incorporated previously documented motivations; its design paralleled other studies focused on blogging motivations. The online questionnaire was short, simple, and easy to answer to lessen many of the drawbacks of online questionnaires (Baron & Siepmann, 2000; Gunn, 2002). It was written in Spanish since it targeted a Spanish-speaking population.

The online questionnaire was divided in three main sections:

1. Bloggers' demographic data: questions in this section addressed the blogger's personal data (such as, age, time blogging, gender and education).
2. Information about the blog: questions in this section addressed the different elements in the blogger's blog (e.g., blogger's identification, updating frequency, forms of contact, and tags that better describe their blog).
3. Motivation for writing the blog: this section included an open-ended question in which bloggers were asked to describe in their own words the reasons why they blog. Questions in this section asked bloggers to rate statements describing different motivations for blogging in a 1-7 Likert scale. The study employed seven categories as examined in Li (2005) to gauge participants' motivation for writing a blog. The seven categories were self-documentation, improving writing skills, self-expression, medium appeal, information sharing, passing time, and socialization.

Sampling

The sample collected for the study consisted of regularly maintained personal blogs written in Spanish. The blogs in the sample were selected from the following two blog directories:

- Blog Directory – www.blogdirectory.com
- Blogalaxia – www.blogalaxia.com

These two directories were chosen among several other blog directories because blogs in these sites were categorized by country and by type, thus allowing the researcher to easily identify personal blogs from different countries. The country pages for Mexico, Colombia, Peru, Chile, Argentina, and Ecuador in both directories were examined to select personal blogs that conformed to the following criteria:

- The blog was classified in the directory as a personal blog.
- The bloggers identified themselves and provided an email address for contact.
- The content of the blog was examined and it was confirmed that it did not serve any commercial or marketing purpose.
- The blog had been updated in the last month.

Three hundred blogs matching the criteria specified above were identified from the country pages in the two directories. This sample represents a census of all personal blogs listed in the specific country pages at two directories. Using the email address provided in the blogs, the researcher sent emails to the bloggers inviting them to participate in the study. The introductory email included a short explanation of the study and the address of the website containing the online questionnaire. Because blogging is an online activity, contacting the bloggers and collecting the data online in their natural setting was considered the most effective approach. Of the 300 bloggers contacted, 90 responded to the invitation to participate in the study, representing a 30% response rate. This response rate echoed response rates in other studies about blogging (Guadano, Okdie, & Eno, 2007; Huang et al., 2007; Yu, 2007). All participants were Spanish-speaking adults (18 years of age and older).

Participants

The bloggers that participated in the study were individuals who had maintained an individually authored personal blog. In general, the demographic characteristics of bloggers in this study were consistent with previous bloggers' surveys (Herring et al., 2005; Viegas, 2005; Yu, 2007) where the majority of participants were young adult males with a college education. Table 1 presents the demographic data on the participants.

The majority of bloggers surveyed were young people from ages 18-35 (61.1%, $n = 55$), mostly men, 62.2% ($n = 56$) with a bachelor's degree (83.3%, $n = 75$) from Mexico, Colombia, Peru, Chile, Argentina, and Ecuador. These data support the findings from three other bloggers' studies that investigated the Chinese (Yu, 2007), the North

Table 1. Description of participants

Bloggers' Demographics	Percent of Total (N)
Age Range	
18-24	27.8% (25)
25-35	33.3% (30)
36-45	17.8% (16)
46-55	12.2% (11)
56-65	6.7% (6)
65+	2.2% (2)
Gender	
Male	62.2% (56)
Female	37.8% (34)
Level of education	
Grade school education	8.9% (8)
High school graduate	7.8% (7)
Bachelor's degree	83.3% (75)
Length of time blogging	
Less than a year	14.44% (13)
1-2 years	37.77% (34)
3-4 years	35.54% (32)
More than 4 years	12.22% (11)

American (Li, 2005) and the Spanish-speaking (*State of the Hispanic Blogosphere*, 2009) blogospheres in which the majority of bloggers were reported to be males between the ages of 18-35 with a college education. In addition, most of the bloggers participating in this study were experienced bloggers who had maintained their blog for more than two years.

Data Analysis

Data analysis was conducted in two phases. In the first phase quantitative responses received from the survey were compiled in a Microsoft Excel document and analyzed using descriptive and comparative statistics. This phase yielded quantifiable demographic data about the participants and the information they provided or presented in their blogs. It also yielded statistical data on the motivations and feelings involved in writing a personal blog. The second phase of the analysis examined the open-ended question in which bloggers were asked to describe in their own words their motivations for blogging. Data were analyzed using content analysis methodology. Phrases as the minimal information unit were identified and then coded into their respective categories by constantly comparing these phrases to the properties of the emerging category to develop and saturate the category.

STUDY RESULTS

RQ1: What motivates bloggers to write a personal blog?

The first research question examined the motivations that drive bloggers in Spanish-speaking Latin American countries to write personal blogs. As noted, seven different types of motivations for blogging were investigated: (1) blogging as a means for self-documentation; (2) blogging as a means for improving the blogger's writing skills;

(3) blogging as a means of self-expression; (4) medium appeal: the easiness of blogging motivates the blogger to write; (5) blogging as a means of sharing and publishing information; (6) blogging as a way of passing time; and (7) blogging as a means of socialization. Bloggers were asked to rate statements describing the different motivations on a 1-7 Likert scale (see Table 2).

Results in Table 2 show that blogging as a means of sharing information with others was the factor that received the highest ratings ($M = 5.52$) by participants. The two individual motivations that were ranked highest were the possibility that blogs provided for Latin American bloggers to freely express their thoughts and feelings ($M = 5.76$) and to publish information on their interests ($M = 5.72$). Self-expression and sharing information in an easy to publish environment are related to what Recuero (2008) calls "creating a personal space in the Internet." A blog becomes a channel for bloggers to "express themselves and to share the knowledge they have" (p. 100).

The inclination for writing ($M = 5.64$) was the individual motivation rated third by Latin American bloggers in this study. According to Li (2005), the motivation bloggers have to improve their writing skills is developed from a prior personal advancement motivation. In spite of the development of other forms of blogs (such as video blogs), text-based blogs are still the most pervasive blog form and blogging is still largely equal to writing. Writing is an enjoyable activity for most bloggers, and they blog to practice writing skills in hopes of refining their thinking process. Nardi et al. (2004) called this "thinking by writing" (p. 227).

The socialization factor was not highly rated ($M = 3.12$). Latin American bloggers were not highly motivated to blog to keep in touch with family and friends ($M = 2.27$) or to meet new people ($M = 3.37$). This finding does not concur with other studies that found that bloggers were highly motivate to blog to keep in touch with friends and family and to socialize (Jones & Alony, 2008; Li, 2005;

Table 2. Motivations for blogging

Motivation Items: "I blog to …"	Factor Score		Cronbach's α	
	Mean	SD		
Factor 1: Self-documentation	3.96	1.61	0.66	
To keep a record of what I learn	4.66	1.97		
To keep track of what I am doing	4.12	2.11		
To document my life	3.09	2.17		
Factor 2: Improving Writing	4.92	1.74	r = 0.50	
Because I like to write	5.64	1.79		
To practice my writing	4.19	2.26		
Factor 3: Self-expression	4.07	1.26	0.62	
To express what I think and what I feel	5.76	1.84		
Because I can get the reactions of others to my feelings and my thoughts	4.28	2.02		
Because it helps me clear my thoughts	3.61	2.16		
To influence the feelings and thoughts of others	3.41	1.98		
To talk about feelings that I could not express out loud	3.30	1.99		
Factor 4: Medium Appeal	4.71	2.15	0.94	
Because I can publish at any time	5.04	2.15		
Because it is easy to update	4.70	2.27		
Because I can access it wherever I am	4.38	2.38		
Factor 5: Information	5.52	1.58	r = 0.67	
To publish information on my interests	5.72	1.67		
To share useful information with other people	5.32	1.79		
Factor 6: Passing Time	2.97	1.88	r = 0.72	
Because it helps pass the time	3.43	2.15		
When I have nothing better to do	2.50	1.90		
Factor 7: Socialization	3.12	1.36	0.69	
To be known by other people	3.66	2.05		
To meet new people	3.37	1.90		
To feel like I am part of a community	3.20	1.94		
To keep in touch with my family/friends	2.27	1.65		

McKenzie, 2008; Nardi et al., 2004; Recuero, 2008). However, such results are consistent with Herring et al.'s (2004) study that concluded that popular accounts frequently overstate "the extent to which blogs are interlinked, interactive, and oriented towards external events, and underestimate the importance of blogs as individualistic, intimate forms of self-expression" (p. 1).

Latin American bloggers were motivated to blog to keep track of what they have learned (M = 4.66) and what they are doing (M = 4.12). Nardi et al. (2004) found that blogs were used as a way to record events in bloggers' lives. According to Jones and Alony (2008), the nature of a blog enables bloggers to document their life experiences in chronologically arranged data entries. Passing

Figure 1. Gender differences in motivation for blogging

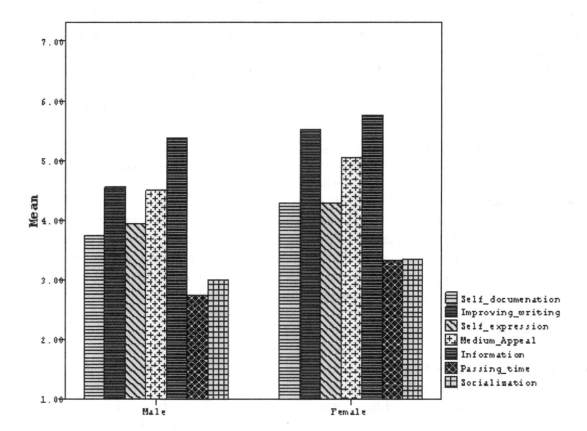

time as a motivation for blogging was the factor rated the lowest in the scheme ($M = 2.97$). Only one study (McKenzie, 2008) claimed that adult bloggers in the United States are motivated to blog to pass the time or entertain themselves.

RQ2: Is there a relationship between gender, age and education levels of the bloggers and their motivations for blogging?

The second research question examined whether a correlation existed between each of the three variables of gender, age and educational level and the seven motivations presented in Table 2. When correlating gender and motivation using a univariate Analysis of Variance (ANOVA), it was revealed that female Latin American bloggers were

more motivated to blog to improve their writing skills ($r = 5.51 \pm 1.48$) than male bloggers ($r = 4.55 \pm 1.80$). In comparison, published studies about Polish and British bloggers showed that female bloggers were more motivated than male bloggers to blog to initiate social interactions (Pedersen & Macafee, 2007; Trammel et al., 2006). Figure 1 shows the results of the correlation analysis of gender and motivations.

Correlation between age and motivation was examined by utilizing Spearman correlation analysis. The analysis showed that younger Latin American bloggers were more likely to be motivated to blog to improve their writing skills ($r = -.38, p < .001$) and to pass time ($r = -.39, p < .001$) while older Latin American bloggers were more likely to be motivated to blog as a means to share and publish information ($r =.22$, $p < 0.05$). In comparison, Li (2005) found that younger North American bloggers were more likely to be motivated to blog to document their lives and to express themselves. Lastly, concurring with Li's (2005) results no significant correlation was found between educational levels and specific blogging motivations.

To further understand motivation for blogging, bloggers were asked to describe in their own words what motivated them to write a blog. The following six themes emerged from the qualitative analysis of the textual data provided in the open-ended question: (a) self-expression, (b) socialization, (c) information sharing, (d) blogging as a writing exercise, (e) blogging to have an effect or impact the readers, and (f) blogging as a means to document one's life.

Self-expression. The first category related to the need to express feelings and thoughts in an uncensored way. Writing a blog as a means of self-expression was revealed as a significant motivation for bloggers. They described this channel of freedom of expression in different ways:

… it is a socially acceptable way of going through life talking to yourself.
(I write a blog)…to channel my frustrations and angers in a positive and artistic way.
(I write a blog)… as an emotional discharge.

Socialization. The second category revealed in the qualitative analysis was the motivation bloggers had to connect and socialize with people who share their interests and hobbies. They explained that they were motivated to blog:

… to find in my readers people who think like me.
… to keep in touch with the people who live in the south, because I live in Buenos Aires
… to get to know other bloggers and their silliness.

Information sharing. The third category revealed in the analysis was the motivation to share information they value with their readers:

… to share what little I know, to share my experiences with others
… to share my experiences as a mother with humor and irony
… to give my readers for free what took me time to find on the Internet.

Blogging as a writing exercise. The fourth category identified in the analysis referred to motivation to practice one's writing skills. Bloggers talked about the benefits they got from writing their blog and how enjoyable they found writing. They explained that they were motivated to write a blog:

[because]… writing relaxes me
… as a writing exercise that develops my creativity
To write is to fire away oblivion. What I write won't change the world, but it will keep the world from changing me.

Blogging to have an effect or impact the readers. The fifth category that emerged from the analysis refers to bloggers' desire to have an impact on their readers, to educate them on different subjects through the information they share:

… to know that my writing will make people laugh, that it will move them (in a good or in a bad way)
… to make someone happy
… to motivate adults to have good habits.

Blogging as a means to document one's life. The sixth category referred to blogging as a means or tool for documenting one's life. Bloggers viewed blogging as a way to preserve ideas, experiences, or thoughts:

... to document my life, things that have happened to me and are important.

... to remember the things I don't want to forget, to rescue my ideas.

... as a way to remember the days that have gone by, things that happened, to remember my experiences, my feelings, my anecdotes.

Overall, the bloggers' statements presented above support the findings from the quantitative phase of the study and further illustrate bloggers' motivations to write a personal blog.

CONCLUSION AND DISCUSSION

Using the theoretical framework of the uses and gratifications theory, this study investigated the motivations of bloggers who authored a personal blog. The basic assumption of the uses and gratifications approach is that people use media to gratify their needs. This study found that bloggers are motivated to blog as a way to fulfill emotional needs (such as self-expression and creativity) and needs for socialization (such as sharing information with others). Results show that blogging is a versatile medium that supports different kinds of behaviors, from the personal and spontaneous release of emotion to the creation of interpersonal relations and the archiving of information. This versatility may be the reason behind the very different ways that bloggers describe the significance of their blog to their lives. A personal blog is an invitation into the personal life of its author. The authors then filter and interpret information for their readers, putting their daily experiences in a wider context without directly targeting or imposing upon their audience to read it. For this reason, blogging is less intrusive than other technologies, and because bloggers do not impose upon others to read their posts, they are often surprised to find that there are people who read them. Because of their particular nature, blogs provide a safe haven for people who need or want to use online technologies to fulfill different needs.

The motivation that received the highest rating among Latin American bloggers was the need to "express what I feel and think." The analysis shows that through blogging, bloggers can talk about their lives, discuss hobbies and other fields of interest, publish their creative work and express opinions on events and issues while managing the degree of self-presentation to their convenience. Such results concur with Yu's (2007) findings on Chinese bloggers who use their blogs as a place to showcase their talents and personalities. Self-expression as a strong motivation for blogging also was revealed in the qualitative analysis when Latin American bloggers described blogging as an emotional outlet or a positive way to channel their feelings and frustrations. In their statements, Latin American bloggers described their blogs as legitimate venues of self-expression where the online identity of the blogger can be created and developed. Self-expression through blogging can help bloggers achieve a deeper understanding of themselves while expressing and disclosing personal information on their blog. This conclusion supported the Pennebaker and Beall's (1986) study that stated that writing about life experiences can help achieve a better understanding of ourselves and to resolve or mitigate personal conflicts.

The freedom of expression that blogging allows also is a salient theme in other studies about blogging (Jones & Alony, 2008; Nardi et al., 2004; Trammell, 2006). Lenhart and Fox (2006) found that three out of four North American bloggers blog to express themselves creatively. Furthermore, Recuero (2008) stated that Brazilian bloggers felt they were creating their own personal space in the Internet when blogging. For Miller and Shepherd (2004) the self-expression inherent in blogging provides "the same opportunity that television talk shows afford their participants: the opportunity to tell stories in a mediated forum to a potentiality large, though distant and invisible audience" (p.10). Thus, by expressing their innermost thoughts to an invisible audience, bloggers become their own private audience and blogging becomes private writing. They called this type of writing "private writing": that is, writing that allows the writer to write freely and value his or her writing without having to worry about the reactions of others.

Blogging as a means to improve the blogger's writing ability also was revealed as a significant motivation for blogging in this study. It is clear from both the quantitative and the qualitative findings that Latin American bloggers enjoyed writing their blogs and found blogging to be an easy way to practice and improve their writing skills. This conclusion confirms Nardi et al.'s (2004) study that described the need to write as "thinking by writing" (p. 227), and claimed that people worked through their writing process by blogging and found out whether they had something interesting to say. Furthermore, Mortensen, and Walker (2002) stated that the "instant publication encourages spontaneous writing rather than carefully thought out arguments" (p. 266). The attractiveness of practicing one's writing skills by blogging is directly related to the medium appeal: that is, to the facility for creating new content and sharing it with others to read and react to it (Li, 2005). Like other social technologies, blogs can be created and updated by anyone with basic information, computer skills, and Internet access, allowing the content published to reach a vast audience.

The motivation to document one's life, to preserve ideas, experiences and thoughts was shown to be significant for Latin American bloggers in this study. Their statements show that they perceived blogging as a way of documenting and safeguarding different aspects of their personal life, a knowledge management tool that allows them to keep a record of their lives. Such finding echoes results from other studies. Lenhart and Fox (2006) found that North American bloggers used their blogs as storage sites or memory devices. Li (2005) noted that "blogs function as a notebook, a

tape recorder and a bookmark collection" (p. 130). He compared bloggers to diarists who write down and reflect on events in their daily lives. Mosel (2005) described blogs as tools that can document the blogger's subjective view of the world by chronologically archiving the personal knowledge appearing in the posts. Nardi et al. (2004) found that by documenting their lives on their blogs, bloggers look to reaffirm their existence.

Writing a blog can be triggered by an intrinsic need for self-expression reflected in what has been called "private writing" and by an extrinsic need to share information with others as a channel of communication and socialization (Walker, 2000). That is why one of the first functions of blogs was to serve as filters of large quantities of information for the readers. Bloggers provide their personal point of view by choosing the items relevant to the topic they wanted to discuss, commenting upon them and analyzing the information (Mortensen & Walker, 2002). In the present study, the Latin American bloggers' desire to share and publish their knowledge for the benefit of others was revealed as one of the most significant motivations for blogging. Hsu and Lin (2008) similarly agreed that bloggers were motivated to blog because they believed that sharing information might enhance their online reputation. They stated that people gained confidence and improved their self-efficacy when sharing useful information with others.

For some bloggers, the need to influence others was the driving force behind the motivation to share information. When asked to describe in their own words the reasons for blogging, they talked about their desire to have an impact on their readers, to educate them on different subjects. This result falls in line with other studies dealing with North American (Lenhart & Fox, 2006), Polish (Tremmell et al., 2006), Japanese (Miura & Yamashita, 2007) and Brazilian (Recuero, 2008) bloggers who were eager to share practical knowledge or skills with their readers. Miura and Yamashita's (2007) study developed this concept by assigning a communication function to blogs. Thus, by sharing information on their blog, bloggers create an opportunity for readers to participate in their behavior and consequently create a relationship with them.

Socialization as a motivation for blogging was not a highly significant motivation for Latin American bloggers in the sample. This contradicts several other studies in which blogs were described as socialization tools through which bloggers maintain existing personal relationships and develop new ones. Part of this socialization occurs when readers comment or provide feedback to the blogger's posts (Li, 2005; McKenzie, 2008; Nardi et al, 2004). Although socialization was not rated high in the quantitative phase of the study, when describing in their own words why they blog, Latin American bloggers stated that they were motivated to blog to keep in touch with family and friends, to meet people who share their interests and to be a part of a community. Likewise, Yu (2007) found that Chinese bloggers expect to meet readers with whom they share common interests or exchange opinions towards certain issues. Li (2005) suggested that the motivation to blog to keep family and friends updated is related to a need to document the blogger's life experiences.

The need to share information and to create online relationships were two motivations for blogging that, according to Brady (2006), have a basis in Maslow's hierarchy. Brady classified these two motivations as third and fourth-level needs that focus on relationships with others. On Maslow's pyramid, social needs are the third level, and these needs are consistent with the need to maintain emotional relationships with others, which the participants listed as a motivation for blogging. Sharing information fulfills the fourth-level need of gaining recognition from others in an effort to promote one's self-value.

Blogging as a way of passing time was not found to be a primary motivation for the majority of Latin American bloggers in this study. This could serve to explain why most participants do not update their blog very frequently. Only 11.11%

of participants reported updating their blog many times a day. While 6.66% update their blogs once a day, 24.4% reported doing it once a week and 14.14% once a month. These findings show support for two other studies (Lenhart & Fox, 2006; Li, 2005) in which passing time was not revealed as a significant motivation for blogging for North American bloggers. Few studies, for example, Trammell et al. (2006) reported entertainment as a significant motivation for Polish bloggers.

Limitations and Future Research

Because participants self-reported the data, information may be potentially biased since the survey measure was not standardized. Moreover, as is the case of online surveys, participants might have responded to the survey without sufficient forethought and therefore their answers might not fully represent their motivations and feelings about blogging. It should also be noted that the findings represent only those bloggers who chose to participate in the study; therefore, the sample might not adequately represent the overall population of bloggers who write personal blogs in Latin America. Finally, participants were bloggers living in Latin America, therefore culture and lifestyle differences may not represent bloggers form other regions of the world. Further research is needed to understand the blogging motivation in different parts of the world. Future studies of blogging motivation should employ a combination of qualitative and quantitative research methods to achieve a clearer picture of the subject. An increased sample size may generate more generalizable data for the blogger population. Moreover, because motivations for media use can be influenced by a series of external and internal factors, those forces should be sorted and examined to offer better predictions for blogging behaviors. The notion of a "protected space" should be further researched in other media to gain a deeper understanding of online behaviors.

REFERENCES

Bar-Ilan, J. (2005). Information hub blogs. *Journal of Information Science, 31*(4), 297–307. doi:10.1177/0165551505054175

Baron, J., & Siepmann, M. (2000). Techniques for creating and using online questionnaires in research and testing. In Birnbaum, M. H. (Ed.), *Psychological experiments on the Internet* (pp. 235–265). San Diego, CA: Academic Press. doi:10.1016/B978-012099980-4/50011-3

Bitacoras.com. (2009). *State of the Hispanic blogosphere.* Retrieved September 11, 2010, from http://bitacoras.com/ informe/09/en

Blood, R. (2002). *The weblog handbook: Practical advice on creating and maintaining your blog.* Cambridge, MA: Perseus Publishing.

Brady, M. (2006, September). *Blogs: Motivations behind the phenomenon.* Paper presented at the Information Communication and Society Conference, University of York, York, UK. Retrieved April 9, 2006, from http://www.essex.ac.uk

Dearstyne, B. W. (2005). Blogs: The new information revolution? *The Information Management Journal, 39*(5), 38–44.

Eighmey, J., & McCoed, L. (1998). Adding value in the information age: Uses and gratifications of sites on the World Wide Web. *Journal of Business Research, 41*, 187–194. doi:10.1016/S0148-2963(97)00061-1

Flynn, S. I. (2003). *Scribe tribes and shape shifters: An ethnographic study of online journal communities.* Unpublished doctoral dissertation, Yale University Department of Anthropology.

Funk, J. B., & Buchman, D. D. (1996). Playing violent video and computer games and adolescent self-concept. *The Journal of Communication, 46*(2), 19–32. doi:10.1111/j.1460-2466.1996.tb01472.x

Guadano, R. E., Okdie, B. M., & Eno, C. A. (2007). Who blogs? Personality predictors of blogging. *Computers in Human Behavior, 24*(5), 1993–2004. doi:10.1016/j.chb.2007.09.001

Gumbrecht, M. (2004, May). *Blogs as protected space.* Presented at the Workshop on the Weblogging Ecosystem: Aggregation, Analysis and Dynamics, New York. Retrieved April 3, 2006, from http://www.blogpulse.com/ papers/www-2004gumbrecht.pdf

Gunn, H. (2002). Web-based surveys: Changing the survey process. *First Monday, 7*(12). Retrieved March 31, 2010, from http://firstmonday.org/htbin/ cgiwrap/bin/ojs/index.php/ fm/article/view/1014/935

Herring, S. C., Scheidt, L. A., Bonus, S., & Wright, E. (2004). Bridging the gap: A genre analysis of weblogs. *Proceedings of the 37th Annual Hawaii International Conference on System Sciences (HICSS'04).* Retrieved April 3, 2006, from http://doi.ieeecomputersociety.org/ 10.1109/HICSS.2004.1265271

Herring, S. C., Scheidt, L. A., Bonus, S., & Wright, E. (2005). Weblogs as a bridging genre. *Information Technology & People, 18*(2), 142–171. doi:10.1108/09593840510601513

Hsu, C., & Lin, J. C. (2008). Acceptance of blog usage: The roles of technology acceptance, social influence and knowledge sharing motivation. *Information & Management, 45*(1), 65–74. doi:10.1016/j.im.2007.11.001

Huang, C., Shen, Y., Lin, H., & Chang, S. (2007). Bloggers' motivations and behaviors: A model. *Journal of Advertising Research, 47*(4), 472–482. doi:10.2501/S0021849907070493

Internet World Statistics. (n.d.). *Website.* Retrieved from http://www.internetworldstats.com

Jeffrey Group. (2008). *The blogosphere in Latin America: An analysis of region's webfluentials.* Retrieved June 17, 2011, from http://www.jeffreygroup.com/ news/blog-1112-eng.pdf

Jones, M., & Alony, I. (2008). Blogs – The new source of data analysis. *Issues in Informing Science and Information Technology, 5,* 433–446.

Katz, E., Blumler, J. G., & Gurevitch, M. (1974). Utilizations of mass communication by the individuals. In Blumber, J. G., & Katz, E. (Eds.), *The uses of mass communication: Current perspectives on gratifications research* (pp. 19–32). Beverly Hills, CA: Sage.

Lenhart, A., & Fox, S. (2006). *Bloggers: A portrait of the Internet's new storytellers* (Pew Internet & American Life Project report). Retrieved April 24, 2010, from http://www.pewinternet.org/ Reports/2006/Bloggers.aspx

Li, D. (2007). *Why do you blog: A uses-and-gratifications inquiry into bloggers' motivations.* Paper presented at the Annual Meeting of the International Communication Association, San Francisco, CA. Retrieved January 15, 2010, from http://www.allacademic.com/meta/p171490_index.html

Lin, C. A. (1996). Looking back: The contribution of Blumler and Katz's uses and mass communication to communication research. *Journal of Broadcasting & Electronic Media, 40,* 574–581.

Lu, H., & Hsiao, K. (2007). Understanding intention to continuously share information on weblogs. *Internet Research, 17*(4), 345–361. doi:10.1108/10662240710828030

McKenzie, H. M. (2008). *Why bother blogging? Motivations for adults in the United States to maintain a personal journal blog.* Unpublished master's thesis, Raleigh, NC: North Carolina State University.

Mendelsohn, H. (1964). Listening to the radio. In Dexter, L. A., & White, D. M. (Eds.), *People, society and mass communication* (pp. 239–248). New York, NY: Free Press.

Mernit, S. (2003). *Blogger classifications: Some thoughts.* Retrieved April 13, 2006, from http://susanmernit.blogspot.com/ archives/2003_10_05_susanmernit_ archive.html#106554742635066352

Miller, C. R., & Shepherd, D. (2004). Blogging as social action: A genre analysis of the weblog. In L. Gurak, S. Antonijevic, L. Johnson, C. Ratliff, & J. Reyman (Eds.), *Into the blogosphere: Rhetoric, community, and culture of weblogs.* Retrieved April 25, 2010, from http://blog.lib.umn.edu/ blogosphere/blogging_as_social_action_a_genre _analysis_of_the_weblog.html

Miura, A., & Yamashita, K. (2007). Psychological and social influences on blog writing: An online survey of blog authors in Japan. *Journal of Computer-Mediated Communication, 12*(4), article 15. Retrieved April 26, 2010, from http://jcmc.indiana.edu/vol12/ issue4/miura.html

Mortensen, T., & Walker, J. (2002). Blogging thoughts: Personal publication as an online research tool. In A. Morrison (Ed.) *Researching ICTs in context.* April, 26, 2010 from http://www.intermedia.uio.no/ konferanser/skikt-02/docs/ Researching_ICTs_in_context-Ch11-Mortensen-Walker.pdf

Mosel, S. (2005). *Self directed learning with personal publishing and microcontent.* Microcontent Conference, Innsbruck, Austria. Retrieved April 24, 2010, from www.microlearning.org/ micropapers/ MLproc_2005_mosel.pdf

Nardi, B. A., Schiano, D. J., Gumbrecht, M., & Swartz, L. (2004). Why we blog. *Communications of the ACM, 47*(12), 41–46. doi:10.1145/1035134.1035163

Newhagen, E. J., & Rafaeli, S. (1996). Why communication researchers should study the Internet: A dialogue. *The Journal of Communication, 46*(1), 4–13. doi:10.1111/j.1460-2466.1996.tb01458.x

Papchirissi, Z., & Rubin, A. M. (2000). Predictors of Internet use. *Journal of Broadcasting & Electronic Media, 44*(2), 175–196. doi:10.1207/s15506878jobem4402_2

Pedersen, S., & Macafee, C. (2007). Gender differences in British blogging. *Journal of Computer-Mediated Communication, 12*(4), article 16. Retrieved August 25, 2010, from http://jcmc.indiana.edu/vol12 /issue4/pedersen.html

Peng, H., & Hsiao, K. (2007). Understanding intention to continuously share information on weblogs. *Internet Research, 17*(4), 345–361. doi:10.1108/10662240710828030

Pennebaker, B. A., & Beall, S. K. (1986). Confronting a traumatic event: Towards an understanding of inhibition and disease. *Journal of Abnormal Psychology, 95*(3), 274–281. doi:10.1037/0021-843X.95.3.274

Recuero, R. (2008). Information flows and social capital in weblogs: A case study in the Brazilian blogosphere. *Proceedings of the 19th ACM Conference on Hypertext and Hypermedia,* Pittsburgh, PA, (pp. 97-107).

Rubin, A. M. (1981). An examination of television viewing motivations. *Communication Research, 8,* 141–165.

Rubin, A. M. (2002). The uses-and-gratifications perspective of media effects. In Bryant, J., & Zillmann, D. (Eds.), *Media effects: Advances in theory and research* (pp. 525–548). Mahwah, NJ: Lawrence Erlbaum Associates.

Rubin, A. M., & Bantz, C. R. (1989). Uses and gratifications of videocassette recorders. In Salvaggio, J., & Bryant, J. (Eds.), *Media use in the information age: Emerging patterns of adoption and consumer use* (pp. 181–195). Hillsdale, NJ: Lawrence Erlbaum Associates.

Sun, T., Zhong, B., & Zhang, J. (2006). Uses and gratifications of Chinese online gamers. *China Media Research, 2*(2), 58–63.

Thelwall, M. (2006). *Bloggers during the London attacks: Top information sources and topics.* WWW 2006 Blog Workshop. Retrieved April 3, 2006, from http://www.blogpulse.com/www2006-workshop/papers/ blogs-during-london-attacks.pdf

Trammell, K., Tarkowski, A., Hofmokl, J., & Sapp, A. (2006). Rzeczpospolita blogów [Republic of Blog]: Examining Polish bloggers through content analysis. *Journal of Computer-Mediated Communication, 11*(3), 702–722. doi:10.1111/j.1083-6101.2006.00032.x

Viégas, F. B. (2005). Bloggers' expectations of privacy and accountability: An initial survey. *Journal of Computer-Mediated Communication, 10*(3), article 12. Retrieved April 8, 2010, from http://jcmc.indiana.edu/vol10 /issue3/viegas.html

Walker, K. (2000). It's difficult to hide it: The presentation of self on Internet home pages. *Qualitative Sociology, 23*(1), 99–120. doi:10.1023/A:1005407717409

Yu, H. (2007). *Exploring the Chinese blogosphere: The motivations of blog authors and readers.* Unpublished Master's Thesis, National University of Singapore.

KEY TERMS AND DEFINITIONS

Blogger: A person who creates, writes and maintains a blog.

Blogging: The act of publishing information on blogs.

Blogosphere: The Internet blogging community.

Journal Blog: The most common form of blog, usually taking the form of a personal diary or journal.

Link: Using hypertext, a link is a selectable connection from one word, picture, or information object to another.

Post: A single unit of content on a blog, usually consisting of at least a title and text; a blog is made up of a collection of posts.

Tags: Labeling or attaching natural language keywords to describe pieces of information such as movies, posts, pictures or links.

Chapter 13
The First Amendment's Impact on Bloggers:
A Legal Perspective

Joshua Azriel
Kennesaw State University, USA

ABSTRACT

This chapter examines the First Amendment's challenges to bloggers in the United States and highlights the potential legal consequences for victimizing someone online. While the First Amendment protects an overall right to free speech, there are certain boundaries to this right. Federal Internet-related speech laws, libel, invasion of privacy, copyright, trademark, and others are analyzed within the context of blogging. The author discusses the potential legal consequences to blogging at work or after hours and how personal blogs can negatively impact the work environment. Several Supreme Court cases are discussed to assist bloggers in understanding the scope of contemporary Internet free speech laws. An analysis of U.S. federal laws restricting online speech and an overview of the following areas of speech law are provided: libel, invasion of privacy, protection for confidential sources, copyright, trademark, true threats, and obscenity.

INTRODUCTION

In the United States bloggers enjoy the same freedom of speech rights as print-based reporters and publishers. In a 1997 pivotal decision examining the constitutionality of a federal law designed to protect minors from online indecency, the Supreme

Court remarked in *Reno v. American Civil Liberties Union* that the Internet is a "unique and wholly new medium of worldwide human communication" (J.S. App., 46a, 81) and that "the content on the Internet is as diverse as human thought" (J.S. App., 43a, 74). The Supreme Court distinguished "Internet communications and communications received by radio or television" (J.S. App. 49a,

DOI: 10.4018/978-1-60960-744-9.ch013

89) due to the ubiquitous and interactive nature of the former. The Supreme Court emphasized the democratic nature of the Internet and considered it as a publishing venue for millions of individuals, not merely as a publishing tool for organizations. In 1997 the Supreme Court made a landmark decision by ruling that Internet communication should enjoy maximum protection under the First Amendment. This decision placed online communication on the same legal foundation as print media: books, magazines and newspapers. In this milestone ruling, the Supreme Court acknowledged that the Internet could be used for a multitude of communication-oriented purposes.

This democratic perspective can be applied to the practice of blogging as one of the Internet-based interactive communication platforms. Bloggers have few First Amendment restrictions, and they are beholden to the same legal restrictions as their print counterparts. For the fast growing number of bloggers, it is important to realize the full scope of the First Amendment related rights and responsibilities that exist in cyberspace.

While the First Amendment to the U.S. Constitution states, "Congress shall make no law abridging the freedom of speech, or of the press," Congress has passed statutes prohibiting certain categories of online speech. These apply to the world of blogging. However, to preserve the freedom of expression on the Internet, bloggers need to understand not only their rights but also their responsibilities. This chapter provides an analysis of U.S. federal laws restricting online speech and an overview of the following areas of speech law: libel, invasion of privacy, protection for confidential sources, copyright, trademark, true threats, and obscenity. Each area of law is discussed in relation to how it applies to blogging.

BACKGROUND

While blogging is a relatively new phenomenon, the concept of it could be dated to the early years of the U.S. when Benjamin Franklin published the *Pennsylvania Gazette* using a lead type printing press. The notion and practice of publishing one's own thoughts without government approval is closely related to blogging. Gillmor (2006) noted that the founders of the early American Republic, such as Thomas Paine and James Madison, published their opinions about the political and social issues of their time and often under an assumed name. According to Gillmor, blogging is fundamentally the same idea. Anyone with a computer and Internet access can start a blog. Bloggers can reveal their identity or use a pseudonym in a similar manner to how James Madison, Alexander Hamilton, and John Jay published the Federalist Papers under the name "Publius."

As with the traditional print media, bloggers do not have an unrestricted right to publish any content they want. There are potential legal consequences to cyberbullying, libeling, invading one's privacy, or posting obscenity. While the First Amendment guarantees a right to freedom of speech and the press, it is not a legal right to harm someone. The laws are not meant to restrict content ideas, but they serve as a means to protect people from harm. Libel, privacy, copyright infringement, trademark, threats, and obscenity are areas of speech law that bloggers commonly and unknowingly violate. They cross a legal line when what they publish impacts a victim's privacy, reputation, or creative works. Whether it is a blog read by just a few people or one that is viewed by thousands or millions, a blogger is just as legally culpable as any mainstream media organization.

Bloggers often work for news organizations or are independent seekers and distributors of information. How First Amendment jurisprudence applies to bloggers can depend on their professional status when it comes to issues related to confidential sources, copyright, and trademark. Yet, in other legal areas (such as libel, invasion of privacy, or obscenity), regardless of a blogger's professional status the laws are applied in the same manner. If a blogger libels a victim and harms his or her reputation, the courts will treat that blogger in the same manner regardless of his or her professional status. As will be discussed in this chapter, there is no one generic, "one size fits all" formula for how the First Amendment applies to blogging. It often depends on the specific set of legal facts in a dispute.

FREE SPEECH LIMITATIONS ON BLOGGING

Federal Laws on Internet Speech

While the Supreme Court has provided legal latitude for online speech compared to what is allowed for books, newspapers and magazines, there are two federal laws that limit an individual's free speech rights in certain circumstances. The first law applies specifically to online communication including blogs. In 1996 Congress passed into law Section 230 of the Communications Decency Act (CDA) as part of the Telecommunications Act. Prior to 1996, there were no federal statutes that criminalized online threats, stalking, and harassment. Instead, prosecutors used existing laws that pertained to telephone and U.S. Postal Mail communication and applied them to Internet communications. Section 230 of the CDA criminalizes threatening, harassing, lewd and other "offensive information" on the Internet. It prohibits online speech that may be "obscene, lewd, lascivious, filthy, excessively violent, harassing, or otherwise objectionable."

An important component of Section 230 is that it legally exempts Internet Service Providers (ISPs) and other "users" for any offensive speech posted on their servers. Many bloggers use ISPs as the host for their sites. Essentially, ISPs and other "users" who offer the server space for others to publish a blog are not responsible for any offensive postings as long as they make a good faith effort to censor these offensive materials (Gillmor, 2006, 195).

Several state and federal courts have enforced this law and exempted ISPs from any legal responsibility for allegations of defamation and invasion of privacy.[1] Section 230's ban on categories of online speech and the exemption for ISPs applies to bloggers if they cross several free speech lines including libel, invasion of privacy, or copyright violations.

In addition to the CDA, the federal law on extortion and threats (18 USCS §875 2010) criminalizes communication in "interstate commerce" related to blackmail, threats of bodily injury, or harming a victim's reputation. The law on extortion and threats applies to online communication including blogging. Federal appellate courts have applied this law for threats made through email communications.[2]

There is little public debate about whether stalking, harassment, obscenity, and extortion should be protected speech. The courts are nearly unanimous in placing these categories of speech beyond any First Amendment protection. While the vast majority of bloggers do not engage in these types of communication, they should know that any attempt to single out an individual for harassment could be grounds for a federal lawsuit. The legal precedent is strong and electronic "paper" trails and Internet protocol (IP) addresses make it possible to find the purveyor of such threats. Simply having an onscreen pseudonym will not disguise anyone who threatens a victim online.

COMMON BLOGGER SPEECH DANGERS

Libel

The U.S. legal approach to libel derives from common law decisions through the court system. At its core libel law is centered on damage to one's reputation and the victim's ability to restore it. In 1964 in the *NY Times v. Sullivan* decision, the Supreme Court outlined the actual malice standard for public officials. *Actual malice* refers to the intentional disregard for the truth, essentially publishing information which is false or intentionally damaging to someone's reputation. In the blogosphere there are many writers who comment on the lives and professional works of public personas. If a public personality believes he or she has been libeled, that person must prove the actual malice standard. The difficulty here is that even a private individual who has been victimized by libel could become a temporary public individual simply by having her or his name known through a blog, which might be viewed by thousands of readers. Depending on a state's specific libel law, that "public" individual might have to prove actual malice or negligence, the lower standard of proof that reflects accidental damage to reputation.

In 1974 in *Gertz v. Welch*, the Supreme Court identified three categories of public figures: all purpose, limited purpose, and involuntary. An "all-purpose" public figure is someone a court stated "occupies positions of such persuasive power and influence that they are deemed public figures for all purposes" (p. 351). The president, a governor, or renowned celebrities are all purpose public figures. No matter what the controversy in question is, the individual claiming to be a victim of libel is well known and may have to prove the actual malice standard.

"Limited purpose" public figures are people who may invite attention to themselves, previously not being in the public eye. For example an unknown individual could run for an elected office. These persons place themselves before the public scrutiny and invite criticism. Other examples of limited purpose public figures are those individuals who appear on reality television programs. They were unknown before the program and after the program may again be out of the public eye. The third category, "involuntary" public figures, encompasses individuals who are drawn into a public controversy through no fault of their own.

These individuals do not seek public notoriety but are often drawn into the spotlight by chance.

Regardless of the public figure category, in any libel incident these individuals often have to prove the actual malice standard. Blogs are fertile ground for creating limited or involuntary public figures. Since a blog could be read by thousands of viewers, previously unknown people could find themselves the victim of a libelous online rant. Bloggers need to understand their responsibilities and the potential consequences for posting potentially libelous comments about individuals in their online forums. Bloggers who believe that hiding their true identity will protect them from libelous charges are mistaken. ISPs can use IP addresses to trace where a blog originates. Even if the blogger's identity is not found, chances are that the computer in question may lead to revealing the individual's true identity.

In a libel lawsuit, the plaintiff, or victim, must prove seven elements to win a legal case: statement of fact, publication, identification, defamation, falsity, fault, and harm (Trager, Russomanno, & Ross, 2010). The statement of fact is the libelous assertion itself. Publication is proof that the libelous statement was made public on a blog. An ISP could be held responsible if it is directly involved in the blog's publication. In most cases, the ISP is simply the conduit for publication and under the CDA law is not responsible for publication.

Identification means that the victim was specifically referred to by name, title, or even from photo or video images. If the third party audience can confirm identification, then it is considered official recognition. Groups of individuals can be libeled but the smaller the group size the more likely a successful identification.

Defamation, the fourth element, is the libelous content. This is an examination of the use of words and the meaning they convey. Typically, the defamatory content would be false, injurious, and possibly expose the victim to hatred or contempt by others. Taken as a whole, the defamatory statement(s) would harm the victim's reputation. The next element, *falsity*, is that the libelous comment(s) in question is not true. With evidence, the victim can prove that the statement(s) are not true.

Fault is the next element in the plaintiff's case. The alleged victim must show that the defendant was at fault, the person responsible for the libelous statement(s). Finally, the victim must prove *harm*. The victim must show in some concrete way that their reputation is tarnished with consequences. Their career may have been negatively impacted, personally become a social pariah, or suffered in some other way.

A blogger who is sued for libel does have a few defense strategies. The first is called *fair report privilege*. Information quoted from official sources, such as government documents, can often shield the blogger from any libel allegations. The blogger must fairly and accurately quote from the record they have obtained and the source be clearly identified.

A second defense strategy for a blogger is *fair comment and criticism*. Bloggers are often critics who comment on the professional works of others. Often, the person critiqued is someone in the public eye: a politician, musician, artist, public advocate, etc. By having their professional works displayed before the public, these individuals open themselves up for criticism about their professional lives.

Good old-fashioned *opinion* is a libel defense. Bloggers, like all other citizens, are entitled to their opinions about an issue. Trager et al. (2010) point out a four-part test to determine if an opinion is libelous based on the 1984 *Ollman vs. Evans* Supreme Court decision. First, is the statement in question verifiable? In fact, opinions are often not verifiable. Secondly, what is the common usage of the word(s) in question? Does society consider these words slanderous in some way? Next, what is the "journalistic context" for the statement(s) in question? The entire blog entry needs to be evaluated to see if it is opinion and not just the specific libelous sentence(s) in question. Finally, what

is the broader social context of the statement(s) in question? Was it made within a blog where opinions often appear or does the blog rely on facts instead of opinion? The answers will help a court decide if the comment(s) in questions are libel or opinion.

Finally, other defenses include the *neutral reportage rule*, *wires service doctrine*, and the *libel proof plaintiff*. *Neutral reportage rule* means two or more individuals or groups are engaged in a controversy where one party libels the other. The media, including bloggers, simply reports a controversy as a neutral, third party. The *wire services doctrine* is when a media organization subscribes to a news organization's wire service, such as the Associated Press (AP). The AP story is posted in its entirety and is unchanged by the blogger. The wire service could be held directly responsible for the libelous posting, not the blogger. A *libel proof plaintiff* is someone whose reputation is already damaged and it could not be hurt further with a libelous claim. These individuals are often already convicted in a court of law for a crime, and therefore, their reputation cannot be further harmed.

Another element related to libelous blog postings are those from third parties who post damaging statements on someone else's blog. Is the operator of the blog responsible for those postings? Although there is no clear cut answer, so far the courts would indicate that the blog operator is not responsible. Section 230 of the CDA could mean that blog operator is classified as an ISP or "user" and, therefore, immune from prosecution.[3]

Privacy

The common law of protecting an individual's privacy has four *torts* or areas of injury: *False Light, Intrusion*, and *Private Facts*, and *Appropriation*. *False light*, as the name implies, means portraying a victim in a false manner. It is similar to libel except that in the eyes of some state courts, a lie may not amount to libel. Libel ruins an individual's reputation, but false light may not technically harm someone's reputation. Instead, it casts someone in a false manner but does not harm their reputation. Despite this subtle difference, 13 state courts reject false light as a privacy tort. Some state courts will allow a victim to sue for both defamation and false light based on the same harm (Trager et al., 2010, p. 218).

Only individuals can sue for false light. Companies and non-profit entities cannot sue. Bloggers need to be careful not to cast anyone they write about in false light. False statements could be both potentially libelous and invade one's privacy. It is important for bloggers to know the laws of the state where they live. Generally, similar to libel law, most states require the plaintiff to prove the falsity of the published material in question that identified the plaintiff with the defendant knowing or suspecting the material was false (Trager et al., p. 219). Some states require the *actual malice* standard set by the Supreme Court in libel issues. In 1967 the Court ruled in *Time vs. Hill* that actual malice can be the standard of proof needed by private individuals to prove a false light case. Eleven states have followed the Court's guideline (p. 224). Most other states require the negligence standard of proof.

Intrusion is a second area of privacy law. This is violated when the media may use untraditional newsgathering tools to violate someone's personal space or seclusion. This may be in the form of undercover reporting. The intrusion can be physical in nature, such as planting a microphone on an unsuspecting individual. New York and Virginia are the only states that do *not* recognize some form of intrusion law (Trager et al., 2010, p. 241).

As a communication tool, the Internet can be used to intrude on a victim's solitude. A blogger could use the Internet to disclose an individual's social security number, bank records, or any other confidential information. Uncovering personal information from an unsuspecting individual could endanger a blogger to an intrusion lawsuit. The technology exists where a blogger could stream live video or audio from an unsuspecting victim. Courts often use what is called the *reasonable person* standard to determine if intrusion has occurred. This standard reflects whether an average person would be offended by the intrusion method in question.

The tort of *private facts* is when the media publishes truthful but private information that courts may not believe is of legitimate public concern. These private facts would be offensive to a *reasonable person*. The private facts in question are usually intimate details about a person's life. Forty-one states and D.C. recognize private facts lawsuits (Trager et al., 2010, p. 248).

While bloggers might claim that private facts are fair game if they are easily obtained online, that does not mitigate the issue of whether they are of legitimate public concern. Intimate facts about celebrities are often placed before the public eye and lawsuits do not result. That does not mean that privacy law does not allow a lawsuit to go forward. Private facts are those areas of an individual's life that should not be made public, such as health, finances, or the intimate details of one's home life.

The *appropriation* tort applies to any blogger who uses a person's name, picture, or overall identity without permission for commercial, specifically profit-making purposes. The appropriation tort has two smaller torts associated with it: commercialization and right of publicity. Commercialization prevents a corporate or business entity from using another's likeness for advertising purposes. The right of publicity protects the monetary value of someone's name and picture. Nearly all appropriation controversies center on a famous individual who did not allow their identity to be used commercially. As the U.S. Supreme Court explained in 1977 in *Zacchini vs. Scripps Howard*, essentially appropriation centers on the rights of performers to protect their income source. Every state court has followed the lead by the Supreme Court in recognizing appropriation as a tort.

Appropriation may apply to any blogger who uses an identity that is identical or nearly identical to a well-known individual. Attempting to capitalize on another's likeness, even indirectly, could be construed as appropriation. Any blogger who may try to use someone's image, video, or audio as a marketing tool to "endorse" his or her blog runs into potential legal trouble within the appropriation area of privacy law.

Protecting Confidential Sources

Whether bloggers work for a media company or are independent information seekers and publishers, they may come across information from confidential sources. These individuals often have access to "inside information" related to a controversy but do not want their identities revealed. If a federal grand jury seeks the identity of an informant, the federal courts have consistently ruled that the First Amendment does not give a reporter the right to withhold the information. This refusal by the federal courts dates back to 1972 in the Supreme Court's *Branzburg v. Hayes* landmark decision. Therefore, if a blogger is subpoenaed to testify and asked to reveal the identity of a confidential source, the First Amendment does not protect him or her under federal law.

In *Branzburg* the Court in a 5-4 vote ruled that there is no First Amendment right for reporters to withhold confidential sources related to a federal criminal matter. The Court did say that states and Congress have the right to pass their own shield laws protecting reporters. To date, Congress has not passed a federal-based shield law though one is pending before the U.S. Senate and another law has passed the House of Representatives. In the U.S., 37 states have enacted laws granting reporters some protection for their confidential sources related to state-based grand juries who seek the identities of informants. These laws vary from absolute confidentiality rights to varying degrees of legal protection. Additionally, state-based appellate courts in the 13 states without shield laws

recognize varying degrees of reporters' right to protect confidential sources.

It is important that bloggers understand that they can be required to reveal the identity of any anonymous poster on their sites. State and federal courts have required ISPs to reveal the identities of anonymous bloggers in defamation and privacy lawsuits. Two legal tests have emerged for when websites are required to reveal their anonymous bloggers or posters: the *Dendrite* and *Cahill* tests. Both require that for a subpoena to be issued that reveals the identity of an anonymous online poster in a libel case, the plaintiff must have unsuccessfully made a good faith effort to contact the defendant and tell the defendant that he or she is the subject of a legal action and to confront that individual with the offensive online comments. So far, courts that have heard cases related to revealing the identity of anonymous bloggers are adopting or modifying the *Dendrite* and *Cahill* tests.

Copyright

While the appropriation area of privacy law focuses on an individual's right to control the profitability of their personal commercialization, copyright law focuses on the individual's actual creative works. Copyright law emanates directly from the Constitution. Article One Section 8 states that Congress has exclusive control over copyright law. State governments cannot create their own copyright provisions. The goal of securing copyright is to encourage Americans to be innovative and secure the rights to their creative works. Creative works include art, music, literature, videos, novels, and plays. These types of works can be uploaded to the Internet. Any blogger who wants to display a creative work must seek permission from the copyright holder unless the work is in the public domain. The *public domain* contains creative works that are no longer copyrighted and are available for use by anyone.

It is up to bloggers to find out what person or company controls the copyright to an item they want to post. In the music industry, ASCAP, BMI, and SESAC are the three main companies that handle copyright permission on behalf of musicians. For a flat rate, bloggers can legally access millions of songs. Use of videos, literature, and other creative works need the direct permission from the individual or company who controls the copyright.

In 1998 Congress passed the Digital Millennium Copyright Act (DMCA) to bring the Internet within the legal boundaries of copyright law. The DMCA includes a provision for ISPs. Similar to provisions in the Communications Decency Act, the DMCA shields ISPs from copyright infringement lawsuits if they make an effort to remove copyrighted materials from their websites. There is no legal protection if the ISP knowingly allows user(s) to violate a copyright owner's materials. If a blogger uses copyrighted materials without permission, he or she cannot sue an ISP that removes these protected materials from the blog.

While bloggers must obtain copyright permission to use photos, videos, and music, as creators of content they have the right to copyright any of their own original works. While facts such as scores, measurements, and dates cannot be copyrighted, *how* they are presented can be. The easiest way to obtain a copyright is for any blogger to post a notice, such as © with the year and name: for example, "© 2011 John Doe." More formally, a blogger can register a copyright online or electronically with the U.S. Copyright Office.[4] The registration price begins at $35 depending on the specific material being copyrighted. Having the creative works officially registered gives any blogger legal protection in any alleged infringements and would have a stronger case in court. Copyright becomes effective the date the U.S. Copyright Office receives the application.

Since blogging is an electronic based activity, the blogger controls the rights to that creative content for life *plus* an additional 70 years after death. If a blog is jointly operated by two or more individuals, then the additional 70 years of copyright ownership starts after the "last surviving author's death."[5] For works made under a contract between a blogger and a company where the blogger retains copyright, then the duration of copyright is 95 years from publication or 120 years from creation whichever comes first. This includes creative works by bloggers who use a pseudonym. This corresponds with the same policy for traditional print works for hire.[6]

Copyright is a personal right, but bloggers can transfer ownership of their copyrighted materials. This is accomplished through a written contract between the two parties. An attorney should review any transfer of copyright ownership. Copyright can also be passed along through a person's will upon death of the original creator. Bloggers should consult an attorney since this ownership right comes under any state's property laws. The U.S. Copyright Office does not directly handle copyright transfers but will store any signed copyright transfer agreements.[7]

Since blogging is an international phenomenon and U.S. based bloggers are read around the world, they receive international copyright protection in any country that is a signed party to the Berne Convention for the Protection of Literary and Artistic Works and/or the Universal Copyright Convention (Radcliffe & Brinson, 1999).

Most countries are members of one or both of these conventions. The member countries agreed to give foreigners the same copyright protections as their own citizens. The protection works the other way too. Foreigners who copyright their creative works are protected under U.S. copyright law as long as their country is a member of either convention.

Any blogger who obtains copyright for a creative work has six exclusive rights: 1) reproducing the work; 2) making derivatives (other creative works based on the original); 3) distribution; 4) public performance; 5) public display; and, 6) digital audio transmission of a sound recording.

This last provision affects bloggers. It is aimed at requiring permission from a recording company to play music online. While bloggers would need to seek permission to incorporate music into their blog site, as copyright holders, they also control any digital retransmission of their own recorded sound creations.

Trademark

While copyright protects a blogger's legal right to her or his creative works, trademarks identify a company's specific product to show how it is different from similar items. Trager et al. (2010) point out that a trademark can be a word, name, symbol or design. Any blogger has the right to create a trademark to distinguish their blog's purpose from similar themed ones. Included in a trademark design are size, shape, color, texture and graphics. A trademark can include one to all four of these factors.

From a customer perspective, a trademark ensures that the products they purchase are original and not generic imitations. Customers are often loyal to brand names and the logos associated with particular brands reassure the customers of the quality they are seeking. Bloggers who trademark their online "product" are assuring their readers (customers) of their unique quality. Trademark holders can register through the U.S. Patent and Trademark Office in order to have statutory protection under the 1946 Lanham Act.[8] The law provides legal protection for trademark holders but also for fair use claims. As with copyright, the trademark holder can file electronically. The filing fees start at $275.

Unlike copyright, the U.S. Patent and Trademark Office does not automatically grant trademark protection. It determines if the logo or symbol in question qualifies as a trademark. It will not register a mark similar to an existing one. During the sixth year, the trademark owner must file an affidavit stating the trademark has been in use. Trademarks have a ten year term but can be renewed.

Bloggers should be aware that they can lessen a trademark's value. Trademark infringement takes place when a customer can be confused about a trademark. But bloggers can refer specifically to a trademarked name for informational purposes. Bloggers run into legal trouble if they use someone's trademark in a way that portrays that product in a negative way or diminishes its effectiveness. This is called *diluting*. According to Trager et al. (2010) dilution occurs when a product name similar to a well-known trademark makes the famous mark less distinctive.

True Threats

While libel, privacy, copyright, protecting confidential sources, and trademark infringement are five areas of speech law bloggers are often sued for, there are other illegal forms of speech that appear online, especially in blogs. *Hate speech* can be racially or ethnically motivated but generally is derogatory of another group. While the courts have time and again constitutionally protected a right to hate speech, what is not protected is speech that threatens, stalks, or harasses an individual or group of people. In 2003 in *Virginia v. Black*, the Supreme Court set out its "true threats doctrine." In a decision that centered on a Virginia law that banned all cross burnings, the Court ruled that threats, such as cross burnings, can be banned if they are directed toward individuals that causes them to fear for their physical well being.

The Court's decision on this case has solidified a true threats legal doctrine that has emerged in recent years and has consequences for the bloggers. In the 1990s the American Coalition of Life Activists (ACLA), a pro-life group, created posters and a website that contained the names, phone numbers, and addresses of doctors who provided abortion services. Several doctors were harmed including three who were murdered. ACLA placed a slash through the names of the murdered and injured doctors in its "Nuremburg Files" website. In *Planned Parenthood of the Columbia/Willamette Inc. v. ACLA* (2002), the Ninth Circuit Court of Appeals ruled en banc that the website acted as a true threat against the doctors and ordered it removed from the Internet.

This ruling, along with the Supreme Court's *Virginia v. Black* decision, has practical implications for bloggers. They can be held accountable for any threat posted on their blogs. If the intended target of the message is actually harmed by the blog's reader(s) or physically threatened by the posting of a harmful message, the victim can sue the blogger to remove the controversial threat message or even have the blog shut down. Any blog posting that incites another to a violent act could be considered outside the boundaries of free speech law.

In addition to court rulings, parallel to the true threats legal doctrine is the CDA's anti-harassment measures. As noted earlier in this chapter, Congress has criminalized online communication that is violent or harassing of a victim. This, in conjunction with the federal extortion and threats law, adds up to a strong legal foundation that threats and harassments posted by a blogger intended for a specific victim are outside the boundaries of free expression.

Obscenity

The Internet era has promulgated a number of pornographic websites. While adult pornography is legal in the United States, child pornography is not. U.S. courts have universally upheld this legal doctrine. Adult bloggers have the right to display pornography and discuss mature sexual matters that do not include victimizing minors. In 1997 in *Reno v. ACLU*, the Supreme Court explicitly stated that adults have the right to access online pornography. The Court has struck down federal laws, such as the Communications Decency Act and the Child Online Protection Act, that attempted to protect minors from accessing adult materials

if those laws also restricted adults from those same materials. The Court has embraced the use of website filters and credit card authorization as the mechanisms for protecting minors from adult sexual materials.

Sexual speech loses any First Amendment value when it crosses to obscenity. Free speech does not include obscene works. Obscenity can be written or visual. It is sexual material that appeals to the *prurient interest*, meaning it arouses unnatural lustful thoughts. Obscenity is difficult to define. Obscenity law in the U.S. is grounded on local and state laws. A work deemed obscene in Toledo, Ohio may not be considered obscene in New York City.

In 1973 the Court in *Miller v. California* provided a definition of obscenity that is still considered the legal standard today. Under the *Miller* test, a creative work is obscene if: 1) the average person, applying contemporary community standards, finds the work, as a whole, appeals to prurient interest; 2) the work depicts in a patently offensive way sexual conduct as defined by *applicable state law*; and, 3) has no literary, artistic, political, or scientific value. *All* three portions of the test *must* be satisfied for any work to be considered obscene and lose its free speech status. For a blog, its entirety must be judged and not just one or two photos, videos, or postings.

The difficulty of the *Miller* test is that it is based on local law and any controversial work must be considered in its entirety. Juries in local communities often decide whether the work in question is obscene. Since blogs are Internet-based, which state or local community's obscenity law is used? Is it where the blogger lives or where one of the blog's readers resides? The answer is both. Federal prosecutors have the right to prosecute and try an obscenity case in either location. If a blogger has sexually explicit material on a blog site, it is recommended that he or she knows the laws in his or her state. Yet, with a blog viewed by hundreds or thousands of people, it becomes nearly impossible for a blogger to know the local obscenity laws across the U.S. Consequently, federal prosecutors have the legal advantage in this area of free speech law.

Blogging on the Job

Companies are free to enforce any policy regarding using work time to blog or even check personal e-mail. With few exceptions, Americans do not have the right for private blogging at work. In many ways our First Amendment rights cease to exist at work. When they are on company time and payroll, employees should follow corporate policies. Many employees understand this and often blog after work hours from the privacy of their own home. Everyone who blogs after hours should be careful about the content they publish regarding their employer. According to Grumban (2008), the growing danger of off-hours blogging worries both small and large companies. The act of blogging after hours would seem like a casual, harmless activity; but, when posting comments about one's work environment and co-workers, there are several potential legal dangers. Many employers fear that they could be criminally liable for any illegal behavior by bloggers even outside the office. Guttman (2003) noted that employers often worry that any libelous or pornographic activity by a blogger could harm the company. Grubman (2008) added other legal dangers, such as leaking corporate trade secrets and proprietary information or releasing copyrighted materials.

The issue becomes more problematic when employees blog on the job. If bloggers use company resources for their own personal postings, then the danger of any negative exposure increases. Using company computers and Internet resources could expose the company to a lawsuit even if they are not an active resource for the blog. The solution to this growing problem is simple: Do not write a personal blog during work hours.

If bloggers publish opinions about their co-workers during personal time, they should be extremely careful. When viewed by others, these words can harm professional relationships and even create grounds for termination. While the First Amendment protects a blogger's rights for free speech, it does not automatically grant a right to libel, invade the privacy of co-workers, or leak corporate confidential information.

If blogging is part of a job, then the employer becomes culpable for any offensive information that is published in the company's name. It is important that organizations create and maintain guidelines that define acceptable blogging topics. Whether individuals post offensive content in their own name or the company's name, it does not matter according to law. The individual and/or the company could be targets of legal action.

FUTURE RESEARCH DIRECTIONS

As social media increasingly become the standard for communication among friends, family and business associates, it will be interesting to see what implications, if any, there are for blogging. Social media sites such as Facebook have an online mechanism for users to post their thoughts and observations as updates. Increasingly, lawsuits based on libel, invasion of privacy, and other controversies stem from postings on social media websites. In a similar vein to how the Internet incorporates email, blogs, and instant messaging, social media sites are offering similar communication platforms for their users. From a legal perspective, it will be interesting to see whether the laws and courts create a new legal paradigm for this form of communication or whether they will apply the traditional forms of law discussed in this chapter to social media communication uses including blogging.

CONCLUSION

As bloggers increase in number, they should realize that from a legal perspective, the danger of retribution for harmful and illegal content published on blogs is real. While libel, privacy, obscenity, and other speech laws can be applied to blogging, future court cases involving offensive, harmful blog postings will determine whether courts continue to apply traditional legal principles to online content. Courts will determine if a new set of common law principles will apply to blogs. They will also determine whether Section 230 of the CDA needs to be revised by Congress if the law is not covering the growing number and types of illegal content.

While the CDA exempts ISPs and other "users" from any offensive content posted on the Internet, Congress may have to refine the law by defining these "users." Under the current legal framework, "users" may be individuals who host a blog but do not author the content in question; in short, they simply host the online forum for third party posts. How courts and Congress approach the issue of who is responsible for illegal content will determine the future of free speech in relation to blogging.

This chapter addressed several areas of free speech law and its application to blogging from the perspective of Internet free speech. As blogging becomes more of an accepted practice both for organizations and individuals, there are several areas of free speech law they should be aware of. While the First Amendment guarantees a right to freedom of speech and the press, the courts, guided by the Supreme Court decisions, have outlined several legal categories of speech outside the boundaries of the First Amendment: libel, invasion of privacy, threats, and obscenity. In addition Congress has stepped into this legal gray area by providing guidelines for who is legally responsible for posting offensive materials on Internet-based platforms, including blogging. Section 230 of the CDA immunizes ISPs and other "users" if they make a good faith effort to restrict illegal materials from their websites.

While bloggers need to be aware of the legal consequences to what they may publish, this chapter has also provided a guide for insuring bloggers' the right to copyright and trademark their creative works. A blog is a creative endeavor and the publisher has every opportunity to secure the rights to that creative expression. At the same time, it is important for bloggers not to impede on the creative works of others but to seek permission to post music, photos, or videos on their sites.

Blogging at work has the potential for creating many problems for the employee. Beyond using employer time for personal writings, blogging about co-workers or exposing work related issues or even confidential projects could be grounds for termination and a lawsuit. The easy choice would be not to blog during work hours nor to blog about the workplace environment since that could open the door to a defamation or privacy oriented lawsuit.

Blogging is an exciting form of online communication because it empowers any user to post observations. Anyone with the means to access the Internet is capable of blogging through a variety of websites. Although this freedom of speech is unique because of its near universal access for users, this chapter has discussed several problematic categories of speech the user should be aware of pertaining to potential, constitutional restrictions on blogging.

REFERENCES

Barrett v. Rosenthal, 40 Cal. 4th 33 (2006).

Branzburg v. Hayes, 408 U.S. 665 (1972).

Communications Decency Act, 47 USCS §230(c)(2)(2010).

U.S. Const. amend. I.

Crimes and Criminal Procedure, 18 U.S.C. §875(c)(2010).

Digital Millennium Copyright Act, Pub. L. 105-304, 112 Stat. 2860 (1998).

Dimeo v. Max 433 F. Supp.2d 523 E.D. Pa. (2006).

Gertz v. Welch, 418 U.S. 323 (1974).

Gillmor, D. (2006). *We the media*. Sebastopol, CA: O'Reilly.

Grubman, S. (2008, Spring). Think twice before you type: Blogging your way to unemployment. *Georgia Law Review (Athens, Ga.)*, *42*, 615–647.

Gutman, P. (2003, Fall). Say what? Blogging and employment law in conflict. *Columbia Journal of the Law and the Arts*, *27*, 145–186.

Limitation on liability relating to material online, 17 USC §512(c) 2010.

Miller v. California, 413 U.S. 15 (1973).

Ollmans v. Evans, 47 U.S. 1127 (1985).

Planned Parenthood of the Columbia/Willamette, Inc., 290 F. 3d 1058 (9th Cir. en banc 2002).

Radcliffe, M., & Brinson, D. (1999). Ownership of copyrights. *Findlaw for Legal Professionals*. Retrieved March 23, 2010, from http://www.library.findlaw.com/ 1999/Jan/1/241478.html

Reno v. ACLU, 529 US 844 (1997).

Time v. Hill, 385 U.S. 374 (1967). New York Times v. Sullivan, 376 U.S. 254 (1964).

Trager, R., Russomanno, J., & Ross, D. S. (2010). *The law of journalism and mass communication*. Washington, DC: CQ Press.

United States Copyright Office. (2010). *Website*. Retrieved March 23, 2010, from http://www.copyright.gov

U.S. Patent and Trademark Office. (2010). *Website*. Retrieved March 25, 2010, from http://www.uspto.gov

U.S. V. Alkhabaz, 104 F.3d 1492 (1997). US v. Newell, 309 F. 3d 396 (6th Cir. 2002).

Virginia v. Black, 538 U.S. 343 (2003).

Zachinni v. Scripts Howard Broadcasting, 433 U.S. 562 (1977).

Zeran v. America Online, 129 F.3d 327 (4th Cir. 1997).

ADDITIONAL READING

Azriel, J. (2009). Social networking as a communication weapon to harm victims: Facebook, MySpace, and Twitter demonstrate a need to amend Section 230 of the Communications Decency Act. *The John Marshall Journal of Computer & Information Law*, *26*(3), 415–429.

Azriel, J. (2007). The California Supreme Court's decision in Barrett v. Rosenthal: How the court's decision could further hamper efforts to restrict defamation on the Internet. *Hastings Communications and Entertainment Law Journal, 30(1)*.

Calvert, C. (2009). Sex, cell phones, privacy, and the First Amendment: When children become child pornographers and the Lolita effect undermines the law. *CommLaw Conspectus*, *18*, 1–65.

Cioli, A. (2007). Bloggers as public figures. *The Boston University Public Interest Law Journal*, *16*, 255–283.

Citizen Media Law Project. (2010). Available at http://www.eff.org

Electronic Frontier Foundation. (2010). Available at http://www.eff.org

Frischmann, B. (2008). Law in a networked world: Speech, spillovers and the First Amendment. *The University of Chicago Legal Forum*, 301–333.

Gillmor, D. (2006). *We the media*. Sebastopol, CA: O'Reilly.

Glasser, C. (2006). *International Libel and Privacy Handbook*. New York, NY: Bloomberg Press.

Gordan, M. (2009). The best intentions: A constitutional analysis of North Carolina's new anti-cyberbullying statute. *North Carolina Journal of Law and Technology Online*, *11*, 48–71.

Grubman, S. (2008, Spring). Think twice before you type: Blogging your way to unemployment. *Georgia Law Review (Athens, Ga.)*, *42*, 617–647.

Gutman, P. (2003). Say what?: Blogging and employment law in conflict. *Columbia Journal of the Law and the Arts*, *27*, 145–186.

Hayward, A. (2008). Regulation of blog campaign advocacy on the Internet: Comparing U.S., German, and EU approaches. *Cardoza Journal of International and Comparative Law*, *16*, 379–408.

Levy, L. (2004). *Emergence of a free press*. Chicago, IL: Ivan R. Dee Publisher.

Medenica, O., & Wahab, K. (2007). Does liability enhance credibility?: Lessons from the DMCA applied to online defamation. *Cardoza Arts and Entertainment Law Journal*, *25*, 238–269.

Reed, C., & Angel, J. (2007). *Computer law: The law and regulation of Information Technology*. New York: Oxford University Press.

Reno v. ACLU, 529 US 844 (1997).

Rustad, M. (2009). *Internet law in a nutshell*. Eagan, MN: West.

Sanders, A. (2009). Defining defamation: Plaintiff status in the age of the Internet. *Journal of Media Law and Ethics*, *3*(4), 155–185.

Times v. Sullivan, 376 U.S. 254 (1964).

Travis, H. (2007). Reclaiming the First Amendment: Constitutional theories of media reform: Of blogs, ebooks, and broadband: Access to digital media as a First Amendment right. *Hofstra Law Review*, *35*, 1519–1581.

Tremayne, M. (2007). *Blogging, citizenship, and the future of the media*. New York: Routledge.

United States Copyright Office. (2010). Available at http://www.copyright.gov

Zeran v. America Online, 129 F.3d 327 (4th Cir. 1997).

KEY TERMS AND DEFINITIONS

Actual Malice: Intentionally harming someone by spreading false information about them knowing it is not true.

Appropriation: One of the four torts of privacy law. When someone uses another's identity for commercial gain without permission, the law on appropriation may be violated.

Contemporary Community Standards: A local community perspective on whether a work is obscene. The community can be a city, town, or county.

Copyright: A legal way to protect creative works that are literary, musical, artistic, or visual from being illegally used for commercial gain by someone other than the original creator.

Cyberbullying: Using the Internet to intimidate victims causing them to fear for their safety.

En banc: A legal term that describes a court session with all the judges on a court rather then the usual quorum.

False Light: One of the four torts or areas of privacy law. When someone is portrayed in the press in a false manner, the law on false light may be violated.

First Amendment of the U.S. Constitution: This is regarded as a legal cornerstone of the freedom of speech and the press in the United States: "Congress shall make no law respecting an establishment of religion, or prohibiting the free exercise thereof; or abridging the freedom of speech, or of the press; or the right of the people peaceably to assemble, and to petition the Government for a redress of grievances."

Intrusion: One of the four torts of privacy law. Physical intrusion by the media often occurs when undercover reporting methods are used to gather information about someone's personal life.

Libel: A defamatory statement expressed to harm a victim's reputation.

Private Facts: One of the four torts of privacy law. These are truthful but often embarrassing pieces of information exposed by the media about an individual.

Prurient: A specific term describing an unusual or abnormal sexual desire and applies to obscenity controversies.

Public Domain: Not a physical location but it is a source of creative content such as music or fiction no longer protected by copyright law. The copyright may have expired on specific content.

Reasonable Person Standard: A hypothetical person used as a legal standard to determine guilt of a crime.

Trademark: A word, phrase, logo, or other symbol that distinguishes a product from others.

ENDNOTES

[1] *Zeran v. America Online* (1997) and *Barrett v. Rosenthal* (2006).

[2] *U.S v. Alkhabaz* (1997) and *U.S. v. Newell* (2002).

[3] *Dimeo v. Max* (2006).

[4] http://www.copyright.gov

[5] http://www.copyright.gov/circs/circ1.pdf

[6] http://www.copyright.gov/help/faq/faq-duration.html#duration

[7] http://www.copyright.gov/circs/circ1.pdf

[8] http://www.uspto.gov

Chapter 14
Analyzing Blogs:
A Hermeneutic Perspective

Richard Fiordo
University of North Dakota, USA

ABSTRACT

An operating public blog was selected as a case for a depth study blending mixed perspectives. The aim of the research was to compare the face value of the blog with social dynamics operating beneath the surface of the blog for which the investigator had special knowledge. The perspectives applied in the study converged from the general fields of communication, philosophy, and other social sciences. Specific theories from semantics, argumentation, and rhetoric were emphasized in the discourse analysis. Especially useful to this research was an analysis of preferred, negotiated, and oppositional readings (or interpretations) of discourse in general and blogs in particular. Blog posts were analyzed, interpreted, and assessed—particularly in light of what was not overtly communicated. The findings of this depth analysis were consistent with empirical studies that have found that blogs may not provide the optimal platform for the deliberative sharing of ideas but may serve to draw likeminded bloggers. Insofar as this study addressed an allegedly helping type of public blog, it may have heuristic value for similar instances. To the extent that this study addressed diverse levels of meaning in a particular public blog, it may contribute to understanding levels of meaning in blogs in general.

INTRODUCTION

In the poetic words of W. H. Auden (1970, p. 6), "To ask the hard question is simple, The simple act of the confused will." Auden later decides: "But the answer Is hard and hard to remember." In this study, a hard question is simply asked to confuse the will less, yet the question may be hard to answer because of its intricate vastness. While truth can be stranger than fiction, fiction can be more believable than truth. For many reasons, fiction can trounce history. Furthermore, art and life may complement each other, and fictional narratives may interact with real narratives. In televised crime dramas, a judge may take an insincere position on a public issue because of a

DOI: 10.4018/978-1-60960-744-9.ch014

bribe or threat. Heroic detectives eventually correct the wrong perpetuated by the bribe or threat. In actual life, although a judge may be bribed or threatened into making a false statement, justice may never flourish or may follow decades from the actual public deception. A whole and true public understanding may be wrongfully assumed. A fictional script can give us insight into a real one and vice-versa (Burke, 1968).

Based on the discourse of a public blog (Urbanski, 2010), the researcher unveils, through interpretive research (Anderson, 1996, pp. 13-15; Griffin, 2003, p. 508), a struggle between truth and fiction as well as between what was expressed and suppressed in a blogging incident. As Keyes (2004) argues, in contemporary life, we seem to be in the post-truth era where dishonesty and deception constitute the norm. In fact, he asserts that dishonesty "inspires more euphemisms than copulation or defecation," thereby helping to "desensitize us to its implication." In the post-truth era, we have statements that constitute truth and lies as well as "ambiguous statements that are not exactly the truth but fall short of a lie." He adds that through "such aggressive *euphemasia* we take the sting out of telling lies" (Keyes, 2004, p. 15).

Space only permits a summary with telling quotes of the blog's content dealing with truth, lies, and euphemistic ambiguities. For this study, the researcher assembled a discourse hermeneutic to decrypt, in considerable complexity (Pagels, 1989), the institutionalized conventionality of blogs and discourse in general. It is held that blogs need interpretation or translation, are polysemic and possibly hyperreal, may camouflage controversial elements, and require extensive investigation into contextual factors to unveil a holistic meaning. To understand blogs more fully, the discourse hermeneutics formulated here considers manifest and cloaked aspects of blogs as well as their contextual relations. While no claim is made that the hermeneutic perspective developed in this study constitutes the Rosetta Stone (or the ultimate interpretive key) for blogs, it does assert that it provides a useful key for interpreting blogs.

In the movie *The Gods Must Be Crazy*, a Coca-Cola bottle is thrown from an airplane and lands unbroken in the Kalahari Desert. Xi, the protagonist, and his band of Bushmen, portrayed idyllically, must interpret its nature and value as a boon or curse from the gods. Their limited knowledge of the bottle makes it special in this tale. The meaning of the bottle is treated eventually as a problem. The solution follows with Xi concluding the bottle is evil since it caused trouble twice and his venturing to dispose of it. As for blogs, the suggestion in this study is that blogs might be safely understood initially as indeterminate or problematic phenomena.

The focus of this study is a public blog of approximately 40 pages that circulated in the blogosphere. A conflict (Hewitt, 2005; Perlmutter, 2008), actually a masked rivalry between blogging and lurking antagonists, is revealed as underlying the overt blogged discourse. Fictionalized narratives pose as sincere ones. Not without its investors (Blood, 2002; Cobb, 1998; Edelman Group, 2007; Negroponte, 1995), the Internet has cautioners (Bowers, 2000; Johnson & Kaye, 2004; Jost & Hipolit, 2006; Price, 2004), and this investigative researcher is one, who recognize the Internet's double bind: that the Internet in general and blogging in particular embody advantages and disadvantages, the disadvantages being highlighted since participants tend to focus on advantages (Bowers, 2000, pp. 2 & 177).

With blogs occurring in the complicated and unfathomable prism of global satellite contexts (Hachten & Scotton, 2007), challenged in this hermeneutic (or interpretive) approach to a case study is an unidentified blogging incident claiming to represent a full and factual account of an event. Motivated by the misuse and abuse of blog technology, transformative (Mertens, 2009, pp. 2-4) elements that address social injustice (p. 14) through ethical responsibility (p. 179) are examined. While numerous blogs may transparently legitimate educational and business goals, socially unjust blogs may foster petty egocentricity, actionable bullying, and sophistic media and symbol manipulation (Dumova & Fiordo, 2010).

Blog abuse and misuse can mirror that of discourse in general (Dumova & Fiordo, 2007; Dumova, Fiordo, & Rendahl, 2008; Fiordo, 1990, 2011; Goldstein, 2007). The partial and partisan content of our undisclosed public blog is unveiled (Fiordo, 2001; 2002; 2010), especially for what it lacked and distorted. The public blog is translated (White, 1990) fittingly from its supposedly straightforward, full account to its actually distorted, limited account. The hermeneutic translates a hyperreal (Eco, 1986) or pseudo-event (Boorstin, 1961) into a real or veracious event.

Viewed as a mode of journalism, the public blog is researched with the depth and breadth attitude of investigative journalism. Levy (1975) explains that investigative reporting "goes beyond the obvious aspects of the story" (p. 1). The investigative reporter optimally has these virtues: 1) a "cynical, suspicious, nongullible, distrustful" state of mind; 2) the nerve to "print a story that disturbs the accepted view of something" to prove the righteousness of the research; and 3) the conviction to "have opinions" of what is right and wrong and the ability to judge that something is wrong with the "official story" (pp. 4-8). Investigative researchers, like investigative reporters, do not: 1) "believe much, until and unless, they have been able to verify it for themselves"; and, 2) distrust what "people say – and the more powerful the people, the greater the skepticism." When given a "choice between accepting something at face value or suspecting its accuracy," investigative reporters "opt for suspicion every time" (p. 4).

Gaines (1997, p. 1) echoes Levy. The investigative story may be contrary to the announced version because it contains information not revealed in earlier accounts. When investigative reporting and insider information are unavailable, reports lack the sophistication that strengthens the total truth of a story. Figuratively speaking, the investigative report works to avoid mistaking the façade of a hollow building in a Hollywood film set for an actual building. When the whole truth can only be found on the other side of investigation, the vacuum created in the absence of a thorough investigation must be filled (Enda, 2010, p. 23). As an investigator reporting and commenting on a blog, this researcher, through an innovative discourse hermeneutic, seeks to unveil stories behind a story in a blog.

HOLISTIC CARTOGRAPHY AND BLENDED PERSPECTIVES

This qualitative study blends theoretical perspectives to bare the whole – or at least the holistic - truth on the content and credibility of the blog in its byzantine contexts. Blog discourse should be deciphered as pragmatically and circumstantially as manageable since the whole truth, ideally, constitutes the hermeneutic discipline endorsed here. The truth in its entirety may be only a legal fiction because truth *in toto* cannot always be known at the moment of adjudication. The holistic truth, the fullest account, may have to serve as an expedient end. Much blogged communication is deceptively elaborate like the proverbial iceberg with most of its mass invisibly beneath the water or like a carrot with its appealing leaves readily apparent and its desired robust, taproot hidden in the earth. In other words, the proportion of what is not communicated in a blog can dwarf, once translated, what is communicated.

Since the blogged incident is problematically complex, a simple solution is not likely. Because they can be labyrinthian, blogs should cause us to consider the perplexing contexts and consequences of what appears to be merely a straightforward sending and receiving of digitized discourse. The critical system used here involves a hermeneutic of translation through cartography. The translation occurs, figuratively, in the vast lane – like an astronomer mapping galaxies in the limitlessness of space. The cartographic method applied in this study maps blogging space to justify a sound, holistic translation. The cartography attempts to determine, with respect to the object of study, all that is known and unknown, symbolized and not symbolized, stated and unstated, accurate and inaccurate, correct and incorrect, unverifiable and verifiable, verified and unverified, declared and performed, decipherable and undecipherable, and deciphered and not deciphered (Korzybski, 2000). When a critic reveals what is known and unknown about a blog, an enlightened translation can follow: the vast, boundless, uncharted unknown metamorphosing into a bounded, demarcated, charted known.

This investigative researcher seeks to assemble the most complete story. The disclosing of problematic, missing, fragmentary, and hidden features of the discourse alerts readers to the particular blog's pitfalls. Though blogs can be cast globally, there is no effort to account totally for the global and personal consequences of the blog studied or of blogs in general. This study alerts bloggers and lurkers that more than is posted on a blog constitutes its unabridged meaning. A blog can reach immeasurable, unintended audiences as well as a measurable, intended one; it is dissimilar from a small group discussion shared for an hour around a campfire. Since a blog can become an intractable entanglement, bloggers and lurkers must beware of the blog, its unabbreviated signification, and its uncut significance.

Fundamental philosophical premises can inform us of the breadth and depth of the blog analysis. Vedanta philosophy (Sivananda, 1998, p. 154) provides us with a theoretical premise for analyzing the multifarious aspects of an elaborate blog. Vedanta teaches that "this world is unreal" and "veiled by Maya" – or, "the illusory power." As the "veils are lifted, the mind becomes clearer" through "constant enquiry into the nature of things." With respect to method, the following didactic Vedanta story guides us. A man was in his garden looking for a dropped needle. A passerby, offering to help find it, asked exactly where the needle might have fallen, and learned that it had fallen in the house. The passerby admonished that he would never find the needle outside when it was dropped inside. The man told the passerby that his house was too dark to locate it, so he decided to search for it outside in the light. The moral of this tale is that, like this man, most of us look in the wrong places for what we wish to find (p. 156). As a popular song admonishes, we look for love in all the wrong places. As regards research efforts, we may also look for answers in all the wrong places – or at least not in enough relevant places. This research edges toward correcting this tendency.

The lifting of veils through research has an analog in film and media narratives generally. This critique probes for items excluded from the final product. The critical instrument employed considers it essential to look holistically in the right places for signification and significance. Even when the right places pose difficulties, they are germane to unmasking meaning. Analogous with film, the right places include our blog for public consumption and extra-blog matters: behind the camera activities, behind the scene activities, inside the studio activities, outside the studio activities, out-takes, bloopers, gag reels, flubs, goofs, gaffe, kayfabes, errata, mistakes, and all activities relevant to making the best total sense possible of the discourse under inspection. The aim is to explore the whole picture by demystifying and demythologizing one public media blog, especially by uncovering what is unstated and missing.

The interest in the study is to search the right places for proper and complete answers. Seeking the truth frees inquirers to look where they must to gain a real understanding of the discourse. Since this study evaluates conventional communication analyses as much as it critiques a particular blog, its holistic critical orientation may deter bloggers from absorbing blogs before considering their concomitant deficiencies. Damage delivered in the name of decency resulting from this blog cannot be undone. Like the BP Gulf Oil Spill Disaster of 2010 or the Japanese earthquake and tsunami of 2011, only damage control, not damage prevention, is possible. The critique is tendered as a cautionary account of uninvited and undeserved woe stemming from the misuse of a, perhaps, well-intentioned blog.

Lehman and Luhr (2005) encourage a "critical process that is, by definition, never finished." As they contend, when "we stop questioning, we are in danger of accepting easy and obvious 'truths' that can, in fact, blind us to important issues" (p. 4). Consistent with Lehman and Luhr, from this researcher's standpoint, communication criticism grows with the theoretical knowledge of the critic. Mixing theoretical perspectives can enhance critical development. Beginning with Aristotle (Cooper, 1932; Kennedy, 1991, pp. 33-35; Ross, 1960), a critic might pose a version of his question about rhetoric: that is, what are the available means of judging discourse in any given situation? Griffin (2003) explains that, like Plato, Aristotle "deplored the demagoguery of speakers using their skill to move an audience while showing a casual indifference to the truth." Aristotle held that "truth has a moral superiority that makes it more acceptable than falsehood." When "unscrupulous opponents of the truth...choose falsehood," the ethical discourse critic must use all available, substantial means to "counter the error" (p. 303).

With Aristotelian ethical sentiments, this blog investigator applies discourse analysis to correct error with fact as fully as possible and to keep the bloggers honest as often as possible. Integrating other theorists into Aristotle's ethical principle increases the potential for insightful appraisals. While Aristotle brings light to communication criticism, other theorists augment the light. Blended perspectives enhance the hermeneutic dynamic of criticism. What the blogger says and does implies, terminologically from Burke's (1968) perspective, what is not said and not done: for example, to direct a reader's attention by declaring "Helmut is innocent" asserts tacitly and complementarily negations of and alternatives to this sentence. To illustrate this through the use of the single word "innocence," the declared sentence semantically excludes many statements such as, "Helmut is *not* "guilty," *not* "accountable," *not* "someone to fear," and so on. With respect to the public blog being examined, the language used and not used, the total meaning symbolized, and the information discovered outside the blog that alters its manifest communication is examined.

Augmenting Aristotle, additional perspectives follow. A philosophical perspective on discourse is derived in part from the behavioral semiotic of Morris (Fiordo, 1977; Morris, 1964; Sebeok, 2001), Burke's (1968; 2007) notion of language as symbolic action, Skinner's (1983) notion of behavioral consequences, Austin's (1987) notion of performative utterances, Toulmin's (1958) argument model, and Foucault's (1982) intellections on hegemony. What a blogger writes is assessed here in part by semiotic actions that are empirically verifiable.

Embracing social disclosures of self, Kanin (1981) respects constructivism's cognitive complexity (Delia, O'Keefe, & O'Keefe, 1982). With willingness to bare their souls, people may manipulate disclosures, in a one-sided way, to hide the whole truth and support a biased image. Detailing facts is commendable. Keeping a story about oneself flowing, details correct in principle may be provided. The goal is to want to be authentic. To do so with impunity, perestroika segues into glasnost. People then talk as fearlessly as celebrities publicizing their personal traumas (Kanin, 1981, pp. 5-6).

Since the blog studied seems to involve *exomologesis* as an underlying theme, this term needs elaboration. Honoring Mowrer (1961) who tried to restore *exomologesis* through his integrity groups - guided by honesty, responsibility, and involvement - to everyday life (Fiordo, 1981), Kanin (1981, pp. 57) explains *exomologesis* as a radical openness with trusted, reasonable others designed to improve oneself personally. *Exomologesis* "requires public confession of mistakes and defects, forgiveness of self and others, group support in correcting these wrongs, acceptance into the community, and fellowship for life"; it involves a shared moral inventory of oneself with a system for "correcting errors of thought and behavior." Mowrer (Kanin, 1981) tried to recreate a fully informed community, "where people helped people and everyone was accepted" and to restore a close sense of community that existed when "extended families were intact" and "people shared material possessions" along with "their troubles." Mowrer offered evidence that *exomologesis* yields honesty which produces individual and societal health (pp. 5-7).

With Rescher's (1977) advancement of dialectics as a controversy-oriented approach to knowledge, two or more perspectives should be considered to insure a relatively unimpaired interpretation of discourse. Eemeren and Grootendorst's (1992) pragma-dialectics requires addressing opposing views as a part of convincing others of the acceptability of a position. Confused or unscrupulous bloggers tend to build cases convincing only to susceptible and likeminded others. A blog may simulate building an exhaustive case, but in fact may not. In the public blog studied, optimistically stated, the bloggers strived toward *exomologesis* to lessen the suffering of an accident survivor and to assuage their suffering with respect to the survivor. Pessimistically stated, the striving of the bloggers toward *exomologesis* languished

from misuse and was counterproductive in helping the victim. As the blogged dialog shows, the noble objective of the bloggers to transcend their shortcomings and generate the ultimate community for *exomologesis* deteriorated.

The non-allness principle of general semantics (Korzybski, 2000, p. 375) underlies this study. No one can say everything about an event. No event can be reported perfectly and completely. Distortion flows from unsubstantiated claims about the thoroughness of information. When information blogged is either misinformation or limited information misperceived as complete information, deception can be deduced. Deception theory (Knapp, 2008) involves intentional concealment, falsification, and equivocation. Since blogs can be fraudulent, self-serving, or fictional, they should be distilled to their undeniably verifiable elements with the remainder functioning as fiction. Morris (1964) addresses the empirical concern through the semantic component of semiotics that relates symbols (Fiordo, 1977, p. 58) to denotata – that is, percepts or "things." Extra-symbolic or empirical factors help unclothe the blog's translation. The researcher uncovered facts from scenes and agents (Burke, 1968) unknown to the bloggers and enjoyed insider information about the content of this blog and external developments. In blog analysis, the underbelly of contextual material evidence may be available, yet may not be found. When unfound, the discourse under examination can be interpreted only from the text. This holistic critique strains to reveal the intact story, pragmatically discoverable.

From the perspective of reception theory, the hermeneutic impulse is fulfilled by how the readers perceive the blog's discourse in comparison with the way intended by its source (Hall, 1997; Lehman and Luhr, 2003). In a *preferred reading* of a form of discourse, its audience reception corresponds to that desired by the source of the message. In a *negotiated reading*, the audience accepts most, but not all, of the dominant meaning of the intended message from the source and adds meaning with special value for certain segments of the readership – for example, bloggers or lurkers. In an *oppositional reading*, the audience receiving the discourse opposes the preferred reading promoted by the message source. Determining an oppositional reading entails knowing how the source wants the audience to accept the message, rejecting the source's desired reception, and embracing a radically different meaning (Lehman & Luhr, 2003, pp. 187-190). In this blog, the bloggers tend to display a preferred reading while the lurkers an oppositional reading.

Lehman and Luhr (2003, p. 289) direct us to the performances of actors, especially characters serving as empowering role models. The authors and this researcher concur in advancing the value of a highly critical, analytical response to every aspect of a mediated message: "However well intentioned the motive, we cannot exempt any element from scrutiny." Role modeling derived from actual people differs dangerously from role modeling derived from "media heroes." As an illustration, the mediated personality of Tiger Woods as a cultural icon, while currently depreciated, labors to rise like the Phoenix.

Misinformation and incompleteness among some bloggers can be easy to detect. The bloggers on this blog deceived themselves; they confounded illusion with reality; and, their hyperreal world denied the verbal and material consequences of their perceptions and actions (Skinner, 1983). As the poet Jeffrey Skinner (1988, p. 15) remarks, "Denial, like whiskey, can work, especially if you drink or lie to yourself with a positive view…"

BLOGGING HYPERREALITY: TRANSLATION IN THE VAST LANE

With the confidentiality of personalities honored, the translation of the public blog in extended contexts unravels with fictional substituting for actual names, dates, genders, or other identifying pieces of information. Fictional and partial blogs can triumph online over factual and thorough accounts. The blog fiction can bypass scrutiny and be misconstrued as fact. When blog readers misread a blog's imaginary and fragmentary portrayal of events as actual and unbroken events, trouble may follow.

The public blog examined here covered a period of approximately three months and a length of about 40 pages printed at 12 font. Postings show that there may have been approximately 25 bloggers and 50 lurkers. The blog initiator, named *Alpha* here, developed the blog supposedly as a means of informing friends and family of the condition of an accident survivor - a popular, professional athlete known to fans, friends, and family in at least three countries - and referred to here as *Omega*. *Omega* is a name with irony since the survivor began at the blog's start as the first concern while by the blog's end appeared to be the last concern. Bloggers are referred to by numbers: *Blogger One, Two,* etc. On one occasion in the history of this public blog, Omega contributed, likely with assistance, a brief single entry, at least nominally, to the script of the blog. All of the bloggers but one praised Alpha. Alpha expressed self-praise. A number of off-camera lurkers to the blog, termed *Lurkers* here, were known to the researcher and were hegemonic opposites of the Bloggers. Although a "lurker" (that is, an Internet user who read the public blog transactions yet never posted messages), this investigative researcher posted nothing on the blog.

The term *Bloggers* designates Alpha's supporters as announced through their postings. Consequently, the term *Bloggers* is synonymous with such terms as: *supporters, followers, flatterers, fans, loyalists, believers, disciples*, and the like. The term *Lurkers* is synonymous with such terms as: *opponents, critics, debunkers, counterhegemonists, antagonists, rebels*, and the like. The researcher learned that conversations, email, and phone calls took place off-camera among the Lurkers as well as between Alpha and the Bloggers – none of which surfaced on the blog's script. While some research estimates that lurkers may constitute as much as 90 percent to online groups (Nonneck & Preece, 2000), the exact volume of off-camera exchanges in this case remains unknown, although the investigator's speculation is that it was high because of the international locations of the bloggers. Hypothetical lurkers may have been in communication with Alpha, Omega, the Bloggers, and the Lurkers. Without confirmation, lurkers from afar in cyberspace are but postulated in this study. Although uncounted, the researcher observed and was informed of extensive off-camera exchanges among the Lurkers. Only one Lurker, designated *Harbinger* and discussed later, blogged once. Harbinger, who had the final posting, deviated, as judged by context, from the chorus of blogged encomium for Alpha.

The encomium for Alpha from the Bloggers parallels the empirical research findings that the Internet may form circles of likeminded people who strengthen their opinions, attack the opinions of others, and close or minimize deliberation from multiple viewpoints (Galston, 2003; Kaye, Johnson, & Muhlberger, 2012; Sunstein, 2001). Blogs can create a feeling of community among Internet users who side with others they perceive to have points of view in common, and a dominant blogger can express opinions and make assertions without evidence while overlooking conflicting views or alternative hypotheses (Barton, 2005; Johnson, Bichard, & Zhang, 2007; Papacharissi, 2004; Poster, 1997; Strandberg, 2008).

The bloggers began listening increasingly to Alpha online about matters that pertained indirectly and superficially to Omega. Alpha and the Bloggers gradually eclipsed Omega as the blog's *raison d'etre* with Omega becoming little more than a pretense for them to advance their interpersonal relationships in Omega's name. The blog fails to document Omega's recovery thoroughly or unerringly. Initiating it without official approval

from relevant sources, Alpha directed the blog and its content. As the hegemonic power with an estimated 70 percent of the posted script, Alpha propagandized her/his way to dominance as author omniscient and "yellow journalist" extraordinaire.

The Bloggers and the blog claimed to help Omega return to health from a near-death situation. The blog proclaimed to help Omega "fight" and win the toughest of battles - the fight for life. The study would end here if the declared intention of the blog unfolded without flaw and with nothing lacking. Deconstruction of the blog's script demonstrates and material findings surrounding the blog evidence that an oppositional reading of the Lurkers complements the preferred reading of the Bloggers, thereby completing its fullest meaning. The holistic critical question surfaces: What is missing? One answer is: plenty of relevant and insightful information.

Alpha's image manipulated on-camera (that is, in view of the public via the blog) contrasted sharply with behavior demonstrated off-camera (that is, out of view of the public via the blog). The imagery of a comforter in residence projected on the blog had its shadow in the observed lowness and meanness displayed in actual face-to-face dealings with Omega: namely, chastisements directed at the survivor for unseemly and pathetic aspects of the survivor's recovery. Off-camera, Alpha demeaned Omega and blocked others who desired to visit her/him from doing so. On-camera, Alpha smiled for photographs blogged and wrote in a sanctified manner about the challenges s/he surmounted in resurrecting the survivor. Fiction trumped fact. The fragmentary picture was portrayed as complete. By the close of the public blog, Alpha's image was one of self-sacrificing, untainted devotion to Omega's welfare.

As the survivor of a life-threatening accident, Omega was, for a time, not conscious of her/his physical condition, the blog, and its global broadcast with ineluctable implications. Without approval from Omega's formal guardians and using a daily journalized format, in the name of decency by the blog's early light, Alpha played the online leading role convincingly to the Bloggers as Omega's blog-master and healer. Alpha's vainglorious creation of the international blog to rally for Omega's life betrayed his/her alleged care of Omega and implicitly Omega's official guardians and cherished ones.

Omega's formal guardians never contributed to the blog. Around the blog's fifth week, Omega started to acknowledge and suffer dissonance over the blog. Recovering from medical stresses, for a multitude of reasons including fear of being disharmonious with Alpha, Omega was inhibited to ask her/him to discontinue the blog. Omega's guardians were equivalently handicapped in terminating the blog because there was no desire to risk troubling Omega further. Content that should never have been publicized was blogged globally in detail.

As the blog dialog evolved, the seemingly decent intention of Alpha to share painful information about Omega with friends and family became more a boasting of the sorrows and triumphs of Alpha than a sensitive account of the painful condition and recovery of Omega. Blogger Three supported Alpha with the line: "[Alpha], Always speak your TRUTH!" With Omega's interaction on the Internet radically limited and of tenuous authorship since s/he was not medically capable of exacting human communication for over a month, Alpha rationalized not controlling the blog's script.

The blog script demonstrated that Omega's recovery served as the battle cry for self-serving and myopic discourse between Alpha and the Bloggers. Omega, the alleged blog protagonist, devolved into a cameo role in its drama. Postings on Omega's ups and downs waned as Alpha, skyrocketing to blog prominence, shared his/her and successes as Omega's super-caregiver. Communicating high identification with Alpha, the Bloggers applauded him/her as the *sine qua non* of Omega's recovery. Elevating her/him to

superstar status, the Bloggers marginalized Omega and underwrote an illusion of *exomologesis*.

From the blog's beginning, nobody contested what Alpha said or did. Harbinger, the counter-hegemonist, became involved twice: once indirectly through a private email to Alpha and once with the final blog posting. Harbinger's delicate email was known to several lurkers off-camera. An excerpt of the email to Alpha respecting Omega will demonstrate its civilized tone: "I have been reading your blog on [Omega's] progress and am happy to hear [s/he] is doing well. I pray for [him/her] every day. However, I do have one request I wish you would consider. I ask that you please take the photos off of [Omega]… I feel they are inappropriate for the Internet, and I would like to explain why. Anyone can come across your blog…To anyone that knows [Omega], they represent this awful accident…but to someone else, they may look at it as a joke… I wonder how [Omega] feels about these photos being online of [her/him] at such a vulnerable time. I appreciate all the support you're giving [him/her]… and ask you consider my request." Incidentally, at the hospital, Omega's medical files and photographs were officially restricted to hospital caregivers and specified family members.

Harbinger served to foreshadow counter-hegemonic energies formerly unexpressed on the blog. Except for the final blog posting that seemed to connote antithetically in context Alpha's possible benignity and malice, Harbinger eventually served Alpha as a scapegoat. Although the private email discreetly indicated to Alpha feelings of discomfort about the unauthorized posting of Omega's postsurgical photographs, the gatekeeper Alpha publically maligned Harbinger's civil request to consider removing the compromising pictures. Based on the number and tone of postings, Alpha's rendition of Harbinger's email as criticism for "something so minor" as "my use of pictures on this blog" stimulated the Bloggers to attack Harbinger and defend Alpha – thereby blessing

Alpha's demagoguery. Alpha showed no signs of awareness that the photographs differed since no two were alike and that some photographs were objectionable in part, some *in toto*, and some not at all. To Alpha, all were reverential and no other view was tolerable.

To illustrate, Blogger Seven said: "Poo Poo on all the mean people in the world… Your pictures captured [Omega's] spirit!!!!!! How sad Mean People can't see it. Their loss! [Alpha], I think everything you're doing is perfect! You owe no explanation to anyone…! Don't let Mean People live in your head rent free, forget and ignore them." Blogger Eight wrote: "[Alpha], if there is anyone you want me to lay the smack down on, just let me know!" Blogger Nine asserted: "And may I say…WTF with the criticism cited in the last entry? [Alpha], …you have every right to be a little perturbed… It makes my blood boil… can't imagine what it's done for you. So, an emphatic and undiplomatic 'piss off' to the naysayers… whoever you are." Blogger Ten announced: "I have no idea how anyone could have the audacity to question anything that you are doing." Blogger eleven concluded: "No one has the right to question you… I wanted to say what a wonderful person you are but that would be an understatement. You are truly [a being] who was sent by god! Hope you are feeling better." And, Blogger Twelve affirmed: "Things need to be kept positive… If anyone is questioning [her/his] support then feel free to come and try it your selves… [Alpha] put [his/her] life on hold… to ensure [Omega] was getting everything possible on a daily basis… I for one think [Alpha] has gone above and beyond what any one else may have done."

With groupthink (Janis, 1982) operating, the bloggers, as a collective, in Gramscian (1971), fashion, conformed merrily and wholeheartedly to grant total command to Alpha. S/he could do no wrong in their eyes. Believing in their inherent morality, feeling invulnerable, and closing their minds to different viewpoints (Janis, 1982, pp. 111, 119, & 256), Bloggers as a group surrendered their consciousness and conscience to Alpha. In the expressed views of the Bloggers, Alpha, now apotheosized, was given, and deserved to be given, supreme credit for improving Omega's medical condition. The Bloggers, some of whom were arm-chair activists as far as helping Omega (that is, friends or family who would be expected to be at Omega's side but were not), deferred their responsibility online to Alpha – despite their limited understanding of Alpha from his/her card-stacking entries. Alpha served to assuage the Bloggers' group and individual consciences by being the suppositious victim at Omega's side.

Inventing a new term may benefit the blog analysis and translation. The apparent purpose of the blog as a helping effort might be called a *functional* or *SOS fallacy*. If there is a declaration that help is being provided but the effort is more dysfunctional than functional (or as dysfunctional as functional), a functional or SOS fallacy has likely surfaced. In the vernacular of English, at least two questions emerge: "With friends like this, who needs enemies?" and "The road to hell is paved with good intentions." Those presumably helping Omega may have had decent intentions, but the intended assistance became dysfunctional and took a downward turn. Reports from several people with significant ties to Omega indicate that they and the survivor were hurt more than helped by the blog. Due to the knottiness of this event in and outside cyberspace, dysfunctional ramifications of the blog will never be accurately measured nor comprehended.

With Alpha as their benevolent dictator, the Bloggers prostrated themselves before him/her. In totalitarian style, Alpha shaped, through one-sided propaganda, the verbal and graphic information the Bloggers received on Omega's strivings and tribulations. Although s/he presented a partial and partisan account of Omega, Alpha's account was perceived as gospel in speaking the whole truth and nothing but the truth. Bloggers Seven through Twelve applauded Alpha's efforts and ascribed saint-like virtues to her/him. Blogger Fifteen declared that Alpha even "deserves the purple heart." Alpha became an icon of purity, goodness, and truth as well as the *sine qua non* of Omega's recovery. With empirical research supporting the extremist direction of the public blog studied here toward "cyber-ghettoes" cut off from outsiders' views (Dahlgren, 2005; Xenos, 2008), the Bloggers consistently posted extremist positions to back Alpha.

Although the Lurkers known to the researcher were outraged by the blogged photographs and would not, so they said, have been as genteel as Harbinger if they were to express their views on Alpha's posted photographs. Omega was not medically stable enough to adjudicate the suitability of the photographs. When Omega regained sufficient consciousness, s/he too was displeased with those whom Harbinger and the Lurkers spurned.

Alpha's framing and rendering of Harbinger's email constituted a gross reversal of the content and intent of Harbinger's email. The investigative researcher read the email and recognized Alpha's calumniation of Harbinger. Alpha's poisoning of Harbinger's email incited the Bloggers to decry Harbinger as a Harpy and celebrate Alpha as a protective archangel. Alpha seemed to have mesmerized the Bloggers and never displayed Harbinger's email for the Bloggers to judge for themselves. Although Alpha lacked material and ethical grounds to counterattack the actual email, s/he chose to misrepresent Harbinger's message. For creating and violating Harbinger as a straw-person, Alpha was lauded by the Bloggers. Factual reporting almost totally abandoned, Alpha embraced yellow journalism with the attitude of Alpha's way or the highway prevailing among the Bloggers.

When Alpha and the Bloggers attacked Harbinger, the Lurkers began an off-camera outcry for a counterattack. After conferring with the investigative researcher, the Lurkers decided to remain silent for Omega's welfare for a short time with a deadline set for a counterattack. If the public blog on Omega were not removed by the deadline, oppositional messages would storm the hegemony of Alpha and the Bloggers. Harbinger entered the final posting and addressed it to Alpha in these contextually antithetical words: "Bravo! Bravo! Dear [Alpha], you are truly [a being] descended from heaven, gifted with the power of healing no less. Such a selfish act you have done, caring for [Omega] like you have, and seeing to it the whole world knows. Godspeed!" With unexpected drama, one day before the deadline, Alpha removed the public blog on Omega.

To this researcher's knowledge, no Lurker informed Alpha or the Bloggers that s/he would soon face the shock and awe of hostile postings on the date specified for the counterattack. Yet, Alpha privatized the blog. When Alpha privatized the blog, s/he did what would have produced less negativity had s/he created a private blog from the start. Once privatized, no effort was made by the researcher or any of the Lurkers to access it. With the public blog removed, the counter-hegemonic Lurkers were partially satisfied. Although several Lurkers leaned toward renouncing Alpha and the Bloggers through petulant blogs, to the researcher's knowledge, none were transmitted.

Once the public blog was closed, about a fifth of the Lurkers speculated that Harbinger's final entry functioned as a draconian warning of animosity to come. It was inferred that Alpha construed Harbinger's final posting on the blog to be ominous. By privatizing the public blog, Alpha saved face publically. It remains unknown whether Alpha read the final entry by Harbinger as a sign that war was looming over false and hurtful blog declamations. While this researcher can make no statement to support the conclusion of perceived poetic justice on the part of some Lurkers, that Alpha was about to inherit a blogging hurricane of a thousand hornets appears to be a safe conclusion. In contrast, Alpha may have decided that all that needed to be said was said or that the error in his/her ways - intimated by Harbinger - had finally been realized. Regardless of intentions, moral or expedient, Alpha's removal of the public blog calmed the Lurkers since Omega no longer suffered unrestricted public display.

Though delayed, the Lurkers saw justice as being delivered. The Bloggers expressed no knowledge of the off-camera activities of the Lurkers. No discourse of the Bloggers hinted that they were conscious of the Lurkers. The Lurkers' perspectives expressed to this investigative researcher particularized their agonies with the blog. If the whole meaning of this blog cannot be rendered, a holistic meaning has been ventured.

DISCUSSION: EXOMOLOGESIS LOST

This study has allowed us to investigate the overt discourse of a public blog and reveal where it might have embodied prosocial and antisocial values. The seemingly kind and decent content resulted in a subculture of adults emoting over a hyperreal account of a painfully real event. In the self-appointed starring role as crusader and rescuer, Alpha engineered the Bloggers to accept her/his preferred reading of the blog. Although a few Lurkers leaned to a slight degree toward a negotiated reading, the supermajority maintained an oppositional reading.

As the first and chief blogger, Alpha orchestrated a blog that resulted in misinformation outweighing information and limited information masquerading as unlimited information. Alpha's voice amplified by the choral accompaniment of the Bloggers blocked divergent voices from being heard on Omega. The online illusion of hegemony without counter-hegemony (Foucault, 1982) ruled the blog's text. The Lurkers' off-camera protests justify a reading of opposition to an unsanctioned gatekeeper's propaganda.

Although the Bloggers provide dauntless loyalty online for Alpha, the counter-hegemony of the Lurkers was potent. Appearing heroic online, Alpha's status off-line was seen as mock-heroic and false-heroic (or simulated heroism) (Keegan, 1987, p. 235). Alpha preached to the choir and manipulated praise from the choir. The erring hyperreality of the blog failed to attain Internet *exomologesis*. The stories behind the story uncover a supermajority of Lurkers who saw Omega and the blog's content as bogus, censored, and ill-suited for public display.

With respect to the blog's text, Alpha presented illusions of reality and wholeness. Heat replaced light with a sophistic rhetoric triumphing over an epistemic one. With Gramscian (1971) zeal, the Bloggers bestowed unjustifiable honors on Alpha, and s/he exploited the undeserved authority granted her. Because s/he remained sinless in the Blogger's eyes, they transmogrified Alpha's vices into virtue. Alpha artfully molded Bloggers into true believers.

According to their statements of oneness with Alpha, the Bloggers characterized Alpha on-camera in terms of honesty, responsiveness, caring, transparency, authenticity, modesty, and enlightenment. The Lurkers characterized Alpha off-camera in terms of dishonesty, narcissism, phoniness, resentment, and deception. The Lurkers saw Alpha as playing gullible Bloggers like pawns. Rather than the writing of a responsible reporter, to the Lurkers, the blog represented the stratagems of a demagogue who shamelessly propagandized his/her subordinates. Although the Bloggers flattered Alpha as a loving, selfless, helpful, and noble human being, the Lurkers excoriated her/him as a spiteful, selfish, hateful, and ignoble human being. With comments about Alpha from Bloggers accenting only the positive, comments about Alpha from Lurkers accented mostly the negative.

To analyze a selection of discourse fully, a discourse interpreter should discover to as high a degree as possible: what was and was not publicly stated, what was communicated privately or coded, what was contradictory, and what was missing. Multiple aspects of the message, if not all, must be found and interpreted. All of the information available, located, and revealed should be disclosed to astute readers for them to judge the entire meaning for themselves. Identifying misinformation, fabrication, equivocation, and missing information alters the total comprehension of the message's truthful representation of the event. While this researcher tried to make some unknowns known, there is no claim here that all the information pertaining to this blog has been uncovered and all standpoints voiced. The analyst remains open to additional substantive information. To translate other public blogs through the amalgamated hermeneutic perspectives applied here should enlighten findings. Blog translators and critics are urged to proceed with holistic wisdom in order to avoid partial folly.

STUDY LIMITATIONS

As a form of public discourse on the Internet, an unidentified public blog is critiqued as a case in this study. When the public blog became private, the private blog was never investigated. After consultation with the Institutional Review Board at the University of North Dakota, it was determined that IRB approval was not needed due to the public nature of the information reported. Due to numerous sensitivities, the researcher safeguarded the anonymity of the blog and the identities of the bloggers. Since the study is exploratory in its hermeneutic perspective, the findings should be interpreted as preliminary and heuristic. What may be a unique blogging event should not be generalized without caution. Additional research, especially quantitative, should be undertaken to confirm tendencies suggested from these findings. This investigative researcher intends to reveal how blog information can be manipulated through

what is and what is not shared. Because the researcher had insider information on the bloggers, the content of the blog, and a group of lurkers, this blog was selected. An expose of the blog and its surroundings is delivered. The investigation evinces the potential for public blogs to be fictitious and antisocial while pretending to be real and prosocial – or, helpful (Dumova & Fiordo, 2007). The content of this blog is interpreted as discourse manipulated in a context of known and unknown bloggers, lurkers, and material factors. Potentially developing with imperfect knowledge, blogs might best be understood in their holistic contexts. Since everything is not uttered in a blog and since the opportunities for blogging nonsense abound, bloggers and lurkers should be wary of blogs.

FUTURE RESEARCH DIRECTIONS

Research pertaining to blogging becomes increasingly important as investigators recognize multiple levels of meanings and contexts. Interpreting with validity the meaning of public blogs and blogs in general grows in relation to the critical filters available and applied. While social scientific methods can be used to support generalizations about blogging, hermeneutic methods can be used to scrutinize and evaluate a specific blog – a specific blog in the context of its expressed history of interactions and circumference of postings as well as likely unexpressed interactions and postings. In many blogs, what is manifestly available to readers and contributors may represent hypothetically but 20 percent of the meaning while what does not appear in the blog may account for 80 percent of the meaning.

Future research on specific instances of blogging can probe the information behind the information. Revealing the stories delivered behind the declared story in any unique blog would advance knowledge of the dynamics of narratives, for it would reveal meaning not communicated overtly through the blog per se. Future research might investigate types of blogs that typically communicate information at a high ratio of explicit to implicit information (perhaps 80 percent or more explicitly stated and 20 percent or less implied or unreported) and blogs that typically express information at a high ratio of implicit to explicit information (perhaps 80 percent or more implied or unreported and 20 percent or less explicitly stated). International, intercultural, gender, religious, education, and age differences can be researched as well. The examination of cases of blogging would epistemologically breathe life into the findings of statistical studies from the perspective of social and behavioral science research methods.

CONCLUSION

Multiple hazards potentially accompany social interaction technologies in general and blogs in particular (Dumova & Fiordo, 2010). Blog discourse should be filtered for illusory, reckless, and missing elements. This hermeneutic study of discourse offers support that blogs can be Daedalian. When readers fail to recognize the imperfections and convolutions of blogs in their vast contexts, misinformation predominates. Blogs should be interpreted and judged through as many methods and from as many perspectives as needed to determine their overall meaning. Blogs can range from those with reasonable entries to those that serve the inclinations of a clique. In the incident examined, with participants less corrupt in their motives and less inept in their methods, the benign intent of the blog might have overcome dysfunctional leadership, groupthink, and other shortcomings. In an attempt to establish far-ranging grounds for judging the comprehensive meaning and value of a blog in light of on-camera and off-camera participants in numerous

contexts, the investigative researcher concludes that this blog fell short of producing the positive consequences of its expressed intention and that careful inquiry into other blogs should keep this flawed blog from masquerading as an exemplary blog. Yet, as Auden prophesied, "the answer Is hard and hard to remember."

REFERENCES

Anderson, J. A. (1996). *Communication theory: Epistemological foundations*. New York, NY: Guilford.

Auden, W. H. (1970). *Selected poetry of W.H. Auden*. New York, NY: Vintage Books.

Austin, J. L. (1975). *How to do things with words*. Cambridge, MA: Harvard University Press.

Barton, M. D. (2005). The future of rational-critical debate in online public spheres. *Computers and Composition, 22*, 177–190. doi:10.1016/j.compcom.2005.02.002

Blood, R. (2002). *Weblog handbook*. Cambridge, MA: Perseus.

Boorstin, D. J. (1961). *The image: A guide to pseudo-events in America*. New York, NY: Vintage.

Bowers, C. A. (2000). *Let them eat data: How computers affect education, cultural diversity, and the prospects of ecological sustainability*. Athens, GA: The University of Georgia Press.

Burke, K. (1968). *Language as symbolic action: Essays on life, literature, and method*. Berkeley, CA: University of California Press.

Burke, K. (2007). On persuasion, identification, and dialectical symbols. *Philosophy and Rhetoric, 39*, 333–339. doi:10.1353/par.2007.0000

Cobb, J. (1998). *Cybergrace: The search for God in the digital world*. New York, NY: Crown.

Cooper, L. (1932). *The rhetoric of Aristotle*. New York, NY: Appleton-Century-Crofts.

Dahlgren, P. (2005). The Internet, public spheres, and political communication: Dispersion and deliberation. *Political Communication, 22*, 147–162. doi:10.1080/10584600590933160

Delia, J., O'Keefe, B., & O'Keefe, D. (1982). The constructivist approach to communication. In Dance, F. E. X. (Ed.), *Human communication theory* (pp. 147–191). New York, NY: Harper and Row.

Dumova, T., & Fiordo, R. (2007). Presenting prosocial TV messages to early adolescents. *The International Journal of Interdisciplinary Social Sciences, 4*, 120–135.

Dumova, T., & Fiordo, R. (2010). Handbook of research on social interaction technologies and collaboration software: Concepts and trends: *Vol. I, II.* Hershey, PA: Information Science Reference.

Dumova, T., Fiordo, R., & Rendahl, S. (2008). Mass media, television, and adolescent socialization: Making peace with TV. *Communication and Social Change, 2*, 174–192.

Eco, U. (1976). *A theory of semiotics*. Bloomington, IN: Indiana University Press.

Eco, U. (1986). *Travels in hyperreality*. New York, NY: Harcourt Brace Javanovitch.

Edelman Group. (2007). *A corporate guide to the global blogosphere*. New York, NY: Edelman Group.

Enda, J. (2010). Capital flight. *American Journalism Review, 32*, 15–31.

Fiordo, R. (1977). *Charles Morris and the criticism of discourse. Lisse, The Netherlands: The Peter de Ridder Press and Bloomington*. IN: Indiana University Press.

Fiordo, R. (1981). Integrity training: A moral code and method for moral education. *The Journal of Educational Thought, 15*(1), 47–60.

Fiordo, R. (1990). *Communication in education*. Calgary, Canada: Detselig Enterprises.

Fiordo, R. (2001, Spring). Charles Morris and the significant revelation. *Recherches Semiotiques. Semiotic Inquiry, 21*, 189–209.

Fiordo, R. (2002). The darkness behind the light: The consequences of communicating extreme deceit. *Mind, Medicine, and Adolescence, 21*, 189–20.

Fiordo, R. (2010). Integrating deception theory into public speaking classes: A study in communication education. *Journal of Communication. Speech & Theatre Association of North Dakota, 23*, 31–48.

Fiordo, R. (2011). *Arguing in a loud whisper: A civil approach to dispute resolution*. Saabrucken, Germany: VDM.

Foucault, M. (1982). *The archaeology of knowledge*. London, UK: Tavistock.

Gaines, W. C. (1997). *Investigative reporting for print and broadcast* (2nd ed.). Chicago, IL: Nelson-Hall.

Galston, W. A. (2003). If political fragmentation is the problem, is the Internet the solution? In Anderson, D. M., & Cornfield, M. (Eds.), *The civic web: Online politics and democratic values* (pp. 35–44). Lanham, MD: Rowman & Littlefield Publishers.

Goldstein, T. (2007). *Journalism and truth*. Evanston, IL: Northwestern University Press.

Gramsci, A. (1971). *Selections from the prison notebooks*. New York, NY: International.

Griffin, E. (2003). *Communication: A first look at communication theory* (5th ed.). Boston, MA: McGraw-Hill.

Hachten, W. A., & Scotton, J. F. (2007). *The world news prism: Global information in a satellite age* (7th ed.). Malden, MA: Blackwell.

Hall, S. (1997). *Representations: Cultural representations and signifying practices.* London, UK: Sage.

Hewitt, H. (2005). *Blog: Understanding the information reformation that's changing your world.* New York, NY: Nelson.

Janis, I. L. (1982). *Groupthink: Psychological studies of policy decisions and fiascoes.* Boston, MA: Houghton Mifflin.

Johnson, T., & Kaye, B. K. (2004). Wag the blog. *Journalism & Mass Communication Quarterly, 81,* 622–642.

Johnson, T. J., Bichard, S. L., & Zhang, W. (2009). Communication communities or cyberghettos? A path analysis model examining factors that explain selective exposure to blogs. *Journal of Computer-Mediated Communication, 15,* 60–82. doi:10.1111/j.1083-6101.2009.01492.x

Jost, K., & Hipolit, M. (2006). Blog explosion: Passing fad or a lasting revolution. *CQ Researcher,* 505-528.

Kanin, R. (1981). *Write the story of your life.* New York, NY: Hawthorn/Dutton.

Kaye, B. K., Johnson, T. J., & Muhlberger, P. (2012). Blogs as a source of democratic deliberation. In Dumova, T., & Fiordo, R. (Eds.), *Blogging in the global society: Cultural, political and geographical aspects* (pp. 1-18). Hershey, PA: Information Science Reference.

Keegan, J. (1987). *The mask of command.* New York, NY: Penguin.

Kennedy, G. A. (Trans. Ed.). (1991). *On rhetoric: A theory of civil discourse.* New York, NY: Oxford University Press.

Keyes, R. (2004). *The post-truth era: Dishonesty and deception in contemporary life.* New York, NY: St. Martin's.

Knapp, M. L. (2008). *Lying and deception in human interaction.* Boston, MA: Pearson.

Korzybski, A. (2000). *Science and sanity: An introduction to non-Aristotelian systems and general semantics.* New York, NY: Institute of General Semantics.

Lehman, P., & Luhr, W. (2005). *Thinking about movies: Watching, questioning, enjoying* (2nd ed.). Malden, MA: Blackwell.

Levy, E. (1975). *By-lines: Profiles in investigative journalism.* New York, NY: Four Winds.

Mertens, D. M. (2009). *Transformative research and evaluation.* New York, NY: The Guilford Press.

Morris, C. W. (1964). *Signification and significance: A study in the relations of signs and values.* Cambridge, MA: MIT Press.

Mowrer, O. H. (1961). *The crisis in psychiatry and religion.* Princeton, NJ: Van Nostrand.

Negroponte, N. (1995). *Being digital.* New York, NY: Vintage Books.

Nonnecke, B., & Preece, J. (2000). *Lurker demographics: Counting the silent (Proceedings of CHI 2000).* The Hague, The Netherlands: ACM.

Pagels, H. R. (1989). *The dreams of reason: The computer and the rise of the sciences of complexity.* Toronto, Canada: Bantam Books.

Papacharissi, Z. (2004). Democracy online: Civility, politeness, and the democratic potential of online political discussion groups. *New Media & Society, 6*(2), 259–283. doi:10.1177/1461444804041444

Perlmutter, D. D. (2008). *Blogwars.* Oxford, UK: Oxford University Press.

Poster, M. (1997). Cyberdemocracy: Internet and the public sphere. In Porter, D. (Ed.), *Internet culture* (pp. 201–218). New York, NY: Routledge.

Price, T. (2004). Do computers and the internet enhance democracy? *CQ Researcher, 14*, 757–780.

Rapoport, A. (1950). *Science and the goals of man.* New York, NY: Harper and Brothers.

Rescher, N. (1977). *Dialectics: A controversy-oriented approach to the theory of knowledge.* Albany, NY: State University of New York Press.

Ross, W. D. (1960). *Aristotle* (5th ed.). London, UK: Methuen.

Sebeok, T. A. (2001). *Signs: An introduction to semiotics* (2nd ed.). Toronto, Canada: University of Toronto Press.

Sivananda Yoga Vedanta Center. (1998). *Yoga: Mind and body.* New York, NY: DK.

Skinner, B. F. (1983). *A matter of consequences.* New York, NY: Knopf.

Skinner, J. (1988). *A guide to forgetting: Poetry by Jeffrey Skinner.* Saint Paul, MN: Graywolf.

Strandberg, K. (2008). Public deliberation goes online? An analysis of citizens' political discussions on the Internet prior to the Finnish parliamentary elections in 2007. *Javnost—The Public, 15*, 71-90.

Sunstein, C. (2001). *Republic.com.* Princeton, NJ: Princeton University Press.

Toulmin, S. E. (1958). *The uses of argument.* Cambridge, MA: Cambridge University Press. Lawrence Erlbaum Associates.

Urbanski, H. (2010). *Writing and the digital generation: Essays on new media rhetoric.* Jefferson, NC: McFarland and Co.

van Eemeren, F. H., & Grootendorst, R. (1992). *Argumentation, communication, and fallacies: A pragma-dialectical perspective.* Hillsdale, NJ: Lawrence Erlbaum Associates.

White, J. B. (1990). *Justice as translation: An essay in cultural and legal criticism.* Chicago, IL: The University of Chicago Press.

Xenos, M. (2008). New mediated deliberation: Blog and press coverage of the Alito nomination. *Journal of Computer-Mediated Communication, 13*, 485–503. doi:10.1111/j.1083-6101.2008.00406.x

KEY TERMS AND DEFINITIONS

Exomologesis: A radical openness with trusted, reasonable others with the end in view of improving personally.

Functional (or SOS) Fallacy: When there is a declaration that help is being provided someone but the effort is more dysfunctional than functional (or as dysfunctional as functional); declared aid that is bogus.

Hegemony: The exercise of power and control among human beings, especially when achieved through consent rather than force.

Hermeneutics: The study or theory of methodical interpretation, especially of texts.

Hyperreality: The human challenge to distinguish what is real from what is artificial or counterfeit, especially in technologically advanced cultures that have the means to characterize the world through refined media that shape and reshape actual events.

Lurker: An Internet user who reads transactions on a blog or other interactive system yet rarely, if ever, posts messages.

Negotiated Reading: Occurs when the audience of a message accepts most, but not all, of the dominant intended meaning of the message from the source and adds meaning with special value for certain segments of the readership.

Oppositional Reading: Occurs when the audience of a message opposes the preferred reading promoted by the message source.

Polysemy: The capacity of words and signs to have multiple meanings.

Pragma-Dialectic: Addressing opposing views in a controversy reasonably as a part of convincing others of the acceptability of a position.

Preferred Reading: Occurs when the audience reception of a message corresponds to that desired by the source of the message.

Semiotics: The theory and study of signs and symbols.

Chapter 15
Social Interaction Technologies and the Future of Blogging

Tatyana Dumova
Point Park University, USA

ABSTRACT

In an age of user-generated content, multimedia sharing sites, and customized news aggregators, an assortment of Internet-based social interaction technologies transforms the Web and its users. A quintessential embodiment of social interaction technologies, blogs are widely used by people across diverse geographies to locate information, create and share content, initiate conversations, and collaborate and interact with others in various settings. This chapter surveys the global blogosphere landscape for the latest trends and developments in order to evaluate the overall direction that blogging might take in the future. The author posits that network-based peer production and social media convergence are the driving forces behind the current transformation of blogs. The participatory and inclusive nature of social interaction technologies makes blogging a medium of choice for disseminating user-driven content and particularly suitable for bottom-up grassroots initiatives, creativity, and innovation.

INTRODUCTION AND BACKGROUND

As we move into the 21st century, a new generation of Internet technologies transforms the information landscape and previously established media usage patterns. Social interaction technologies, or Internet-based tools and techniques designed to initiate, share, and maintain interactive and collaborative activities online (Dumova & Fiordo, 2010), have penetrated multitudinous aspects of people's lives. When applied to the realm of media and communication, these technologies are commonly referred to as social media and include weblogs, microblogs, social networks, wikis, discussion forums, audio and video podcasts, Web feeds, social bookmarking services, and virtual

DOI: 10.4018/978-1-60960-744-9.ch015

worlds. The term "blogging" refers to the practice of publishing user-generated content on the Web in a journal-type format that can be easily updated and commented on. Blogs permit people to engage in social interactions, build connections, maintain conversations, share ideas, and collaborate with others. Above all, blogs and blogging advance the creation of user-centered, user-driven, and user-distributed content.

Social media development concurs with the grand vision of the World Wide Web as "more a social creation than a technical one" (Berners-Lee, 1999, p. 133). To draw attention to the paradigm shift in how Internet users collaborate and share content online, the concept of Web 2.0 was introduced (O'Reilly, 2005). However, there is no separation barrier between Web 1.0 and Web 2.0; rather, there is a symbiosis of emerging and already-established Internet technologies. There are many definitions of social media and most of them emphasize the creation and exchange of user-generated content (Kaplan & Haenlein, 2010). Powered by new technologies with blogging at their core, social media are taking the world by surprise. A recent worldwide poll conducted by a global media planning and marketing company, Universal McCann, demonstrates that the social media universe is growing exponentially. The primary adopters and participants of social media are more than 600 million active Internet users who go online every day in various parts of the world (Wave 4 Social Media Tracker, 2009). Reading and writing blogs remain the most common social media activities, along with managing personal profiles, visiting friends' social network pages, sending and reading short messages, sharing photos, and watching and uploading video clips (Wave 5 Social Media Tracker, 2010). It is not accidental that the website hosting the popular blog service Blogger (blogspot.com) is the world's fifth most visited site after Google, Facebook, YouTube, and Yahoo.[1]

In just one decade, blogging has taken off and become nearly omnipresent with millions of blogs published worldwide. There are numerous blog classifications: public blogs and those hidden beyond the intranet firewalls (private or limited access), single-authored blogs and multi-authored, or collective blogs. Blogs differ by ownership (personal, organizational, or corporate), by genre (political, educational, sports, military, law, current events, fashion, "mommy" blogs, etc.), by multimedia type (photo, video, and audio blogs), and by platform (moblogs). The origin of blogs as communication systems is mired in the history of Usenet groups and the Bulletin Board Systems of the 1980s, as well as the first World Wide Web communities of the1990s. Early self-expressive websites gave birth to a well-known dimension of blogs as a cyber-equivalent of a personal diary. The adoption of WWW brought popularity to the collections of hyperlinks, which users composed, updated, and shared with one another. These linklogs became common and there was just one step from a linklog to a linkblog (link plus commentary) and finally to a weblog.[2] In essence, "personal foraging sites" (Blood, 2000, p. 20) merged with personal Web pages, and the rest was history. Ultimately, hyperlinks and self-expression defined the nature of blogs and turned blogging into the medium that we know today.

The concise history of blogging pioneers still has to be written by Internet historians.[3] However, there are several innovations that separate modern blogging from the early days. Among them, the incorporation of trackbacks by the MovableType blog publishing platform and the introduction of the commenting feature in the Open Diary blog hosting service. On its first day of operation Open Diary had twelve visitors; three of them started their own diaries. One of the three users happened to be from Turkey (Locken & Loughnane, 2005, p. 291), an early signal that blogging was destined to become a global enterprise. In 1999 the introduction of Pitas.com's and Blogger.com's easy-to-use and free blog hosting and publishing services made the blogging revolution inevitable. Interestingly enough, its vanguard was located in the Netherlands with "the highest number of we-blogs per capita in the world" (Blood, 2002, p. 5). Recognizing the international flavors of blogging, the first Weblog Awards in 2001 included such categories as best American, Canadian, European, Asian, Australian, and New Zealand blog.[4]

Bloggers have created a new world—a global blogosphere—populated by technology and lifestyles gurus, heads of state and multinational corporations, politicians, celebrities, opinion leaders, information purveyors of all kinds, activists, volunteers, human and animal rights defenders, civil liberties experts, corruption fighters, and truth seekers. It appears that the "noosphere" imagined by Vladimir Vernadsky as a special realm of existence for human thoughts has been finally located. The global blogosphere, as well, reflects the contradictory nature of humanity since it not only accommodates the human need to communicate, connect, and share, but also encompasses some questionable and even antisocial practices. Nonetheless, blogging has firmly entered society's everyday existence and has become an essential part of politics, business and marketing, public relations and advertising, social and public services, nonprofit organizations operations, various professional activities, as well as other political, social, economic and cultural dimensions of life. However, the greatest impact of the blogging revolution can be seen in the domain of human and media communication.

In 1999 one technology enthusiast characterized weblogs as: "the pirate radio stations of the Web, personal platforms through which individuals broadcast their perspectives on current events, the media, our culture, and basically anything else that strikes their fancy from the vast sea of raw material available" (Katz, 1999). Since that time blogging has evolved into an industry. Thus Rick Calvert, founder of the BlogWorld & New Media Expo, a major international social media event, thinks of blogs as the center of the social media universe. Calvert elaborates, "The blog is the hub and all these other things—Facebook, LinkedIn,

Twitter, Flickr, YouTube—are spokes that lead back to the center" (as cited in Black, 2011, p. 14).

This chapter aims to evaluate the future direction of blogging as a social media phenomenon by surveying the global blogosphere landscape for current trends and assessing their implications and potential impacts. It should be noted, however, that the author considers the shoes of H. G. Wells too large to step in, and therefore avoids the promise of drawing a vision of the blogosphere's future; rather, she sees her task as alerting the scholarly community and interested readers about the important transformations that herald challenges and opportunities for blogging. Blogs can provide fascinating insight into the functioning of human communication in the digital age, and the author hopes that the current study will encourage students of media and communication to continue pursuing this line of research.

LITERATURE

Even though blogs are a newborn medium—if one compares their short existence with more than a 300-year history of newspapers—political commentators, social observers, and cultural critics have all praised the value and impact of blogs on society and culture. Among social scientists, blogs have received general acclaim for raising the levels of political participation (Kaye, 2005; Pole, 2010) and serving as gatekeepers in campaigns and elections (Garris, Guillory, & Sundar, 2011); empowering citizens (Papacharissi, 2007); encouraging civic engagement (Rheingold, 2008); fostering public discourse (Benkler & Shaw, 2010; Etling et al., 2010); creating a new form of journalism (Johnson & Kaye, 2004; Wall, 2005); building community (Kervin, Mantei, & Herrington, 2010); harnessing collective intelligence (Gregg, 2010); and rendering knowledge (Park, Jo, & Moon, 2010). What's more, blogs have been viewed as one of the most striking developments of the early twenty-first century (Sunstein, 2009, p. 138).

In addition, the study of motivations for blogging has turned into an interdisciplinary area of inquiry of its own, providing insight into bloggers' individual differences and reasons for blogging (Guadagno, Eno, & Okdie, 2010; Herring, Scheidt, Kouper, & Wright, 2007; Hollenbaugh, 2011; Kaye, 2007). A recent study by Larsson and Hrastinski (2011), "Blogs and Blogging: Current Trends and Future Directions," utilized a sample of 248 scholarly articles indexed in an academic citation database, ISI Web of Knowledge. The study documents an increase in scholarly interest in blogs within the social sciences and the humanities: from 2 articles appearing in 2002 to 101 articles published in 2008. Overall, the existing research indicates that blogs are a highly multifunctional and versatile medium of communication and allows to identify the following major functions of blogging: (1) personal narrative and self-expression, (2) information sharing and message relaying, (3) public discourse, (4) citizen journalism, (5) educational, (6) business and professional, and (7) entertainment. Blogs are playing an increasingly influential role in politics and civic engagement. Musing on the future of political blogs, Farrell and Drezner (2008) predict that they will continue to maintain their pervasive role in public discourse as a tool "through which politicians and others will seek to influence political debate" (p. 29). Pole (2010) similarly draws the conclusion that political blogs "will remain prominent" (p. 138). In the journalism realm, Tremayne (2007) seems to agree that blogs are altering the nature of journalism and that collectively blogs can affect mainstream news coverage of politics. Thriving in the new media environment, blogs make the old model of mass communication, "which allowed little voice for the audience" (p. 271) obsolete. Tremayne believes that although blogging will not replace the functions of traditional journalism, blogs on politics, war, sports, technology, health, entertainment, and the like will continue to occupy important niches and present serious competition for mainstream media.

Focusing primarily on personal journals, Barlow (2008) confirms that blogs are changing people's individual relationships with technology, particularly in the areas of politics and journalism, and that bloggers do not live in a virtual, make-believe world, but deal with real-world problems around them. "Technology is part and parcel of the cultural whole" (p. 124), argues Barlow, who is optimistic about the changes that blogs, as a new public sphere, are bringing with them. Raising the question, "What's next for blogging," Bruns (2006) presciently writes that technology itself "does not guarantee the eventual success of a blogging genre" (p. 251) and places the future of the medium into the hands of bloggers.

While scholarly research on blogs is growing, addressing the future of blogging as a medium presents a motivating challenge. Thus, Jensen and Helles (2011) believe that "the future of many-to-many communication on a massive scale, across different groups, institutions and sectors in society, is still in the process of taking shape" (p. 529). They posit that the specific potentials of the so-called "many-to-many" forms of communication, such as blogs, can be evaluated only in relation to future outcomes.

Harold Lasswell, one of the founders of communication science, emphasized that any communication process can be examined in "two frames of reference, namely, structure and function" (1948, p. 38). To address the question of the future of blogging, the author of this chapter uses a structural-functional approach and focuses on the place of blogs among social media. The underlying premise of the chapter is that unlike the traditional "Big Four" media (i.e., print, film, radio, and TV), blogging should not be analyzed in isolation and should be viewed holistically, as an integral part of the social media cluster that function together to sustain the whole.

THEORETICAL FRAMEWORK

Despite a large body of empirical research delineating the growth of specific social media applications, there is still a lack of theoretical conceptualizations of these developments that can help identify the role and place of blogging as a communication channel within the greater context of modern society and estimate its future. Two theoretical frameworks are particularly relevant to this task, specifically: *media convergence* developed by Henry Jenkins of the University of Southern California Annenberg School for Communication & Journalism, and *cultural technology* proposed by James Lull of San Jose State University.

Most generally, media convergence can be viewed as the integration of multiple media types meant to enable technological innovations, produce better content that can be disseminated more effectively, and to facilitate two-way communication between content producers and consumers. Many authors have discussed the idea of media convergence through digital technologies. In the 1990s, "convergence" was defined as "the coming together of all forms of mediated communication in an electronic, digital form, driven by computers" (Pavlik, 1996, p. 132). The term "digital convergence" is frequently used to imply that not only new and emerging media, but also traditional media (such as newspapers, books, magazines, radio, TV, film) are part of the process (Pavlik, 2008). With the proliferation of social media applications on mobile platforms, it became apparent that media convergence ultimately blurs the boundaries between traditional media formats allowing them to flow across platforms and multiple media channels (Jenkins, 2001, 2006a). A key characteristic associated with the process of media convergence is the participatory nature of convergent media. From the user perspective, convergence provides new levels of engagement with mediated realities. Users are learning to master the attributes of new and enhanced technologies "to bring the

flow of media more fully under their control and to interact (and co-create) with others" (Jenkins & Deuze, 2008, p. 6). "Consumption becomes production; reading becomes writing; spectator culture becomes participatory culture," explains Jenkins (2006b, p. 60), and this trend has been noted by many observers. For instance, Bruns (2009) emphasizes the birth of a new culture that supports active user participation in the creation and distribution of content—participatory culture. Lull (2007) similarly indicates, "consumers are producers; audiences are authors; users are developers" (p. xii). At the global level, however, because of the international flow of information and media content, convergence routinely results in the "cultural hybridity" of the mediated environment (Jenkins, 2001).

Media convergence dramatically expands opportunities for social interaction, improves access to distant cultural resources, and diversifies cultural experiences. Lull (2007) introduces the notion of cultural technology, given the enormous popularity of the Internet around the world and its profound impact on culture. As articulated by Lull, the key principles of cultural technologies entail: (a) "blurring the distinctions between social life and technology," (b) "convergence of technological components and functions," and (c) "melding of normative social behaviors" facilitated by technology (p. 61). Echoing Jenkins, Lull stresses the interconnectedness of technological mechanisms that enable the production of user-generated content and support the social dimension of cultural technologies. To Lull, these mechanisms involve the full spectrum of media, with social networking, blogging, photo and video sharing, and instant messaging to name a few. As a cultural technology tool (Lull, 2007), blogging lets users obtain cultural knowledge (p. 65), participate in the global public sphere (p. 75), foster shared public communication, and promote global consciousness (p. 157). Cultural technologies also allow for the routine blending of traditional cultural influences such as language with the attitudes and behaviors generated in the Internet's cultural spaces. However, Lull cautions that universal values broadcast in mediated forms can "clash with actual practices in many parts of the world" (p. 63, 68). Overall, the theoretical frameworks of media convergence and cultural technology allow for a better understanding of the dynamic interrelationship between blogs and other components of the social media cluster.

METHOD

To answer the question of what the future holds for blogging, this chapter utilizes the method of environmental scanning drawn from the methodological toolbox of futures studies. Futures research is a fast growing, multi-disciplinary field of knowledge which builds on the foundation of management, economics, political science, sociology, and human ecology to address pertinent problems associated with the growth of a modern industrialized society (see Ackoff, 1974; Dator, 2002; Fowles, 1978; Morrison, Renfro, & Boucher, 1983). Samet (2009) distinguishes between three types of futures research: (a) projective futures and forecasting; (b) prospective futures and scenarios; and (c) evolutionary futures. Applying evolutionary futures research approach to the global blogging environment, this chapter critically analyzes the current issues, trends, and their implications with the purpose of identifying important challenges and opportunities facing blogging.

The method of environmental scanning (ES) originates from the business world where it is imperative to analyze competition and the overall market for tactical and strategic purposes (Aguilar, 1967; Kroon, 1995). Currently, it is frequently utilized for a thorough and comprehensive examination of emerging technologies (Alexander, 2009). This type of analysis is done through a wide-angle lens and allows mapping of the dynamic interplay of many technological and societal factors and identifying the driving forces behind

them, both centripetal and centrifugal. In sum, the technique of environmental scans "provides a macro-image of the environment and indicates how different environments function" together (Kroon, 1995, p. 77).

As it applies to blogging, the key elements of ES utilized in this chapter include evaluating statistical data, events, industry reports, white papers, survey results, expert reviews along with a wide range of ideas, issues, and perspectives originating from the scientific community. The author also considered views and opinions expressed in top technology blogs and forums, such as: ReadWriteWeb, Mashable, Slashdot, TechCrunch, Wired, Engadget, and Ignite Social Media. Advantages of the environmental scanning method come from the use of multiple and diverse sources of information (Alexander, 2009) as well as the interdisciplinary nature (Morrison, Renfro, & Boucher, 1983) of inquiry that it provides. Finally, the method utilizes a systems approach that allows focusing on the entire cluster of social media and tracing the interaction between the platforms and tools that operate as a whole.

A broad and all-inclusive environmental scan can be realized through an exhaustive review of different factors and components such as social, economic, technological, political, regulatory, and cultural, and it can be conducted as a stand-alone examination or a series of analyses. The current study utilized processed-form scanning relying on existing secondary data. Ideally, however, ES should be supplemented by gathering new data (through surveys or other means), systematic longitudinal scanning, or ad-hoc scanning of issues under investigation. To minimize the subjective factor, further investigations may apply a series of environmental scans or combine ES with other techniques such as the Delphi method, alternative futures scenarios, or prediction markets (Alexander, 2009).

BLOGGING AS A GLOBAL PHENOMENON

After the appearance of the first English-language weblogs in the 1990s, blogging has quickly turned into an international phenomenon: over 60% of all blogs are written in a language other than English (Wyld, 2007, p. 52). Internet users across the world are utilizing blogs as one of the most ubiquitous social media tools to establish human contacts, build connections, share opinions, follow conversations, collaborate, and interact with others. According to the *State of the Blogosphere* report (Technorati, 2010), two-thirds of all bloggers are male, and 65% are between ages 18 and 44.[5] Another study shows that worldwide, women bloggers prevail despite the fact that women occupy 46% of the global Internet population. In addition, the share of women's online time spent on blogs is greater than men's (ComScore, 2010). The prevalence of women among blog users is also evident from the analysis of user demographics for specific blogging and microblogging services, for example, LiveJournal, Xanga, Twitter, and Tumblr (Ignite Social Media, 2011). It should be noted, however, that global statistics of blog authorship and readership can be misleading and regional, geographic, and cultural differences should always be considered (see Table 1 for top ten global blog markets). In India, for example, women compose only 20% of all Internet users while North American online population is split evenly (ComScore, 2010).

The author would like to draw the attention to the intricacy of assessing the overall scope of the blogging universe because of the incomplete and sometimes conflicting estimates provided by Internet metric services, social media monitoring companies, blog search engines, and bloggers themselves. According to BlogPulse (2011), an automated trend discovery system for blogs owned by the Nielsen Company, there are currently 168 million blogs. In comparison, in May 1999 there were only 23 known weblogs (Blood, 2000. p. 70). EatonWeb, one of the earliest blog directories on the Web and Technorati's predecessor in blog indexing, listed less then 50 blogs in the same year. After the year 2008, Technorati's annual *State of the Blogosphere* analysis no longer reported a total number of blogs in the global blogosphere, and the latest available estimate was 133 million blogs (Technorati, 2008). Other specialized blog search engines and directories (such as Google Blog Search, IceRocket, Regator, and

Table 1. Top ten global blog markets by country (average minutes per visitor and percent reach)

Top Markets by Average Minutes per Visitor on Blogs	Average Minutes per Visitor	Top Markets by Percent Reach of Blogs	Percent Reach
Japan	62.6	Taiwan	85.5%
South Korea	49.6	Brazil	85.2%
Poland	47.7	South Korea	84.9%
Indonesia	33.1	Turkey	81.9%
Brazil	32.5	Japan	80.5%
Vietnam	30.3	Peru	77.3%
Sweden	29.2	Portugal	76.0%
Malaysia	26.6	Argentina	73.3%
Portugal	24.8	Singapore	73.2%
Taiwan	24.1	Chile	72.3%

Source: Adopted from ComScore, 2011.

Bloglines) do not disclose the overall number of blogs that they index. According to WordPress. com (2011), there are 57.8 million WordPress sites in the world, with 294 million people reading blogs hosted and published by this service. Finally, BlogScope (2011), a research project of the University of Toronto, tracks 56 million blogs. However, there has been a paucity of inquiries into the blog abandonment rate and the proportion of active and inactive blogs. In addition, the issue of spam blogs cannot be ignored.

Even though the adoption of blogging in Western countries might have reached a critical mass and is decelerating, it demonstrates a rising trend in many other parts of the world. As evident in Tables 1 and 2, blog reading and writing are popular in such diverse geographies as Japan, China, South Korea, U.S., Poland, Sweden, India, and Brazil. China's blogging community is by far the largest in the world. While instant messaging and social networking compete with blogging to become "the social glue" of the Chinese Internet, which currently encounters about 485 million users (Internet World Stats, 2011), blogging remains one of the most popular activities for online audiences in China. According to the Nielsen Company (2009), 90% of Chinese netizens read blogs and microblogs and 81% write and post comments, a much higher percentage than in the U.S. or Western Europe. The state-run China Internet Network Information Center (2010) gives a more modest estimate of the total number of net citizens in

China as equal to 420 million and the number of blog users as nearing 231 million or 55%. South Korean blogs are read by 88% of active Internet users. In Brazil, 62% of online users read blogs, and over 50% write them (Wave 4 Social Media Tracker, 2009).

At the same time, Western countries display a different and more complicated picture. For example, only 57% of Internet users in Germany read blogs, and even less contribute to them (Wave 4 Social Media Tracker, 2009). The Pew Research Center reports that blogging in the U.S. displays a downhill tendency among young adults but remains steady among the older population. Currently, one in ten American adults maintains a blog, and this trend has been fairly consistent during the past five years (Lenhart, Purcell, Smith, & Zickuhr, 2010). It is possible that blogging in the U.S. has already reached saturation levels and is giving way to more popular activities such as social networking. Yet, the world's blogging community is expanding as Internet users discover and adopt blogs in various geographical areas such as Central and South America, Eastern Europe (including Russia), the Middle East, and Africa. Thus, in the five years after the appearance of the first Russian-language post on LiveJournal in February 2000, the number of Russian bloggers grew to 235,000 (Gorny, 2006, p. 335). The Berkman Center for Internet & Society estimates that there are about 35,000 active Arabic-language blogs (Etling et al., 2009), and this number continues to grow. Multi-language

Table 2. Blogging and other types of social media activity by country (percent of online users)

	U.S.	U.K.	Germany	Brazil	India	China	South Korea
Blog Readers	66	58	57	62	79	90	88
Blog Writers	33	25	28	51	54	81	61
Create Social Networking Profiles	59	64	47	69	78	70	62
Visit a Friend's Social Network Page	67	71	53	84	82	82	76
Video Watchers	83	79	74	93	87	89	83

Source: Adopted from Wave 4 Social Media Tracker, 2009.

support is already increasingly incorporated into blog software. It is possible that bloggers will enjoy "on-the-fly" translation services with embedded automated language detection in the near future, an upgrade that will turn blogs into versatile cultural technology tools.

The following example demonstrates the immense power and potential of blogging as a cultural technology in promoting a social cause such as global education. In 2009, Rania Al Abdullah, the Queen of Jordan, launched a fundraising campaign in support of primary education in developing countries. An active social media user, she began the campaign by addressing bloggers gathered at Le Web'09, the leading Internet forum in Europe. Due to the support of the blogging community, the campaign was joined by 18 million people and was successful in raising global awareness of the issue (1GOAL, 2011). One participant noted:

Finally, the Internet is breaking the cultural barriers and history heritage that for so long has separated people in Europe. Finally, different cultures are working together to keep those links alive. Finally, we are starting to be one, and not many. (Guest post, 2009)

While the practice of blogging permeates the barriers of space and time, the worldwide trajectory of blog penetration depends on many socioeconomic, cultural, technological, and demographic factors. The overall spread of blogging and other social media is tied to the global efforts of bridging societal divides.

BLOGGING: TRENDS AND IMPLICATIONS

Evolution of Blogging Platforms

Early blogs were crafted manually as simple Web pages with hyperlinks. Thus, blogging at the early stages required basic knowledge of HTML programming, which created entry barriers for potential bloggers. The appearance of free blog hosting and publishing services made blogging available to anybody with a computer and an Internet connection. The pivotal role in the blogging revolution belongs to Blogger.com, a web-publishing service launched in 1999 by San Francisco-based technology startup Pyra Labs, purchased by Google, Inc. in 2003. It offered ready and easy-to-use, customizable templates for blog entries that could be updated from any stationary computer or mobile device. The Pyra Labs software was a breakthrough in the complexity typical of early Web programming; it allowed ordinary Internet users without intimate knowledge of computing to effortlessly publish content and incorporate links and multimedia. In addition, Blogger quickly developed a range of enhancements: such as the commenting feature, permalink, blog roll, trackback, calendar, archive, and RSS feed. According to Alexa Internet, U.S.-based Blogger and WordPress are among the most popular weblog publishing platforms in the world (see Table 3), while Twitter and Tumblr are the most popular microblogging services.

Despite the dominance of large players, there is healthy competition among the providers of blog hosting services and software. As a technological innovation, blogging originated in the United States; however, in many countries domestic platforms and services also appeared, for example Weblog.nl, BlogNL, and Blogeiland in the Netherlands. LiveJournal, developed in 1999 in the U.S. and purchased by the Moscow-based company SUP Fabrik in 2007, powers the Russian-language blogosphere (Alexanyan & Koltsova, 2009). To attract new users, LiveJournal continuously experiments with new features, for example voice posts, and emphasizes the creation of communities of bloggers. Even in the U.S. there are functioning communities of bloggers gathered around small providers (e.g., Open Diary and DiaryLand) that compete with giants such as Blogger and WordPress. Edublogs is the biggest

Table 3. Top ten popular blog publishing platforms by Alexa Internet ranking

Blog Publishing Platform	Alexa Global Traffic Rank
1. Blogger	5
2. Twitter	9
3. Tumblr	46
4. WordPress	75
5. LiveJournal	79
6. TypePad	201
7. Webs	355
8. Weebly	362
9. Drupal	390
10. Posterous	479

Source: Alexa Internet, The Web Information Company, August 12, 2011.

Note: The rankings were generated by Alexa Internet search analytics based on a three-month comparison of the number of daily visits to the site and the number of page views.

international provider of educational blogging, and operates from Australia. It is likely that this trend will persist in the future, and the diversity of blogging platforms and services will be sustained. The Dutch blogosphere presents a case of such diversity. Weltevrede and Helmond (2011) utilized an innovative approach for examining "the nationality" of blogs through URL, source code, and link analyses, as well as the use of the Internet Archive's Wayback Machine. They discovered that there is a growing preference for domestic platforms in the Dutch blogosphere. Perhaps this can be explained by certain centripetal sociocultural tendencies in the national blogosphere that counterbalance the centrifugal forces of cultural globalization. Such an assumption also concurs with Lull's (2007) notion of cultural technologies which points out that technology is merely a tool in people's hands.

Network-Based Peer Production and Blogging

As blogging platforms continue to evolve, new participatory modes of content production dem-

onstrate their growing power with the emergence of widely accessible online distribution channels. At its core is the user-driven nature of convergent media where traditional distinctions between consumers and producers of information and content have started to dissolve. Viewing the Internet as a platform for human connection, Benkler (2006) draws attention to the new ways of citizen engagement enabled by participatory media leading to the "social production" of content (p. 91) or "commons-based peer production" (p. 60). Bruns (2009), who has coined the term "produsage," emphasizes the blending of the roles of producers and users of information. In this new information landscape, a new culture that supports active user participation in the creation and distribution of content is being born (Jenkins, 2009).

The ongoing evolution of networked technologies supports effective interaction among communities of interest allowing them to participate in public discourse, negotiate agendas, and voice opinions at previously unknown levels of engagement (Benkler, 2006). "The value of any bit of information increases through social interaction," writes Jenkins (2006b, p. 140). Indeed, the value of social interaction technologies in fostering a participatory culture can hardly be negated. A recent London-based study of the social impact of citizen-run neighborhood websites and blogs found that these sites play a critical role in the local communication ecosystem (Harris & Flouch, 2010). They cultivate information sharing, raise awareness of local issues, reinforce local identity, stimulate the growth of social capital, strengthen social cohesion, and contribute to citizen empowerment. Established through free blog services, social networks, and discussion forums, these websites effectively function as public social third spaces (e.g., Whampstead), local agoras (e.g., Stroud Green), or civil social networks (e.g., Harringay Online). They can also operate as blogazines (e.g., Transpontine) or placeblogs (e.g., Brockley Central). Scientists (Gordon & de Souza e Silva, 2011) emphasize the importance of Web 2.0 tools (including blogs for community engagement), but warn that adding a networked component to neighborhood life cannot be viewed as a universal remedy for urban ills. Merely having access to technology is not sufficient for bridging the "participation gap" in a modern industrialized or developing society (Jenkins, 2006a); knowing what to do with technology is what really matters.

Researchers have already pointed out a recent massive growth of information startups such as the online community and neighborhood based publications often discussed in the context of Internet-based participatory media, citizen media, or alternative media (e.g., Carpenter, 2010; Metzgar, Kurpius, & Rowley 2011). These publications focus on small geographical areas and aim to fulfill the information demands of niche groups of people at the local and hyperlocal, or neighborhood, level. "Hyperlocal blogging" refers to blogging about issues, people, and events that affect local communities, neighborhoods, and suburban areas that do not find adequate coverage in "big" media. Well-known hyperlocal blogging and news sites—such as Baristanet (Montclair, New Jersey), NEastPhilly (Philadelphia), Live Here Oak Park (Chicago), Monroe Scoop (Monroe, North Carolina), Greensboro101 (Greensboro, North Carolina), Next Door Media (Seattle, Washington), and Capitol Hill Seattle (Seattle, Washington)—have been at the forefront of the hyperlocal news explosion. Numerous other lesser-known locally focused blogs, called "placeblogs," have also emerged to meet the needs of local audiences.[6]

Driven by the demand for local news, participatory community news sites, such as the community oriented blog Frankford Gazette (Philadelphia), bridge the gap between mainstream media and innovative grassroots initiatives by identifying new modes of gathering and disseminating information and giving voice to ordinary people. Blogazines and placeblogs actively solicit feedback and contributions from the public, and establish easy mechanisms for distributing user-generated

content. The Huffington Post founder Arianna Huffington reflects:

The content provider is no longer at the center of the universe. ... At the center of the universe is now the news consumer. People want to be part of the story of their time. They want to participate—both in small ways and in big ways, both in small issues and in big issues—with what is happening in our world. (as cited in McMains, 2010)

Despite the fact that hyperlocal blogs provide content of interest to relatively small audiences, when compared with such Internet giants as Facebook, Twitter, or YouTube, they still attract sizeable readership. For example, Next Door Media, a local news portal and a network of North Seattle neighborhood blogs, attracts 200,000 visitors monthly.[7] Baristanet, a grassroots blog based in Montclair, New Jersey, receives 9,000 visits per day and 80,000 unique visitors every month (as cited in George & Peters, 2010). Launched in 2004, Baristanet targeted three communities in New Jersey and quickly established itself as one of the national forerunners in hyperlocal blogging. The site presents an innovative mix of community news, original reporting, video interviews, and readers' comments. Baristanet has served as a model for other hyperlocal sites in these locales: Pittsburgh, PA; Brooklyn, NY; New Haven, CT; Watertown, MA; and Red Bank, NJ. Analysis of "mentions" by Regator.com, a specialized cross-platform blog directory and search engine, shows that local topics can receive more interest than national news.[8] The emergence of networks of hyperlocal news sites and blogs similar to Greensboro101 or "Next Door Media: Seattle Neighborhood Blogs and Hyperlocal News" demonstrate a growing trend. At the international level, full-fledged participatory news sites—such as OhmyNews (South Korea), NowPublic (U.S.), and ThirdReport (U.S.)—already feed the blogosphere with local news generated by citizen journalists. Although the business model of hyperlocal blogging at the time of writing is still uncertain, some hyperlocal sites (for example, Greensboro101 or Baristanet) are able to sustain themselves through a combination of community fundraising and advertising.

Social Media Convergence and Blogging

According to Jenkins, media convergence is more than another technological shift, for it alters the relationship between "existing technologies, industries, markets, genres and audiences" (2004, p. 34). To take this further, convergence encompasses not only legacy media, but also the social media cluster. Notably, social media convergence speaks to the principle of the interconnectedness of technological mechanisms that underlie the operation of cultural technologies conceptualized by Lull (2007). For example, convergent media become part of Internet products and services, as is the case with China's Tencent Holdings, which operates one of the biggest Web portals in the country and provides blog hosting and publishing services. Known mostly for its instant messaging (IM) service, Tencent's QQ, the company gradually added a lineup of innovative products. Three examples follow: (1) Tencent's Qzone, a pseudonym general-purpose social networking service (SNS); (2) Tencent's PengYou ("friends" in Chinese) with the real-name SNS; and (3) Tencent Weibo microblogging service. In Tencent's corporate philosophy, the Internet is viewed as a utility similar to electricity,[9] and for many people in China, Tencent has indeed become a daily necessity. Tencent Qzone, which accounts for 26% to 28.7% of the SNS market in China, also allows its members to create and maintain blogs (Cheung, 2011, p. 28-29). On Qzone, subscribers can update their status, post blogs, pictures, and video, play social games, receive the latest news, and chat with their friends. This trend of re-bundling existing social media tools is likely to continue.

In contrast, social media convergence can take completely new directions, as with the short-form blog or microblog, which allows users to share text (originally limited to 140 characters),[10] hyperlinks, pictures, and re-post quotes from other sources. Unlike traditional blogging, microblogging presents a unique format that is hard to classify under the existing categories; it merges synchronous ("push") and asynchronous ("pull") communication models, utilizing the best of both realms. Microblogs become effective catalysts of online communities which then tend to merge into networks. It is because of this effective convergence of blogging and social networking functions that Twitter and similar platforms substitute other online communication channels such as instant messaging, chat, and discussion forums.

There is yet another trend; currently, many microblogging sites have shifted their emphasis from simple message relaying to providing more opportunities for interactivity. For example, Tumblr offers a balanced combination of short-form blogging (allowing users to post messages that are longer than 140 characters) and options to integrate multimedia content. Tumblr's re-blogging feature (a blend of reposting and forwarding) has become especially popular. Perhaps due to its distinct versatility, four-year-old Tumblr already has 25 million subscribers (Tumblr, 2011). Generally, while the traditional format of blogging places emphasis on self-expression and content sharing, microblogging encourages conversation, interactivity, and user engagement and thus can be categorized as *social blogging*.

At present, microblogging is the fastest growing social media platform (Wave 5 Social Media Tracker, 2010). It originated as a crossover between instant messaging, chat, and traditional blogging tailored to teenage audiences. Because microblogging offered a shorter and faster format for exchanging blog posts, it was quickly adopted by Internet users of different age cohorts worldwide. Launched in 2006, Twitter allowed users to quickly post short text entries about their daily activities over the Internet or a cellular network. Immediacy, simplicity, and constraint were at the core of Twitter's original concept (Sagolla, 2009). Twitter gained nearly instant popularity in the United States and around the world and currently has 100 million active users (Sysomos, 2011). Approximately 140 million short messages or "tweets" are sent through the Twitter network every day (Sysomos, 2011). According to a Pew Research Center's report (Lenhart & Fox, 2009), by the year 2009, one in five Americans between 18 and 24 years of age had used Twitter or similar services. Twitter redefined short-form communication in the age of information overload but, paradoxically, there are now complaints about "Twitter overload."

Twitter's success brought to life other similar microblogging services around the world. Jaiku, based in Finland, and Soup.io, operating from Austria, are popular in Western Europe. The Plurk network is widespread in Taiwan, the Philippines, and Indonesia. A special version of Twitter has been created for Japanese users. Tencent's and Sina's Weibo ("weibo" stands for "microblog" in Chinese) dominate the Twitter-like scene in China. Sina Weibo is China's biggest microblogging network with 200 million registered users (Dayal & Liu, 2011).[11] Tencent Weibo claims to have 160 million registered users and 93 million active users; however, it is common for Internet companies in China to inflate their statistics (iChinaStock.com, 2011). Analysts report that compared to Twitter, Sina Weibo provides more opportunities for interaction: it allows for commenting on other users' posts and sending audio, images, video, and emoticons as attachments (Zhang, 2011). In response to a post, Twitter users can create a new tweet, re-tweet, or reply using a private message function. Uploading and sharing images on Twitter have become a popular pastime. A number of specialized microblogging platforms dedicated to education have also been developed, for example, Edmodo and Twiducate. Regardless of their geographical origin, microblogging

platforms provide rich opportunities for content sharing and peer interaction.

One of the reasons behind the immense popularity of Twitter, Sino Weibo, and the like is the fact that in addition to providing an innovative blog platform for sending and receiving short messages in a near real-time mode, microblogging performs a social networking function. Having gained a critical mass, Twitter-like microblogging platforms are evolving into social networks of their own, although they remain in the shadow of Facebook which has more than 500 million users (Sysomos, 2011). Energized by the shift in functionality from relaying messages and content to maintaining connections, microbloggers engage in creating small and big networks of followers (Twitter) or fans (Sina Weibo). The user-centric and many-to-many nature of microblogging offers bright prospects for its adoption in many walks of life.

Twitter has turned into a global cultural phenomenon; among its converts are 35 heads of state and nearly half of the world's top religious leaders including the Pope and the Dalai Lama (Twitter blog, 2011). Twitter's international success became possible after it integrated multi-language support: microblogs can now be written in 17 languages. Sina Weibo also announced plans to attract more subscribers from across the globe, and we may witness the appearance of an intercultural bridge that will meet halfway between the West and the East in the near future. Recognizing the cultural significance of microblogs, the Library of Congress has begun archiving Twitter content. In addition, along with Facebook and YouTube, Twitter remains the primary source of online referral traffic (see Table 4).

There is no limit to the creative adaptations of new media technologies, and blogging is no exception. For example, live blogging allows for posting real-time updates to a blog during an event while it is taking place rather than blogging about it after the fact. Live blogging is particularly effective for covering meetings, conferences, key-

Table 4. Top ten sources of website referral traffic (percent of all referrals)

Source of Referral Traffic	Percent of All Web Referrals
1. Facebook	0.64574
2. YouTube	0.28394
3. Twitter	0.11363
4. StumbleUpon	0.06609
5. LinkedIn	0.03062
6. Reddit	0.00534
7. Google+	0.00354
8. Del.icio.us	0.00097
9. Mashable	0.00071
10. Flickr	0.00057

Source: NetMarketShare, 2011.

note speeches, and community or sporting events. It can be done by using specialized services (such as CoverItLive) or by adding a plugin to an existing blog publishing platform (as with WordPress). Live blogging allows end-users to create a single blog post that can be updated without reloading the browser window. CoverItLive streams live content directly into a blog homepage. To view the stream, blog visitors do not need to register at the site or download any additional software. The console window displays: writers' entries, readers' comments, graphics, photographs, video, quick polls, and a range of ready-to-use messages, such as "Be right back in 5 minutes." The WordPress live blogging plugin uses AJAX technology and supports integration with Twitter: if activated, the first 139 characters of each live blog entry will be posted to the Twitter network. ScribbleLive is another platform designed specifically for collaborative live blogging. Live blogging merges the functions of instant messaging, chat, e-mail and online video conferencing, and seamlessly integrates Web searches to navigate to YouTube and other multimedia sites.

Video blogging also utilizes the Internet to deliver entertainment content, news, and commentary that can be viewed in a Flash video format (FLV), or downloaded as WMV and MP4 video files. Capitalizing on the ideas behind Internet TV and video streaming, video blogs (vlogs) deliver local news, investigative reporting, and video footage from citizen journalists. Video blogging can serve other purposes, for example, provide intracasts through organizations' intranets. To make video distribution services even more effective, video blogs often utilize RSS or Atom syndication formats which allow for automatic aggregation and playback on personal computers and mobile devices. Examples of video blogging are abundant on YouTube and vary in formats. For example, a weekly talk show, "The Partners Project," features interviews of YouTube stars whose videos have attracted millions of global viewers (Stelter, 2011). Unedited transcripts of all interviews are published on a complimentary blog.[12] Some popular video blogging channels like Bloggingheads.tv record dialog matchups between the hosts, conducted via webcams, and post them for viewing and commenting. These discussions often involve scientists, writers, journalists, and A-list bloggers. One could argue that we should expect new innovative forms of video blogging to materialize in the future. Accordingly, the *State of the Blogosphere* analysis (Technorati, 2010) indicates that in the next five years, more people will receive their news and entertainment from social media than traditional media. Interactive features of social media create particularly fruitful grounds for future innovative developments.

DISCUSSION

During the last decade, blogging has witnessed remarkable growth around the globe, having wide-ranging implications for many people regardless of their geographical location, socioeconomic status, age, gender, education, or cultural background. Yet the future of blogging cannot be assessed without taking into account the critical voices questioning the impact of Web 2.0-associated media on the written word, reading, and culture in particular (Carr, 2010; Keen, 2007; Lanier, 2010; also see Andersen & Rainie, 2010). Sunstein (2008), for example, emphasizes that "a dramatic increase in individual control over content and a corresponding decrease in the power of general interest intermediaries, including newspapers, magazines, and broadcasters" (p. 95) should not be automatically viewed as a step towards deliberative democracy. Since social media allow for an unprecedented level of control over the selection of content, such control can lead to a dramatic reduction of the political horizon for a given individual and thus "reduce the importance of the 'public sphere' and common spaces in general" (p. 96) since these individuals are exposed only to partisan points of view. Goldman (2008) similarly remarks that blog readers prefer to seek out those blogs that adhere to their own political views, which can negatively affect the blogosphere's role in fostering citizen involvement. Others note that blogging is particularly suitable for disseminating "exaggerated, distorted, incorrect or downright deceitful" information and rumors (McNair, 2006, p. 131) and for spreading "mean-spirited, overtly personal" attacks (Powazek, 2002, p. 6).

In 1995 in his seminal book "Being Digital" Nicholas Negroponte, the MIT Media Lab founder, envisaged a customized online news channel—*Daily Me*. Hardly could Negroponte predict that highly personalized news aggregation could produce the so-called "echo chamber effect" leading to political polarization and cultural tribalization of the news media. The media echo chamber is characterized by social scientists as a "bounded, enclosed media space that has the potential to both magnify the messages delivered within it and insulate them from rebuttal" (Jamieson & Cappella, 2008, p. 76). Jamieson and Cappella, unlike Sunstein, find that this phenomenon has not only negative, but also positive effects, since it "encourages engagement and increases the audiences' ideological coherence" (p. 247). Alter-

nately, they point out that media echo chambers have the potential "to undercut individual and national deliberation" (p. 247).

Despite mainly positive accounts of user-generated media (Bruns, 2009; Bruns, & Jacobs, 2006; Jenkins, 2009; Russell & Echchaibi, 2009), Shirky (2008) thinks that most user-generated content is not content at all and that the blogging phenomenon is completely misinterpreted. Shirky argues that most blogs are public only in appearance since they are usually intended for small audiences with close social ties. He uses a metaphor of a person sitting in the mall's food court next to a group of youth communicating with each other: The person can hear what they talk about, but that doesn't make him a part of their group. Shirky also claims that blogs confuse broadcasting and communication functions: "dozens of weblogs have an audience of a million or more, and millions have an audience of a dozen or less" (p. 84) and that weblog world is not universal and cannot be viewed as such. Pioneer technologist and computer scientist, Lanier (2010) uses harsh words to describe the "open culture" of Web 2.0:

Anonymous blog comments, vapid video pranks, and lightweight mashups may seem trivial and harmless, but as a whole, this widespread practice of fragmentary, impersonal communication has demeaned interpersonal interaction. (p. 4)

Most of the attempts to define the future for blogging view blogs either from the technological determinist or the social construction of technology point of view. Both of these approaches represent the extreme ends of the pendulum by overly emphasizing either the role of technology in shaping people's values, attitudes, and behaviors or the degree of human control over technology. No one would deny that media technology affects people, as it is the case with television. However, there are reasons to believe "that the hysteria over the dangers of the online extensions of our world will begin to die down" (Barlow, 2008, p. 159).

Despite the warnings of cultural critics, empirical research does not provide evidence of the social isolation of Internet users. Recent Pew Internet Research Center's polls show that Internet usage does not reduce real-life social interactions as it is commonly assumed. One such survey (Rainie, Purcell, & Smith, 2011) found that the majority of Internet users (80%) are engaged in real-life social groups, as compared with 56% of non- users (p. 2). Interestingly, micro-bloggers turned out to be the most social (85%).

While new information and communication channels continue to emerge, social interaction technologies make it possible for global citizens to obtain and share information in a variety of formats and forms that are crossing the traditional divides of time, location, and geographical borders. Some refer to the plethora of emerging online participation channels as *Web 3.0* and even *Web 4.0*, or the *Semantic Web* to emphasize the unprecedented level of interactivity the new generation of Web-based technologies and applications brings with them. An industry analysis of semantic Internet technologies documents that the old information-centric patterns of media consumption have reached their limit, giving way to the "ubiquitous Web of connected intelligences" (Davis, 2008, p. 4). Mills Davis, the author of the report, elaborates:

The semantic wave embraces four stages of internet growth. The first stage, Web 1.0, was about connecting information and getting on the net. Web 2.0 is about connecting people—putting the "I" in user interface, and the "we" into Webs of social participation. The next stage, Web 3.0, is starting now. It is about representing meanings, connecting knowledge, and putting these to work in ways that make our experience of internet more relevant, useful, and enjoyable. Web 4.0 will come later. It is about connecting intelligences in a ubiquitous Web where people and things reason and communicate together. (2008, p. 3)

As with every new technology, in blogging, humans face the dilemma of maximizing the positive effects and minimizing the potential negative impact. The future of blogging, therefore, depends on whether or not people will be able to overcome the challenges associated with "the dark side" of this communication technology and put it to work to fulfill legitimate human needs. Overall, the proliferation of blogging provides testimony to humanity's continual desire to maintain the free flow of information and to advance innovative means of social connectedness and engagement across the barriers of geographical space, cultural preferences, and political divides.

STUDY LIMITATIONS AND FUTURE RESEARCH

In this chapter, the author concentrated on blogging as an integral part of the overall cluster of social media. This study is not free of limitations. The author utilized a wide-angle view adopted from evolutionary futures research which provides a broad perspective but might leave aside some of the aspects that would emerge in a narrowly focused analysis. Future studies could focus on women's blogging activities across different social and cultural environments, and blogs as a tool to promote gender equality. According to the results of one analysis co-sponsored by BlogHer and Ketchum, 55 million American women or 63% of all female Internet users in the U.S. read blogs on a monthly basis (Collins, 2011). "Mommy" blogging, niche blogging, blog-based brand communities, professional blogging, and collaborative blogging could also be analyzed in detail.

Moblogging, or the ability of users to engage in blogging via a mobile device, promises to become the next big trend and is already predicted to become "the wave of the future" (Wave 5 Social Media Tracker, 2010). Mobile blogging, therefore, is another important venue for future research. According to Technorati (2010), one fourth of all bloggers are already engaged in mobile blogging using a smartphone or a tablet device, and this shift needs further investigations. Another limitation of this study that could be addressed in future analyses is a more in-depth focus on negative forms of blogging (such as spam blogs), as well as the downsides of blogs which may include: inaccuracy of information, subjectivity, bias, lack of credibility, breaches of the unwritten ethics code, and issues associated with intellectual property rights.

CONCLUSION

Aimed to assess the future direction of blogging, this chapter surveyed academic and professional literature and examined the status quo of the global blogosphere in the context of the contemporary information landscape. Two theoretical frameworks, media convergence and cultural technology, provided a useful approach to understanding the phenomenon of blogging and its place among other social media viewed through the lens of social interaction technologies. The method of environmental scanning shed light on the current state of the information ecosystem and helped evaluate the direction that blogging, as an evolving social media phenomenon, might take in the future. The analysis of a wide range of data obtained from scholarly research, industry statistics, white papers, polls, and expert reviews indicates that the worldwide trajectory and specific patterns of adoption depend on a combination of socioeconomic, technological, political, cultural, and demographic factors.

The global blogosphere does not recognize national borders and easily transcends geographical constraints. The international adoption of blogs has been slowly eroding North America's status as the center of the global blogosphere. Currently, the growth of blogging continues in Asia, Eastern Europe, Latin America, and the Arab world. However, international bloggers are still impeded by language barriers, the digital divide, and state firewalls in their attempts to turn the global blogosphere into "the fourth estate" of the digital age. Simultaneous translation services embedded into blog software are foreseeable in the future and promise to turn blogs into ultimate cultural technology tools. Currently, language-bound blog galaxies in the blogging universe are connected through systems of so-called "bridge" blogs, run by bloggers with the knowledge of two or more foreign languages. Global bloggers gravitate towards others through common interest and passion and create international communities such as Global Voices, a nonprofit group that with the help of volunteer translators connects 30 national blogospheres.

The results of the analysis confirm that network-based peer production and social media convergence are the driving forces behind the current transformation of blogs. Taken as a whole, the social media explosion symbolizes an important shift from the user vs. producer paradigm to the social production of content. From Barista-net to Plurk to Bloggingheads.tv, the diverse implementations of the social Web uncover the emergence of a new wave of user-centric, user-driven practices: producing, searching, sharing, publishing, and distributing information at all levels and in various modes, from synchronous to asynchronous. Advantages of participatory modes of content production have become especially visible in hyperlocal blogging which meets the demands of local communities, neighborhoods, and small groups of people. Hyperlocal news sites, for instance, present a new model for gathering and disseminating information and bridge the gap between mainstream media and grassroots initiatives. Hyperlocal blogging demonstrates a lasting trend as it reinforces the social dimension of technology through community building.

Social media are in constant Brownian motion, giving life to new features, genres, and forms. At first glance, it may resemble a random mingling of elements. However, if one takes a closer look, there are distinct patterns that become visible in the overall development of the social media cluster. Currently, social networking is flourishing among all social media platforms, which affects all other types of social media (Wave 5 Social Media Tracker, 2010). Such developments, however, do not seal the fate of other social media applications; due to their digital nature, they easily morph and merge with one another. Online social networks compete with blogging for users and increasingly integrate new features, including growing multi-language support and higher levels of interactivity. In turn, microblogging, currently the fastest growing social media platform, is incorporating social networking aspects and evolving into social blogging.

The convergence of various social media formats such as blogs, social networks, podcasts, forums, and online chat blurs the boundaries between platforms and tools and greatly expands their overall functionality. Short-form blogs successfully merge synchronous ("push") and asynchronous ("pull") modes of communication. While Twitter leans towards social networking, Tumblr focuses on multimedia-rich content. Although it may still be too early to predict the results of the "platform wars," the convergence of social media is likely to persist in the near future. At the same time as traditional weblogs incorporate audio posts, video blogs experiment with adopting TV formats such as talk shows. Photo, video, and audio blogs converge into new types of blogging with rich multimedia features. Many hybrid forms have already emerged: for example, hyperlocal blogs and live blogs. Even though cultural critics diverge in their predictions of the future of blogging, innovative implementations of social interaction technologies offer positive prospects for further adoption of blogs in many walks of life. The participatory and inclusive nature of the underlying social interaction technologies makes blogging especially suitable for bottom-up initiatives, creativity, and innovation.

Yet, despite newspaper claims about the waning of the blogs, bloggers themselves stay optimistic about the future prospects of their favorite medium, since they believe that blogging will continue to have a lasting impact on political and social life. In fact, many bloggers plan to blog more frequently in the future (Technorati, 2010). With the world population approaching 7 billion people and the total number of blog posts nearing 1 million per day (Technorati, 2009), there is sufficient room for blogging to expand. It would be reasonable to conclude that blogging, whether in its standalone or convergent form, is here to stay and that its outlook aligns with the Internet's overall prospects. What the future holds for blogging depends on whether or not humanity will be able to solve pressing societal issues and whether or not the functionality of social media will continue to increase social capital, build community trust, and help people to advance towards the "good society." However, blogs should not be viewed as the cure-all for societal ills. The blogging revolution will continue to face the challenges of "the dark side" of human nature and inappropriate uses of technology, whether it is a propensity for gossip, spreading falsehood, defamation, cyberbullying, trolling, sock puppetry, or comment spam. Overall, the results of this study concur with the conclusion made by the McKinsey Global Institute (2011): The Internet has become an essential part of the global modern economy, society, and culture, and the way to move forward involves embracing new technologies. Among the variety of online channels powered by social interaction technologies, blogging has the potential to perform as a means to generate societal benefit, improve community, build cultural bridges, and create a more connected world.

REFERENCES

Ackoff, R. L. (1974). *Redesigning the future: A systems approach to societal problems*. New York: Wiley.

Aguilar, F. J. (1967). *Scanning the business environment*. New York: Macmillan.

Alexander, B. (2009, May/June). Apprehending the future: Emerging technologies, from science fiction to campus reality. *EDUCAUSE Review, 44*(3), 12–29.

Alexanyan, K., & Koltsova, O. (2009). Blogging in Russia is not Russian blogging. In Russell, A., & Echchaibi, N. (Eds.), *International blogging: Identity, politics, and networked publics* (pp. 65–84). New York: Peter Lang.

Andersen, J., & Rainie, L. (2010, February 19). *The future of the Internet*. Washington, DC: Pew Research Center's Internet & American Life Project. Retrieved from http://www.pewinternet.org/Reports/2010/Future-of-the-Internet-IV.aspx

Barlow, A. (2008). *Blogging America: The new public sphere*. Westport, CT: Praeger.

Benkler, Y. (2006). *The wealth of networks: How social production transforms markets and freedom*. New Haven, CT: Yale University Press.

Benkler, Y., & Shaw, A. (2010, April). *A tale of two blogospheres: Discursive practices on the left and right*. Cambridge, MA: The Berkman Center for Internet & Society. Retrieved from http://cyber.law.harvard.edu/publications/2010/Tale_Two_Blogospheres_Discursive_Practices_Left_Right

Berners-Lee, T. (1999). *Weaving the web: The original design and ultimate destiny of the World Wide Web by its inventor*. San Francisco, CA: HarperSanFrancisco.

Black, T. (2011, September). Navigating the new online universe. *Inc. Magazine*, 14. Retrieved from http://www.inc.com/magazine/201109/social-media-for-small-business.html

BlogPulse. (2011, August 24). *BlogPulse stats* (The Nielsen Company). Retrieved from http://www.blogpulse.com

BlogScope. (2011, August 24). *BlogScope preview* (Department of Computer Science, University of Toronto). Retrieved from http://www.blogscope.net

Blood, R. (2002). *The weblog handbook: Practical advice on creating and maintaining your blog*. Cambridge, MA: Perseus.

Boyer, A. (2011, August 24). *The history of blogging: 12 years of blogs*. Retrieved from http://www.blogworld.com/2011/08/24/the-history-of-blogging-12-years-of-blogs/comment-page-1/

Bruns, A. (2006). What's next for blogging? In Bruns, A., & Jacobs, J. (Eds.), *Uses of blogs* (pp. 249–254). New York: Peter Lang.

Bruns, A. (2009). *Blogs, Wikipedia, Second Life, and beyond: From production to produsage*. New York: Peter Lang.

Bruns, A., & Jacobs, J. (Eds.). (2006). *Uses of blogs*. New York: Peter Lang.

Carpenter, S. (2010). A study of content diversity in online citizen journalism and online newspaper articles. *New Media & Society, 12*(7), 1064–1084. doi:10.1177/1461444809348772

Carr, N. G. (2010). *The shallows: What the Internet is doing to our brains*. New York: W.W. Norton.

Cheung, W. (2011, May 17). *Tencent Holdings* (Credit Suisse China SNS survey report). Retrieved from http://www.penn-olson.com/2011/05/27/tencent-infographic/

China Internet Network Information Center. (2010, July). *Statistical report on Internet development in China.* Retrieved from http://www.cnnic.cn/uploadfiles/pdf/2010/8/24/93145.pdf

Collins, J. K. (2011, April). *Social media matters study* (Co-sponsored by BlogHer and Ketchum). Retrieved from http://www.ketchum.com/files/BlogHer_2011_Social_Media_Matters_Study.pdf

ComScore. (2010, June). *Women on the Web: How women are shaping the Internet.* Retrieved from http://www.comscore.com/Press_Events/Presentations_Whitepapers/2010/Women_on_the_Web_How_Women_are_Shaping_the_Internet

ComScore. (2011, August 24). *Japan Internet users spend most time on blogs worldwide* (Press release). Retrieved from http://www.comscore.com/Press_Events/Press_Releases/2011/8/Japan_Internet_Users_Spend_Most_Time_on_Blogs_Worldwide

Dator, J. A. (2002). *Advancing futures: Futures studies in higher education.* Westport, CT: Praeger.

Davis, M. (2008). *Project 10X's semantic wave 2008 report: Industry roadmap to Web 3.0 & multibillion dollar market opportunities* (Executive summary). Retrieved from http://www.project10x.com

Dayal, A., & Liu, C. (2011, September 9). *Signs of good things to come for Sina.* Retrieved from http://online.barrons.com/article/SB50001424052702304715104576559002445683400.html

Dumova, T., & Fiordo, R. (2010). Preface. In Dumova, T., & Fiordo, R. (Eds.), *Handbook of research on social interaction technologies and collaboration software: Concepts and trends* (*Vol. 1*, pp. xl–xlvi). Hershey, PA: Information Science Reference.

Etling, B., Alexanyan, K., Kelly, J., Faris, R., Palfrey, J., & Gasser, U. (2010, October). *Public discourse in the Russian blogosphere: Mapping RuNet politics and mobilization.* Cambridge, MA: The Berkman Center for Internet & Society. Retrieved from http://cyber.law.harvard.edu/publications/2010/Public_Discourse_Russian_Blogosphere

Etling, B., Kelly, J., Faris, R., & Palfrey, J. (2009, June). *Mapping the Arabic blogosphere: Politics, culture, and dissent.* Cambridge, MA: The Berkman Center for Internet & Society. Retrieved from http://cyber.law.harvard.edu/newsroom/Mapping_the_Arabic_Blogosphere

Farrell, H., & Drezner, D. W. (2008). The power and politics of blogs. *Public Choice, 134*, 15–30. doi:10.1007/s11127-007-9198-1

Fowles, J. (Ed.). (1978). *Handbook of futures research.* Westport, CT: Greenwood Press.

Garris, K., Guillory, J., & Sundar, S. S. (2011). Does interactivity serve the public interest? The role of political blogs in deliberative democracy. *International Journal of Interactive Communication Systems and Technologies, 1*(1), 1–18.

George, E., & Peters, J. (2010, July 23). *Hyperlocal blogging* (The Brian Lehrer Show podcast). Retrieved from http://www.wnyc.org/shows/bl/2010/jul/23/hyperlocal-blogging/

1GOAL. Education for all. (2011). *About 1GOAL.* Retrieved from http://www.join1goal.org/about-1GOAL.php

Goldman, A. (2008). The social epistemology of blogging. In Hoven, J., & Weckert, J. (Eds.), *Information technology and moral philosophy* (pp. 111–122). New York: Cambridge University Press.

Gordon, E., & de Souza e Silva, A. (2011). *Net locality: Why location matters in a networked world.* Malden, MA: Wiley-Blackwell.

Gorny, E. (2006). *A creative history of the Russian Internet*. Unpublished Doctoral dissertation, University of London.

Gregg, D. G. (2010). Designing for collective intelligence. *Communications of the ACM, 53*(4), 134–138..doi:10.1145/1721654.1721691

Guadagno, R. E., Eno, C. A., & Okdie, B. M. (2010). Personal blogging: Individual differences and motivations. In Dumova, T., & Fiordo, R. (Eds.), *Handbook of research on social interaction technologies and collaboration software: Concepts and trends* (pp. 292–301). Hershey, PA: Information Science Reference.

Guest post: Why do we need things like LeWeb? (2009, December 14). Retrieved from http://2010.leweb.net/blog/guest-post-why-do-we-need-things-leweb

Harris, K., & Flouch, H. (2010). *The online neighbourhood networks study*. London: The Networked Neighbourhoods group. Retrieved from http://blog.e-democracy.org/posts/1078

Herring, S. C., Scheidt, L. A., Kouper, I., & Wright, E. (2007). Longitudinal content analysis of blogs. In Tremayne, M. (Ed.), *Blogging, citizenship, and the future of media* (pp. 3–20). New York: Routledge.

Hollenbaugh, E. E. (2011). Motives for maintaining personal journal blogs. *Cyberpsychology, Behavior, and Social Networking, 14*(1-2), 13–20.. doi:10.1089/cyber.2009.0403

iChinaStock.com. (2011, May 6). Tencent's microblog claims 93 million monthly active users, but are its numbers accurate? Retrieved from http://news.ichinastock.com/2011/05/tencent%E2%80%99s-microblog-claims-93-million-monthly-active-users-but-are-its-numbers-accurate/

Ignite Social Media. (2011). *2011 social network analysis report*. Retrieved from http://www.ignitesocialmedia.com/social-media-stats/2011-social-network-analysis-report/

Internet World Stats. (2011). *Internet usage in Asia*. Retrieved from http://www.internetworldstats.com/stats3.htm#asia

Jamieson, K. H., & Cappella, J. N. (2008). *Echo chamber: Rush Limbaugh and the conservative media establishment*. Oxford: Oxford University Press.

Jenkins, H. (2001, June). Digital renaissance: Convergence? I diverge. *Technology Review*. Retrieved from http://www.technologyreview.com/Biztech/12434/

Jenkins, H. (2002, March). Blog this: Online diarists rule an Internet strewn with failed dot coms. *Technology Review*. Retrieved from http://www.technologyreview.com/Biztech/12768/

Jenkins, H. (2004). The cultural logic of media convergence. *International Journal of Cultural Studies, 7*(1), 33–43. doi:10.1177/1367877904040603

Jenkins, H. (2006a). *Convergence culture: Where old and new media collide*. New York: New York University Press.

Jenkins, H. (2006b). *Fans, bloggers, and gamers: Exploring participatory culture*. New York: New York University Press.

Jenkins, H. (2009). *Confronting the challenges of participatory culture: Media education for the 21st century*. Cambridge, MA: The MIT Press.

Jenkins, H., & Deuze, M. (2008). Convergent culture. *Convergence: The International Journal of Research into New Media Technologies, 14*(1), 5–12. doi:10.1177/1354856507084415

Jensen, K. B., & Helles, R. (2011). The internet as a cultural forum: Implications for research. *New Media & Society, 13*(4), 517–533. doi:10.1177/1461444810373531

Johnson, T. J., & Kaye, B. K. (2004). Wag the blog: How reliance on traditional media and the Internet influence credibility perceptions of Weblogs among blog users. *Journalism & Mass Communication Quarterly, 81*(3), 622–642.

Kaplan, A. M., & Haenlein, M. (2010). Users of the world, unite! The challenges and opportunities of Social Media. *Business Horizons, 53*, 59–68. doi:10.1016/j.bushor.2009.09.003

Katz, J. (1999, May 24). *Here comes the Weblogs*. Retrieved from http://slashdot.org/story/99/05/13/1832251/Here-Come-The-Weblogs

Kaye, B. K. (2005). It's a blog, blog, blog world: Users and uses of Weblogs. *Atlantic Journal of Communication, 13*(2), 73–95. doi:10.1207/s15456889ajc1302_2

Kaye, B. K. (2007). Blog use motivations: An exploratory study. In Tremayne, M. (Ed.), *Blogging, citizenship, and the future of media* (pp. 127–148). New York: Routledge.

Keen, A. (2007). *The cult of the amateur: How today's internet is killing our culture*. New York: Doubleday/Currency.

Kervin, L., Mantei, J., & Herrington, A. (2010). Blogs as a social networking tool to build community. In Dumova, T., & Fiordo, R. (Eds.), *Handbook of research on social interaction technologies and collaboration software: Concepts and trends* (pp. 685–700). Hershey, PA: Information Science Reference.

Kroon, J. (1995). *General management*. Pretoria, South Africa: Kagiso Tertiary.

Lanier, J. (2010). *You are not a gadget: A manifesto*. New York: Alfred A. Knopf.

Larsson, A. O., & Hrastinski, S. (2011). Blogs and blogging: Current trends and future directions. *First Monday, 16*, 3–7. Retrieved from http://firstmonday.org/htbin/cgiwrap/bin/ojs/index.php/fm/issue/view/334.

Lasswell, H. D. (1948). The structure and function of communication in society. In L. Bryson (Ed.), *The communication of ideas: A series of addresses* (Religion and Civilization Series, pp. 37-51). New York: Harper & Brothers.

Lenhart, A., & Fox, S. (2009, February 12). *Twitter and status updating* (Pew Internet & American Life Project data memo). Retrieved from http://www.pewinternet.org/Reports/2009/Twitter-and-status-updating.aspx

Lenhart, A., Purcell, K., Smith, A., & Zickuhr, K. (2010, February 3). *Social media & mobile Internet use among teens and young adults*. Washington, DC: Pew Internet & American Life Project. Retrieved from http://pewinternet.org/Reports/2010/Social-Media-and-Young-Adults.aspx

Locken, E., & Loughnane, E. (2005). *Net success interviews*. S.L.: InterviewBooks.com.

Lull, J. (2007). *Culture-on-demand: Communication in a crisis world*. Malden, MA: Blackwell.

McKinsey Global Institute. (2011, May). *Internet matters: The Net's sweeping impact on growth, jobs, and prosperity*. Retrieved from http://www.mckinsey.com/mgi

McMains, A. (2010, March 1). 4A's: Huffington embraces consumer control. *AdWeek*. Retrieved from http://www.adweek.com/news/television/4as-huffington-embraces-consumer-control-101728

McNair, B. (2006). *Cultural chaos: Journalism, news and power in a globalised world*. London: Routledge.

Metzgar, E. T., Kurpius, D. D., & Rowley, K. M. (2011). Defining hyperlocal media: Proposing a framework for discussion. *New Media & Society, 13*(5), 772–787. doi:10.1177/1461444810385095

Morrison, J. L., Renfro, W. L., & Boucher, W. I. (Eds.). (1983). *Applying methods and techniques of futures research.* San Francisco, CA: Jossey-Bass.

Negroponte, N. (1995). *Being digital.* New York: Knopf.

NetMarketShare. (2011, July). *Social media referrals.* Retrieved from http://www.netmarketshare.com/social-media.aspx?spider=1&qprid=89

O'Reilly, T. (2005). *What is Web 2.0: Design patterns and business models for the next generation of software.* Retrieved from http://oreilly.com/web2/archive/what-is-web-20.html

Papacharissi, Z. (2007). Audiences as media producers: Content analysis of 260 blogs. In Tremayne, M. (Ed.), *Blogging, citizenship, and the future of media* (pp. 21–38). New York: Routledge.

Park, J., Jo, S., & Moon, J. (2010). Towards understanding the successful adoption of blog-based knowledge management systems: A socio-psychological approach. In Dumova, T., & Fiordo, R. (Eds.), *Handbook of research on social interaction technologies and collaboration software: Concepts and trends* (pp. 486–495). Hershey, PA: Information Science Reference.

Pavlik, J. V. (1996). *New media technology: Cultural and commercial perspectives.* Boston, MA: Allyn and Bacon.

Pavlik, J. V. (2008). *Media in the digital age.* New York: Columbia University Press.

Piper Jaffray Companies. (2007, February 23). *Piper Jaffray predicts global online advertising revenue to reach $81.1 billion by 2011 in new report: 'The user revolution'* (Press release). Retrieved from http://www.piperjaffray.com

Pole, A. (2010). *Blogging the political: Politics and participation in a networked society.* New York: Routledge.

Powazek, D. M. (2002). What the hell is a weblog and why won't they leave me alone? In Rodzvilla, J. (Ed.), *We've got blog: How weblogs are changing our culture* (pp. 3–6). Cambridge, MA: Perseus.

Rainie, L., Purcell, K., & Smith, A. (2011, January 18). *The social side of the internet.* Washington, DC: Pew Research Center's Internet & American Life Project. Retrieved from http://pewinternet.org/Reports/2011/The-Social-Side-of-the-Internet.aspx

Rheingold, H. (2008). Using participatory media and public voice to encourage civic engagement. In Bennett, W. L. (Ed.), *Civic life online: Learning how digital media can engage youth* (pp. 97–118). Cambridge, MA: MIT Press.

Russell, A., & Echchaibi, N. (Eds.). (2009). *International blogging: Identity, politics, and networked publics.* New York: Peter Lang.

Sagolla, D. (2009). *140 characters: A style guide for the short form.* Hoboken, NJ: John Wiley & Sons.

Samet, R. H. (2009). *Long-range futures research: An application of complexity science.* North Charleston, SC: BookSurge.

Shirky, C. (2008). *Here comes everybody: The power of organizing without organizations.* New York: Penguin Press.

Sino Daily. (2010, December 22). *Creator of China's Great Firewall forced to remove microblog.* Retrieved from http://www.sinodaily.com/reports/Creator_of_Chinas_Great_Firewall_forced_to_remove_microblog_999.html

Stelter, B. (2011, January 9). *YouTube introduces weekly talk show*. Retrieved from http://mediadecoder.blogs.nytimes.com/2011/01/09/youtube-introduces-weekly-talk-show/?src=twt&twt=mediadecodernyt

Sunstein, C. R. (2008). Democracy and the Internet. In Hoven, J., & Weckert, J. (Eds.), *Information technology and moral philosophy* (pp. 93–110). New York: Cambridge University Press.

Sunstein, C. R. (2009). *Republic.com 2.0: Revenge of the blogs*. Princeton, NJ: Princeton University Press.

Sysomos. (2011). *Social media statistics: Changes in the social sphere from 2009 to 2011*. Retrieved from http://sysomos.marketwire.com/report-sysomos-social-media-statistics.html

Tai, Z. (2006). *The Internet in China: Cyberspace and civil society*. New York: Routledge.

Technorati. (2008). *State of the blogosphere: Introduction*. Retrieved from http://technorati.com/blogging/article/state-of-the-blogosphere-introduction/

Technorati. (2009). *State of the blogosphere: Introduction*. Retrieved from http://technorati.com/blogging/article/state-of-the-blogosphere-2009-introduction/

Technorati. (2010). *State of the blogosphere 2010*. Retrieved from http://technorati.com/blogging/article/state-of-the-blogosphere-2010-introduction/

The Nielsen Company. (2009, March). *Global faces and networked places: A Nielsen report on social networking's new global footprint*. Retrieved from http://blog.nielsen.com/nielsenwire/wp-content/uploads/2009/03/nielsen_globalfaces_mar09.pdf

Tremayne, M. (Ed.). (2007). *Blogging, citizenship, and the future of media*. New York: Routledge.

Tumblr. (2011). *About us*. Retrieved from http://www.tumblr.com/about

Twitter blog. (2011, September 8). *One hundred million voices*. Retrieved from http://blog.twitter.com/

Wall, M. (2005). 'Blogs of war': Weblogs as news. *Journalism*, 6(2), 153–172. doi:10.1177/1464884905051006

Wave 4 Social Media Tracker. (2009). *Power to the people* (Universal McCann survey report). Retrieved from http://universalmccann.bitecp.com/wave4/

Wave 5 Social Media Tracker. (2010). *The socialization of brands* (Universal McCann survey report). Retrieved from http://www.umww.com/global/knowledge/view?id=128

WordPress.com. (2011, August). *WordPress stats*. Retrieved from http://en.wordpress.com/stats/

Wyld, D. C. (2007). *The blogging revolution: Government in the age of Web 2.0*. Washington, DC: IBM Center for the Business of Government. Retrieved from http://www.businessofgovernment.org/report/blogging-revolution-government-age-web-20

Zhang, J. (2011, August 18). *Sina's Weibo: Better than Twitter, but monetization is key*. Retrieved from http://seekingalpha.com/article/288127-sina-s-weibo-better-than-twitter-but-monetization-is-key

KEY TERMS AND DEFINITIONS

Blogging: (a) The practice of publishing user-generated content on the Web in a journal-type format that can be easily updated and commented on; (b) The act of creating, writing, maintaining, and/or contributing to blogs.

Blogosphere: A metaphor relating to online environments that equal the sum of all blogs and the interactions between blog creators and an audience.

Blogazines: Websites similar to placeblogs but having a greater focus on human-interest stories and neighborhood profiling.

Hyperlocal Blogging: Blogging about local issues, people, and events that affect local communities and neighborhoods.

Linkblog: Links plus commentary.

Live Blogging: Posting real-time updates to a blog by a participant in or witness to an event.

Microblogging: An act of sending and receiving short (usually under 140 characters) messages over the Internet or a cellular network. Also known as short-form or mini-blogging, an example being Twitter.

Moblogging: The ability of users to engage in blogging activities via a mobile device or a tablet computer.

Noosphere: In Vladimir Vernadsky's vision, a special realm for human thoughts existing along with the geosphere and biosphere.

Participatory Media: Refers to bottom-up, grassroots ways in which media consumers are involved in the production of media content.

Placeblog: A local weblog covering social, cultural, political, and other news of a place.

Social Interaction Technologies: Internet-based tools and techniques designed to initiate, share, and maintain interactive and collaborative activities online.

Social Media Convergence: Refers to the convergence of various social media formats which blurs the boundaries between individual platforms and tools while expanding considerably on their functionality.

Web 2.0: Refers to a broad spectrum of second-generation service-oriented Internet applications, platforms, and tools.

Weibo: Microblog in Chinese.

ENDNOTES

[1] The popularity ranking was retrieved from Alexa Internet traffic measuring company (http://www.alexa.com/topsites) on August 12, 2011. The ranking was established through a three-month comparison of the number of daily visits to the site and the number of page views.

[2] Today's popular Delicious social bookmarking service is in fact an old practice that has flourished in the broadband age.

[3] BlogWorld, an official blog of the annual BlogWorld & New Media Expo, provides an illuminating timeline of major events in the history of blogging complied by Allison Boyer (2011). Available at: http://www. blogworld.com/2011/08/24/the-history-of-blogging-12-years-of-blogs/comment-page-1/. Another helpful blog entry, "A short history of blogging" written by Duncan Riley and published by The Blog Herald (March 6, 2005), is available at: http://www. blogherald.com/2005/03/06/a-short-history-of-blogging/

[4] The Weblog Awards, also known as Bloggies, were first introduced in 2001 and turned into an annual event. The Bloggies represent one of the longest running blog contests decided by public voting (http://2001.bloggi.es).

[5] These results are based on a survey of 7,200 English-language bloggers with 33% of them from the United States.

[6] Placeblogger.com offers a directory of local weblogs.

[7] The numbers are provided by the Next Door Media blog at http://www.nextdoormedia. com/.

[8] The creation of a specialized search engine, Bloglines Local (www.bloglines.com), focused on hyperlocal blog content is also indicative of a growing demand in hyperlocal blogs.

9 See Tencent corporate website at: http://www.tencent.com/en-us/cc/culture.shtml.

10 This limitation (140 characters) is due to the fact that the protocol for sending text messages over cellular networks was standardized in the mid-1980s. The length of the message was kept at 160 characters. Bearing in mind primarily mobile users, Twitter developers limited the length of tweets to 140 characters leaving the remaining 20 for the unique address and username.

11 China's Sina Weibo achieved an unprecedented level of adoption over the period of two years. Such rapid growth can be partially explained by the fact that access to Facebook, YouTube, and Twitter is currently denied to the Chinese netizens by Internet governing authorities in China. An interesting fact illustrates how people in China regard this ban. In December 2010, Fang Binxing, the developer of China's Internet filtering system dubbed "the Great Firewall" and the president of Beijing University of Posts and Telecommunications, started a microblog on Sina Weibo. Flooded under the wave of angry comments by the Chinese netizens, it lasted only a few days. One comment said: "Before, the GFW deprived people's right to freely access the Internet, now people will deprive your right to use a microblog. You should not regret this, should you?" (Sino Daily, 2010). For more details about the Great Firewall of China, see Tai (2006), p. 102-103.

12 The videos and transcripts are available at: http://partnersproject.com/.

About the Contributors

Tatyana Dumova (PhD, Bowling Green State University) is an Associate Professor in the School of Communication at Point Park University (Pittsburgh, Pennsylvania) where she teaches undergraduate and graduate courses in digital media. Her research focuses on the social implications of information and communication technologies and the role of technology in teaching and learning. She has presented and published her research nationally and internationally. Recently, she has lead-edited a two-volume *Handbook of Research on Social Interaction Technologies and Collaboration Software: Concepts and Trends* (Information Science Reference). Dr. Dumova is the Editor of an interdisciplinary scholarly journal, the *International Journal of Interactive Communication Systems and Technologies.*

Richard Fiordo earned his PhD at the University of Illinois at Urbana after completing his dissertation on the American philosopher Charles Morris. He is a Professor of Communication at the University of North Dakota, has served in administration at several universities, and has taught and performed research at universities in the USA and Canada—including the University of Calgary, Athabasca University, and Royal Roads University. His current research includes computer-mediated communication, semantic and communication theory, and dialectical theory. His publications are diverse with a concentration in *Semiotica, Recherches Semiotiques/Semiotic Inquiry*, and *ETC: A Review of General Semantics*. Dr. Fiordo teaches traditional and online courses in communication at the University of North Dakota.

* * *

Joshua Azriel, PhD, is an Assistant Professor of Communication at Kennesaw State University, Georgia where he teaches news reporting and media law. He earned his PhD in Journalism and Communications from the University of Florida. His current research focuses on the First Amendment's impact on the Internet including social media. He has published chapters and articles in *Communication Law and Policy, Hastings Communications and Entertainment Law Journal*, and the *Handbook of Research on Social Interaction Technologies and Collaboration Software: Concepts and Trends.*

Sitthivorada Boupha received his MA in Communications from the University of Arkansas and BA from the Lao-American College in Laos. Apart from his current work as a Human Resource Executive for Recruitment at Millicom Lao Co., Ltd, a telecommunication services company in Vientiane, the capital city of Laos, he continues to research cross-cultural communication, particularly in relational and organizational contexts, as an independent scholar.

Jenny Bronstein, PhD, is a Lecturer in the Department of Information Studies at Bar-Ilan University, Israel. She teaches courses in theories of information behavior, information retrieval techniques, business information, information literacy, and information skills. Among her research interests are blogs as information systems, children's information seeking behavior, tagging, and current trends in library and information science education.

Lori F. Brost, PhD, is an Assistant Professor in the Department of Journalism at Central Michigan University where she teaches courses in online journalism, diversity in the media, and mass communication and society. She earned a Bachelor of Science degree from the University of Wisconsin-Stevens Point, a Master's degree from Brooklyn College, and a PhD from Indiana University.

Heather J. Carmack, PhD, is an Assistant Professor in the Department of Communication at Missouri State University. She received her Bachelor's degree in Communication Arts from Truman State University in Kirksville, MO and her Master's degree and Doctorate in Health Communication from Ohio University. Her teaching interests include health communication and qualitative communication research methods. Her research explores the ways health care is delivered, medical mistakes, patient safety, and the issues of death and dying. She has published in *Health Communication, Qualitative Health Research, Journal of Medical Humanities,* and *Qualitative Research Reports in Communication.*

Thomas F. Corrigan is a Doctoral Candidate in Pennsylvania State University's College of Communications. He is a research assistant for the John Curley Center for Sports Journalism, and instructor for the College's Sports, Media & Society course. Corrigan received his Bachelor's and Master's degrees from Florida State's University College of Communication and Information. His research interests are within critical/cultural studies of the media, with specific focus on media and sports, and the political economy of sports. His dissertation centers on the routine practices of bloggers in a major sports blog network. He has published in the *Journal of Sports Media* and *International Journal of Sport Communication*, with a forthcoming publication in *Journalism: Theory, Practice, & Criticism.*

Jocelyn M. DeGroot, PhD, is an Assistant Professor in the Department of Speech Communication at Southern Illinois University Edwardsville. She earned her Bachelor's degree in Communication Studies and Theatre and Master's degree in Communication Studies and Journalism from South Dakota State University in Brookings, SD, and her Doctorate in Interpersonal Communication from Ohio University. Her dissertation examined how people utilize Facebook memorial groups as a means of grieving and mourning. Her teaching interests include interpersonal communication, computer-mediated communication, and small group communication. Her current research focuses on computer-mediated communicative issues of death and dying. She has published in communication journals such as *Communication Research* and *Communication Teacher.*

Sherine El-Toukhy is a Doctoral Candidate in the School of Journalism and Mass Communication at the University of North Carolina at Chapel Hill. She received her BA in Broadcast Journalism and MA in Mass Communication from Cairo University. Her research interests include international and political communication, public opinion, news coverage, political dissent in countries of limited or non-existent press freedom, and the potential of new media for political participation. She has taught broadcast journalism at Egyptian universities for a decade and was a visiting scholar at UNC at Chapel Hill in 2006-2007. While at UNC, she was awarded a William R. Kenan Jr. Fellowship by the Royster Society of Fellows for accomplishments in research.

Tiffany E. Fields obtained her MA from the University of Arkansas and BA from the University of Central Arkansas. She is currently pursuing a Juris Doctor and a Master of Education degree at the University of Arkansas. Among her research interests are sports and social media, sport law, and alternative dispute resolution.

Naomi Gold received a PhD from St. Michael's College, University of Toronto and an MA in Religious Studies from Washington University in St. Louis. She is currently a reference, research, and outreach librarian at Samford University in Birmingham, Alabama, and an Adjunct Professor at the University of Alabama School of Library and Information Studies. Her research interests include depth psychological perspectives on religious belief, varieties of Jewish fundamentalism, and new religious movements. In 2006, she was the recipient of an Institute of Museum and Library Services (IMLS) fellowship.

Marie Hardin (PhD, University of Georgia) is Associate Professor of Journalism and Associate Dean for Graduate Studies and Research in the College of Communications at Pennsylvania State University. She is also Director of the Arthur W. Page Center for Integrity in Public Communication and Associate Director of the John Curley Center for Sports Journalism. She teaches classes in reporting, editing, ethics and sports media. Her research concentrates on diversity, ethics, and professional practices in mediated sports. Her work has been published in *Mass Communication & Society, Journalism & Mass Communication Quarterly, Sociology of Sport Journal, Sex Roles, Newspaper Research Journal, Journal of Sports Management* and *The Howard Journal of Communications*, among others.

Thomas J. Johnson (PhD, University of Washington, 1989) is the Amon G. Carter Jr. Centennial Professor in the School of Journalism at the University of Texas at Austin. Johnson's work has focused on the credibility of the Internet and its components, uses and gratifications of the Internet and its components, selective exposure and the Internet, the degree to which the Internet has served as a substitute for traditional media, the agenda-building role of the media, and how factors influence journalistic frames. His studies have also concentrated on the political effects of the Internet. Johnson has authored or co-edited three books. His most recent co-edited book, *International Media Communication in a Global Age* (Routledge), examined key issues regarding global communication, focusing primarily on international news as well as strategic communication. Johnson has 50 refereed journal articles published or in press, 19 book chapters, and more than 100 papers at academic conferences.

Barbara K. Kaye (PhD, Florida State University) is a Professor in the School of Journalism & Electronic Media, University of Tennessee at Knoxville. Her research interests include media effects, consumer uses of new communication technologies, and the influence of the Web, blogs, and social media on political attitudes and media use. She has co-authored three textbooks: *Electronic Media: Then, Now, and Later, Just A Click Away: Advertising on the Internet,* and *The World Wide Web: A Mass Communication Perspective.* She has published over 30 articles in such journals as *Journalism & Mass Communication Quarterly, Journal of Broadcasting & Electronic Media,* and *Harvard Interna-*

tional Journal of Press/Politics. Additionally, she has contributed chapters to 11 scholarly books. She has taught abroad in Italy and Austria, and was named a NATPE (National Association of Television Program Executives) fellow in 2000.

Treepon Kirdnark earned an MA in Mass Communication from California State University, Northridge. He is currently an Instructor at Bangkok University where he teaches journalism and investigates media representations of minority groups in Thailand. He has presented his research at the International Communication Association and the Association for Education in Journalism and Mass Communication conventions. At California State University Northridge, he was part of a graduate student team awarded a grant to produce content about topics such as globalization and homelessness in Los Angeles for "Indy Media On Air," a radio show on KPFK Pacifica Radio aired in Southern California.

Anastacia Kurylo has a PhD in Communication from Rutgers University and is an Assistant Professor in the Communication Arts Department at Marymount Manhattan College, New York City. Kurylo is a multi-method, cross-disciplinary social scientist who uses content, conversation, and thematic analyses, as well as experimental and survey methods in her research. She studies the variety of social interactions in which stereotypes are communicated interpersonally and their implications for interpersonal, intercultural, and organizational communication. Her recent publications have appeared in *Communication Teacher* and *Qualitative Research in Psychology.* Kurlyo's current projects include editing an inter-cultural communication textbook with SAGE and writing a book on communicated stereotypes, which is also the topic of her blog at TheCommunicatedStereotype.com.

Michael Kurylo is an independent American sportswriter and blogger. He is the founder of a popular sports blog, KnickerBlogger.Net, which is a charter member of ESPN's True Hoop blog network. He has a BS in Mathematics from Stony Brook University, New York, and uses a combination of advanced statistical outlook and visual observation to provide expert analysis of the National Basketball Association. In addition to KnickerBlogger.Net, he has written for *Sports Illustrated* and *Dime* magazines, participated in ESPN Daily Dime online chats, and was interviewed by the national sports media.

Justin D. Martin is the CLAS-Honors Preceptor of Journalism at the University of Maine and a columnist for Columbia Journalism Review. His research and writing focus on international journalism, particularly free speech in developing countries. Martin, a Fulbright scholar who speaks several dialects of Arabic, spent 2005-2006 in Jordan. Over the last seven years he has written for nearly forty news publications on four continents, including *The San Francisco Chronicle, The Chronicle of Higher Education, The Jerusalem Post,* and others. His Ph.D. is in journalism and mass communication from the University of North Carolina-Chapel Hill.

Carol McGinnis is an Instructor in the Department of Journalism at Central Michigan University where she teaches courses in online journalism, media writing, and advertising. She has written numerous articles for newspapers and magazines as well as three reference books about genealogy.

Peter Muhlberger (PhD, University of Michigan) is a Research Assistant Professor and Director of the Center for Communications Research in the College of Mass Communications at Texas Tech University. Professor Muhlberger designed and directed research on Carnegie Mellon University's Virtual Agora Project, a National Science Foundation (NSF) funded grant project investigating the political, social, and psychological effects of computer-mediated deliberative democracy. He was also principal investigator on the Deliberative E-Rulemaking Project, an NSF-funded project to apply natural language processing and multi-level deliberation to federal agency online rulemaking. He has authored multiple academic papers on the political psychology and communication aspects of online political engagement.

Gwen L. Shaffer, PhD, is a Postdoctoral Research Fellow in the Bren School of Information and Computer Sciences at the University of California, Irvine. Her current research focuses on how to incorporate telecommunications policy and economics into the Internet architecture—particularly as these issues relate to traffic management and adhering to net neutrality principles. Shaffer earned her PhD from Temple University in Philadelphia. Her doctoral dissertation, supported by a grant from the National Science Foundation, examined the potential of peer-to-peer networking for bridging the digital divide. She has previously examined the sustainability of municipal wireless networks; the need for a national broadband policy in the United States; and how urban planners are addressing the use of mobile devices in public spaces, as "ubiquitous connectivity" blurs the line between our physical and virtual spheres.

Matthew N. Stell (MA, University of Arkansas) received his Bachelor of Applied Health from Drury University, in Springfield, Missouri. He continues to delve into social science studies as an independent researcher exploring how classical and Neo-Aristotelian rhetoric pertains to popular culture.

Zixue Tai (PhD, University of Minnesota-Twin Cities) is an Associate Professor in the School of Journalism and Telecommunications at the University of Kentucky. He teaches undergraduate and graduate courses in media effects, global media systems, advanced multimedia, and video game studies. His research interests address a multitude of issues in the new media landscape of China. He is the author of *The Internet in China: Cyberspace and Civil Society* (Routledge), and has also published in premier journals such as *International Communication Gazette*, *Journalism & Mass Communication Quarterly*, *New Media & Society*, *Journal of Communication*, *Sociology of Health & Illness*, and *Psychology & Marketing*.

Melissa Wall (PhD, University of Washington), is an Associate Professor at California State University, Northridge and a former reporter and newspaper columnist whose alternative media experience includes reporting for Seattle's homeless newspaper and serving as a videographer for the Los Angeles-based online literary magazine, *Guerrilla Reads,* among others. She organized a student radio project that produced content for KPFK Pacifica Radio, taught journalism in Ethiopia, studied township publications in Zimbabwe, and reported and produced a radio documentary about Taiwan's media reform movement. Her research, focusing on international news and social media, has been published in journals such as *Media, Culture & Society, Journalism, New Media & Society, International Communication Gazette, Journal of Middle East Media, Journal of Communication Inquiry, Journal of Development Communications*, and *Journalism Studies*. She was a Research Fellow at the Berglund Center for Internet Studies at Pacific University, Oregon.

Lynne M. Webb (PhD, University of Oregon) is a Professor of Communication at the University of Arkansas. She previously served as a tenured faculty member at the University of Florida and University of Memphis. Dr. Webb is the author of over 50 essays published in scholarly journals and edited volumes as well as over 100 conference papers. Her recent research examines both blogging and computer-mediated communication in personal relationships. Her work has appeared in *Computers in Human Behavior*, *Communication Education*, *Health Communication*, the *Journal of Applied Communication Research*, and the *Journal of Family Communication*. Dr. Webb has received five teaching awards during her 30+ years as a college professor. She is a Past President of the Southern States Communication Association and has held numerous offices in the National Communication Association.

Bu Zhong (PhD, University of Maryland) is an Assistant Professor and Senior Research Fellow of the John Curley Center for Sports Journalism at the College of Communications, Pennsylvania State University. His research concentrates on decision-making in media use, media ethics, and psychological effects of information consumption, including news, sports, and social media. Special attention has been paid to analyzing the interactions between consumption of news and sports information and people's political, ethical views and psychological well-being. Before joining the Pennsylvania State University faculty, he had worked as a journalist for over a decade at China Daily in Beijing, CNN Bureau in Washington, DC, and CNN World Center in Atlanta.

Index